The Ellen Clarke Bertrand Library
Bucknell University
Lewisburg, Pennsylvania

THE APPOINTED HOUR

DEATH, WORLDVIEW, AND SOCIAL CHANGE IN BRITTANY

Ellen Badone

University of California Press
Berkeley · Los Angeles · London

University of California Press
Berkeley and Los Angeles, California

University of California Press, Ltd.
London, England

© 1989 by
The Regents of the University of California

Library of Congress Cataloging-in-Publication Data

Badone, Ellen.
  The appointed hour: death, worldview, and social
change in Brittany / Ellen Badone.
    p. cm.
  Bibliography: p.
  Includes index.
  ISBN 0-520-06369-4 (alk. paper)
  1. Death—Social aspects—France—Brittany—History.
2. Death—Religious aspects—Christianity—History.
3. Social change—History.   I. Title.
HQ1073.5.F8B34   1989
306.9′0944′1—dc19
                                              88-19903
                                                   CIP

Printed in the United States of America
1   2   3   4   5   6   7   8   9

For my parents

Contents

List of Illustrations	ix
Preface	xi
Acknowledgments	xv
1. *Le Pays de la Mort*	1
2. The Social Context of Aging and Death in La Feuillée	29
3. Death as a Rite of Passage	51
4. Mourning and Masses for the Dead	103
5. The Cemetery	131
6. Religion and Death I: Orthodox Models and Local Interpretations	158
7. Religion and Death II: Faith and Anticlericalism in the Nineteenth and Twentieth Centuries	189
8. The Living and the Dead	245
9. Death and the Supernatural	281
10. Conclusion	328
Bibliography	341
Index	353

Illustrations

Following page 130

Fig. 1. Statue of the Ankou in the parish church at Ploumilliau, Finistère
Fig. 2. The *place* and *monument aux morts* in La Feuillée
Fig. 3. Elderly women, La Feuillée
Fig. 4. The *lit de mort*
Fig. 5. Detail of tomb monument with boxwood
Fig. 6. Funeral procession
Fig. 7. Mission *tableau:* Purgatory
Fig. 8. The *catafalque* in the parish church at Loqueffret
Fig. 9. Tomb monument
Fig. 10. Mission *tableau:* Deadly Sins
Fig. 11. Mission *tableau:* Death of a Sinner
Fig. 12. The procession with statues of the *petits saints, pardon de saint Michel*, Plouguerneau
Fig. 13. Prayer and benediction of the tombs after the Toussaint Mass, La Feuillée
Fig. 14. Preparing the cemetery for Toussaint, La Feuillée
Fig. 15. Flowers in the cemetery at Toussaint, La Feuillée

Preface

When I first traveled to Brittany, in 1981, I did not suspect that my brief trip would lead me to confront the issue of death in profound and personal terms. Like many of my North American contemporaries, I had at that time, and continue to have, reactions of fear and uncertainty in the face of death. I avoid thinking about my own death and become tongue-tied or awkward in expressions of sympathy on the deaths of others. In my experience cemeteries are places that evoke painful memories and are best avoided. So, during my 1981 stay in Plouguerneau, a community on the north Breton coast, it was with surprise and some anxiety that I found myself accepting my companion's matter-of-fact suggestion that I accompany her to the cemetery after the Sunday morning Mass we had just attended.

Anna Le Guen, the forty-five-year-old woman with whom I was boarding, had recently been widowed, and as we walked toward the cemetery she explained that she wanted to make a visit to her husband's grave. As we walked past the neat rows of polished granite tombstones decorated with flowers, commemorative plaques, and photographs of the deceased, I was amazed to discover that Anna and I were not alone. The cemetery appeared to be the focal point for a small pilgrimage after the Mass, with people moving about the tombs, pausing to meditate for a moment or to replace withered flowers with fresh bouquets. Those in the cemetery, mostly women, were not strained and silent with sorrow as I would have expected. Rather, they engaged in relaxed conversations, exchanging local news and speaking of the dead. Their familiar approach to death perplexed me, but what struck me most about this first visit to a Breton cemetery was an unobtrusive rite performed by Anna at her husband's grave. Carved into the granite monument and filled with water was a dishlike circular concavity approximately fifteen centimeters in diameter. A small twig with a sprig of green leaves rested in the dish. Bending down, Anna picked up the twig and with it she traced the sign of the cross in the air, sprinkling water on the tomb. In so doing, she said, one "blesses" the deceased.

Later I was to discover that this rite is linked to an ancient complex of Indo-European and Semitic folk beliefs about the nature of the dead, in which water and other liquids serve as symbols of regeneration. I was also to find out that death has long been recognized by folklorists, historians, social scientists, and popular writers as a dominant motif in Breton culture. These discoveries motivated my return to Brittany for an extended period of fieldwork in 1983–1984, during which death became the principal theme of my research.

In reflecting on my 1981 visit to the cemetery, I was puzzled by the juxtaposition of the ritual I had witnessed there with the "modern" aspect of local material culture, including architecture, cars, and agricultural machinery. Social change in rural Brittany has moved at a rapid pace since World War II. I asked myself how a people's response to death is affected by changes in other aspects of their cultural system. Like the fieldwork on which it is based, this book represents an attempt to provide an answer to that question. In general terms, the book explores the relationships among worldview, religious beliefs, and social organization, against the backdrop of the material environment. More specifically, through a process of "thick description" (Geertz 1973a), it seeks to interpret for the reader the ways in which individuals within a particular cultural context, contemporary Brittany, make sense of their lives and give meaning to their deaths.

It is my suspicion that most, if not all, academic research constitutes, at some fundamental level, an effort to resolve basic anxieties, concerns, or contradictions within the personality of the researcher. This, at least, is how I now see my own case. Looking back, I realize that although I did not set out to study death in Brittany, it was no accident that I finished by doing so. Between my tenth and twenty-fifth years I lost three members of my close family. I know at first hand the sense which death can bring that the world has radically altered. I have felt the emotions—grief and anger, but also fear, guilt, and ambivalence—that come in the wake of loss. I also know what it is to repress the idea of death, to be unable to talk about it or accept its reality. In a sense I can see my work in Brittany, which explored both familiarity with death and what some have called its "denial" in contemporary Western culture, as an attempt to come to terms with my own experience of loss. Perhaps fieldwork and writing was for me an extended and belated period of catharsis. However, beyond speculating that a subconsciously felt need for such catharsis was a contributing factor in my research, I do not wish to probe further. I have no desire to oversimplify the complex and multilayered process of causality that led me to spend fifteen months in Brittany thinking and talking about death, and listening to others voice their emotions in the face of it. There is no direct correspondence between my own experiences of bereavement, my own denial of death, and my decision to study death in Brittany. The links in the chain are much more subtle and ill-defined. Nonetheless, I know that having been touched by death myself, I was able to empathize more fully with those in Brittany who honored me by sharing their understandings of this transition that awaits us all.

Some readers will doubtless regret that I do not describe in greater personal detail either the deaths that have taken place in my own family or those of people I knew in Brittany. To do so, I feel, would be to lay bare and exploit the emotions of people to whom I am close, both in Brittany and at home. In the urban, Anglo-Canadian cultural milieu in which I grew up, to expose one's innermost feelings publicly was to cheapen them. One talks with difficulty about those sentiments and events that have the greatest personal significance. Moreover, the act of putting such emotions into words on paper inevitably freezes them and gives them determinate form, when in reality they are amorphous, complex, and virtually impossible to fathom completely.

Writing about people is a tricky business at best, and perhaps even an unethical one. The author is always open to charges—and self-accusations—of voyeurism or lack of humanity. Cognizant of the dangers and pitfalls inherent in the task, I have nonetheless sought throughout my work to portray death in Brittany, as well as those who talked to me about it, with respect, sensitivity, and an awareness of our common mortality.

Acknowledgments

This study is based on fifteen months of fieldwork in two Breton communities, Plouguerneau and La Feuillée. Without the help of the people of these communities it could never have been carried out. I am deeply indebted to them for their enthusiastic assistance and warm welcome. In order to assure the anonymity of people in both communities who so generously gave of their time and knowledge, all names of persons from Plouguerneau and La Feuillée used in the text are pseudonyms. Original place-names have, however, been retained in most cases.

In addition to residents of Plouguerneau and La Feuillée, many other people throughout Brittany shared with me their hospitality, their memories and their everyday lives. Too numerous to mention individually, they are all thanked here.

For their scholarly advice and friendship during fieldwork, I extend my thanks to Yann Daumer of the Société Bretonne d'Ethno-Psychiatrie; Abbé Dibit; Fanch Elégoët of the Université de Haute-Bretagne; Dr. J.-L. Floch of the Centre Hospitalier Général de Morlaix; Robert Gessain of the Musée de l'Homme; Anne Henry; Donatien Laurent of the Centre de Recherche Bretonne et Celtique at the Université de Bretagne Occidentale; René Le Corre; Patrick Le Guirriec; Fanch Postic; Fanch Roudaut of the Université de Bretagne Occidentale; Bertrand Roux; Janine Sanquer; Abbé Michel Scouarnec; and Martine Segalen of the Musée National des Arts et Traditions Populaires. I am especially grateful to M. le Chanoine Le Floc'h of the Diocesan Archive in Quimper, who very kindly made available archival sources and assisted me in photographing the *tableaux* shown in figures 7, 10, and 11. Steve Hewitt and Abbé Yves Troal provided invaluable assistance with Breton grammar and orthography.

Financial support for fieldwork from the Wenner-Gren Foundation and the Social Sciences and Humanities Research Council of

Canada, as well as from the Humanities Graduate Research Grants program and the Lowie scholarship fund at the University of California, Berkeley, is gratefully acknowledged. I would also like to thank the Department of Anthropology and Sociology at the University of British Columbia and the Institute of French Studies and Department of Anthropology at New York University for hosting me as a visiting scholar and research associate during part of the period when the final manuscript was written. A grant from the Arts Research Board at McMaster University helped to cover incidental costs associated with preparing the manuscript for publication.

Stimulating discussions with Nelson Graburn, Alan Dundes, Eugene Irschick, Stanley Brandes, Susan Carol Rogers, and Caroline Brettell helped immeasurably in clarifying my thinking about social change, folk belief, and attitudes toward death. This book has also benefited greatly from the intellectual insight and critical reading of Stephen Jones. His moral support, good humor, and willingness to participate in all aspects of my research have helped me through many dark moments during the course of fieldwork and writing.

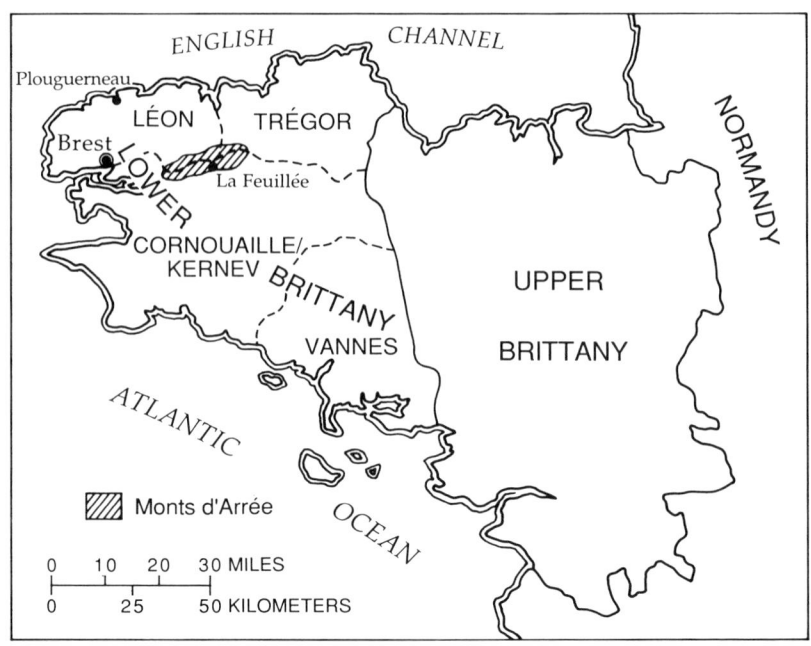

Map 1. Brittany: Subregions and locations of fieldwork communities

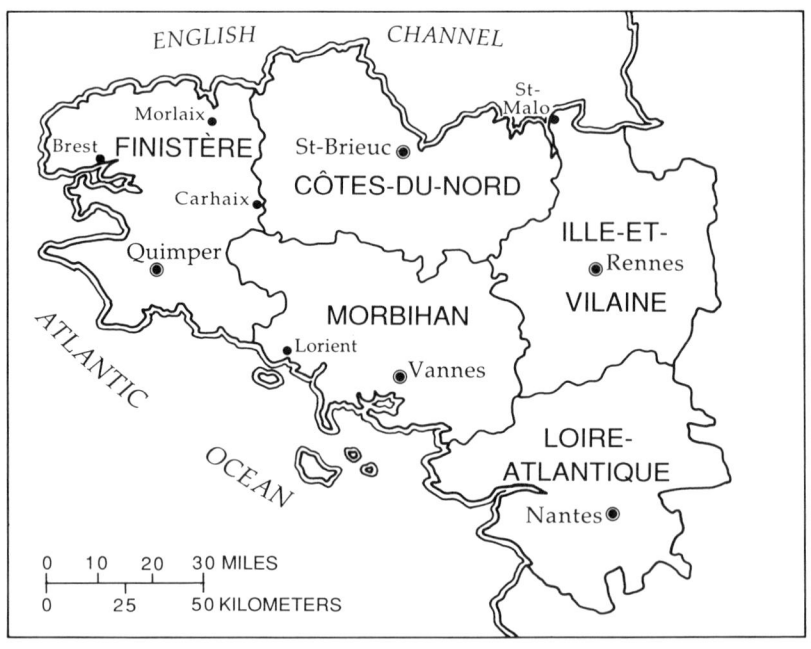

Map 2. Breton departments and major cities

1

Le Pays de la Mort

Brittany, the roughly triangular peninsula at the northwesternmost extremity of France, has been noted throughout its history for its cultural and linguistic distinctiveness. Geographically isolated, Brittany remained largely a peasant "part-society" and "part-culture" (Kroeber 1963:92) with respect to metropolitan France until the 1960s.

Linguistic criteria divide the region into two subregions, Upper and Lower Brittany (see map 1). To the west, Lower Brittany comprises those areas where Breton, one of the Celtic family of languages, has traditionally been dominant. Breton continues to be used along with French in rural areas of Lower Brittany (Timm 1973: 284). To the east, in Upper Brittany, which borders on Normandy and the Vendée, both French and Gallo, a Breton-influenced *patois*, have historically been spoken. A north-south boundary traversing the peninsula roughly between Vannes and Saint-Brieuc marks the historical division between Gallo- and Breton-speaking populations (Siegfried 1913:75–77). My exploration of Breton deathways focuses on Lower Brittany, which includes the department of Finistère and the western sectors of the departments of Morbihan and the Côtes-du-Nord.

For over two centuries, observers of Breton national character have drawn attention to the importance accorded in this region to death and to the dead. An account written in 1794 states that "the Breton nation is remarkable for its piety for the dead" (Cambry [1836] 1979:1280).[1] At a slightly later date, Jean-François Brousmiche, a departmental administrator who traveled throughout

---

1. All translations from French or Breton publications cited in the text are my own. When quoting Breton phrases from published works, I have followed the spelling used by the author. Elsewhere, with the exception of some words and usages specific to the La Feuillée area, I have followed the *Nouveau dictionnaire breton-français* (Hemon 1978).

Finistère in 1829, 1830, and 1831 observes: "Nothing is more sacred in Lower Brittany than the type of veneration given to the dead, than the religion of the tomb" (1977:108). One hundred and twenty years after Brousmiche, in a study entitled *Le caractère breton dans le culte des morts et la religion des saints*, Stéphane Strowski claims: "One can truly say that this people loves its dead. . . . The dead have not become strangers to the human condition; they continue to be men, to live in this terrestrial world, to become involved daily in the material life of their successors" (1948:368). Similarly, contemporary Breton author Pierre-Jakez Hélias, recalling his boyhood in Lower Brittany, comments: "There are certain regions in which the people experience joy more profoundly than mourning. In my own, the climate is such that at times it favors an obsession with death and consequently the Cult of the Dead" (1978:104).

During the 1980s, the theme of death in Brittany has received attention from historians Alain Croix and Fanch Roudaut, who view death as the *fil conducteur* or master key to the essential quality of Breton culture from the sixteenth century to the present (Croix 1981; Croix and Roudaut 1984). As Croix (1981:935–936) has pointed out, an abundant "harvest" of customs and oral narratives relating to death was reaped by folklorists in Brittany during the last quarter of the nineteenth century and the first quarter of the twentieth. These materials provide an excellent base for comparative research on Breton responses to death before and after the social upheavals of the post–World War II era.

Some of the most important figures in the development of French folklore scholarship, including Sébillot, Souvestre, Luzel, and La Villemarqué, were instrumental in collecting Breton deathlore during the nineteenth century.[2] More than anyone, however, it is Anatole Le Braz (1859–1924) who established Brittany's reputation

---

2. Souvestre's works include *Les derniers Bretons* (1843) and *Le foyer breton* ([1844] 1887), a volume of narratives associated with the four major *pays* or subregions of Lower Brittany. La Villemarqué, himself a Breton, was influential in shaping the French romantic interest in folk literature with the publication of his *Barzaz Breiz: Chants populaires de la Bretagne* in 1839 (La Villemarqué [1839] 1963). Sébillot published the monumental four-volume *Le folk-lore de France* between 1904 and 1907, as well as several works devoted exclusively to folklore from Upper Brittany (Sébillot 1882, 1886, 1899–1900). François-Marie Luzel, from the Côtes-du-Nord, was responsible for the collection and publication of a large body of folklore materials from Lower Brittany (Luzel 1868–1874, 1887, 1890, [1879] 1980).

as *le pays de la mort*, or the land of death (1928:1:xliii). Born in the Côtes-du-Nord, educated in Saint-Brieuc and at the Sorbonne, folklorist, literary historian, and poet, Le Braz is best known for his *Légende de la mort chez les Bretons armoricains*. First published in 1893, this two-volume, thousand-page work is an exhaustive compilation of Breton funerary customs, folk beliefs, and legends concerning death and the dead. So great was the interest provoked by the book that it was republished and augmented four times, in 1902, 1912, 1922, and 1928. Abridged editions of the work appeared in 1966 and 1974 and a reprint of the 1928 edition was published in 1982, testifying to the continued relevance of its theme. Le Braz himself collected the materials presented in his study over a fifteen-year period in communities throughout Finistère and the Côtes-du-Nord.

Regarding the Breton worldview of his time, Le Braz concludes that "at base, the whole conscience of this people is oriented toward things related to death" (1928:1:l). In his view the "quasi-perpetual promiscuity of life and death is one of the most striking things about this region" (1928:1:xlvii). As Le Braz points out, the souls of the deceased were believed to continue the type of existence they had known during life (1928:1:liv–lv). One legend he records describes the ghost of an old man who died several years after marrying a young wife who had borne him seven children in rapid succession. No sooner is the old man in his grave than his spirit reappears in his former household, where—sometimes visible, sometimes invisible—it delights in playing practical jokes on his family and their servants. Not only does he flirt with an attractive young servant and punish the taciturn older housemaid for her sour disposition, but he continues to sleep with his wife, who duly bears him an eighth child, posthumously conceived! (1928: 2:149–163).

For nineteenth-century Bretons, the dead existed in a domain parallel to that occupied by the living. This community of the souls, known as the Anaon, was never far away, as folk beliefs from the era reveal. "As crowded as the blades of grass in the fields or as the drops of water in a storm are the souls who do their penance on earth," writes Le Braz (1928:2:26). The ubiquitous souls must be warned when the activities of the living might disturb them: "When one is about to pass over an embankment planted with gorse, it is necessary to take care, first of all, to make some noise—to cough, for example—in order to warn the souls who may be doing penance there and to give them a chance to move away" (Le Braz 1928: 2:25). Likewise it is courteous before harvesting a field of wheat to inform the spirits with the ritual formula, "If the dead are there, peace to their souls!" (Le Braz 1928:2:25). Walking on country roads by night, one might hear the *scrigerez noz,* or night crier, a lost soul who follows the living with plaintive cries (Sébillot 1904: 158), and the *bugel noz,* or night child, wailing piteously for its mother, "Ma Mamm! Ma Mamm!" (Le Braz 1928:2:223). At rivers or washing pools, travelers risk encountering the *lavandières de la nuit,* ghostly washer-women. Those who agree to help them wring out the sheets they wash are likely to be caught up in the cloth and twisted to death (Sébillot 1905:428–429). One finds, wandering the fields by night, the souls of those persons who enlarged their property by displacing the stones marking the boundary between their own land and that of their neighbors. These spirits are condemned to carry the heavy boundary stones until they rediscover the original location of the stones (Le Braz 1928:2:28–29; Sébillot 1904: 147).[3] Should a hare be seen in the vicinity of an abandoned château, it is probably the spirit of the *seigneur* who formerly lived there. In retribution for terrorizing their tenants during life, such wealthy landlords serve their penance in the guise of hares, "the most timid of animals" (Le Braz 1928:2:39).

As these folk beliefs attest, the omnipresence of the dead among the living typified worldview in nineteenth-century Brittany. Moreover, in this cultural context death itself was not merely an abstract concept or an event but a personified, animate force with a will of its own, known as the Ankou, or Death (see fig. 1).

According to Le Braz's nineteenth century informants, "the Ankou is depicted sometimes as a very tall, thin man with long white hair, his face shadowed by a large felt hat; sometimes in the form of a skeleton draped in a shroud, whose head turns ceaselessly at the top of his spine . . . in order that he can encircle in a single glance the entire region that it is his mission to travel through. In either

---

3. Legends concerning ghosts condemned to "wander" for displacing boundary stones are common in other regions of France and elsewhere in Europe (Sébillot 1904:147; Goldey 1983:6–7).

case he holds a scythe in his hand" (1928:1:112–113). The Ankou travels in a cart pulled by two horses and accompanied by two companions. One of these leads the horses and the other places the dead whom the Ankou has reaped in the cart. The sound of the squeaking wheels of the Ankou's cart presages a death in the neighborhood. To meet the Ankou signals that one's own death is imminent (Le Braz 1928:1:115–116; Sébillot 1904:152–158).

In addition to the Ankou, other presages of death, or *intersignes*, commonly recognized in nineteenth-century Brittany involve mysterious noises and visions or the actions of birds and animals in the natural environment (Le Braz 1928:1:1–12). Dogs howling in the neighborhood, the owl calling outside one's house, or the cock crowing by night all foretell an impending death (Sauvé 1883–1885: 495–496). Likewise, the sound of boards being cut with a saw accompanied by the noise of hammering, heard at night in the home when no workmen are present, is another infallible omen: "One of your close kinsmen is dying, and the invisible carpenters are at work for him" (Sauvé 1883–1885:495).

The legends and folktales recorded by Le Braz and his contemporaries about *intersignes*, the Ankou, the Anaon, and the otherworld belong to a culture that has been radically altered by social change in the twentieth century (Berger 1972; 1977; Burguière 1977; Morin 1970). In order to interpret contemporary Breton responses to death, it is important to understand the nature of these changes and to examine in detail those that have occurred since the end of World War II.

Social Change in Brittany: 1945–1980

Since 1945, rural Brittany has changed from a region characterized by small peasant polyculture to one of specialized, intensive cash-crop and livestock production. Farmers have become integrated into a broad-reaching network of industrial, financial, and service infrastructures (Chevalier 1983:82–83). Agricultural mechanization has changed the social organization of production, decreasing the need for reciprocal assistance among neighbors to accomplish tasks such as haying or harvesting, and making agricultural labor more and more solitary (Chevalier 1983:88).

In response to the high cost of mechanization, informal arrangements for the co-ownership of agricultural machinery have developed among farmers in rural Brittany.[4] Elsewhere in France the existence of such informal cooperation among local farmers has been read as evidence that mechanization has not in fact undermined relations of reciprocal assistance or *entraide* among agriculturalists (Gröger 1981). However, at least in the Breton context, it seems important to stress the qualitative differences between co-ownership of machinery and traditional forms of communal labor and *entraide*. Informal arrangements to purchase equipment collectively can be contracted between producers living at some distance from one another. The traditional pattern of *entraide* was, in contrast, based on the neighborhood. Physical proximity was an important consideration in determining who engaged in *entraide* relationships. With respect to the co-ownership of machinery, greater freedom of choice can be exercised, and farmers seek to participate in such arrangements with counterparts owning similar-sized operations, who need and can afford similar types of equipment (Segalen 1985:320–321). In addition, sharing ownership of machinery does not imply the same level of interdependence, mutual assistance, and sociability as did the sharing of labor which took place in the past. As Segalen (1985:321) points out:

> Multiownership of agricultural machinery does not substitute for the traditional forms of cooperation. Threshing used to take place at the farm, and several farms were mobilized for this task, [with] parents, children, neighbors, servants, animals in a festive ambience.... With modern equipment, even if eight farms are grouped together [i.e., sharing machinery], there are never more than three people in a field. Instead of human contact there is a telephone call to find out if the machine is free on a certain day. No meal for the co-owners: a rapid settling of accounts over a cup of coffee, and the transfer of equipment for the next use is organized.

It would be erroneous to claim that face-to-face social interaction among agriculturalists on the local level in Brittany has disappeared. However, with the decline of neighborhood-based communal labor, the degree to which face-to-face relationships are

---

4. These informal associations have generally been more successful than the government-sponsored Coopératives d'Utilisation de Matériel Agricole (CUMAs) organized for the same purpose (Segalen 1985:320).

maintained has also declined. Paralleling this trend since the 1960s has been the development of new forms of solidarity among farmers through regional or national agricultural syndicates, cooperatives, and producers' associations (Berger 1972; Chevalier 1983:89–94; Segalen 1985:321). As in the case of co-ownership of machinery, however, the type of social relations which these institutions make possible are qualitatively different from the traditional relationships of *entraide*.

The character of local-level social interaction has also been altered by the *exode rural*, or rural depopulation, which has occurred as a result of rural poverty and overcrowding throughout Brittany and elsewhere in France during the twentieth century. The massive abandonment of the countryside for the industrial centers of metropolitan France took place at different periods in different parts of Brittany. In some regions the *exode* began prior to World War I, while in others it did not reach significant proportions until the interwar years or after World War II. Numerical loss of population undercut the ability of Breton peasant society to maintain and reproduce its traditional institutions. In particular, depopulation has contributed to the decline of neighborhood-based *entraide*: "Now . . . where one could once count two to ten farms, there remains but one farmer, which makes traditional neighborly cooperation difficult" (Segalen 1984:173).

Other developments have transformed the system of class stratification in rural Brittany. Landless laborers, sharecroppers, and small peasant producers have left the land for jobs in the industrial sector. The disappearance of this body of cheap labor has weakened the position of the landed proprietors, who formerly occupied the highest rung of the stratified social order. Property ownership is no longer a prerequisite for wealth and status. The expenses associated with succession duties as well as other financial difficulties involved in maintaining large estates have motivated this class to sell much of their property. Buying this land, the former middle peasantry is currently emerging as the dominant rural class, in agriculture as well as in the professional and political life of the rural milieu (Elégoët 1983:110–112).

The post–World War II period has also been marked by a general decrease in levels of religious practice. Historically, Brittany has been one of the regions of France where the Catholic church was most firmly entrenched. Most parts of Brittany resisted the republican, anticlerical trends that developed in French society after the Revolution. Until the 1960s the region was characterized by a high degree of adherence to the church. During the 1950s, in over half of rural Breton cantons, at least 50 percent of the adult population attended Mass on a regular basis. Only in 11 out of 215 rural cantons did fewer than 20 percent of adults attend Mass regularly, and in certain areas well over 80 percent attended Mass weekly (Croix and Roudaut 1984:200; Lambert 1985:8). Since the 1960s, however, the level of regular religious practice has fallen by approximately one half (Lambert 1983:224–225; 1985:245). Over the same period, the number of Breton men and women taking up vocations in religious orders has also dropped dramatically (Lambert 1985:265–66). Although apparent in all age categories, the rupture with the church is most notable among the young (Lambert 1985:318).

Since 1945, family structure in rural Brittany has been reorganized, partly as a result of a new emphasis on individualism. Influenced by the teachings of the progressive Jeunesse Agricole Chrétienne movement, the generation that grew up in the 1950s places a high value on the residential autonomy of the nuclear family (Elégoët 1983:108). The extended or stem family pattern of co-residence with parents and/or siblings, formerly a stage in the household cycle and the intergenerational transmission of property, has been largely rejected (Elégoët 1983:108; Segalen 1984:168, 185). This rejection has led to a dramatic increase in the number of "solitary" households, composed of elderly widowed persons who are no longer housed with their married children and grandchildren (Segalen 1984:166–167). The multigenerational household no longer represents an important unit of agricultural production. To some degree the current importance accorded to nuclear family residential autonomy reflects the unwillingness of younger Bretons to accept the traditional domestic power structure, which favored the authority of the elderly (Elégoët 1983:108).

Although kinship remains central to Breton social organization, the post–World War II period has seen a contraction of the family, with ties between parents and their married children strengthened and those linking collaterals and more distant relatives weakened. In household tasks and child care, for example, a high degree of cooperation between mothers and their married daughters is maintained even though they no longer live together. Likewise, as Segalen (1984:170, 173, 184) points out, the level of cooperation in agricultural work between parents and married children residing separately has probably increased relative to the nineteenth century, a phenomenon that may be related to the current decline in neighborhood-based cooperation.

In the contemporary pattern the nuclear family, together with the parents of one or both spouses, has increasingly emerged as the most significant unit of kinship (Segalen 1984:179; 1985:359–360, 362–363, 374).[5] Accompanying this process has been a decline in the size of the nuclear family as the use of contraceptives has become more widely accepted (Elégoët 1983:109). Interaction with kin other than parents and children, including married siblings, cousins, and the siblings of parents, tends to be of secondary importance, although these larger kinship networks do facilitate informal economic exchanges involving labor, home-produced foodstuffs, and information about employment opportunities (Segalen 1984:179; 1985:352–358).

In addition to the changes in patterns of interpersonal relationships, the material conditions of everyday life in rural Brittany have altered significantly since 1945. Running water, indoor plumbing, and electricity are available in all areas. Local roads have been paved and long-distance superhighways constructed. Car ownership has increased dramatically. By 1975, 53.7 percent of Breton households owned one car and a further 11.1 percent owned two or more (INSEE 1979:14). In the same year 20.4 percent of households had installed telephones and 48.7 percent were equipped with water, indoor toilet, shower or bath, and central heating (INSEE 1979:14). An increasingly diverse range of consumer goods has become available. Television has become general since the early 1970s, and by providing entertainment in the nuclear family home it reinforced the decline of *veillées*, neighborhood evening gatherings of dancing, storytelling, and card games, which had started to disappear some years previously. Likewise, running water and automatic washing machines have displaced two of the

---

5. "On observe un resserrement sur le groupe domestique et la génération ascendante" (Segalen 1985:374).

traditional foci for social interaction among women neighbors: the well and the *lavoir,* or washing pool.

Changes in material culture have had the effect of insulating rural Bretons from the intimate relationship with natural forces— winds, rain, and tides—experienced by their nineteenth-century predecessors. This alienation has had important consequences for the interpretation of supernatural significance in phenomena of the natural world. In the social domain, although face-to-face relationships still characterize small rural communities, the intensity of local-level interaction has diminished. Contemporary Bretons have been progressively integrated into the larger universe of metropolitan French society and have also become increasingly aware of cultural diversity on the international level. This process has been accompanied by a heightened consciousness of regional identity, reflected during the 1970s by a renaissance of interest in Breton linguistic and cultural traditions and by the development of political movements promoting separatism or greater regional autonomy for Brittany within France (Berger 1977; Fortier 1980; Lebesque 1970; McDonald 1986; Morin 1970:46, 251–252; Reece 1977; 1979). In addition, despite the widening of social horizons to include regional, national, and international levels, many rural Bretons have retained a strong sense of belonging to more local foci of identity such as the parish (Badone 1987).

As the works of Le Braz, Croix, and other observers attest, familiarity with death and the supernatural was a key feature of Breton culture up to the mid-twentieth century. Indeed, the opposed categories of "supernatural" and "natural" as we commonly understand them probably held little meaning for Bretons of that era. Rather, the two domains were seen as being inextricably interconnected. Phenomena or events which the contemporary Western observer might describe as "supernatural" were probably considered by many Bretons in the past to be completely natural. To some extent this perspective persists in present-day Brittany. I am therefore cautious about using the term "supernatural" and also about drawing a distinction between the natural and the supernatural in my discussion of Breton worldview. As Benson (1977) points out, it is all too easy for the ethnographer to project such folk categories from Western culture onto the cosmological systems of other peoples. In addition, the term "supernatural" is often used ambiguously. To avoid this problem, I have followed Benson's suggestion that the Western category "supernatural" can best be defined as those phenomena that transcend the laws of nature as they are currently understood. Benson further argues that it is worthwhile to retain the natural-supernatural dichotomy "when we can demonstrate that the natives make use of a similar opposition or when we explicitly desire to point out that they do not" (Benson 1977:51). I have chosen to discuss Breton worldview in terms of the natural-supernatural opposition because it seems to me that the lack of a strong distinction between these categories was a hallmark of Breton worldview in the past. Conversely, the developing recognition of a separation between these domains is one of the key features that distinguishes worldview in contemporary Brittany.

Since World War II, attitudes toward death and folk ideas about the connections between the natural and supernatural worlds have responded to other aspects of cultural transformation in Brittany. The relationships between changes in relatively easily observable features of social organization and those involving less tangible realities, such as values and eschatological beliefs, are complex and difficult to elucidate. They can be grasped only through close attention to the explanations offered and the actions performed by individuals in particular ethnographic contexts. These observations must, however, be set in a theoretical framework that enables them to be perceived as parts of a coherent pattern.

Theoretical Considerations

The work of French historian Philippe Ariès provides a useful starting point for research concerning death and social change. As a historian of *mentalités,* Ariès has undertaken a comprehensive study of attitudes toward death in Western culture from the medieval period to the present (Ariès 1982). Influenced by structuralism, he sees the opposition between nature and culture as a critical theme throughout Western history. Nature, for Ariès, represents a violent, dangerous force inimical to human society. Culture, in contrast, demarcates a "safe" zone for human activity, in the form of a symbolic defense system against nature through institutions such as religion, kinship, and law (1982:393). In Ariès's view sexuality and death constitute the weak points in this system of defense, because they are "natural" physiological phenomena that humans share with other animal species. For this reason, throughout the course of Western history rituals and taboos have developed around these areas of experience to control, or, in Ariès's terms, "domesticate" them (1982:394).

Basing his analysis on literary and iconographic sources, Ariès argues that death during the early Middle Ages was "tame." It was accepted with resignation as a natural, familiar occurrence and accompanied by collective rituals that emphasized the permanence of the social group over the loss of an individual life. In this way, death was integrated into the fabric of community social existence. Medieval literature suggests that a "good" or desirable death was one that gave advance warning, either through natural signs, such as the symptoms of disease, or supernatural presentiments, such as visions. These omens gave the dying the opportunity to arrange their worldly affairs and compose themselves for the passage to the otherworld, where the state of the dead as most commonly depicted was analogous to sleep (Ariès 1982:5–28).

In mapping the history of Western responses to death, Ariès constructs an evolutionary, or what might more properly be called a devolutionary, model in which death reverts through several successive stages from the tame to the savage state. According to Ariès, in late twentieth century postindustrial Euro-American society, death has broken through the system of cultural defenses erected against nature during earlier periods. Our own society is characterized by the "denial of death." No longer familiar, death has become unmentionable, for it inspires fear and horror. The idea of death is repressed, and death as an event is pushed to the margins of social existence. The dying, placed in medical institutions, are prevented from knowing the finality of their condition. Cemeteries and funerals are avoided, and public expressions of mourning are discouraged (Ariès 1982:559–601). This theme of death denied in contemporary Western culture has been the focus of much research in the social sciences since the 1960s (Blauner 1966; Bowman 1959; Dempsey 1975; Goody 1975; Gorer [1965] 1967; Griffin and Tobin 1982; Huntington and Metcalf 1979; Jackson 1977; Stannard 1975).

In the context of this study it is impossible to do more than present a brief and partial summary of Ariès's complex analysis of the historical stages through which Western attitudes toward death have progressed. He traces the loss of the tame death initially to an increasing awareness of individual identity and a corresponding decline in the importance of the community, which he dates to the later Middle Ages (1982:208–209, 285–286, 293). Between the sixteenth and the eighteenth centuries the denial of death was given further impetus by the new theological doctrines of Protestantism and the Counter-Reformation, which deemphasized the ritual importance of the moment of death for salvation. For Calvin and Erasmus, it was necessary for the Christian to devote an entire lifetime to piety and personal communion with God. Therefore death itself was accorded no sacred or special quality (Ariès 1982:300–305). Although this theological stance was originally intended both to purge Christian sacraments of their "superstitious" elements and to inspire a more rational, lifelong meditation upon death, its outcome was to distance death from the realm of everyday experience by reducing the significance of physical death as an event (Ariès 1982:314–315).

During the seventeenth and eighteenth centuries, the "first manifestation of the great modern fear of death" appears, in the form of widespread anxiety concerning premature burial (Ariès 1982:397–401, 403). Romanticism, in the following era, marked a "revolution in affectivity," which Ariès claims has important consequences for reactions in the face of death. At this period, he argues, the nuclear family pattern becomes dominant in Western society. Henceforth intense emotional investment is concentrated in a few individuals, whereas formerly affectivity was distributed more diffusely among members of the extended family and the larger community. With the nuclear family pattern, the death of close relatives becomes extremely difficult to cope with emotionally. Thus, during the late eighteenth and nineteenth centuries, death begins to be depicted as the precursor to reunion with loved ones in the afterlife. Moreover, at this period belief in an afterlife becomes increasingly independent of formal religious faith (Ariès 1982: 471–472).

For Ariès the development of the denial of death is also linked to the declining belief in evil in Western culture (1982:610). Furthermore, he suggests that as Western society has become more and more capable of dominating nature through technology, the perceived need for symbolic defenses against nature has decreased. Death, as a weak point in the cultural defense system, has been left unguarded. Ariès argues that the subject of death is repressed in contemporary Western consciousness because it is one of the few natural phenomena that modern technology has proved unable to control. The medicalization of death has generated a view of death as disease that can be overcome. Technology, however, has failed to provide a cure (Ariès 1982:583–588, 595, 611–614).

Despite some questioning of his chronological schema (Stone 1981), many historians credit Ariès for having grasped the broad outlines of the changing patterns of death-related *mentalités* in Western history (McManners 1981:118; Whaley 1981:7–8). His emphasis on the development of individualism and family affections as critical factors shaping responses to death is generally well accepted (McManners 1981:121). Nevertheless, Ariès has come under criticism for failing to explain how particular attitudes, such as the tame death, come into being, and for neglecting to specify the mechanisms that lead them to alter. He makes no attempt to analyze transformations of *mentalités* in relation to material, economic, or demographic variables that might promote a clearer understanding of the causes of change (Whaley 1981:8). His analysis thus appears to rely on some poorly defined evolutionary or devolutionary tendency inherent in culture as the causal factor underlying the appearance of new *mentalités*. In addition, like most unidirectional models, Ariès's devolutionary paradigm tends to oversimplify social and cultural reality. He has difficulty, for example, in reconciling the denial of death with the recent renewal of interest in death and dying on the part of health-care professionals and social scientists, best exemplified in the work of Elisabeth Kübler-Ross (1969). Moreover, Ariès's model does not adequately cope with the persistence of features of the tame death through to the present. As he recognizes, the "tame" acceptance of death is recorded in literary contexts as diverse as nineteenth-century American settlers' letters and Solzhenitsyn's *Cancer Ward* (Ariès 1982:16, 447). Yet he is able to explain this type of "survival" or prolongation of a *mentalité* beyond the historical epoch to which it supposedly corresponds only through reference to disparities between elite and popular culture, or to differing rates of social evolution in urban and rural areas (1982:16, 28, 410, 447–450).

In spite of these shortcomings, Ariès provides the anthropologist interested in death with some important insights. In my own work on Brittany I have attempted to build on these insights and combine them with theoretical perspectives formulated by social anthropologists interested in religion and symbolic systems. In my view it is useful to retain Ariès's categories of the "tame death" and "death denied" as heuristic devices, bearing in mind that real-world responses to death probably never completely correspond to either category. In addition, rather than place these conceptually opposed responses at two endpoints on an evolutionary or devolutionary scale, it is more instructive to view them as linked to different types of social structural conditions, which are not confined to any particular historical period. To some extent, therefore, I take a Durkheimian approach in suggesting that in any given society, religion—broadly defined to include both responses to death and eschatological beliefs—corresponds to that society's system of social organization. However, I do not share Durkheim's rather mechanical, sociologically deterministic interpretation of religion, which portrays religious systems as simple reflections of social processes. Rather, I suggest, together with Peter Berger, that "the same human activity that produces society also produces religion, with the relation between the two products always being a dialectical one" (Berger 1967:48).

My view of religion and social structure has also been influenced by the work of Clifford Geertz, who argues that equal weight must be given to social and cultural processes and that neither should be viewed as the "'mirror image' of the other" (1973b:143). Only in this way can the functionalist oversimplification of reducing religion's role to the maintenance of social institutions be avoided. While religion undoubtedly does perform this role under certain circumstances, it can also be a potent force for structural change. Alternatively, religious beliefs and rituals may themselves be transformed to correspond to new social situations. As Geertz contends, religion and social organization are "independent, yet interdependent, variables" (1973b:169).

In the chapters that follow I hope to demonstrate that there has been such an interdependent, dialectical, or mutually reinforcing relationship between changes in Breton social organization over the past thirty to forty years and changes over the same period in

Breton responses to death. Specifically, I suggest that the latter have moved in the direction of Ariès's "denial," although this movement is far from definitive and complete. Moreover, as later chapters demonstrate, while the concept of a growing denial of death explains some of the recent changes that have taken place in Breton worldview, it fails to provide an adequate interpretation of others.

The complex pattern of change and continuity which typifies contemporary Breton attitudes toward death cannot be understood without considering the issue of secularization. Secularization, or the weakening of what Geertz (1973c:110) has called the "religious perspective," is intimately connected to the emergence of new patterns of reacting toward death, for it is religion's role to provide meaningful explanations of reality in the face of such anomic experiences (Berger 1967:42, 44, 51–52). Although frequently associated exclusively with modernization, urbanization, and the development of scientific thought, the secular worldview has more fruitfully been linked to particular social-structural conditions. Specifically, Douglas ([1970] 1978) has argued that one aspect of secularization, the negative evaluation of ritual, corresponds to nonhierarchical social settings, where individual autonomy is emphasized and pressures to conform to community norms are weak. In contrast, where ritual is positively valued, the community is tightly knit and exerts strong controls over its members. Roles and social obligations in this type of society are determined by position within the hierarchical social structure.

In Douglas's view the characteristics of social structure typical of secular and ritualistic societies are also correlated with differing conceptions of sin. In the ritualistic setting, the idea of sin refers to specific formal acts and offenses against the Deity. For example, prior to Vatican II, Catholics considered it a sin to eat meat on Friday. In the more secular context, where ritual is negatively valued, sin involves, to a greater degree, states of mind. Wrongdoing is subject to reasoning, and morality becomes a question of personal decisions rather than obligations. In such a social situation, ethical values are emphasized over specific prescriptions and proscriptions.

The deritualization described by Douglas is one facet of the process of secularization occurring in contemporary Brittany. I use the term "secularization" with caution, since it is clear from other European contexts that declining levels of participation in church rituals do not necessarily correspond to a decline in religious faith. The expression of faith may be moving from the realm of public observance into more private and personal domains (Freeman 1978: 104–105, 118). Nonetheless, in Brittany as in many other parts of rural Catholic Europe, religion is becoming a discretionary domain. In the past, powerful sanctions made it difficult for rural Europeans to live outside the religious norms of the Catholic church, especially in contexts such as Salazarist Portugal and Franco's Spain (Brandes 1976; Riegelhaupt 1973, 1984). Now, however, religion is increasingly perceived as something the individual can elect to pursue or ignore. In Brittany, as in southern Europe, many are choosing the latter option.[6] Diminishing levels of church attendance in contemporary Brittany have been accompanied by widespread questioning of the traditional Catholic cosmological system. Related to this process is the displacement, at least to some extent, of folk-religious beliefs that deviate from Catholic orthodoxy. Popular conceptions relating to the Anaon, the Ankou, and omens of death fall into this category of unorthodox beliefs which, while ignored or condemned by the church, are nevertheless considered "religious" by those who subscribe to them and which serve, like formal church doctrines, to impose a meaningful order on individual experiences of tragedy or death. As Freeman (1978) and Riegelhaupt (1973, 1984) have argued, definitions of religion in European society must include such popular beliefs alongside the authorized rituals and theological tenets of the established churches.[7]

The displacement of folk beliefs and orthodox Catholic doctrines are both facets of the process of "rationalization" or "disenchantment of the world," which, according to Weber, involves the ascendancy of modes of thought based on empirical observation, technical mastery, and scientific knowledge (Weber 1946). In juxtaposing and contrasting the rationalized, scientific view of the

---

6. See Behar (forthcoming) for discussion of the "contestability" of religion in contemporary rural Spain.
7. On this point I disagree with Devlin, who argues in her recent study of nineteenth-century French superstitions that the unorthodox practices and beliefs of the period had little to do with religion and functioned primarily to provide psychological reassurance, escapism, and release from frustration in the face of hostile natural and social environments (Devlin 1987). Devlin implicitly presents a view of "true" religion as being concerned exclusively with morality and spirituality.

world with the supernatural perspective throughout this study, I do not mean to imply a devaluation of the latter. Neither do I intend to suggest that the two represent radically separate modes of thought which cannot coexist in the same culture and within the same individual. It is my position that people in all cultures at all historical periods employ both "scientific" and "supernatural" ways of dealing with the world. Contemporary Bretons are themselves clearly aware of the distinction between the supernatural and scientific or naturalistic modes of interpreting reality. They frequently claim that there has been a shift within living memory in their culture away from the one and toward the other mode. In my view this transition has not led to replacement of the supernatural or religious perspective by the scientific one. People in rural Brittany continue to adhere to both supernatural and scientific models. Often each functions in a different context. However, I share my respondents' perception that in general terms, over the course of the twentieth century in Brittany, scientific or naturalistic explanations have increasingly been accepted as more credible than supernatural explanations.

In order to outline ways in which different responses to death might be connected to specific features of social organization, I have chosen to combine elements of Ariès's work on death with approaches from Douglas's analysis of secularization. In so doing, I seek to link worldview to other aspects of society and culture and emphasize the interconnections between changes in attitudes toward death and changes in related sociocultural domains. Such an approach avoids the pitfalls of treating changes in deathways as if they occurred in a vacuum or resulted from some evolutionary impulse towards modernity.

Specifically, I suggest that Ariès's tame response to death is likely to be dominant in a hierarchically organized social context where religion and ritual are important and where a sense of sin as inherent in formal transgressions is strongly developed. In this face-to-face setting social control is relatively inflexible, and concomitantly, individuals perceive their lives to be governed by destiny or fate. Both formal and informal religious systems in this type of society are marked by the perception that the natural world is closely connected to the supernatural and that to a large extent the two domains interpenetrate. Conversely, Ariès's denial of death is most likely to be found in a secular society where humanistic ethical values are emphasized and where face-to-face social interaction is minimized. Social control is less rigid in this individualistic setting, and personal autonomy predominates over obligations to the community. Here it is believed that each person shapes his or her own fate. According to this rationalized worldview the natural and supernatural realms are perceived as being sharply demarcated. To quote Weber, such a society has undergone the "disenchantment of the world."[8]

In attempting to understand the ways in which attitudes toward death in Brittany have changed over the past forty years, it is useful to think in terms of a shift away from the first type of society described above and toward the second. However, this shift has by no means been total, irreversible, or without exception. Moreover, although, roughly speaking, much of contemporary Anglo-American society could be said to approach the latter characterization, whereas Breton society of the nineteenth and early twentieth centuries could be compared more closely to the former, the transition that has taken place in Brittany should not be conceived of as the result of some inevitable trend toward cultural homogenization. Death in Brittany during the 1980s is far from identical to death in contemporary Toronto or London, but it is also different from death in the Brittany of the 1880s. The changes in Breton responses to death cannot be viewed in isolation but must be seen as part of a complex pattern of mutually reinforcing and interdependent transformations in many different domains.

Five major themes emerge as central to the complex pattern of change and continuity which characterizes contemporary Breton deathways. The first is the development of the denial of death in a region where, until recently, death was accepted as a natural phenomenon and integrated into community social life. A second theme is the gradual transition from a religious view of the world to one based on naturalistic, empirical science. In this process of "disenchantment" certain features of death-related ritual are decreasing in importance, both socially and in terms of their ability to respond meaningfully to the needs of the bereaved.

Both secularization and the growing denial of death in Brittany

---

8. "Entzauberung der Welt" (Weber 1958:105n. 19).

are closely related to a third domain in which change has occurred: that of social organization. The post–World War II period in Brittany has witnessed, in Durkheim's terms, the replacement of mechanical by organic solidarity, at least to some degree (Durkheim 1933). A fixed, hierarchical, class-based society is giving way to more fluid structures permitting greater social mobility, and the importance of the community is waning with the growth of individualism. These changes in Breton social structure have been accompanied and to some extent precipitated by transformations in the material conditions of rural life. The mechanization of agriculture, improvement of transportation facilities, and increasing access to the communications media constitute a fourth important domain in which changes have affected both Breton worldview and cultural constructions of death.

A fifth theme stands out in the rich and intricate mosaic of contemporary Breton responses to death. In spite of religious change, modernization of material culture, social-structural transformation, and the impingement of national and international levels of culture on local Breton levels of identity, death remains an important cultural preoccupation in this region. Its importance is seen, for example, in the continuing demand for Catholic funeral services, the frequency of "visits" to the cemetery, and the increased elaboration of tomb monuments since the 1950s. Moreover, elements of the "enchanted" worldview, which draws little distinction between natural and supernatural categories, continue to be meaningful, particularly for the elderly in rural areas. All of these factors suggest that social transitions and changes in *mentalités* are complex processes that may occur in varying rates and in varying forms, even within a single region.

My awareness that cultural change can assume different patterns in different local contexts was reinforced by my experience in two Breton communities representing highly contrasting subregions of Lower Brittany. During the initial two months of fieldwork I lived in Plouguerneau, on the northwest coast of Brittany, approximately thirty kilometers from Brest. Following this, I spent thirteen months in La Feuillée, a smaller center in the Monts d'Arrée area of interior Finistère. I also made shorter visits to cities such as Morlaix and Brest in order to gain a perspective on death in Breton urban settings. In addition, social networks in both Plouguerneau and La Feuillée extend to neighboring communities. Therefore, although my research focuses on these two centers, it is in no way limited to them. However, these communities were my "home base" in Brittany. Much of my understanding of the ways in which contemporary Bretons attempt to deal with death is a product of my experiences in Plouguerneau and La Feuillée. For this reason it is important to introduce the differing cultural backgrounds of both communities and the Breton subregions in which they are located.

Plouguerneau and La Feuillée

Typical of rural Brittany, the pattern of settlement in Plouguerneau consists of a central *bourg* surrounded by rural "villages" or *quartiers*. The church, municipal administrative offices, post office, and stores are located in the *bourg*. Here too, the local professionals including the doctors, nurse and notary have their homes and offices. The outlying villages vary in size from two or three to ten or twelve, primarily agricultural, households. *Bourg* and villages constitute a single administrative unit, the commune.

According to the 1983 census, Plouguerneau numbers 5,388 inhabitants. Relative to most communities in rural Brittany, for Plouguerneau the major period of social upheaval and population loss, the *exode rural*, came late, during the 1960s (Elégoët 1983:103). Plouguerneau lost half its agricultural labor force between 1968 and 1975. Despite this loss, the commune remains densely populated, with 130 people per square kilometer (Elégoët 1983:103–104). This high population density has been maintained as a result of Plouguerneau's diverse economic base. In addition to agriculture, which now occupies one quarter of the commune's active labor force, tourism and fishing provide employment. Those living along the coast harvest seaweed, which is sold for use in the pharmaceutical and food processing industries. A significant proportion of Plouguerneau men are enlisted in the French navy or receive navy retirement pensions (Elégoët 1983:104; Hernin 1983:18). Other men and women from the community commute to jobs in Brest.

In terms of both population and geographical extent (4,333 hectares), Plouguerneau is one of the largest communes in Finistère. Whereas most Breton communes comprise only a single parish, the post-Revolutionary communal boundaries having been established along earlier parish lines (Croix and Roudaut 1984:197), Plouguerneau includes three parishes. In addition to the central church in the *bourg* of Plouguerneau, there are churches in Lilia, five kilometers to the northwest on the coast, and in Grouanec, four kilometers inland to the southeast. Each of these parishes has its own cemetery. Both Lilia and Grouanec are small *bourgs* and commercial centers in their own right, although they lack administrative autonomy. A third center of population is located along the coast slightly to the east of Lilia, at Saint-Michel. Here a weekly Mass is celebrated in the seventeenth-century chapel. Lilia and Saint-Michel are more heavily populated than the Grouanec area, partly because most of the 850 secondary residences in the community, occupied during the summer months by tourists from Germany, Paris, and Brest, are located along the coast.

The Lilia–Saint-Michel and Grouanec subdivisions of the commune correspond to two different types of traditional subsistence adaptations. On the coast, small-scale agricultural production was supplemented by fishing and seaweed harvesting. Oriented toward the sea, people from Lilia also made careers in the navy to a greater extent than those from other areas of the commune. The inland, Grouanec sector has always been dominated by farming. Until the 1950s these two worlds remained largely distinct, and relations between *les gens de la mer* and *les gens de la terre* (sea folk and land folk) were marked by antipathy.

For a variety of reasons, including Plouguerneau's size and the massive influx of summer tourists that made fieldwork unmanageable, I decided after two months to move to interior Brittany. Although I made several short return visits to Plouguerneau, my remaining time in Brittany was spent in La Feuillée.

Located sixty kilometers east of Plouguerneau and forty kilometers inland, La Feuillée presents a striking contrast to the seaboard community. Whereas Plouguerneau is situated on the flat coastal plain, La Feuillée boasts the highest point in Brittany, Roc'h Trévézel, which at 384 meters above sea level is the summit of the chain of hills known as the Monts d'Arrée. With slightly over six hundred inhabitants and a surface area of 3,176 hectares, La Feuillée is sparsely populated. While there are one hundred or more commercial enterprises in Plouguerneau, the *bourg* of La Feuillée has only four stores, a garage, a hotel, a bank, and a *crêperie* (see fig. 2).

Several tradesmen, including two carpenters, a mason, and a roofer, live and work in the commune. In addition to the *bourg*, there are thirteen villages. The largest of these, Kerelcun, contains fifty-five inhabited houses and has its own *café-boulangerie*, which also serves as a general store. Each village is surrounded by its fields, many of them identified by name and separated from one another by *talus*, low walls of earth and stone, upon which flourish blackberry bushes, gorse, and trees such as hawthorn, willow, and hazelnut.

Unlike Plouguerneau, La Feuillée began to experience the effects of the *exode rural* as early as the last quarter of the nineteenth century. Between 1801 and 1876, the population of the parish increased from 1,300 to 2,100. With population growth and an egalitarian pattern of inheritance, existing small landholdings were divided and subdivided, becoming increasingly less economically viable. As a response to poverty and overcrowding, emigration from La Feuillée first becomes apparent between 1876 and 1914, when the population dropped overall from 2,100 to 1,800, despite periodic reversals of the downward trend. The year 1911 marks a watershed after which the population of La Feuillée entered a period of uninterrupted decline. Over the seventy-three-year period between 1911 and 1984, the commune lost 66.8 percent of its population. The sharpest drop occurred directly after World War II, between 1946 and 1954, when an average of thirty-five people left the commune each year. The number of inhabitants decreased from 1,269 to 989 over these eight years (Chaussy, Emeillat, and Messager 1976:17–24, Annexe 1). By 1984 the population had reached a low point of 627.

Prior to the opening of the Roscoff-Lorient *voie express* in 1983, which passes through the commune, La Feuillée was bypassed by major lines of communication. The new highway, which connects the north and southwest coasts of Brittany, provides access from La Feuillée within half an hour by car to the two main cities in the area, Morlaix (population 20,532) to the north, and Carhaix (population 8,949) further south in the interior. The cantonal administrative and commercial center, Huelgoat (population 2,230) is located thirteen kilometers southeast of La Feuillée.

In both Plouguerneau and La Feuillée, I was welcomed into all aspects of community life, from agricultural labor to *festoù-noz*, evenings of Breton music and dance popular in the Monts d'Arrée. Although I was at first hesitant to attend wakes and funerals, I soon discovered that people in Plouguerneau and La Feuillée considered it quite natural that I should do so. The rituals associated with death in rural Brittany are much more public than those I had experienced in North America. In La Feuillée, where I developed especially close ties, my presence at funerals was easily accepted and, indeed, in some cases expected. People spoke naturally to me about their experiences of death and bereavement. La Feuillée is largely a community of the elderly, and perhaps this explains in part why death and grieving are such frequent topics of conversation there. During the fall and winter months, when the pace of outdoor work slackens, I spent many afternoons of conversation over coffee at kitchen tables in La Feuillée. Mostly I listened, as widows and elderly persons told me about their solitude and described for me the deaths of those whom they had loved. I suspect that there are some things that can be said more easily, or in different ways, to an outsider than to one's close neighbors and kin. Whatever the case, I found myself drawn into many lives and a participant in many griefs. Often, if I asked questions about aspects of Breton death ritual, I was myself questioned in turn: "How did *you* feel? What do people do in Canada?" The similarities and differences that such comparisons highlighted stimulated people to reflect on their own culture and share their insights with me.

Although death and grieving were often part of daily conversation, my companions in Plouguerneau and La Feuillée were much more reticent about ghosts, *intersignes,* and witchcraft. People in rural Brittany are very guarded when it comes to revealing their feelings about such occult phenomena, especially to outsiders, who, it is suspected, will ridicule such "foolish and old-fashioned superstitions." Consequently, it was important to make clear that I did not share this kind of deprecating attitude. Often my ability to use Breton terms proved that I was already somewhat privy to inside knowledge and helped gain the confidence of those with whom I talked. Sometimes, while doing farm tasks or at meetings of the La Feuillée senior citizen's club, I sought to pose questions about aspects of the supernatural such as *intersignes.* In certain situations, during evenings of cardplaying or at coffee parties, men and women enjoyed relating narratives about experiences with the supernatural because these stories are intrinsically interesting and provide good entertainment. As much as possible I recorded this type of narrative on tape to enable accurate word-for-word transcription. For less detailed folklore materials such as proverbs, and other types of information, I relied on notes taken during and after conversations.

At the beginning of my fieldwork, as a North American with a tendency to "deny" death, it was difficult for me to explain that death was the primary focus of my research. However, as time went on, particularly in La Feuillée, it became apparent that Bretons themselves are well aware of the centrality of death in their culture. My half-embarrassed efforts to explain why I was interested in attitudes toward death in Brittany typically met with the response, "Oh yes, that's very important. Here we have the *culte des morts*."

Differences between the Plouguerneau and La Feuillée Regions

Lower Brittany encompasses four main subregions, whose boundaries are coterminous with those of dioceses established by the Catholic church during the Middle Ages. Although the departmental boundaries established after the Revolution crosscut the older ecclesiastical organization of territory, the medieval dioceses retain symbolic significance as foci of identity in Breton political, academic, and popular discourse (Badone 1987; Croix and Roudaut 1984:196–197; Kuter 1985; Simon 1979). Geographical, economic, and historical circumstances have led to the development of strikingly different *mentalités* in each of these regions. An observation made by political analyst André Siegfried in 1913 remains relevant to the present day. Writing of the former dioceses, he states: "They bracket the four principal dialects of the Breton language and, above all, they correspond to four political, religious, and psychological temperaments so clearly distinct that it is necessary to see in them, at least as far as politics is concerned, the four essential compartments of the peninsula" (1913:133).

As shown on map 1, the medieval dioceses of Lower Brittany are the Léon and Trégor in the north, and the Cornouaille (known as Kernev—pronounced *Kerné*—in Breton) and Vannes in the south. This study is concerned with only two of these subregions: the

Léon and the Kernev, where Plouguerneau and La Feuillée respectively are located.

As Siegfried states, "The political unity of the department of Finistère is facetious. The reality is the opposition between the Cornouaille and the Léon" (1913:164). Traditionally the Kernev has been predominantly *rouge*, or red—republican and anticlerical—in its political orientation. The Monts d'Arrée represents the most radical, democratic area of the subregion. Historically in the Monts d'Arrée an ideology of egalitarianism was conditioned by the fact that, unlike the Léon, this was a region of independent small landholders with very few nobles (Siegfried 1913:174, 177). The power of the clergy, who exerted a strong influence over temporal affairs in the Léon, was muted in the Monts d'Arrée: "At base, the population of the mountain is not very religious. The mayors keep a close watch over the curés and know how to prevent them from overstepping the boundaries of their functions" (Siegfried 1913:176).

In addition, overcrowding and poverty on the small farms of the region and the infertility of the soil made it necessary for its inhabitants either to emigrate, finding employment in the French navy and civil service, or to adopt a secondary employment to supplement returns from agriculture. Both these alternatives exposed La Feuillée to the outside world and to republican political ideas. In the first case, those who left the Monts d'Arrée to work as civil servants naturally developed close ties to the French state. The social milieu of these *petits fonctionnaires* was particularly progressive and left-wing during the early part of the twentieth century. The émigrés maintained contact with relatives in La Feuillée and frequently returned to the community on retirement, bringing with them an awareness of cosmopolitan intellectual trends. The second alternative, that of taking a supplemental employment, generally involved some form of entrepreneurial activity requiring travel into other regions of Finistère. Thus, this pattern also brought people from La Feuillée into contact with external influences and new ideas (Siegfried 1913:176). These influences found expression in voting patterns. From the Revolution to Siegfried's time, La Feuillée, like the entire canton of Huelgoat in which it is located, consistently cast the majority of their votes for left-wing or extreme left candidates in legislative elections (Siegfried 1913:177–78). Currently the Parti

Communiste Français (PCF) and the Parti Socialiste (PS) enjoy a broad base of support in the Monts d'Arrée.

The Léon, in contrast, displays the opposite *blanc,* or white, political tendency. Along with most other Léonard cantons, the canton of Lannilis, where Plouguerneau is located, had never given a majority to a left-wing candidate in any legislative election prior to Siegfried's study (Siegfried 1913:191). These patterns have persisted to the present (Lambert 1983:208).[9] The dominant political parties in the contemporary Léon are the Union pour la Démocratie Française (UDF) and the Rassemblement pour la République (RPR). Jean-Marie Le Pen's extreme right-wing Front National has also gained some ground here in elections during the 1980s.

The traditionally conservative political orientation of the Léon was largely the result of its domination by the Catholic church: "The Léon is, above all, a Catholic society, where political life, like spiritual life, is supremely governed by its clergy" (Siegfried 1913: 181). Although a noble class existed in the Léon, it was not particularly rich or influential. Rather, Léonard society of the late nineteenth and early twentieth centuries was controlled by a coalition between the church and the *juloded,* or wealthy landed peasantry. Comfortably affluent, capable of hiring servants and agricultural laborers, the *juloded* were a proud, self-conscious class within which intermarriages were common. They encouraged their sons to pursue higher education at local Catholic colleges. Close ties of kinship and mutual interest were established between this upper peasantry and the church, since many sons and daughters of *juloded* families took up religious vocations (Siegfried 1913:182–183; Le Gallo 1980:79–83). The clergy was able to maintain its social power in the Léon, even as late as the 1950s, through a clerical discourse that emphasized death, the Last Judgment, and retribution for one's sins in the afterlife (Croix and Roudaut 1984). As Siegfried points out, Léonard priests felt free to intervene in the political life of their parishes, threatening refusal of absolution to those who did not vote for the *candidat du presbytère* (Siegfried 1913:184). Similar sanctions were carried out against those who sent their children to the republican state-run schools or subscribed to newspapers whose

---

9. Although, in an exception which may signal the beginning of a changing trend, Plouguerneau elected a socialist mayor in the 1983 municipal elections.

ideological stance conflicted with that of the church. Such people could risk losing their jobs, farms, and social status as a result of boycotting and ostracism initiated by the clergy. The curé frequently went so far as to dictate details of his parishioners' personal lives, such as the choice of marriage partners or godparents (Siegfried 1913:184). The social power of the clergy was accepted primarily because priests were feared and revered as representatives of God, the Supreme Authority:

> Popular belief depicts the representative of the church as the formidable dispenser of the favors of heaven and the punishments of hell. Between his sovereign hands, like Saint Peter, he holds the keys to paradise; he holds those to the abyss as well. . . . Who, in effect, in this Léon, would bypass the curé? Those who dare confront death without his aid are rare; hardly less rare are those who resign themselves to living without him.
> (Siegfried 1913:183, 185)

It would be an oversimplification to state that all Plouguerneau residents are *blanc* and all those living in La Feuillée are *rouge*. The diverse religious orientations of Plouguerneau and La Feuillée are discussed with greater attention to their complexity in Chapter 7. However, in each community differing experiences of Catholicism have been influential in shaping both worldview and attitudes toward death.

Plouguerneau and La Feuillée have followed different trajectories of social change throughout the course of the present century. Paradoxically, despite its earlier exposure to outside influences, La Feuillée appears more "traditional" than Plouguerneau in terms of material culture. Whereas Plouguerneau is characterized by newly built modern houses, for example, many La Feuillée houses are stone-walled cottages built in the nineteenth century. Although many La Feuillée residents have spent significant portions of their lives living and working in cities, the community as a whole is currently less integrated into the culture of urban Brittany than is Plouguerneau, with its proximity to Brest. Neither Plouguerneau nor La Feuillée represents a pristine peasant community isolated from larger cultural forces and trends. However, each community is distinctively "Breton." Moreover, like a core around which other issues crystallize, death emerges as a dominant theme of local culture in both Plouguerneau and La Feuillée.

2

The Social Context of Aging and Death in La Feuillée

> *Ar yaouankiz a zo ur boked*
> Youth is a bouquet
> *Ha ne bad ket pell*
> And it does not last long,
> *Ma ne teuit ket d'e guitaat*
> If you do not leave it
> *Eñ a zeu d'ho tilezel*
> It will abandon you.
>
> (Told by Catherine Hamon,
> aged seventy-six,
> La Feuillée)

Introduction

It is an autumn afternoon in La Feuillée. The few tourists who stray into the commune during the summer have long since returned to Holland, England, or Germany. Throughout the month of August, most of the elderly residents of La Feuillée have entertained children or grandchildren on vacation. Like the tourists, they too have gone home, to jobs and school in Paris, Brest, and Marseille. Most of the time the *bourg* is quiet. This afternoon, however, there are cars parked around the central square, and small groups of men and women walk purposefully in the fading sunlight toward the schoolhouse, halfway up the hill on the road leading out of the *bourg* toward the main highway. Today is Wednesday, when schools are closed during the afternoon, and the La Feuillée *club du troisième âge,* or senior citizens' club, is coming together for its weekly meeting.

The school is an imposing structure, erected to house over a hundred students during the interwar years. Now, with under thirty-five children attending classes in the commune, the school stands virtually empty. Currently the elderly make the most use of the building, for the activities of their club. The same people who entered the school fifty years earlier to learn the skills that would provide them with jobs in the world outside La Feuillée now return to their former classrooms to reminisce about the past, exchange news about the present, and renew old friendships.

How do the people of La Feuillée interpret the course of their lives, and how do they come to terms with their inevitable aging and death? This chapter seeks to answer these questions, focusing primarily on the elderly. For many of those who belong to the *club du troisième âge,* death continues to be "tame," like a familiar companion. However, in Breton society as a whole, this response is currently transforming, and new ways of dealing with death and dying are emerging.

The *Retour au Pays*

As in all cultures, death in Brittany is a social process that begins well in advance of the actual physical event. For many people born in La Feuillée the process of death begins on retirement, with a residential transition back to the natal community from the towns and cities of metropolitan France where they have spent their working lives. This pattern of return migration, the *retour au pays,* or return to the home region, is the mirror image of the rural depopulation, the *exode rural,* which has drained the commune of its young people throughout the twentieth century.

Demographic studies indicate that impoverished upland areas of interior Brittany such as the Monts d'Arrée typically show high mortality rates and low birthrates as a result of the emigration of young people to urban centers and the return migration of the elderly (Beuchet 1982:6; Trégouët 1982:28). A survey conducted in the Côtes-du-Nord indicates that a majority of those who choose to return to Brittany on retirement are motivated to do so by family connections or the desire to live in their geographical region of origin (Cormier 1979:34).

In La Feuillée the *retour au pays* is linked to a consciously articulated imperative to die and be buried in the place where one was born. As one forty-seven-year-old man living and working in Brest explains, he hopes to be buried in La Feuillée because "I was born here, and one must end up in the *terre natale* for eternity." A woman of the same age living in the outskirts of Paris describes the need to return to La Feuillée for burial as *un cri du coeur*, a cry from the heart. Many people in La Feuillée expressed a sympathetic interest in the funeral of singer Tino Rossi, who was flown back for burial to his native Corsica after his death in September 1983. As Marie-Thérèse, an elderly La Feuillée woman commented, "He was Corsican. He was born there. That was his *pays*." No further explanation is needed for his desire to be buried in Corsica. Marie-Thérèse's comment is clearly a projection of her own feelings and those of other people from La Feuillée. They were born in the commune, it is their *pays*, and they will return to die, or at least to be buried in the *terre natale*. Such attitudes suggest that the worldview of the elderly in La Feuillée is characterized by a cyclical perception of time, in which birth and death are symbolically linked through return migration. From this perspective, the thirty or forty years spent living and working in cities appear as an insignificant interval bridging the critical moments at the beginning and end of life. Young people in La Feuillée share this cyclical interpretation of the life course. A twenty-four-year-old man from the commune who has recently completed his military service and accepted a job in Paris regretfully calculates that he has thirty-six years to wait before retirement will enable him to return permanently to La Feuillée.

For some returned émigrés readjustment to rural life comes easily. M. Mahé, who has returned to La Feuillée in his seventies after a career in Paris, Toulon, and Brest explains, "It's an imperative to return *au pays*. You find the friends of your childhood again. Their characters have not changed and we talk about the old days, about our youth. We get along very well." Others, accustomed to the cosmopolitan environment of the city and the rapid pace of urban life, find themselves socially isolated, sharing few interests with neighbors who have never lived outside of La Feuillée.

The sometimes ambivalent emotions associated with the *retour au pays* are summed up in a proverb quoted by the middle-aged and elderly in La Feuillée:

> *Piv 'zo ganet e gwall vro*
> He who is born in a miserable country
> *War zu henni a zistro*
> Always returns.

No matter how great were the poverty and hardships which drove them from the Monts d'Arrée in the past, it is believed that those who leave are always inexorably drawn back. "Once they reach a certain age, they all return," observes one woman fatalistically.[1]

The symbolic importance of the *retour au pays* in La Feuillée reflects the influence of the romantic perception of death documented by Ariès for the nineteenth century, which emphasized the loss of beloved relatives and the hope of reunion in the afterlife. Many émigrés express the desire to be buried in La Feuillée "because all the family is there." The natal commune becomes the locus for the reunion of the family, both living and dead. Families frequently make difficult and expensive arrangements to ship the bodies of relatives who die abroad or elsewhere in metropolitan France back to the Monts d'Arrée for burial in the family tomb. Even people in their early thirties voice their unwillingness to be buried in the large, anonymous cemeteries of cities such as Paris, "where we have no roots."

The desire to be buried in La Feuillée is equally strong among the elderly who have spent their entire lives there. These people have maintained a closer ongoing relationship with the cemetery in the commune and with those buried there than have the returned émigrés. Eighty-six-year-old Marie-Thérèse, who has lived in the same house in the *bourg* of La Feuillée over the past fifty-three years, remarks, "There are three in my tomb, waiting for me." Similarly her neighbor, eighty-two-year-old Marguerite Prévost, observes that four people—her husband, her parents, and a son-in-law—are already buried in her tomb. She would not want to be interred elsewhere and separated from them. The son-in-law's body was transported to La Feuillée from Paris, where he died in a hospital. Marguerite explains that each time she visits her grandchildren in the city of Lorient, on the Breton south coast, she tells them, "Now,

---

1. This perception does not accord with social reality, for only a small percentage of those who emigrate do in fact return to La Feuillée on retirement.

if I die while I am here with you, make sure you get your mother to send me back to La Feuillée." Although said partly in jest, this admonition stems from a deeply felt concern.

Acceptance of Death: The Traditional Response

> *Div ha teir amzer*
> Two and three seasons
> *En deus an den*
> Has a man,
> *Ha n'e ket henvel*
> And it is not the same
> *An eil hag eben*
> From one to the other.

Told by eighty-two-year-old Madeleine Bleunven in La Feuillée, this proverb reflects a conception of life as a threefold process evolving through youth and maturity to old age. The unfolding of life from season to season, ultimately ending in death, is accepted by the elderly as an inevitable aspect of the fundamental order of nature. Reflecting on death, Marie-Thérèse observes, "You have to die. It's the most natural thing there is." Similarly, Madeleine Bleunven remarks, "Everyone will go that route. No one is eternal. The respiration stops. It is the same with animals." Having lived all her life in La Feuillée, Madeleine has become accustomed from childhood to the deaths of farm animals and the deaths of people around her. "Getting older, one gets used to sad things," she states, simply.

For Madeleine, like many elderly people in La Feuillée, the state of being dead is not a source of fear. One eighty-eight-year-old woman remarks that she spends days when she feels she would be better off dead than sitting alone in her house with nothing to do. Others see death as a welcome deliverance from physical ailments. Many express the desire to die before they reach their late eighties or nineties, when the prospect of senility looms large. "If only I can keep my mind," says Madeleine, "and not be reduced to worse than a child." Yet before one can achieve the welcome release of "being dead," one must pass through the process of dying. The physical suffering associated with dying constitutes the primary source of anxiety about death for the elderly. As Marie-Thérèse says, "The worst hardship we will have will be when we leave from here. Everyone has to have something to depart from this world." Likewise, Marguerite Prévost confides that it is at night, when she cannot sleep, that she starts "to think black thoughts." She wonders how she is going to die and whether she will suffer greatly beforehand. "At my age one can't help but think about it," she explains. Death sends its messengers in the form of small things like moles and warts that appear on her skin for no apparent reason: "The doctor says it's age that does it." Marguerite observes that each time she shops for things that come in large quantities but are rarely used, such as garden fertilizer, she thinks, "This is surely the last time I'll ever buy that. I won't run out of that again before I die."

The elderly in La Feuillée express their acceptance of death by preparing in advance for the rituals that will mark their own passing. In the armoires of many elderly women one can find carefully wrapped parcels, sometimes marked "In Case of Death," containing fine white linen sheets and pillowcases. At their own wake this linen will be placed on the *lit de mort*, the bed where the body is displayed. Often these parcels of linen contain intricately crocheted white bedspreads made by the women themselves for their *lit de mort*. Some have knitted the white shawls or sweaters they hope to be dressed in during the wake. Advance preparation of burial vaults and tombstones, discussed in detail in Chapter 5, represents another aspect of the acceptance of death. In making these material preparations the elderly come to terms with the fact of their own deaths. Death becomes something over which one can exert some degree of control. Thus it becomes a familiar, less terrifying prospect.

For the elderly in La Feuillée, death continues to be "tame." Their conversations about death are typified by realism and occasional humor. One eighty-seven-year-old woman feels that at her age it is "too late" to have the hip operation that could alleviate her difficulties in walking. *"Tant pis!"* she says lightly, "It's time to die now." Groups of women neighbors chatting together joke with one another about which of them will be the first "to go to the cemetery." "Die today or die tomorrow, it's all the same," claims one woman, in a matter-of-fact tone. Such an acceptance of death and its inevitability for those of her generation is expressed in a proverb quoted by Marie-Thérèse:

> *Ar re yaouank a varv lod eus outo*
> The young die sometimes,
> *Met ar re gozh a varv atav*
> But the old always die.

Fear of the process of dying and acceptance of the state of death itself make attitudes toward euthanasia generally positive among older people in La Feuillée. As one woman phrases it, she would prefer to have "a good injection" than to suffer at length from cancer. However, the elderly also express the desire to know the truth about the likelihood of their dying from the illnesses they suffer. Says one woman, "I told the doctor, 'If it's cancer, I would prefer to know.' You have to endure it."

Aging entails a reassessment of one's position in the community. At eighty-two Madeleine Bleunven observes, almost incredulous, that when she was young she used to think that people of sixty or sixty-five were very old. "And now I've gone beyond them," she notes. Many people in their late seventies and eighties feel that their closest social ties are with the community of the dead. "Everyone around me is in the cemetery," says Madeleine. Similarly, others claim that "now we know more people among the dead than among the living." Each death in the community alters the social points of reference. As one's older neighbors die, one finds that it is oneself who is the oldest person in the *quartier.*

Among the elderly in rural Brittany, age classes continue to be meaningful. In conversations with older women from La Feuillée one frequently hears comments such as, "She is the same age as me. We are from the same class." It is with members of one's age cohort that one passes through all the major rites of passage: baptism, school, First Communion, catechism class, confirmation, marriage, the founding of a family, and, ultimately, death. Says Marie-Thérèse, "Yes, when a group of us get together, one says, 'I'm getting close to the grave,' and we say, 'I'm two years younger, I won't be much longer after you.' We're all going to be there at the same time." Just as those in the same age class make the transition from one social category to another together, so too will they pass from the community of the living to that of the dead at the same time. Death is further "tamed" by the knowledge that one faces it alongside friends in one's age class.

The death of an age-mate serves as a reminder of one's own mortality. At each funeral there are people who turn to each other and say, "He was the same age as us. We are from the same class." Learning of the death of a La Feuillée man slightly older than herself, Marie-Thérèse was visibly shaken. Reflectively, she commented, "One by one, each in turn, we depart." As others die, it becomes apparent that one's own turn cannot be far in the future.

Writing of his youth during the 1920s in rural southern Finistère, Hélias comments, "While I was still in school, death itself was accepted with a kind of fatalism that was not resignation but rather a simple submission to what everyone called his 'star'" (1978:106). His observation applies equally well to the elderly in La Feuillée during the 1980s. Here too, older persons maintain that

> *Pep hini en deus e blanedenn*
> Each one has his destiny (planet).

One dies when one's appointed hour has come.

The cyclical conception of time held by the elderly in La Feuillée links birth with death through return migration. In the same way the cycle of the seasons provides a metaphor for death, regeneration, and the succession of generations. Autumn is associated with death in La Feuillée. It is said that "here, more people die when the leaves fall."[2]

New Responses: The *Troisième Age*

Throughout France, the increase in life expectancy over the course of the twentieth century has contributed to recognition of the need to provide special social and medical services for the elderly (INSEE

---

2. Although autumn is perceived to be the time when many people die, according to a local general practitioner there is little seasonal variation in mortality rates, an observation confirmed by INSEE (1980:64) statistics for Brittany as a whole. The tendency to link individual deaths to a larger natural order was also apparent in La Feuillée after several deaths during the first two weeks of May 1984. People attributed the succession of closely spaced deaths to the circumstances that 1984 was a leap year and that the deaths had occurred during the *lune rousse*, the first lunar month after Easter, which is often a period of nightly frosts that kill newly sprouting plants.

1979:3). This recognition has come with particular force in Brittany. As demographic statistics reveal, this is a region of aging population. While the proportion of people over sixty-five in the four Breton departments as a whole, at 14.6 percent, is not appreciably higher than the national average of 14.3 percent, there are striking demographic variations within the region, partly resulting from different patterns of migration and return migration. In the majority of cantons in interior Finistère, Morbihan, and the Côtes-du-Nord, for example, over 18 percent of the population is older than sixty-five. More than 21 percent of the population is over sixty-five in ten cantons in Finistère, twelve in the Côtes-du-Nord, and four in the Morbihan. In the canton of Sizun, just west of La Feuillée, 28.7 percent of the population is over sixty-five (INSEE 1979: Map 2). The commune of La Feuillée itself represents an extreme example of these demographic characteristics. Of its 627 inhabitants in 1984, 227 (36.2 percent) were over sixty-five years of age.

Brittany's current demographic situation has given rise to the local assimilation of a new social category recognized elsewhere in France, the *troisième âge*. Literally translatable as "third age," *troisième âge* is more closely analogous in meaning to such English euphemisms for old age and the elderly as "the golden age" and "senior citizens." Use of the term *troisième âge* in Brittany reflects the progressive distancing of the processes of aging and death from the center of Breton social life.

Prior to the introduction in 1962 of the *indemnité viagère de départ*, a compensation payment for aging agriculturalists who cease farming and turn their land over to another producer, the majority of farmers continued to work their land as long as health permitted. Cultural norms stressing the residential autonomy of the nuclear family were less developed before the 1960s, and many rural households combined two or three generations, with elderly parents assisting in the agricultural exploitation until physical ailments made them dependent on their children for care (INSEE 1979:9–10; Segalen 1984:167). With the subsequent decline of the extended family, the institution of pensions permitting farmers to retire at sixty-five, and the acceleration of the *retour au pays* since the 1970s, the *troisième âge* in Brittany has become a new category or social compartment with its own needs and activities, set off from youth and middle age.

The demand for specialized pursuits for the elderly has led to the formation of *clubs du troisième âge,* or senior citizens' clubs, in over a hundred communes in the department of Finistère. Founded in 1978, the La Feuillée *club du troisième âge* is seen by its members as relatively successful in combating the problems of loneliness among the elderly in the commune and providing them with social activities. The club's weekly meetings are held in the unused classrooms of the La Feuillée primary school. During the winter the men in the club play *pétanque* indoors in a downstairs classroom, where a bar is set up. The game moves outdoors into the school courtyard in warmer weather. Upstairs the women play whist or dominoes. For three francs members receive afternoon coffee at four o'clock, complete with fresh bread from the La Feuillée baker, butter, and jam. Special events such as New Year's are celebrated by a more elaborate coffee party, featuring singing and entertainment by members of the club. Three or four times annually the club charters a bus for a trip to the seaside or another regional attraction. These day trips usually feature a large meal at an elegant restaurant, with singing, toasts, and speeches by club members and officers. The trips are eagerly anticipated, and the sites visited, the quality of the meal, and the general ambience are discussed for days afterward.

Although it helps the elderly of La Feuillée to overcome solitude,[3] the *club du troisième âge* also has a darker side. One member comments, "This is a dying region. The young people all leave. All that people talk about here are the *clubs du troisième âge*. The clubs aren't going to reinvigorate the *pays.*" Another member acknowledges that she finds the meetings and the day trips depressing. In her view, it is sad to see people who sang beautifully in their youth now losing their voices and unable to remember the words to their songs. Despite its euphemistic title, the club is a reminder that she and her contemporaries have become part of the marginal social category of those who are slowly but inevitably moving toward death.

---

3. Writing of southern Finistère, Segalen (1984:167) also observes that the growth of old-age clubs is directly related to loneliness among elderly people living alone.

In contemporary Brittany the development of institutions that provide organized leisure activities for the elderly, such as the *clubs du troisième âge,* reflects the decreasing role of family and neighborhood in meeting the needs of the aging population. In addition, compartmentalization of the elderly into a distinct social category, the *troisième âge,* indicates the lessening integration of aging and death into the fabric of community social life. The growth of specialized institutions for the elderly is one facet of the increasing division of labor in post–World War II Brittany. This trend toward specialization also typifies the provision of health care and support services for older persons.

In the past the needs of the elderly who were no longer capable of caring for themselves were met by the family and, to a lesser extent, by neighbors. To some degree this continues to be the case. Neighbors in the *bourg* in La Feuillée do shopping for elderly shut-ins. Others routinely do laundry for elderly neighbors who do not own washing machines. If there are no family members in the community, a neighbor woman will frequently take on the short-term responsibilities of looking after an elderly person who has contracted a minor illness. In farming families with numerous children, one child may remain on the farm or return to maintain its operation and to look after aging parents. A number of elderly, incapacitated persons in La Feuillée are cared for in the homes of their middle-aged children. Many of the women providing such care explain that they have chosen to do so rather than "abandon" their parents to hospitals or geriatric institutions such as the local retirement home, or *maison de retraite,* in Huelgoat.

Social pressures against the institutionalization of the elderly remain strong in La Feuillée, and people often assert that it is desirable to maintain elderly persons in the community for as long as possible. In many families, however, the *exode rural* has made home care for elderly relatives difficult from a practical standpoint. Several couples from La Feuillée who live in Brest keep secondary residences in the commune and return each weekend with shopping and clean laundry for their aging parents. People from La Feuillée who live in Paris return less frequently, but during summer vacations they are likely to cut wood and do minor household repairs and shopping to help prepare their parents for the coming winter.

Among the elderly living alone in La Feuillée, the possibility of institutionalization is a constant source of anxiety. As a Breton psychiatrist explains, "For the old, it is very important to die at home. It is a total disgrace, the loss of one's identity, to die in the hospital." In a village located two kilometers from the *bourg* of La Feuillée, Madeleine Bleunven lives alone in a large stone house built in the nineteenth century. The traditional beaten earth floor has not been covered over with tiles or cement, and although she cooks over a gas stove, Madeleine's fireplace and wood stove serve as the only sources of heat. There is no running water or toilet in the house. Despite its discomfort in the winter, Madeleine is attached to her home, which she inherited from her parents. Her greatest worry is that failing eyesight or senility will prevent her from finishing her days where she has lived all her life. She does not want to spend months helpless in a hospital.

Marie-Thérèse shares her friend Madeleine's attitudes toward institutionalization. Pointing to the house in the La Feuillée *bourg* where she has lived for most of her life, she explains: "I brought my father here to die, too. After my mother's death, he couldn't stay alone anymore. In those days, there weren't any hospitals or old people's homes. Now it's *allez-hop!* Get rid of the elderly!" Although rarely mentioning the possibility directly, with failing health and her family in Paris, Marie-Thérèse is clearly troubled by the prospect that she herself might die in the *maison de retraite*. According to her logic, it is obvious that people now want to "get rid of the elderly." "Otherwise," she asks, "why would they have spent all the money they have on hospitals and old people's homes?"

The Medicalization of Death

As Marie-Thérèse's comment suggests, public spending on medical facilities in general, and on geriatric facilities in particular, has increased dramatically since the 1960s. The medicalization of society in the Monts d'Arrée underwent a marked acceleration during the 1970s, when an infrastructure of medical facilities was developed in the region. In 1984 there were eight to ten doctors and eight nurses practicing in a sector of roughly thirty square kilometers centered on La Feuillée. During the 1960s, in contrast, a single general practitioner had responsibility for all medical problems in the area. Prior to the opening of the Centre Hospitalier Général de

Morlaix in 1971, surgical operations were performed in the doctor's office and births and deaths took place in the home. Referrals to outside specialists in Paris or Brest were rare.

The expansion of the medical infrastructure in rural Brittany in the 1970s both reflected and precipitated changing attitudes toward the use of medical services. People have become more willing than in previous generations to approach a doctor with their health problems. This increased acceptance of medical care is also related to changes in state health insurance programs. Implemented as early as 1928 for certain occupational groups, health coverage was not extended to farmers until 1961 (Rodwin 1984:86–87). The increased availability of both medical services and health insurance has radically altered the social context of death in rural areas of Brittany, making institutional care viable for the elderly and the dying. As one middle-aged La Feuillée woman observes, "We have modernized death."

The primary medical institutions serving elderly people from La Feuillée are the *centre hospitalier* in Morlaix and the *maison de retraite* in Huelgoat. The *centre hospitalier* in Morlaix started a program of expansion during the late 1960s, which culminated in the opening of a new 1,700-bed facility in 1971. Many doctors with established reputations were attracted to the hospital at this period. The rise in the number of annual admissions to the *centre hospitalier*, from 1,387 in 1956 to 7,891 in 1971 and 16,506 in 1983, attests to the increasing medicalization of Breton society over the past thirty years.

The *centre hospitalier* includes a thirty-bed geriatric service. Most of the patients arrive in the service as transfers from the main hospital following surgery or other treatment. The average length of stay is three weeks, although some patients remain in the service for up to three months. Some die in the geriatric ward. Others return to their homes or to those of their children. If home care is not possible, patients are transferred to a facility providing long-term care, such as a retirement home.

The *maison de retraite* in Huelgoat was founded with a private legacy in 1893 as a shelter for elderly indigents from the region. In 1947 management of the institution was passed to the public domain. As with the *centre hospitalier* in Morlaix, the postwar expansion of the *maison de retraite* reflects the development of state health planning, health insurance, and pension programs for the rural sector.[4] New buildings were added to the *maison de retraite* complex in 1958, 1973, 1978, and 1981. The number of resident pensioners increased from 60 in 1947 to 90 in 1957 and 144 in 1973. Since 1978 there have been 160 pensioners, of whom 136 are invalids. Eighty more elderly people currently have their names on a waiting list to enter the institution. These statistics clearly document an increasing institutionalization of the elderly in contemporary Brittany. As a result of this trend the processes of aging and dying are becoming progressively isolated from the social world of the living. It might be argued that elderly persons are choosing to enter institutions and not being "exiled" by society. However, at the Huelgoat retirement home the director observes that usually the families of pensioners, not the old people themselves, take the initiative in the placement process.

The director of the *maison de retraite* in Huelgoat notes that most of the pensioners in his institution have no close family members living in the area who are able to look after them. In his view the combined effects of the *exode rural* and the changing structure of the family have created the gap in care filled by the *maison de retraite*. The rise in the proportion of working women has also had an effect, for it is diffficult to maintain home care for an elderly parent in addition to a full-time job. Nonetheless, the director observes that women who do not work also place their parents in his institution.

At a meeting of staff members from several old people's homes in interior Brittany, several of those present voiced surprise at the small number of letters and telephone calls received by pensioners from outside family members. "They put the elderly with you there and then it's up to you to do everything," says one woman who works at a small institution in the Côtes-du-Nord. She notes that many pensioners receive only a single annual visit, when their children come to Brittany from Paris on their summer vacation. From the point of view of the exterior, those inside the *maison de retraite* have "lived too long," she maintains. Even the pensioners develop a tendency to view themselves in this light, asking the

---

4. See Rodwin (1984:84–116) for a historical survey of national health insurance and the establishment of public medical facilities throughout France since 1945. The medicalization of French society is evident in the statistics that Rodwin cites (1984: 100): "Between 1960 and 1980, the total consumption of medical services in France almost doubled from 4.0 to 7.5 percent of G.D.P. (gross domestic product)."

staff, "Why haven't I died yet? Why am I still alive? When will *le bon Dieu* come to get me?" For the children of such pensioners, their elderly parents represent a disturbing memento mori. As a social worker from a Finistère retirement home remarks, "Death becomes something terrifying the more it gets pushed to the edges of society."

The creation of institutional facilities since the 1960s to cope with the process of dying attests to the increasing specialization of social functions in Brittany. This process has fostered the denial of death by segregating the elderly and the dying from the social space occupied by other members of the community. Changing patterns of caring for the old and the dying have not, however, led exclusively to the denial response. The twenty-year period between the mid-1960s and the mid-1980s which has witnessed the expansion of geriatric facilities has also seen an attempt to meet the problems of the elderly outside the institutional context in rural Brittany, through the introduction of *aides-ménagères,* or home helpers for elderly people. A privately operated organization, Aide à Domicile en Milieu Rural (ADMR), provides the home-helper service. The ADMR *aides-ménagères* program represents an alternative pattern of specialized care for the elderly, in which paid workers within local communities replace the older networks of family and neighborhood support.

Founded in 1945, the ADMR originated under the sponsorship of Action Catholique, the social reform program of the Catholic church. However, the association no longer retains any religious affiliation. The ADMR was initially intended to assist rural women to cope with farm work and family responsibilities in the face of social upheavals that were undermining the preexisting system of reciprocal aid among relatives and neighbors. In 1970 a special home-helper service for the elderly was created within the context of the organization. The goal of the home-helper service is "to defend the right of the elderly to live in their own homes. *Gardons nos vieux chez eux!*" (*Bulletin de Liaison* 1984). In La Feuillée there are two women in their early fifties employed by the ADMR as home helpers. They provide essential care for at least twenty-five to thirty older people in the commune.

The home helper spends between one and two hours with each of several elderly persons in their homes, six days a week. Her work includes shopping, housecleaning, preparation of meals, laundry, and attention to personal hygiene for her elderly clients. The ADMR emphasizes that in addition to providing material services, the home-helper program seeks to restore a sense of dignity to elderly shut-ins and to reintegrate them into the social networks of the communities in which they live. The program is financed partly by a contribution from the elderly persons themselves, which varies according to income, and partly by the pension funds to which the elderly contributed during their working lives. The Direction Départementale de l'Action Sanitaire et Sociale pays for those with low incomes and for others, including certain agriculturalists, who have never contributed to a pension fund. The home helper is paid at a rate slightly higher than minimum wage. At the level of local administration, the ADMR is largely run by volunteers.

The development of the ADMR *aides-ménagères* program represents another facet of the transition from care for the elderly by relatives and neighbors based on relationships of generalized reciprocity to paid care provided on a contractual basis. Like the expansion of geriatric facilities, the *aides-ménagères* program is related to the growth of the division of labor in contemporary Brittany. However, unlike geriatric institutions, the *aides-ménagères* program works to maintain the tame response to death, by integrating the process of aging within the sphere of community-level social interaction.

From Public to Solitary Death

Of death in the early Middle Ages, Ariès states: "Familiar simplicity is one of the two essential characteristics of this death. The other is its public aspect, which is to last until the end of the nineteenth century. The dying person must be the center of a group of people. . . . One was never physically alone at the moment of death" (1982:18–19).

Likewise, death in Brittany during the early twentieth century was a public event. Many recall that the death of a neighbor implicated all those living in the *quartier*. Neighbors were involved in relationships of reciprocal aid, helping one another look after the sick. Since the *quartier* provided the focal point for social interaction, the death of one of its members created a genuine void in the social fabric and generated a deeply felt sense of loss. In La Feuillée it is remembered that

> When there was a tragedy in the village, everyone knew about it. . . . The sick person, he was there. He was suffering. There was nothing to soothe the pain. There were no doctors. There wasn't any morphine. Those who were in pain used to cry out. . . . It was a tragedy for everyone. We used to be united, much more united, one to the other. So, everyone used to gather together in the home of the dying person. We even used to go from one house to the other, saying, "He's going to die, he's going to die." And then everyone would group together around him. One was never alone to die.

Similarly Louise Vaillant, a woman in her late fifties from the Plouguerneau area, recalls that the entire neighborhood was present at the death of her grandfather in 1955. Nieces living two kilometers away came on foot to be with the dying man: "The relatives stayed all day long. We used to call all the neighbors in to say prayers." In Louise's village this pattern of attending the dying remained the norm as recently as the mid-1970s. However, in 1980, when another of Louise's elderly relatives passed away during the night, the nearest neighbor was not informed until the next morning. As Louise and her husband explain, new values of individual and family privacy cause one to think twice before "disturbing" one's neighbors on such occasions. All aspects of social interaction within their *quartier* have changed. The purchase of agricultural machinery, financed by loans from the Crédit Agricole, permits farmers to operate almost totally independently of help from their neighbors. States M. Vaillant, "We don't need to help one another out anymore. Everyone has equipment now." In the past, evenings after days of labor in the fields were spent in the company of the neighbors with whom one had worked. Now "there is the television, and everyone stays home by themselves." As the way of life has been transformed, so has the way of death. The dying individual is increasingly isolated. "In the past," observes M. Vaillant, "people died in public. That happens less and less. Now, half the time people die in the hospital."

The trend toward increased hospitalization of the dying did not appear in rural Brittany before the late 1960s. Hospital deaths did not exceed 15 percent of the annual deaths in La Feuillée until 1971. As Ariès points out, death in the hospital isolates the dying person.

Relegated to the social space of the institution, death is "hidden" from the living (Ariès 1982:570–571). Moreover, with medicalization, a view of death as disease—something potentially curable—has been fostered in Breton society.[5] This attitude directly contradicts the acceptance of death characteristic of the older generation.

The elderly who are hospitalized almost universally express the desire to return "to die at home." Where feasible, it is recommended by the hospital staff. Yet often fear of coping with a death in the home and the desire to provide the sick person with all the advantages of modern medical care combine to make even those families in a position to maintain home care for the dying unwilling to do so.

Death in the hospital often means death alone. In the geriatric service of the *centre hospitalier* in Morlaix, no systematic attempt is made to stay with and provide emotional support for the dying. Explains one nurse, "We check on them often, but we cannot stay an entire day with a dying person." With only four nurses' aides and two nurses responsible for a thirty-bed ward, there are no extra hands to attend exclusively to the needs of the dying. Neither have the personnel, with the exception of one nursing sister, been specially trained to do so. While the geriatric service nurses realize that, more and more, they are being called upon to replace the family in this role, there is a general expression of helplessness and reluctance to take responsibility in the face of deaths that occur in the ward: "The nurses' aides definitely do not think it is up to them to provide support for the dying, and the nurses would like the doctors to be there more often." The families of the dying are encouraged to be present as much as possible. An extra bed may be provided in the room of the dying person, enabling relatives to remain at the hospital on a twenty-four-hour basis. Thus, to some extent the "public death" has been maintained, despite its transfer to the institution. Nevertheless, in certain cases the family cannot, or will not, remain with a dying relative.

Significantly, in a movement that parallels the creation of the ADMR home-helper service for the elderly, attempts are being

---

5. See Ariès (1982:563–567) for more general discussion of the development of the tendency to view death as disease in Western culture.

made to develop new institutional resources to aid the dying which will replace the traditional family and neighborhood networks of support. The Centre d'Etude et d'Action Sociales, based in Saint-Brieuc, organizes regular seminars on support for the dying to train personnel in hospitals and geriatric institutions throughout Brittany. The theoretical approach advocated is primarily based on that pioneered by Elisabeth Kübler-Ross (1969; 1974; 1975). Similar death-awareness workshops are offered by the center for continuing education at the Université de Bretagne Occidentale in Brest. In Brittany as in other parts of the Western world, the development of the denial of death has generated, at least to some degree, a reaction in the form of a rediscovery of death, led by health-care professionals.[6]

Conclusion

As in all cultural contexts, death in rural Brittany is a social process as well as a physiological event. For those who die in old age the process of death begins with the recognition—on both social and personal levels—of the individual's status as elderly. In La Feuillée this change in social status is marked for many people by the *retour au pays*. This pattern of return migration is linked to a circular interpretation of the life course, in which it is seen to be important to end one's days, or at least to be buried, in the place where one was born. In emphasizing the significance of burial in the family tomb, the *retour au pays* is also closely associated with the romantic view of death as a prelude to reunion with beloved family members.

Among the elderly in La Feuillée, the tame acceptance of death as part of the cyclical order of nature has been maintained. Such acceptance forms part of a worldview in which the hour of one's death is perceived to be appointed or foreordained, according to some preexisting, supernatural design. Ariès's tame approach to death, somewhat influenced by the romantic response, has been dominant in rural Breton communities like La Feuillée up to the

---

6. Ariès (1982:588–593) and Huntington and Metcalf (1979:2–3) describe parallel death-awareness movements in Europe and the United States.

present. Since the 1960s, however, social circumstances have contributed to changes in this pattern. More and more the process of death is being set apart from the mainstream of community life.

This segregation of aging and dying has occurred on both psychological and physical levels. Psychologically, death has been distanced through the development of the *troisième âge* as a distinct social category. To a much greater extent than in the 1950s, the elderly in the rural Brittany of the 1980s have their own circumscribed range of social activities. The euphemistic quality of the term *troisième âge*, with its connotations of "golden age," reflects a growing trend in Breton culture toward repression of the idea of aging as a memento mori. The medicalization of society in contemporary Brittany has also diminished the immediacy of death. Death is increasingly conceptualized in terms of illness, which medical specialists, aided by technology, are able to cure. In addition, medicalization has contributed to the physical distancing of death, by removing it to institutions on the margins of the community, such as hospitals or retirement homes.

The development of specialized facilities to deal with the process of dying is a feature of the elaboration of the division of labor in present-day Brittany. Geriatric institutions and hospitals staffed by specialized personnel have expanded to meet the needs of the sick and the elderly who can no longer be cared for through family and neighborhood networks of support. In recent years, structural changes have altered the intensity of face-to-face social interaction and relationships based on generalized reciprocal aid within *quartiers*. The *exode rural* has left many elderly people without the assistance of children and grandchildren residing locally. Even in those cases where family members have remained in the rural milieu close to elderly relatives, increasing pressures on younger women to engage in salaried labor make it difficult for them to perform the role of primary care-givers.

These transformations in Breton social organization have influenced contemporary responses to death by generating a need for specialized death-related institutions. Medicalization has fostered Ariès's denial of death by facilitating the removal of aging and death from the social world occupied by the living. The tame, public death, in the company of neighbors and family members, has been replaced to a large extent by the solitary death in a hospital.

Although it is important to recognize that this shift in responses to death has occurred, we should avoid endowing it with negative moral connotations. From the perspective of local people, the level of access to health care permitted by the expansion of medical infrastructure and insurance coverage in Brittany since the 1960s has had an unequivocally positive effect on the quality of life in this region. Rural Bretons keenly appreciate the new possibilities available to them for high-quality health care. Few would advocate a return to the era when it was impossible for the majority of peasant families to afford the medicines and professional care that could have alleviated suffering and saved lives. The past should not be portrayed as an idyllic period when care for the elderly and dying was managed without conflict by family and neighbors in harmoniously functioning communities. Often the needs of the elderly are actually better served in geriatric institutions than in the traditional family-based context of care, where arguments over inheritance portions and personal enmity between parents and children can result in neglect or maltreatment of the aged.[7] Moreover, looking after an elderly, incapacitated parent is a heavy drain on the economic and emotional resources of a household. As those in La Feuillée who are currently providing in-home care for aged relatives are quick to point out, the psychological and physical burdens of assuring such care fall most heavily on the women members of the family: daughters and daughters-in-law. The well-being of the elderly who are cared for at home is often achieved at the expense of their middle-aged children. Now, as in the past, the task of looking after elderly parents frequently becomes the exclusive responsibility of one child, as others in the sibling group refuse to participate in care-giving. Given the unavoidable tensions inherent in the older, nonspecialized pattern of caring for the aging and dying, it is not surprising that as soon as alternatives in the form of institutional care became available in Brittany, they were adopted with increasing frequency. However, the institutional context has had the effect of distancing death from the ordinary experience of the majority of people in both urban and rural settings.

Close scrutiny of the processes of aging and dying in rural Brit-

---

7. See Behar (1986:89–103) for a moving account of how these factors can undermine family care for the elderly in a community in northern Spain.

tany suggests that denial is becoming the most common contemporary reaction in the face of death. Nevertheless, the situation is extremely complex. Elements of Ariès's tame and romantic responses are also clearly apparent. Moreover, at the same time as the denial of death is growing, countervailing forces are also developing. Health care professionals are becoming aware of the need for training to provide support for the dying in institutions. Likewise, the *aides-ménagères* program of the ADMR attests to the recognition that geriatric institutions are not the only solution for the needs of the elderly. Neither the ADMR nor death-awareness training for medical personnel can re-create the tame response to death, linked as it is to face-to-face social interaction and to a community pattern in which single individuals have multiple, nonspecialized roles and obligations as members of kin and neighborhood social groups. Nevertheless, these current developments suggest that a new kind of rapprochement with death, which does not seek to repress its reality, can be achieved in Brittany under contemporary social conditions.

3

Death as a Rite of Passage

Introduction

A short line of dark-clad men and women winds its way across the open square in the center of the La Feuillée *bourg*, moving in the direction of the church. The procession is led by a gray-haired man bearing an ornate gold and silver cross held aloft on a two-meter-long pole. His work-worn hands grip the pole tightly to prevent the cross from swaying in the gusts of wind and rain which buffet the mourners. Following the cross, six men escort a coffin draped in a black cloth. Auguste Cadic, a retired agriculturalist, has died, and his relatives and neighbors are accompanying him on his final pilgrimage through the *bourg* to the church for the funeral service. Later, carrying wreaths and pots of flowers, they will follow his body to the cemetery. The curé of La Feuillée, wearing a soutane covered by a long, black woolen cape with a hood, walks directly behind the coffin. He alone chants the "Kantik ar Baradoz," or Hymn of Paradise, to a dismal, haunting melody. The other members of the procession walk in silence, heads bent against the rain. The brightly colored umbrellas of the women make a poignant contrast with their dark raincoats and the sad strains of the priest's hymn.

The funeral is but one of a sequence of rites surrounding death in La Feuillée. According to van Gennep's model for the structure of rites of passage, some features of the ritual complex associated with death in rural Brittany can be seen as rites of separation, setting the deceased apart from the living. Others serve as rites of transition, changing the social status of various actors, including the deceased. A third aspect of the process involves rites of incorporation, which reintegrate both the community of the living and that of the dead. As Danforth (1982:35) has observed in his study of Greek funerary ritual, each stage of the sequence of rites of separation, transition, and incorporation can be further subdivided.

Often there are "rites within rites," such as subrites of transition and incorporation within the context of a rite of separation.

Funerals in La Feuillée differ in some respects from those in Plouguerneau. Urban funerals present yet a third ritual pattern. All of these must be examined in order to understand contemporary Breton responses to death. Furthermore, it is important to consider the differences between present-day death rituals and those of the nineteenth century, as well as those dating from the more recent past. Certain features of contemporary Breton funerary ritual continue to express the tame response to death, while others indicate that change is occurring in the direction of denial.

Like many of the recent developments associated with care for the elderly and the dying, a number of the innovations in Breton funerary ritual since World War II reflect the growth of a specialized division of labor. Other changes in the rituals surrounding death are part of the broader trend toward secularization in contemporary Brittany. As described in Chapter 1, the changes associated with secularization can be linked to the transition from a ritualistic to an ethically based religious system. This transition is in turn related to social factors, which include the weakening of community-level social interaction and social controls, the corresponding increase in individual autonomy, and the disappearance of a rigidly hierarchical form of social organization with a strong emphasis on group cohesion. Among the developments in Breton funerary ritual that are related to secularization, one of the most striking is the changing meaning ascribed to the Roman Catholic rites for the dying.

The Moment of Death

Extreme Unction

From the mid-seventeenth century to the mid-twentieth century, the moment of physical death was marked in Brittany, as in other Catholic regions, by the rite of extreme unction.[1] Following van

---

1. Croix (1981:949) observes that the custom of receiving extreme unction in Brittany increased greatly as a result of the efforts made by the post-Tridentine church during the mid-seventeenth century to regularize practices concerning the sacraments. Prior to that period, parish registers reveal more numerous cases in which the dying did not receive the last rites.

Gennep, extreme unction may be interpreted as a rite of separation, signaling the departure of the dying person from the community of the living and the beginning of his or her transition to the community of the dead.

In La Feuillée it is remembered that "in the past we used to call the priest rather than the doctor." With medical care beyond the means of most rural people, and the perception of death as inevitable and incurable, the spiritual needs of the dying assumed great importance. Considered essential for salvation, extreme unction was linked to an ethos in which sin consisted of specific transgressions that could be ritually expiated, even during the last moments of life. For the dying individual, receiving this sacrament confirmed the finality of his or her condition. As one elderly woman recalls, "Well, the man or the woman, the sick person, he knew very well when he saw the priest coming that he did not have much more time." Extreme unction thus marked the boundary between life and death.

Following a modification of Catholic liturgy in 1972, extreme unction was renamed the anointing of the sick, or the *onction des malades*. The sense of the ritual has been significantly altered along with its name (Isambert 1975). The *onction des malades* may now be administered to anyone suffering from a serious illness or about to undergo major surgery. It may also be received by all those of advancing years. In a liturgical manual used by the priest in La Feuillée, the *onction des malades* is described as "a gesture of friendship, a gesture of brotherhood, a step on the part of the Christian community toward one of its suffering members" (AELF 1977:25). The new liturgy emphasizes themes of healing on both spiritual and physical planes.

Contemporary Catholicism, inasmuch as it addresses the issue of salvation, stresses that it depends on ethical behavior throughout one's life. Unlike extreme unction, therefore, the *onction des malades* is not considered uniquely capable of improving the condition of the soul in the afterlife. In this respect the change from extreme unction to the *onction des malades* resembles the theological innovations of the Reformation and Counter-Reformation which sought to discourage reliance on deathbed rituals by promoting the view that salvation can be achieved only through a lifetime of piety (Ariès 1982:303–305). As Ariès notes, however, these sixteenth-century reforms were largely limited to a small group of Catholic and Protestant intellectuals, whereas popular beliefs concerning the importance of extreme unction remained strong, particularly during the nineteenth century (1982:303).

In contrast to the ritualistic character of extreme unction, the *onction des malades* reflects an intellectual approach to faith. As discussed in Chapter 1, for Douglas ([1970] 1978) such a transition away from ritual is an important indicator of secularization. The church favors administration of the *onction des malades* to the elderly while they are still in moderately good health, in possession of their mental faculties and able to comprehend the significance of the rite. The sacrament is frequently given collectively, on the occasion of pilgrimages to Lourdes or at church festivals such as Easter, when attendance at Mass is high. It is noted that the rite should not be postponed until the moment of death, when the sick person can no longer understand its meaning or take an active role in the event: "It is very important to receive this sacrament under the best conditions. It is not advised to wait too long. When a sick person is too tired, he finds it difficult to participate in this process, and those around him hesitate to propose it" (AELF 1977:26).

By deemphasizing the ritual significance of the moment of death, contemporary Catholic liturgy, in Brittany as elsewhere, provides both a "model of" and a "model for" the denial of death in society at large (Isambert 1975; the terms are discussed in Geertz 1973c: 93–94). The *onction des malades* has been well accepted by priests, whom it relieves of the role of annunciator of death to the moribund. However, as with certain of the other reforms in Catholic liturgy introduced by the Second Vatican Council in the early 1960s, the new sacrament has not been universally welcomed by lay people in rural Brittany, many of whom continue to consider the priest's presence essential at the bedside of the dying.[2] Thus, the change from extreme unction to the *onction des malades* demonstrates that the rituals of the church can actively promote change and not simply reflect preexisting social developments in Brittany.

Like other social institutions in contemporary Brittany, the church no longer uses a vocabulary that approaches the topic of death in a direct manner. As the priest in La Feuillée explains, the words "extreme unction" frighten the dying. He prefers the more

2. This issue will be discussed more fully in Chapter 7.

neutral term *onction des malades*. The language of contemporary religious manuals alludes to death in the same euphemistic fashion as does the term *troisième âge*. It is not the dying person, but the "sick person" who is "too tired," who is considered unable to receive the sacrament "under the best conditions."

Une Belle Mort—A Good Death

In the past extreme unction, as a rite of separation, marked the moment of death and gave it ritual significance. Moreover, the socially ascribed meaning of the "last rites" made the sick person aware that his or her death was at hand. Foreknowledge of and preparation for one's own death were integral features of the tame death documented by Ariès for the early Middle Ages. Sudden deaths without warning were considered abnormal and frightening and were interpreted as divine retribution for the sins of the deceased (Ariès 1982:10–13). According to the tame response, therefore, the ideal or "good" death involved the dying individual's awareness of the imminence of his or her death. Such awareness was made possible through natural or supernatural signs and confirmed through the ritual of extreme unction.

The tame vision of the *belle mort*, or good death, can be seen in a legend collected by Le Braz in late nineteenth-century Brittany (1928:1:142–147). Set in the community of Pleyber-Christ, fifteen kilometers north of La Feuillée, the legend tells of a rich farmer who decided to invite the entire parish to a feast at his home. The farmer announced the time and date of the celebrations in the churchyard at the end of Sunday Mass. As he finished speaking, a stranger came up to him and asked for an invitation. The farmer replied that there was food for everyone. At the feast two days later, the stranger sat motionless before an upturned plate and glass. Finally the farmer approached and spoke to him. The stranger raised his head to reply, revealing the gaping eye-sockets of a dead man's skull. He was the Ankou, death personified. Addressing the farmer, the Ankou explained: "Because you have been generous to me, inviting me with all the others to your feast, I want to give you for my part a proof of friendship. I have come to warn you that you have but eight days to put your affairs in order. In eight days I will pass by here again with my cart, and, ready or not, I have orders to take you with me" (Le Braz 1928:1:146). With these words the Ankou disappeared. The farmer, seemingly unperturbed by this warning, spent his last week dividing his property among his children. The legend continues: "On Sunday, at the end of the Mass, he made his confession; on Monday he asked the priest of Pleyber-Christ to bring the sacraments; and on the Tuesday night he died. His generosity had enabled him to die a good death. May it be likewise for each one of us" (Le Braz 1928:1:146–147).

Among certain people in La Feuillée, awareness that one is going to die continues to be an important part of the definition of the good death, as it was during Le Braz's time. At eighty-two, Madeleine Bleunven describes her conception of the ideal death: not too sudden, but not too slow. An illness of three or four days' duration would provide enough advance warning without unnecessary suffering. Even some young people share this desire to be prepared in advance. One twenty-four-year-old, afraid of sudden death in a car crash, explained that even if the warning came only an hour beforehand, he would like to be aware of death's approach.[3]

Increasingly, however, it is the sudden death which is defined as *la belle mort* in La Feuillée. When an elderly woman from the community suffered a heart attack and died while doing her household chores, her neighbor stated: "She had a good death. I would like to die that way." Similarly, when seventy-five-year-old Hervé Jestin was found dead Monday morning after having spent Sunday playing *boules* in the place du Bourg, his *belle mort* was contrasted with the death of his wife, who had lingered for two years in the hospital following a stroke. As Isambert observes of contemporary French society in general, the good death has become "that in which the deceased does not see himself dying and does not know he is dying" (1975:100). This new vision of the good death is a striking reversal of the earlier tame model, in which sudden deaths evoked horror and suspicion (Ariès 1982:10–13, 587).[4]

---

3. Likewise, in northern Portugal, the "good death" continues to be defined as one that gives advance warning, enabling its victim to prepare: "A man should die in his home, surrounded by family and neighbors, and with time to settle his affairs, both spiritual and temporal" (Goldey 1983:2).

4. To some extent, the recent redefinition of the good death as sudden death may be related to the contemporary medicalization of death, which can prolong the suffering experienced by the dying. The desire for a sudden death expressed by many of the elderly in La Feuillée seems to stem less from fear of death itself than from fear of lengthy and painful illness. As noted earlier, elderly people in rural Brittany are reluctant to accept the possibility of dying in hospitals or geriatric institutions, which is most likely to occur in cases of prolonged illness or incapacitation.

In addition to the concept of *la belle mort*, several types of death are perceived to be *triste*, or sad. *Triste* deaths shake the community as a whole and evoke special grief among those close to the deceased. Deaths characterized as *triste* include suicides, accidental deaths, and the deaths of young people.[5] All funerals are well attended, but it is on the occasion of a *triste* death that the community demonstrates its solidarity with the bereaved to the greatest extent, through attendance at the funeral and wake and through the giving of flowers and Masses for the soul of the deceased.

One of the most traumatic and *triste* deaths of recent years in La Feuillée was that of twenty-two-year-old Jeannie Kervao. The daughter of a La Feuillée family, Jeannie had returned to the community for a week's vacation from her job in Paris. Two days after her arrival in La Feuillée, while walking across the highway outside the *bourg*, Jeannie was hit by a speeding car. She died several hours later at the hospital in Morlaix. Friends and relatives were stunned by Jeannie's unexpected death. There was no room in the church for the three hundred mourners who attended this funeral. As one woman stated, "I have never seen so many people at church in La Feuillée. This has shocked everyone." For Françoise Tanguy, an elderly neighbor of Jeannie's grandparents, the death of the young woman raised implicit questions about the existence of a just order in the universe. "And to think that there are so many old people just waiting to die! The senile. Why did death have to take her?" The traditional answer to such questions is provided by a Breton proverb that likens death to the felling of a tree:

> *N'e ket dre oad*
> It is not by age
> *E vez pilet ar c'hoad*
> That wood is cut,
> *Dre ezhomm eget pilet ur wezenn*
> (But) through need that a tree is felled.
> (Told by Marie-Thérèse,
> aged eighty-six, La Feuillée)

---

5. Similar accidental or violent deaths are classified as "bad deaths" in other cultural contexts, as Fox (1973) and Middleton (1982) point out for the Rotinese and the Lugbara. *Triste* deaths in Brittany do not, however, carry the same symbolic connotations as do "bad deaths" among the Lugbara and the Rotinese. For example, the ritual treatment of those who suffer *triste* deaths is no different from that of

Just as the tree falls to the axman, so too must men and women give way before the Ankou's scythe. "It was her destiny," commented many in La Feuillée, in response to Jeannie's early death.

The *Veillée Mortuaire*

In La Feuillée the passing of a community member marks the beginning of a liminal period that extends for the twenty-four to forty-eight hours between death and burial. This stretch of time is consecrated by the wake, or the *veillée mortuaire*, a rite of separation during which the deceased person belongs neither completely to the community of the living nor to that of the dead. The *veillée mortuaire* is initiated by a subrite of separation, the washing and laying out of the corpse, or the *toilette des morts*.

The *Toilette des Morts*

As in the provision of care for the dying, a specialized division of labor and the concomitant distancing of death have developed in conjunction with the *toilette des morts*. In the past there were one or two women from each *quartier* in La Feuillée who regularly took responsibility for the *toilette*. They were compensated with gifts: articles of clothing belonging to the deceased or a length of material with which to make a blouse. More recently, some of these women were paid a token amount. When men from La Feuillée died, the carpenter who supplied the coffin or a male neighbor helped to wash and shave the deceased.

There are still women who perform the *toilette des morts* in certain *quartiers* of La Feuillée. In other *quartiers* it is the family, with the help of close neighbors, who do the task. The primary feature of this traditional response is that all those performing the *toilette* are community members well known to the deceased and the bereaved. The service was, and continues to be, done in a spirit of

---

those who die a *belle mort*. The two terms are not conceptually or structurally opposed. Moreover, in contrast to the Rotinese case, in contemporary Brittany it is not believed that the ghosts of those who experience *triste* deaths are more likely than other ghosts to return and harm the living. Le Braz (1928:2:207–216, 296–307) does record two legends in which people who died accidentally or at an early age return as malevolent ghosts, which suggests that this idea may have been more important in the past.

generalized reciprocity rather than one of commercial exchange, even in cases where a small payment is provided. Recently, however, a nurse moved into the commune. To an increasing extent it is she who is called upon to perform the *toilette* for those who die at home. Significantly, people in La Feuillée consider it "better," or more appropriate, for the nurse, in her role as a medical specialist, to do the *toilette*. This perception may be related to the fact that if death occurs in the hospital, the *toilette* is performed there by nurses' aides before the body is returned to the family. Thus, whereas formerly it was someone from within the community—a neighbor, the carpenter, or a family member—who did the *toilette*, the present trend is for this task to be done by outside representatives of institutionalized medicine. Here again, the development of the medicalized death can be clearly demonstrated for rural Breton society. In urban areas the *toilette* is the responsibility of another type of specialist, the employees of the municipally operated undertaker service, or *pompes funèbres municipales*.[6] The role of this institution will be considered more fully in the discussion of funeral organization.

On one level the *toilette des morts* serves the purely practical function of ensuring that the body of the deceased is clean and aesthetically attractive for display during the wake. However, this washing of the dead is also a rite of separation, reaffirming the fact that the deceased has undergone a change of social status. By removing substances such as sweat and dirt which accumulate on the bodies of living individuals, the *toilette* ritually sets apart the deceased, who has been cleansed, from members of the living community.[7]

Cross-culturally, washing and ritual purification are frequent features of the rites of passage associated with both birth and death (van Gennep 1960:52, 164). The use of water at baptism in the Western Christian tradition is a widely recognized example. The parallels between washing at birth and at death suggest that the newborn infant and the newly deceased are perceived to occupy analogous symbolic states. In research based in Minot, a village in northern Burgundy, Yvonne Verdier (1976, 1979) draws particular attention to the symmetry in this community between ritual wash-

---

6. In some Breton cities there are both the publicly run *pompes funèbres municipales* and the privately operated *pompes funèbres générales*.

7. Compare Verdier (1976:110, 115–116) on this point.

ing at birth and at death. In Minot it is the same woman, *la femme-qui-aide*, or the "helping woman," who both washes the newborn infant and performs the *toilette des morts*. This duplication of roles is not found in La Feuillée. Nevertheless, here too, people recognize parallels between earliest infancy and death. One of these similarities concerns the state of the terminally ill person in the days immediately prior to death. In La Feuillée it is said that such invalids often smile faintly while staring aimlessly into the distance or looking at a wall. This smile, called the *sourire aux anges*, or "smile to the angels," is considered similar to the smile of young babies. In the words of one La Feuillée woman, the dying smile because "they think they see something. They are drawing closer to their relatives on the other side of the bridge. They're going to take a step toward the other side. They are half in this world, half in the other." The dying, at the threshold of the community of the dead, share the smile of the newly born, who have just entered the world of the living.

The second symbolic link between death and infancy in La Feuillée is seen in the preparation of the body during the *toilette des morts*. The possibility of physical decay during the *veillée* evokes a practical, earthy concern in the Monts d'Arrée, where embalming and other techniques of preservation are rarely practiced. In order to prevent fluids that exude from the body from soiling the *lit de mort*, the pelvic area is enveloped in sponge material and the whole lower body is "swaddled" in somewhat the same fashion as infants were swaddled in the past. As one of the La Feuillée women who continues to perform the *toilette des morts* explains, she wraps a sheet around one of the legs of the deceased. It is passed under the legs and lower body, folded around once or twice, and fastened with safety pins. She did the same kind of partial swaddling for her children thirty-five years ago, enveloping their legs and torso from the waist down in a diaper. That hers is a traditional rather than an idiosyncratic analogy is indicated by a statement from one of Le Braz's informants: "As for the actual shrouding, it consists of wrapping the body in a clean sheet up to the waist, a bit like the way one swaddles an infant" (1928:1:248).

After the *toilette* has been performed, the body is dressed and displayed on a bed, the *lit de mort*, which is arranged in one of the main rooms of the deceased person's home (see fig. 4).[8] In the past the body was fully dressed and shod for the *veillée mortuaire*.[9] Women were dressed in the local costume, and men in their best suits. A special effort was made to arrange the hair and *coiffe* if the deceased was a woman. Until approximately 1978, the dead in La Feuillée continued to be dressed completely during the wake. At present, however, this is extremely rare. Women are dressed in a simple white nightdress or blouse and a sweater. Men wear a white dress shirt and a tie. If the family are practicing Catholics, a rosary is wound around the clasped hands of the deceased. The lower body is covered by the sheets and the coverlet on the *lit de mort*. Many people in La Feuillée feel that the aesthetic impact of the *veillée* has been diminished now that the deceased are no longer fully dressed: "It looked better when we used to dress them completely. Some people are beautiful on their *lit de mort*."

The *Veillée* as Sacred Time

The term *veillée* means a night of watching. In the past the family and neighbors of the deceased maintained a vigil beside the body throughout the one or two nights between death and burial. The wake represented a ritual period of "time out of time," distinct from and structurally opposed to "everyday time" (Leach 1961; Turner 1969). Prohibitions for the bereaved family against engaging in quotidian activities such as work and sleep confirmed the distinctive quality of this period of ritual time. Nineteenth-century sources record that no dust or sweepings should be thrown out of the house during the *veillée mortuaire*. According to some variants of this belief, to do so risks ejecting the soul of the deceased (Le Braz 1928:1:255–256). Other variants state that if anything that was in the house at the moment of death is put outside, the soul will be forced to wander without peace until it has collected all the objects touched by its last breath (Le Calvez 1888:46). Mirrors in the house of the deceased were covered or turned to face the wall

---

8. During the nineteenth century the body was laid out on the kitchen table (Le Braz 1928:1:245).

9. However in the 1920s, Pérennès (1924:3–4) suggests that the custom of dressing the deceased completely was then relatively recent, and that previously the corpse was simply shrouded in two sheets.

(Pérennès 1924:4), and receptacles containing liquids other than milk were emptied or covered to prevent the soul from drowning (Le Braz 1928:1:256).[10]

The sense of the extra-ordinary generated by these ritual precautions was reinforced in the past by aesthetic signifiers within the context of the *veillée*. Like the body of the deceased, the *lit de mort* and the room in which the *veillée* took place were the focus for aesthetic attention. A canopy of fine linen sheets was arranged over the *lit de mort*. Sheets were also nailed up around the walls of the room in which the body was displayed, in order to cover smoke stains or places where the plaster was in poor condition. Many rural Breton houses consisted of only one main room with a granary above. Thus there was no *salle*, or parlor, in which the *veillée* could be held. By nailing sheets over the walls of the main room, everyday space was converted into aestheticized, sacred space. The name given to the canopy of sheets arranged over the *lit de mort*—*chapelle blanche*, or white chapel—further emphasizes the sacred, ritual quality of the *veillée* (Le Braz 1928:1:245).

In contemporary La Feuillée the *veillée* continues to be a period of ritual time and the occasion for attention to aesthetic detail. At present most houses in La Feuillée contain several rooms, and the deceased is generally laid out on a bed in a ground-floor bedroom or on a bed specially moved into the *salle*. The bed is covered with the fine white sheets and white crocheted coverlet which have been kept ready for use by the women of the household. Occasionally the wall behind the *lit de mort* may be covered with a sheet, but this practice is becoming increasingly rare. The desire to convert everyday space into sacred space for the *veillée mortuaire* is now expressed in different ways. For example, after one death in 1984, a family in La Feuillée spent several hours repapering the walls of their *salle* before admitting visitors to the wake.

---

10. In La Feuillée mirrors were formerly covered with a white sheet during the *veillée mortuaire*, and during at least one wake in 1984 this custom was still followed. I was also told that in some cases the reflecting surface of mirrors was covered with *blanc d'Espagne*, a calcium carbonate powder that was mixed with liquid. According to one woman, these practices prevent people from seeing two corpses, the deceased and his or her reflection, in the house. Should both be seen, another death would occur. Croix (1981:953) reports the interpretation that mirrors were covered because the soul, which could not distinguish between reflection and reality, might fly into the glass surface and hurt itself.

Flowers function as aesthetic signifiers during the *veillée mortuaire*. Floral arrangements or potted plants are often placed around the *lit de mort*. Roses or carnations may be scattered on the coverlet itself. These flowers are generally bought from a florist, rarely culled from home gardens. They are out of the ordinary, either because they are difficult to grow or because they are out of season. Flowers as "ephemeral art" (Salvador 1981) thus heighten the sacred, liminal quality of the *veillée*. The wake represents aestheticized, ritual time and space.

Visits

Once the *toilette des morts* is finished and the *lit de mort* arranged, "visits" may begin. Friends, acquaintances, family, and neighbors come to "say a prayer" before the deceased. Attendance involves reciprocity. One attends *veillées mortuaires* in the families of those who have attended *veillées* for the deceased in one's own family. Visits permit family members, neighbors, and friends to demonstrate their respect for the deceased and their solidarity with the bereaved. The wake thus reaffirms the continuity of collective existence in the face of the loss of an individual life.

Upon arrival at a wake, visitors stand next to the *lit de mort* for a moment to meditate on the deceased and say a prayer. Next to the bed a crucifix and candle, together with a white saucer filled with holy water, are placed on a small table covered with a white lace or linen cloth. A sprig of boxwood is placed in the saucer. Each visitor in turn uses the boxwood to "bless the corpse," tracing the sign of the cross with the twig in the air above the *lit de mort* and simultaneously sprinkling holy water on the body.[11]

Identical to the rite performed by Anna Le Guen in the Plouguerneau cemetery, this gesture derives from a long-established Indo-European and Semitic folk tradition that depicts the dead as thirsty and dry. Literally essential for the maintenance of life, water is also metaphorically represented as a fertilizing, regenerative element in folklore motifs such as the "fountain of youth" and "water of life" (Dundes 1980:108–109).[12] The practice of providing liba-

---

11. This rite is not unique to Brittany. In the Basque country, a shallow dish of holy water and a sprig of laurel are placed next to the body at wakes to enable visitors to bless the corpse (Douglass 1969:24).

12. Thompson (1955–1958): Motifs D1338.1.1, Fountain of Youth; and E80, Water of Life.

tions for the dead is well known from classical sources. Likewise, graveside containers for water and other liquid offerings to the dead are known from both archaeological and ethnographic contexts in Palestine and other parts of the Near East and the Mediterranean world (Canaan 1929; Deonna 1939; Onians 1951). In Brittany, blessing with holy water figuratively regenerates the dead and symbolically grants them immortality.[13]

The boxwood used to sprinkle the water on the corpse, at the wake and in the cemetery, is also linked to the concept of regeneration. Boxwood is blessed annually at the Mass on Rameaux, or Palm Sunday. A sprig of blessed boxwood is kept in the home, "for good luck," throughout the year. It is often tucked surreptitiously behind the crucifix on the kitchen wall, bearing witness to the intermingling of Christian and pre- or non-Christian elements in Breton folk religion. As recently as the early 1970s, pieces of boxwood blessed at Rameaux were placed in each room of the home, in all outbuildings and stables, and in gardens and grainfields to ensure a good harvest. When asked to explain this custom, La Feuillée Catholics invariably state that it is done in memory of the palm branches strewn in Christ's path on his entry to Jerusalem at the beginning of Holy Week. "Here there are no palm trees," it is said, "so we bless boxwood branches instead." However, Rameaux, falling as it does in early spring, and the boxwood that serves as a key symbol in this festival would also appear to be linked with popular, non-Christian rites of increase and renewal of plant and animal life.[14] As an evergreen, boxwood flourishes throughout the winter, making it an appropriate symbol of immortality. Boxwood is used in connection with the dead at Rameaux as well as at *veillées mortuaires*. On Dimanche des Rameaux, sprigs of the plant that have been blessed at Mass are taken to the cemetery and placed on tomb monuments or stuck into the adjacent gravel, symbolically regener-

---

13. Croix (1981:938–939), apparently unaware of the literature linking this rite to earlier Indo-European and Semitic folk traditions, offers the interpretation that it is of relatively recent origins, dating only to the mid-sixteenth century in Brittany. For description of analogous rituals from Greece involving the provision of water for the dead, see Danforth (1982:106–112). Danforth also discusses Greek funeral laments that depict the dead as suffering from dryness, heat, and thirst.

14. Van Gennep (1947:1158–1206) suggests that the festival of Rameaux developed through the convergence of orthodox Catholic and non- (but not necessarily pre-) Christian folk religious practices. See further discussion of this festival in Chapter 6.

ating the dead (see figs. 5 and 9). Many families reserve a piece of the same boxwood blessed at Rameaux for use at *veillées mortuaires* throughout the year.[15]

Despite its non-Christian associations, in La Feuillée the blessing of the dead with water and boxwood is linked to Catholicism. The rite is dispensed with at Communist *veillées*. Occasionally ordinary tap water rather than holy water is used for the blessing. For certain community members this devalues the ritual. As eighty-six-year-old Marie-Thérèse observes, "There are some people now who don't use holy water. You can use any kind of water, but it's not the same."

In Plouguerneau further changes in the form of the rite indicate the questioning of previously unchallengeable assumptions about the correct ritual treatment of the dead. Plouguerneau women explain that "we don't bless the body with holy water anymore. That stains the fine sheets on the *lit de mort*. Now we bless the corpse with a sprig of boxwood, and we leave the boxwood in a saucer, but there is no more water." Clearly the symbolic content of the gesture is radically altered, and the modification raises questions about contemporary beliefs concerning the afterlife. These will be discussed at greater length in Chapter 7.

The Wake as a Social Occasion

In the Monts d'Arrée, the *veillée mortuaire* is an essential part of local ideas about the "right way" to look after one's dead. To hold a *veillée* is considered a duty owed by the living to their deceased family members. Jeannette, a La Feuillée woman in her seventies, explains, "At least when my brother-in-law died, my niece did her duty. She brought her father home from the hospital for the last night." Jeannette's phrase "the last night" has special significance. It is the *veillée mortuaire*, not the eve of death, which is conceived of as the deceased's "last night." For Jeannette, as for many of her generation, the wake is "the last night that one spends with one's relatives." It is as though the deceased were not definitively dead until placed in the cemetery. During the *veillée* the deceased is "betwixt and between" categories (Turner 1969:95). He or she is in some senses "still there" as an actor in the social world of the

---

15. Identical traditions concerning boxwood blessed at Rameaux are reported for the Morvan by Gueusquin-Barbichon (1981), including its usage at *veillées mortuaires*.

living. In fact, the deceased is the principal actor during the *veillée mortuaire*. Even those who have exercised no social power or influence during their lives are displayed "in state." Many people seem to receive more visitors at their *veillée mortuaire* than on any other single occasion during their lifetime.

In death, one becomes an object of respect. As a Breton proverb quoted with ironic humor by a young man from the Léon states:

> *Dimeziñ evit bezañ droukprezeget*
> Get married in order to be criticized
> *Ha mervel evit bezañ meulet*
> And die in order to be praised.
> (Told by Marc Vaillant,
> aged twenty-three)

The respect accorded to the dead may be linked to the folk belief recorded in the nineteenth century that "it is not good to speak evil of a dead person; by doing so, one exposes oneself to his vengeance!" (Le Braz 1928:1:287). In contemporary Brittany conversation during the *veillée mortuaire* emphasizes the positive qualities of the dead person's character. Likewise, writing of funerary ritual in the Spanish Basque country, Douglass observes that "the social personality of the deceased is 'laundered'" during the wake (1969:28). Only by ignoring former misunderstandings with or grudges against the deceased can the neighbors who attend the wake provide his or her family with the support it needs during bereavement (Douglass 1969:28). Likewise, in La Feuillée a man recalls that in his boyhood, "even if there were bad feelings, even a legal process between families like that, when there was a funeral, they were all in agreement. There the fighting was finished." Now as in the past, long-standing arguments and rivalries are temporarily suspended in the face of a death in the community.

For those who die in the hospital, the *veillée mortuaire* represents a final homecoming. "I've come to take you home," an elderly woman from La Feuillée reassured her dying husband at the *centre hospitalier* in Morlaix. It is as though the deceased must be brought home for his or her own sake. Not only does the *veillée mortuaire* permit the community to bid farewell to one of its members, but it also allows the deceased symbolically to take leave of the home where the important events of his or her life took place. When

Pierre Rozec, the hotel owner in La Feuillée, died, his widow decided not to hold a *veillée,* and the coffin was brought directly from the hospital to the church. To Marie-Thérèse, Mme Rozec's decision deprived her husband of his right to spend a last day and night at home: "I found it hard to watch Pierre Rozec pass by his house without entering it." The idea that the *veillée* allows the deceased to say farewell to familiar objects and places is expressed in the legend "L'âme vue sous la forme d'une souris blanche," published by Le Braz. In this legend the soul of a dead man leaves his body during the wake in the form of a white mouse and makes a final visit to familiar places in the household, bidding farewell to fields, outbuildings, and the tools he had used during life (1928: 1:216–226).

Until the mid-1970s, legal restrictions frequently conflicted with the desire of families to hold wakes for relatives who died in the hospital. Up to 1976, French law prohibited transport across communal boundaries of corpses not placed in closed coffins. With the increasing trend toward hospitalization of the dying, this ruling often created difficulties for families wishing to display the body outside the coffin at the wake in the home. In practice, hospital and police authorities turned a blind eye to most infringements of this law and permitted transport without a coffin over short distances, provided it was done as quickly as possible after death. Patients were discharged from the hospital as "living" minutes after death occurred to be returned to their family home. Official death certificates for these *morts-vivants* were later filled out as though they had died in their home communes. This practice both permitted the maintenance of the traditional *veillée mortuaire* and circumvented criticism from those who disapproved of "abandoning" a relative to die in a medical institution. One could effectively hospitalize the dying and yet make it appear as though death had occurred in the home.

Although the wake is considered important for the sake of the deceased, it is also significant as a social occasion for the living. Attendance at wakes in the La Feuillée area is generally high. For the neighbors and acquaintances who come "to pay a visit," the *veillée* is marked off from everyday time by a change from ordinary work attire into better clothes. This is particularly true for those who attend during the evening, for daytime visits tend to be shorter and more informal. The serving of alcohol also elevates the *veillée* into an extra-ordinary occasion and promotes a sense of *communitas* (Turner 1969). Mourners may adopt a cheerful, almost festive manner on their way to a *veillée*, stopping at friends' homes to drink an aperitif *pour arroser le mort*, or "to moisten the deceased." This linkage of alcohol and the dead—like the blessing of the corpse with holy water—relates again to the folk conception of the "thirsty dead."

Often the social space at the *veillée* is divided into serious or solemn and festive areas. The close family of the deceased remains in the room where the *lit de mort* is arranged. Here the priest, who attends the wakes of all but the most deeply committed Communists in La Feuillée, recites the rosary at half past eight on the evening preceding the funeral. Mourners remain silent in this room out of respect for the emotional distress of the bereaved. The visitors sit or stand quietly around the walls. The atmosphere is strained and conversation is conducted in whispers, if at all. Conversation may be slightly more animated in the hall outside this room, but it is in the kitchen that people gather to discuss the circumstances of the death, reminisce about the deceased, or simply exchange gossip about the events of the day. Often there will be refreshments provided there, such as coffee and bread or crêpes with butter. Lively conversation also takes place outside the house, where men in particular gather in small clusters in the dark. Depending on whether the death is considered *triste* or not, the atmosphere, even in the room where the *lit de mort* is arranged, may oscillate between solemnity and festivity throughout the evening. If the deceased is an elderly person who was expected to die, an effort will be made to engage the bereaved family in conversation. At certain *veillées* conversation may be very animated, touching on topics such as weddings in the community, neighborhood scandals, and reminiscences about the past. The conversation ceases abruptly with each new arrival, and the mood of the gathering reverts to gravity while the newcomer blesses the corpse and says a prayer. Then slowly conversation is resumed, integrating the new visitor. As the talk gradually gains in pace and volume, the atmosphere of lively *communitas* is re-created. At midnight this festive ambience is heightened when a small meal—consisting of coffee, bread and butter or pâté, wine, and *lambig*, or apple brandy—is served to those who remain at the wake.

At present most La Feuillée families request the priest to attend their *veillées* to lead the mourners in thirty minutes of prayer. Formerly, however, in this region as in many parts of Lower Brittany, representatives of established religion did not attend *veillées*.[16] Prayers were said by lay *diseurs* or *diseuses de grâces,* "sayers of prayers." These men and women could be found in many rural Breton communities (see, for example, Hélias 1978:111–113). Folk religious leaders, they possessed a stock of prayers that they recited from memory, often without stopping for an hour or more. These *grâces* were probably learned in part from the *Heuriou brezonnec ha latin,* a Book of Hours written in Breton and Latin. Composed by a priest and first published in 1760, this book was widely available in the Breton countryside during the nineteenth century (Le Braz 1928:1:265; Pérennès 1924:5). However, the unofficial character of the *grâces* remembered in the Monts d'Arrée suggests that some were also invented and transmitted in the oral tradition. In the La Feuillée area, people recall that the *grâces* contained a mixture of Breton and Latin phrases. Sentences were often fitted together in an ad hoc manner, with more concern for rhyme than for religious orthodoxy. One *diseuse* in the Monts d'Arrée is reputed to have offered a prayer "for the three mothers of Jesus Christ."

The following text, spoken in a rapid monotone, is one La Feuillée man's reconstruction of a *grâce* he heard in the region approximately twenty-five years ago.

> *Pa vije Mai, pa vije krog er mod-se da lar(et) he gras*
> When Marie, when she started this way to say her *grâce*
> *neuze, pa vije aet dreist ar skalier, 'barzh ar vered,*
> then, when (the soul) had gone over the steps, into the cemetery,
> *goude-se neuze ez ae 'vat ha ne arrete tamm 'bet,*
> after that she was still going and didn't stop a bit,
> *tamm 'bet, hag a yae d'ar penn all*
> not a bit, and it (the soul) went to the other end (of the cemetery)
> *da glask he flas, goude-se neuze hag ez ae da glask*
> to look for its place, after that and it went to look for

---

16. Pérennès (1924:4) observes that priests occasionally did attend *veillées* to perform prayers in certain Breton parishes, but the clerical role at *veillées mortuaires* was traditionally minimal (Croix and Roudaut 1984:41–42).

> *he flas 'barzh ur vered, hag ez a hag e zeu*
> its place in the cemetery, and it goes and it comes
> *ha goude-se neuze tout an dud a zeue er-maez d'ar ger*
> and after that then, everyone comes out from the town
> *dreist ar skalieroù, 'barzh ar vered, 'barzh ar vered.*
> over the steps, into the cemetery, into the cemetery.
> *Hennezh 'zo war hent ar Baradoz.*
> This soul is on the road to paradise.

The *diseuse*, Marie, describes the scene as the soul of the deceased searches for its "place," or tomb, in the cemetery, while the mourners gather to bless the corpse. Again, the unorthodox nature of the "prayer" is apparent. As many recall, the *diseuses de grâces* "used to tell all sorts of tales. They mixed up everything. It didn't make any sense. You couldn't understand what they were saying. The main thing was not to stop, even to breathe! The *grâces* prevented people from falling asleep during the *veillée*." The *diseuses de grâces* were recompensed with gifts of clothing and liberal servings of rum or *lambig*. Speaking of Marie, the *diseuse* whose prayer is paraphrased above, people recall with humor, "Sometimes she would come even if she hadn't been asked. She used to come for the rum!"

The most recent *diseuses* and *diseurs de grâces* in the La Feuillée area died during the early 1970s, although the clergy had started to take over the role of leading the prayers at *veillées mortuaires* by the 1960s. The Monts d'Arrée must be one of the last areas of Brittany where lay *diseurs* continued to practice. With the decline of the oral tradition, a book of *grâces* assembled by Breton author Yeun ar Go was published in 1945 under the auspices of the Capuchins. It contains some of the earlier *grâces* published in the *Heuriou brezonnec ha latin*. Used at *veillées* by some families in the Monts d'Arrée as well as in other regions of Brittany, the prayers in the 1945 publication reflect official Catholic doctrine of the pre–Vatican II era. The Pater, Ave Maria, and De Profundis are interspersed with Breton prayers to specific saints and exhortations to those present at the *veillée* to meditate on the state of the soul of the deceased, as well as their own upcoming death.

> Here is the body of one who has given up his life in this world. Pay attention, then, every one of us, at the sad state we would be in if God came to call us and to inflict death upon us. We will be nothing,

shortly afterward, but rotting flesh and food for the worms. Alas! Our bones and all our members will be between the ossuary and the cemetery. But our poor soul, as soon as death has closed our eyes to this world, must go before God's court to give a faithful account of our life from end to end. It will be judged without pity by the grand and just Judge who will reveal with severity all the offenses and affronts to His honor that it has committed. Oh, the account we will have to give of the life we have led will be a terrible thing! If we are found worthy of the truth of paradise, that will be for eternity; but what agony if we find ourselves condemned to hell. There we will be left to burn eternally until the end of time.

O my soul, think often about eternity, about whether you will find true happiness there or the suffering that lasts forever. Sooner or later we must end up there, after having passed only a very short time in this world.

A Pater and an Ave Maria for the soul of this deceased person here, and for the next man or woman among us here to die. May it please blessed Jesus Christ and the Virgin, His Mother, to give him or her the grace to die a good and happy death, and to give the soul of this deceased person here the grace to go immediately among the saints, to God's pleasant palace.

(Yeun ar Go 1945:28–30)

The Capuchin publication is no longer in use. However, small pamphlets containing prayers and hymns for *veillées mortuaires* are issued by the church in certain parishes. Such pamphlets are used in Plouguerneau, where the priest is too busy to attend *veillées*. The prayers in current use differ significantly from those published in 1945. They emphasize themes of hope, resurrection, and God's presence during suffering rather than hell and damnation. No longer the "grand and just Judge," God is portrayed as the Dieu d'Amour, or God of Love. In addition, all but one of the hymns and prayers in the Plouguerneau booklet are in French rather than Breton. Like the liturgical changes associated with the transition from extreme unction to the *onction des malades*, the prayers now recommended by the church for use at *veillées* advocate an approach to death based on a reasoned understanding of religious principles rather than simple acceptance of an authoritarian supernatural order.

Changes in the *Veillée Mortuaire*

Despite the disappearance of *diseurs de grâces* and a few changes in details concerning the arrangement of the body, wakes in La Feuillée continue to be celebrated much as they were forty years ago. However, since the mid 1970s, there has been one major change in the form of this ritual. The vigil with the deceased has been abbreviated. It is increasingly rare for mourners to remain with the body throughout the night. Neighbors and friends generally depart at one or two in the morning, following the refreshments, which are served at midnight. When they leave, the family members themselves go to bed. Although some elderly people consider it sad to leave the deceased alone, in most cases, as people in La Feuillée explain, "Now the door is shut on the deceased."

The current reluctance to spend the whole of the "last night" with the deceased is justified by a practical concern for the physical and psychological welfare of the bereaved. It is difficult to withstand the emotional ordeal of the funeral service after a sleepless night. A middle-aged La Feuillée woman recalls, "We weren't any further ahead to stay up all night. It was hard on the family, especially if they had been spending sleepless nights while the person was sick before he died."

In the shortening of the *veillée* it is possible to see evidence for the rigidification of the boundary between the natural and supernatural realms in contemporary Breton worldview and for the increasing exclusion of the dead from the social world of the living. Formerly the deceased person remained a participant in the community of the living for the duration of the wake. To some extent this is still true. Nevertheless, the shortening of the wake indicates that this outlook is currently being replaced by one in which social death coincides with physical death. Among middle-aged and younger people in La Feuillée, the conception that the deceased is "still there" during the wake is disappearing. Thus it is no longer considered essential to attend the body throughout the night.

It is also important to note that mourners were motivated to remain with the body from fear, as well as respect and affection for the deceased. The unburied body crosscuts boundaries dividing the living from the dead, and in this liminal state it represents a potential danger. Thus one stayed by the body to watch it and to prevent it from exerting some vaguely defined malign influence on the living. That one can now safely leave the body unattended suggests a decline in fear of the dead and changing ideas about their relationship to the living. The conceptual distance between the worlds of the living and the dead is increasing. This change is further suggested by the observation, to be discussed at greater length in Chapter 9, that legends about revenants are now rarely told in La Feuillée. Ghosts are currently considered by many to belong to that category of past culture rejected as "things believed in by the ignorant people in the old days."

The shortening of the *veillée mortuaire* is also related to the deritualization of death. Because one no longer ignores the ordinary physical need of the body for sleep, the abridged wake is less of an extreme departure from the everyday realm into ritual "time out of time." The shortening of the *veillée* suggests that in rural Breton communities death is being displaced from the level of the sacred.

In the abridgment of the wake, as in the Plouguerneau practice of blessing the corpse without holy water, the questioning of a formerly unquestionable ritual structure is apparent. In urban Brittany the wake has been further challenged. Wakes are now rarely held in cities like Brest. In the Monts d'Arrée as well, some people express doubts about the propriety of the wake as an institution. They think that grief should be a private experience and condemn the "intrusion" of neighbors and acquaintances into a household that has lost one of its members. Those who hold this position argue that many people who attend wakes through obligation are hypocritical and feel no genuine grief for the deceased. This criticism, voiced most strongly among those under forty-five years of age, clearly echoes Douglas's ([1970] 1978:74) assertion that ritual is devalued in contemporary society because it is not conceived to provide a vehicle for the expression of authentic emotions.

In La Feuillée the claim is also made that many people attend *veillées* solely "out of curiosity," to see how other people's houses are arranged. The *veillée mortuaire* presents one occasion when people can legitimately enter homes they would normally have no reason to visit. A La Feuillée man in his forties recounts angrily, "After Henriette Tanguy died last week, I was standing next to two women in the *boulangerie*. The one was saying to the other, 'I've never been to the Tanguy house before. If you want, why don't we go and make a visit?' That's disgraceful!" Similarly, a woman in her thirties says that should she die, she would not want "visits" except those of family and close friends: "I don't want those people who have criticized me all my life to come, nor those who just come out of curiosity." She suggests that those of her generation and younger will choose not to hold *veillées mortuaires*, just as many of them have chosen not to marry in church and baptize their children.

The criticism of the wake by younger people in La Feuillée is part of the more general rejection of ritual in contemporary Breton society, a rejection associated with secularization. As Douglas suggests, both processes are also linked to the modification of a stratified social order that permitted little mobility and emphasized group cohesion. As forces of social control within the face-to-face community become less rigid, fewer pressures are exerted to conform to community norms. It becomes possible to shorten the wake or dispense with it altogether.

The questioning of the wake also reflects the privatization of responses to death in Brittany. The desire of certain younger people in La Feuillée to be "left alone" after a death "with just close family and friends" further confirms the growing separation of the individual and the nuclear family from non-kin and neighbors within the larger community. As the public ritual associated with death is rejected, death is becoming an aspect of experience which is approached with delicacy and taboo. This movement toward denial of death in Brittany is also suggested by the predominantly negative attitudes toward children's attendance at *veillées mortuaires*. Formerly children were regularly taken on "visits," and many people over forty have vivid memories of being asked to kiss deceased relatives on their *lit de mort*. In the nineteenth century sickly children in particular were encouraged to touch and kiss the dead, since this physical contact was believed to improve their health (Le Braz 1928:1:262). Although some people in contemporary La Feuillée state that they would take their children to the wake of a close relative or family friend, many feel it would be too traumatic, that "it would scare them." The result, as one Breton priest observes, is that "our children and teenagers are no longer socialized to react in the face of death as they were in the past. They do not know what to say or how to behave."[17]

---

17. A relationship between familiarity with death and early exposure to death through attendance at wakes is noted for the Basque country by Douglass (1969:23), who observes that Basque children are encouraged to attend wakes.

Organizing the Funeral

In La Feuillée it is during the liminal period of the *veillée mortuaire* that arrangements for the funeral, or *enterrement*, are made. One of the first people in the community to be informed of a death is the priest. Generally a male relative of the deceased—a son-in-law or nephew rather than someone from the immediate family—visits the rectory to schedule the funeral service. At this time the holy water that will be used to bless the body at the *veillée mortuaire* is brought to the home, together with the large gold and silver cross from the church, which is placed next to the *lit de mort*. Once the priest has been informed of the death, the representatives of secular authority, the mayor and his secretary, must also be notified. A death certificate must be filed and a plot in the cemetery bought for the tomb, if one has not been bought already.

The second step in organizing a funeral involves informing the community that a death has occurred. Traditionally the ringing of the *glas*, or death knell, served this purpose. In contemporary La Feuillée the priest still rings the *glas* on the day preceding a funeral. Formerly the bells were rung in a characteristic fashion to indicate whether the deceased was a man or a woman. However, since the electrification of the church bells in La Feuillée in the 1970s, the distinction is no longer made. This change reflects the decline of sex-based social classification as rural Breton society becomes more individualistically oriented.

The mournful tones of the *glas* arrest activity and attract attention whenever they are heard in La Feuillée. The death knell serves to alert those who do not yet know that a death has taken place in the community. When they hear the *glas*, people make an effort to find out the identity of the deceased, either through reading the obituary notices in the local newspapers or through conversations with their neighbors. In both Plouguerneau and La Feuillée, obituary notices are read with avid interest. People jokingly comment that one of the two local newspapers, the *Télégramme*, has a wider circulation than its rival, *Ouest-France*, because its fee for obituary notices is lower and there are consequently more to read. Upon receiving their newspaper, many people, especially the middle-aged and elderly, invariably turn first to the obituaries page and peruse it at length, giving local and international news only secondary attention.

The fascination evoked by the obituary pages reflects the close ties of kinship and acquaintance which existed in the past and to some extent continue to exist within and among rural Breton communities. The notices are classified by locality. The commune in which the deceased had been living and where the funeral will take place is listed first, followed by the names of the communes where the relatives of the deceased live. Thus, when reading obituary notices, one can rapidly pick out those communities where one has a family connection. The names of the deceased and his or her relatives enable one to place the family in relation to one's own or to those of one's acquaintances. This in turn makes it possible to determine whether or not one has an obligation to attend the funeral or the *veillée mortuaire*. Moreover, the working out of genealogical ties holds its own special interest. As one man new to the La Feuillée area observed with surprise, "Here people talk about genealogies in the same way as other people talk about the weather."

The obituary notice provides information about the age, status, roles, and religious beliefs of the deceased. It is published on the part of the bereaved family, and names of children, grandchildren, brothers, sisters, nieces, nephews, and parents may be included. One can tell at a glance whether the deceased was the generator of a large family or a spinster leaving no one behind to mourn. If the deceased or his children belonged to a voluntary association, such as the local football club, this group will publish a second obituary notice, requesting its members to attend the funeral. Similarly, the local municipal council will often publish an obituary notice for those who have held public office and for members of their families. If the deceased was a war veteran (*ancien combattant*) or a former naval officer, this information will be included in the obituary. Sometimes an additional notice will be published on behalf of the employers or colleagues with whom the deceased worked. Thus the social status and roles of the dead are displayed on the obituary pages. A long obituary notice, or several published together on the part of a number of different groups, is considered "better" than a short one. The length of the notice to some degree provides a measure of the extent to which an individual's passing has ruptured local social networks. Moreover, especially in Plouguerneau, where competition among families with respect to wealth is a primary concern, a long obituary notice listing numerous names of distant relatives indicates that the family of the deceased is prosperous, or *riche*, for one pays by the line. Like other aspects of death-related behavior, obituary notices offer an opportunity for conspicuous display of wealth.

Despite the great interest in reading obituary notices, in La Feuillée one generally learns about a death within the commune by word of mouth. In fact, to find out about a funeral only by reading the obituary notice indicates that one is not well integrated into the community's informal networks of information transmission. These networks include one's neighbors and, more important, the local shopkeepers. By virtue of the constant coming and going in their stores, the shopkeepers are in an excellent position to find out and pass on information about community events in general and deaths in particular. As Soazic, the La Feuillée grocer explained, it is important to find out about a death in the area, because one may have obligations to the deceased or to the bereaved family. One of the informal services Soazic provides is to tell her clients of deaths that concern them. She will exclaim as a customer enters her store: "Listen, your little neighbor died this morning in the hospital." For the elderly or the sick who cannot leave their homes, the *aides-ménagères* serve as intermediaries, keeping their clients informed of events in the wider community.

In the large towns and cities of Brittany, such as Morlaix or Brest, all aspects of funeral arrangements are overseen by the *pompes funèbres*, municipally or privately operated funeral directors.[18] The offices of the *pompes funèbres* are generally located close to the city hall, so that the bereaved can visit them conveniently after registering a death with the municipal authorities. In Breton towns and cities, as in all French urban centers, the municipal government awards a legal monopoly to one *pompes funèbres*. This institution then has the sole right to provide most of the goods and services required for funerals within the municipality. Legally, therefore, all funerals must be organized through the *pompes funèbres*. In addition to transporting the coffin and corpse from the hospital or

---

18. The *pompes funèbres* exists in larger centers throughout France. It is not a uniquely Breton institution.

home to the church and cemetery, the *pompes funèbres* schedules the funeral Mass. Employees of the *pompes funèbres* perform the *toilette des morts* and arrange the body if there is to be a wake in the home, which is unusual in urban centers. If requested, the *pompes funèbres* will also provide services such as embalming and cosmetic restoration of the corpse. Coffins are supplied through the *pompes funèbres*, and a catalogue is made available to the bereaved in order that they may select the desired model. Uniformed employees of the *pompes funèbres* serve as pallbearers at the funeral and act as ushers, seating the mourners appropriately in the church.

It is clear that in urban areas anonymous, paid specialists are responsible for the organization of funerals. As with the development of specialized medical personnel and facilities to cope with death and dying, the role of the *pompes funèbres* at urban funerals is a product of the increased division of labor in contemporary Breton society. The creation of paid funeral specialists has had the effect of distancing death from the social experience of urban dwellers. In contrast, those living in La Feuillée and similar rural communities are frequently called upon to participate actively in the organization of funerals for neighbors or family members. Thus, in these social settings where face-to-face relationships have been maintained to a greater extent and the specialized division of labor is not highly developed, death remains a more familiar phenomenon than in the urban context.

In La Feuillée the coffin is purchased during the *veillée mortuaire* from a carpenter who resides in the commune. Normally a male relative of the deceased comes to place the initial order with the carpenter, and a woman from the family makes a second visit to decide what color and quality of material will be used to line the inside of the coffin. This sharing of responsibility corresponds to the gender-based definition of roles apparent in other facets of everyday life. Usually it is the women in a family who are concerned with things "interior": the decoration of the house, the choice of furnishings, and the running of the household. The outside world of agricultural markets, bistros, and politics is the male realm.

In preparation for funerals in La Feuillée, a temporary work group must be mobilized to serve as pallbearers, or *porteurs du corps*.

Ideally, it is said, all of the pallbearers should be neighbors from the deceased individual's *quartier*. Often the male neighbor who lives nearest to the deceased or another close male neighbor asks others from the *quartier* to serve in the work group. In other cases a representative of the bereaved family makes the request. The rule concerning the choice of pallbearers from the *quartier* of the deceased continues to be observed as much as possible. However, in some of the more depopulated neighborhoods of the commune it is difficult to find the six men needed for this temporary work group, and men from neighboring *quartiers* are asked to help.

Until recently in La Feuillée it was customary to choose persons of the same sex and age category as the deceased to be pallbearers. Men were thus asked to serve as pallbearers when the deceased was a man, and women performed this role for other women. Likewise, if the deceased was a middle-aged individual, the pallbearers would also be of middle age. Married persons were chosen to carry the coffins of other married persons. This pattern of selection for pallbearers was the dominant one in nineteenth-century Brittany, as Le Braz records: "These pallbearers . . . must belong to the same social category as the deceased; that is to say that married persons must be carried by married persons, young people by young people, agricultural workers by agricultural workers, sailors by sailors" (1928:1:292). As Le Braz indicates, occupational and class distinctions were also important considerations in the selection of pallbearers.

In contemporary La Feuillée, men who made their careers in the navy continue to be chosen as pallbearers at the funerals of former sailors. However, other social distinctions, including those of occupation, sex, and age, are no longer as clearly expressed through the choice of pallbearers as in the past. Regardless of the sex of the deceased, men serve as pallbearers at almost all funerals in La Feuillée. Ostensibly women are no longer chosen because modern coffins are too heavy for them to carry. This practical concern only partly explains the change, however, since coffins are no longer actually carried but are wheeled on a type of cart specially devised for the purpose. On a deeper level, the changing norms concerning women pallbearers in La Feuillée suggest that the local social universe is no longer so rigidly structured in terms of age and sex classes as it was in the past. Increasingly people are coming to perceive themselves and others as individuals rather than as members of a particular age class or sex group.

Between July 1983 and August 1984 in La Feuillée, women served as pallbearers at only one woman's funeral. In the neighboring commune of Loqueffret, however, women continue to "carry" at funerals of women, evidence that patterns of social change are subject to highly localized variations. Women in La Feuillée do continue to carry the wreaths of flowers at funerals of other women from their *quartier,* and it is always women who are asked to carry the coffin at infant burials, even when the deceased child was a boy.

In general, pallbearers at funerals in La Feuillée are currently chosen from age classes younger than that of the deceased. As life expectancy increases, the contemporaries of those who die are increasingly elderly and feeble and cannot be expected to undergo the emotional and physical strain of serving in a temporary work group for a funeral. When a young person from the community dies, however, a strong effort is made to recruit pallbearers from among his or her age-mates. At the funeral of Jeannie Kervao, the twenty-two-year-old woman who was killed while crossing the highway, the pallbearers were young men from her peer group, friends with whom she had spent Saturday evenings at the *crêperie* in La Feuillée. If the deceased is young, it appears to be more important to choose pallbearers from the same age cohort than to choose people from his or her neighborhood. The *exode rural* has drained most *quartiers* of their young people, and it becomes necessary to look beyond the *quartier* to the commune as a whole as a source of potential pallbearers. Conversely, it is generally the neighborhood rule that takes precedence if the deceased is an older person.

In the face-to-face context that has to a large extent persisted in small rural communities such as La Feuillée, social ties and obligations among past neighbors are retained despite changes in residence. If a former La Feuillée resident dies elsewhere and is returned to the community for burial, his or her previous neighbors in the commune are asked to serve as pallbearers. When her elderly aunt died in a retirement home near Rennes, Hélène Roux organized the dead woman's former neighbors to carry the coffin for the funeral in La Feuillée. Hélène commented, "I thought people might refuse. It has been so long since she lived here. But no, everyone from the *quartier* agreed. 'She and her family were always from here,' they said."

While neighborhoods continue to function as cohesive social units in La Feuillée, in the Plouguerneau area the neighborhood has become less important as an arena for social interaction. This tendency is reflected in new norms concerning the choice of pallbearers. In Plouguerneau and Lannilis, the adjacent commune to the south, pallbearers were formerly chosen from the neighborhood of the deceased. Over the past decade, however, with the pattern of social relationships within *quartiers* based on reciprocal aid in agricultural work beginning to change, it has become more difficult and embarrassing to ask neighbors to serve as pallbearers. To do so means asking them to lose a day or half-day of work, something particularly unattractive to the growing number of salaried workers who commute to Brest from this area. In response to this situation, the *pompes funèbres* from Brest moved into the region and began to direct the majority of funerals.

More recently there has been a reaction against the impersonal, often hurried quality of funerals managed by this agency. Regardless of the family's preferences, the funeral Mass must be scheduled when the *pompes funèbres* can conveniently make the twenty-five-kilometer trip from Brest to Lannilis. In addition, the services of the *pompes funèbres* are expensive. For these reasons members of the immediate family of the deceased, such as grandchildren, have in recent years regularly been serving as pallbearers in Lannilis. This is a sharp break with tradition. In La Feuillée the participation of the family in temporary work groups associated with a funeral is strongly condemned. Critical gossip followed one local funeral where the son-in-law of the deceased helped lower the coffin into the grave: "What did people think? It looked as if he were in too much of a hurry to put his father-in-law into the tomb!" As the comment implies, people thought that the son-in-law looked as if he were both emotionally unaffected by the death of his wife's father and overly eager to take possession of her inheritance portion.

The progression from neighbors to outside specialists to family members as pallbearers in the Plouguerneau-Lannilis area follows the decline of *entraide* between non-kin within the neighborhood or *quartier*. With the emergence of specialized medical facilities and personnel, as well as the development of funerary specialists, it has become less and less necessary to engage in reciprocal relationships beyond the family in order to find support and assistance during life-crisis rites. This new social reality is apparent in another feature of funerary ritual which is currently undergoing modification in Plouguerneau: the selection of men to carry the cross that leads the funeral procession.

In addition to pallbearers, the temporary work group organized for a funeral includes two men who head the funeral procession carrying the large gilt cross supplied by the church. In La Feuillée there is no clearly defined rule to guide the choice of those men. Frequently two moderately young men from the *quartier* are picked, since it requires some physical stamina to carry the heavy metal cross on the three-quarter-kilometer route from the church to the cemetery. In two *quartiers* unmarried men are preferred, which means that the same two bachelors are asked to carry the cross whenever a death occurs in the neighborhood.[19] In other *quartiers* it is those men who have maintained a connection with the church, the *blancs*, who are called upon to fill this role. The obligation to carry the cross in Plouguerneau, however, traditionally falls to the two nearest male neighbors of the deceased. It is considered an honor to carry the cross, and one cannot decline without insult. Nevertheless, with the decreasing significance of neighborhood *entraide*, there have been recent funerals at which the closest neighbor has refused to carry the cross.

In Plouguerneau the funeral of Anna Le Guen's husband in 1981 was marred by the failure of the nearest neighbor to meet his obligation to carry the cross. To understand the context of the neighbor's refusal, it is important to point out that Anna's house is located on the outskirts of the *bourg* of Plouguerneau, in Kerarmor, a hamlet that was, until the 1970s, inhabited by peasant agriculturalists. In some Kerarmor families, like the Le Guen's, the husband

---

19. In the La Feuillée area, as in European folk tradition more generally, there is a strong symbolic association between weddings and funerals (see, for example, Bernabé 1980:62, 84; Kligman 1988; Lawson 1964:546–61, 597, 601–602; Linebaugh 1975:112–115). This folk association would appear to underlie the selection of bachelors to carry the cross. Those who have never been in the position of honor at a wedding are compensated with an important role in the community's funeral processions.

was employed by the navy or received a navy pension. Although most of the household income came from this extra-agricultural source, the Le Guen family and others in similar circumstances continued to work their land, producing much of their own food. In the 1970s some of the agricultural land in Kerarmor across the road from the Le Guen house was subdivided and used for the construction of new houses. It is in this new subdivision that M. Riou, the neighbor who refused to carry the cross at M. Le Guen's funeral, lives. Differences of occupation and lifestyle separate the Riou and the Le Guen families, despite their residential proximity. The Riou family does not work agricultural land in the hamlet. M. Riou commutes to a white-collar job in Brest. His refusal to carry the cross appears to have been motivated in part by unwillingness to take unpaid leave from work to attend the Le Guen funeral. Moreover, the Rious seek to distance themselves from the "old-fashioned" and "backward" lifestyle of their agriculturalist neighbors. Considering themselves more sophisticated, the Rious interact very little with the agriculturalist families in the *quartier*. In the past, when all families living in neighborhoods like Kerarmor were engaged in small-scale agricultural production, differences in lifestyle and values among close neighbors were less extreme than those that now separate the Rious and the Le Guens.

Since her husband's death Anna has cut all social ties with the Riou family. She denounces them angrily, claiming that "They think they're superior, richer than everyone else. Well, they'll see, when they need help and there is no one there to give it!" Despite this reference to the norm of reciprocal assistance among neighbors in cases of sickness and death, the traditional system is less and less operative. As another Plouguerneau woman states, the nearest-neighbor rule may cease to be workable now because one has less contact with one's neighbors. Whereas in the past it was a simple matter to ask one's nearest neighbor to carry the cross, because it was with him that one had "the closest relations," this certainty is no longer guaranteed. That one can now refuse to carry the cross in Plouguerneau also indicates that informal processes of social control, such as gossip, are less effective than they once were in coercing community members to abide by social conventions. In addition, families like the Rious need no longer rely on their neighbors to look after them during illness, for with medical insurance and the availability of institutional care, hospitalization now provides an alternative.[20]

The *Enterrement*

The *enterrement*, or funeral, is a rite of transition for the deceased. It begins with a subrite of separation, the *mise en bière*, or placing of the body in the coffin. The funeral ends with burial, which as a rite of incorporation marks the entry of the deceased into the community of the dead.

The *Mise en Bière*

The *mise en bière* takes place in the home of the deceased. The body is transferred to the coffin from the *lit de mort*, where it rested during the wake. Although the dead person remains until burial in a liminal state, between the worlds of the living and the dead, the *mise en bière* widens the gulf that divides the deceased from the living community. Prior to placement in the coffin, the deceased remains visible. On the *lit de mort* he or she appears to be in a deep sleep, undisturbed by the conversation of the mourners in the house. After the *mise en bière*, however, the deceased is much less a physical presence among the living.

---

20. A more detailed system of mortuary obligations among "first neighbors," defined on the basis of geographic proximity, exists in the Basque country. In many French Basque villages, as in Plouguerneau, the male first neighbor carries the cross and leads the funeral procession (Ott 1981:124). Additional mortuary services performed by Basque first neighbors include the *toilette des morts*, preparation of the house for the wake, paying for annual Masses for the deceased, and assisting the bereaved household with daily agricultural tasks (Ott 1981:117–130, see also Douglass 1969:145–163). Describing a village in the French Basque region during the mid-1970s, Ott (1981:122) documents one case in which close relatives provided the bereaved with the assistance in daily chores that has conventionally been the responsibility of the first neighbors. She suggests that although this case is locally considered somewhat aberrant, it may herald the disappearance of the system of first-neighbor mortuary obligations. The same pattern of change from neighborhood-based to family-based participation in funerary ritual and support during bereavement observed in Plouguerneau may also be occurring in Basque communities. In addition to mortuary obligations, Basque first-neighbor relationships were part of a complex system of rotation based on house order that formerly included the exchange of blessed bread (Ott 1981). More research would be required to determine if the nearest-neighbor mortuary obligation which is currently disappearing in Plouguerneau is part of a larger system of rotation and turn-taking similar to those documented for Iberia (Freeman 1987), which may have existed in Brittany in the past.

The *mise en bière* is often described as "the hardest moment" for the bereaved family. The separation between the deceased and his or her living relatives becomes definitive when the body is placed in the coffin. At the *mise en bière*, as at the lowering of the coffin into the grave, a similar moment of separation, grief is difficult to contain. In La Feuillée the priest says a prayer at the home of the deceased just prior to the arrival of the carpenter and his assistant, who bring the coffin. The priest remarks that some families, finding it difficult to watch the *mise en bière*, leave the room at this point. In many families, however, he notes that "they stay, and often here people kiss the person who has died." Many friends arrive to make a visit just before the *mise en bière*, so the home of the deceased may be very crowded during the last moments of the wake.

In La Feuillée and Plouguerneau, as in many rural Breton communes, the carpenter who provides the coffin also performs the *mise en bière*. The carpenter in La Feuillée, Gaston, is aided by the younger of the two municipal employees, who serves as grave digger for the commune. The *mise en bière* is considered to be a particularly stressful task. Gaston acknowledges that "one gets used to it, but it's hard, especially if it's someone you knew well." Perhaps for this reason, many families provide Gaston and his assistant with a shot of hard liquor after their work is finished. Jean-Luc, an older, retired carpenter from the Monts d'Arrée, recalls how he and his assistant always fortified themselves with a glass of rum in a local bar before a *mise en bière*. Afterward they were also served rum. Even now it is rare to be offered rum in this poor rural area, and in the past this drink must have been still less common. The provision of a *pourboire*, or tip, that is "out of the ordinary" emphasizes the sacred quality of the ritual.

Jean-Luc and Gaston express an understated pride in their responsibility for a task that many others in their communities would find disturbing. Discussing local funerals, Jean-Luc comments that he is rarely troubled by morbid thoughts after he has performed a *mise en bière*. On one occasion, however, he was deeply disturbed by dreams of the deceased. Jean-Luc attributes these unsettling dreams to the fact that he had not himself touched the corpse during that particular *mise en bière*. This casual observation is highly significant, for it attests to the continuity of folk beliefs recorded during the past century. According to Le Braz (1928:1:261), "There is a way of assuring that you will never encounter a dead person again in your path; it is to kiss his body before it is placed in the coffin." The La Feuillée priest's comment that "often here people kiss the deceased" takes on new meaning in the light of this belief. Analogous traditions from Scotland relate even more closely to the contemporary Breton carpenter's case: "In the West of Scotland, the belief in touching the dead to prevent dreaming of them or having any uncomfortable sensations afterwards, is common among the older people" (Carson 1900); "When one comes into the presence of a corpse, it is wise to lay one's hand upon it; otherwise one may have to *see it again*" (Goodrich-Freer 1902:60).

After the *mise en bière*, the deceased leaves his or her home for the last time. In La Feuillée neighbors, family, and pallbearers assemble at the house and form a procession to go to the church. If the distance between the church and the home of the deceased is not far, the procession goes on foot, headed by the cross, after which comes the coffin followed by the priest. The neighbors and friends of the deceased chosen to carry wreaths of flowers walk behind the priest, followed by the bereaved family. Family members join the procession roughly in order of their relationship to the deceased. The closest relatives—those from the nuclear family—walk ahead of more distant relatives, with acquaintances coming at the rear (see fig. 6).

If the deceased is from one of the outlying villages of the commune, Gaston, the carpenter, who owns a large station wagon, transports the coffin, cross, and flowers to the church. The procession is organized at the church door, and the pallbearers wheel the coffin into the church. Prior to widespread car ownership in rural Brittany, the coffin was transported from distant hamlets to the funeral on a cart drawn by a horse or oxen (Le Braz 1928:1:292). Mourners followed on foot. At each village, as the procession passed on its way to the church, more people joined the crowd from behind.

The Funeral Service

Like the wake, the funeral itself is designed to make an aesthetic impact on those who participate in the ritual. As one seventy-two-year-old La Feuillée woman states, "The curé here does the most beautiful funerals in the region." The priest attempts to ensure that the funerals he conducts are both aesthetically and spiritually satisfying. In the church at La Feuillée there is no organ, only a simple harmonium, which the curé plays while singing the funeral hymns. In order that he may provide this musical accompaniment, the curé often asks a priest from a neighboring parish to help officiate at the ceremony. Relative to the usual Sunday Mass, funerals have more elaborate music and ritual, owing to the presence of a second priest. The curé of La Feuillée also uses tape-recorded music to enhance the sacred atmosphere in the church. Themes such as the "Ave Maria" are played as people wait for the funeral to begin.

The flowers carried into the church and placed on or around the coffin during the service also heighten the aesthetic effect of the ceremony. So does the ornate gold cross, placed in an upright position in front of the altar at the head of the bier, and the black velvet cover draped over the coffin. These artifacts, together with the lighted tapers in the chancel and, in some cases, the flags of the Union Nationale des Anciens Combattants or the Anciens de la Résistance, war and Resistance veterans, lend a solemn and sacred air to the tableau created at the front of the church.

As at the wake, those who attend funerals mark the liminal nature of the occasion by a change of dress. People wear their best clothes to a funeral, and women carry small purses rather than the large handbags used for mundane chores like shopping.

Attendance at funerals in La Feuillée is high. Funerals are one of the few occasions on which men attend church. Men are particularly likely to be present if the deceased is a man. Similarly, if the deceased is a young person, there will be many young people who otherwise rarely attend Mass in the congregation. For the middle-aged and the elderly, funeral attendance is an obligation incurred through kin and neighborhood ties. One has a duty to attend the funerals of one's neighbors. This obligation holds even if the deceased has not been resident in the community for some time or if one has oneself moved away. Once part of a *quartier,* one remains part of that *quartier,* and the phrase "We were neighbors in the past" is frequently offered as the rationale for attending a funeral. In La Feuillée the elderly and middle-aged explain that "everyone" attends funerals because "everyone knows everyone. We were young together, we did our Communions together." Moreover, people "like to attend funerals" even when there are no close ties with the deceased. Indeed, some of those present at a funeral may have rarely visited the deceased during the last years of his or her life.

To some young people in La Feuillée the local tradition of funeral attendance appears hypocritical. Anne-Marie, a twenty-five-year-old La Feuillée woman who teaches at a regional secondary school, remarks critically that her father goes to every funeral in the parish, "even if he doesn't know the person who has died. It's disgusting. For my part, I go when I really feel something for the deceased or for the family. But not each time. That horrifies me." As in the case of the wake, such criticisms stem from the rejection of public ritual associated with death in favor of less formal, more individualistic responses to bereavement, which are conceived to be more emotionally authentic.

Among older people in La Feuillée, however, it is not considered hypocritical or morbid to attend funeral ceremonies. Rather, it is believed to be *triste*, or sad, and a somewhat shameful reflection on the bereaved family if there are too few people in attendance. Clearly, funeral attendance has different meanings for members of different generations. For the middle-aged and the elderly, attendance at a funeral demonstrates one's solidarity with the living. One also attends because one hopes that people will reciprocally attend for one's own funeral and for those of one's relatives. Moreover, in such a small, isolated community, where a majority of the population is elderly, there are few "events." A funeral provides an "outing" where one can catch up on news from neighboring villages and parishes. It is also the occasion for family reunions. As people explain, "There are some relatives that one sees only at weddings and funerals." However, funerals are replacing weddings as foci for family gatherings for two reasons. First, large weddings are expensive, and in addition, as La Feuillée grandparents comment, "young people don't get married anymore." Numbers of both religious and civil marriages performed in Brittany have decreased steadily since 1972, partly as a result of the increased numbers of couples who live together without formal union (Grignon 1983). The trend toward deritualization in contemporary Breton society extends to weddings and other life-cycle transitions as well as to funerals and wakes. Furthermore, weddings are smaller than funerals because membership in a kin group is self-ascribed for the purposes of a funeral, whereas it is prescribed, by invitation, for a wedding. In La Feuillée all relatives of the deceased and bereaved family feel an obligation to attend a funeral, whereas invitations to a wedding stop at first cousins. Thus, people explain, it is at funerals that one encounters distant family members, those who are "a little bit related" whom one has not seen for some time.[21]

Family members living far away make great efforts to journey to La Feuillée for a funeral. On one occasion in the 1970s, several of Marie-Thérèse's relatives were seriously injured and one was killed in a car accident on the way from Paris to La Feuillée for a family funeral. Recounting the tragedy, Marie-Thérèse reflects: "They would have done better to take the train." She does not question the necessity of their decision to attend the funeral. The idea that "they would have done better not to come" is unthinkable.

Funerals in La Feuillée are scheduled in the afternoon, usually for three o'clock. By two-thirty the center of the *bourg* near the church has become a focus of activity. Small groups of women converge on the place du Bourg from all directions, pausing to exchange news. Men gather in the *bureau de tabac*, or tobacconist's shop and bar, across the road from the church. A funeral presents "the occasion to chat among friends and to drink a glass of wine" before and after the ceremony. Along both sides of the road, groups of people stand on the sidewalk as they wait for the procession to arrive. Waiting is customary, because it is considered impolite to enter the church before the coffin. People file into the church after the bereaved family and those carrying flowers. Nevertheless, in bad weather, or when the funeral is a large one and seating space will be at a premium, a number of people will enter the church early.

When the funeral procession arrives, it is greeted by the priest at the church door. Those already inside stand as the cross, coffin, and other mourners file in. The coffin is wheeled to the front of the chancel, directly facing the altar in the center. The carpenter and grave digger function as funeral directors, draping the black velvet cloth over the coffin and placing the flowers on top. At the front of

---

21. Compare Segalen's (1985:362) observation about the *pays* Bigouden: "Ceremonial relationships with the kin group stop at weddings: at funerals, often attended by more than a thousand people, one knows one is related, but one does not know how. Each person feels an ultimate family obligation in the face of death."

the church the bereaved family is seated, on both the left and right sides of the coffin. Often the church is overcrowded, and those who have waited outside to follow the coffin into the church cannot find a place to sit. However, there is always a place reserved for the immediate family.

The priest begins the Mass with a short introduction naming the deceased: "Brothers and sisters, we are assembled here today to say our last goodbye to . . ." During the course of the Mass several hymns are sung. In contrast to many of the Breton funeral hymns of the past, which emphasized sin, penitence, and the wrath of God, the contemporary hymns, in French, stress themes of resurrection and reconciliation with God:

> *Donne-leur Seigneur le repos éternel*
> Give them, Lord, eternal rest,
> *Et que brille sur eux la lumière de ta face*
> And let the light of Your face shine on them.
> (Diocèse de Quimper 1975:375)

Instead of the Latin *Libera* with its "Dies irae, dies illa," describing the Last Judgment as a "day of wrath," the La Feuillée priest prefers to use the hymn "Sur le seuil de sa maison":

> *Sur le seuil da sa maison, notre père t'attend*
> On the threshold of His house, our Father waits for you,
> *Et les bras de Dieu s'ouvriront pour toi*
> And the arms of God will open out for you.
> (Diocèse de Quimper 1975:376)

Some people regret the passing of the *Libera*, but in line with contemporary Catholic theology, the priest contends that it was an outmoded vestige of "the religion of fear" initiated with the Breton missions of the sixteenth century. "The words were terrifying," he says. "People didn't understand what they were singing." The modification of the hymns used for funerals is one aspect of the rationalization or "disenchantment" of religion in Brittany, which will be discussed at greater length in Chapter 7.

Prior to the Communion at La Feuillée funerals the priest presents a short reading from the Scripture, often from the Book of Job. The reading may be varied according to the context of the death. For example, when a six-month-old baby in the community died, the text chosen was "Suffer the little children to come unto me, and forbid them not, for of such is the kingdom of God" (Mark 10:14). Similarly, the priest's eulogy, although generally short, is tailored to the particular circumstances of each funeral.

In La Feuillée an offertory is collected during the funeral service. Many resent this, claiming that the priest "earns enough with funerals. He doesn't need to pass the plate." In protest, some *rouges* place only "a few little coins to make some noise" in the collection plate, giving the church their unwanted five-, ten-, and twenty-centime pieces. The funeral Mass by itself, paid for by the family, costs 350 francs. Those who request prayers for the soul of the deceased pay 50 francs for a Mass and 10 francs for a service. Not all of this money remains within the parish. Nevertheless, the priest is perceived to profit from deaths in the community. "He sings while the others cry," complains one woman, in reference both to the musical accompaniment provided by the curé at *enterrements* and to the supposed reason for his singing: good spirits occasioned by the money pouring into the church treasury.

This comment underscores another significant feature of funerals in La Feuillée. In contrast to *blanc* Plouguerneau, where social pressure favors participation in church rituals and the congregation sings funeral hymns loudly and with emotion, in La Feuillée it is almost literally true that only the curé sings. As noted earlier, funerals are one of the few occasions on which people attend church in this predominantly left-wing and anticlerical community. Almost all the men and three-quarters of the women who attend funerals maintain a hostile silence throughout the Mass. They are there physically, and their presence is partly an expression of solidarity with the bereaved, but it is not to be interpreted as an endorsement of the Catholic church. Thus, people refrain from singing the hymns, refusing to commit themselves more than minimally to the ritual. Some even refuse to stand at the requisite times in the ceremony. A more extreme form of protest exists in Huelgoat, where Communist tradition is even more deeply entrenched. Here there are numerous comings and goings within the church throughout the funeral Mass. The door creaks open frequently, particularly toward the end of the Mass when the men, gathered on the street corner opposite the church or in the cafés of the *quartier*, enter at the last minute, in order to be present when the congregation files past the coffin to bless it for the final time. In Scrignac, another strongly *rouge* commune in the Monts d'Arrée, the café next to the cemetery where men gather to await the arrival of the funeral procession is locally known as the Ti an Diaoul, or House of the Devil. In name as in function, this café is a veritable "antichurch."[22]

For the majority of the congregation, the most important part of the funeral ceremony is the reading of the list of names of those who have requested Masses or services for the soul of the deceased. People listen attentively, both for their own names and for the names of others in the community who have paid for these prayers. To give a Mass or a service is somewhat equivalent to leaving a calling card with the bereaved family. It demonstrates one's presence and one's sympathy. One gives Masses and services for relatives, neighbors, and reciprocally for those who have given them for someone in one's own family. Thus the list read by the priest displays the networks of social relations and kinship ties within and beyond the parish. It is for this reason that the congregation takes so active an interest in the list. One listens for the answers to mental questions such as, "Did the estranged brother, or the cousins from Paris, give a Mass?" Moreover, the length of the list in itself is, like the length of the newspaper obituary notice, a measure of the popularity, status, and social influence of the deceased and his or her family.

The reading of the list of Masses and services is followed by the blessing of the coffin.[23] At this point in the service a brass container filled with holy water (a *bénitier*) and an aspergillum are placed at the foot of the coffin. The priest is the first to do the blessing, tracing the sign of the cross in the air with the aspergillum, which sprinkles the coffin with holy water. In this rite water again becomes a symbol of immortality and regeneration. This symbolism is affirmed in the hymn that is generally sung immediately before the blessing of the corpse. As one of its verses states:

---

22. See Le Bras (1976:178–179) for more general discussion of the historical position of the café as *contre-Eglise* and the café owner as the *anti-curé du village* in France.

23. In some parishes the priest first circles the coffin with a censer containing burning incense. The rising smoke is said to symbolize the soul of the deceased rising toward heaven. This rite is no longer practiced in La Feuillée.

> *L'eau qui t'a donné la vie lavera ton regard*
> The water that gave you life will cleanse your vision,
> *Et tes yeux verront le salut de Dieu*
> And your eyes will see the salvation of God.
> (Diocèse de Quimper 1975:376)

Here an explicit parallel is drawn between the holy water used to bless the coffin at the funeral and the water of baptism, without which, according to traditional doctrine, salvation is not possible. As one of the prayers during the funeral Mass states in reference to the deceased, "Because he has been baptized in the faith, allow him to participate in eternal life." A less explicit symbolism equating the water used in the blessing with amniotic fluid is also operative in this rite. As with the parallels between infancy and death in the wake, a symmetry between birth and rebirth is created at this point in the funeral ceremony. This symmetry can be seen in another verse of the hymn quoted above:

> *Comme à ton premier matin, brillera le soleil*
> As on your first morning, the sun will shine
> *Et tu entreras dans la joie de Dieu*
> And you will enter into God's joy.
> (Diocèse de Quimper 1975:376)

In Plouguerneau holy water is no longer placed in the *bénitier* during the funeral ceremony. The gesture of blessing the coffin is retained, but the aspergillum is dry. As at wakes in Plouguerneau, the blessing has lost some of its symbolic significance. To some extent this modification reflects a declining belief in the Catholic conception of the afterlife and a loss of certainty that the funeral does indeed accomplish the rebirth of the deceased into "God's joy." The decision to abandon the use of water in this rite in Plouguerneau is rationalized by the need to prevent marking the black velvet cloth used to cover the coffin during the Mass. As with the wake, where the desire to avoid water stains on the fine sheets covering the *lit de mort* is expressed, this-worldly concerns predominate over those related to the afterlife.

Like the giving of Masses and services, the blessing also fulfills a "calling card" function. The congregation files up the side aisles of the church past the coffin, which each person blesses in turn, and then leaves the church by the center aisle. In crossing from the side aisles to the coffin, one must pass in front of the pews where the bereaved family is seated. This enables one to ensure that the family has noticed one's presence at the funeral. Moreover, the act of blessing represents a last farewell to the deceased. During the blessing of the coffin, the "Kantik ar Baradoz," with its haunting minor-key melody, is sung again to the accompaniment of the harmonium.[24]

Some members of the congregation do not bless the coffin in the church. The family and close associates of the deceased accompany the coffin to the cemetery, where the priest says a short prayer and the mourners do the blessing before the actual burial. Those who will go to the cemetery remain seated while the others bless the coffin in the church. The funeral procession, headed by the cross, is re-formed for the walk from the church to the cemetery. In general, those who do not follow the procession to the cemetery do not stand by the roadside to watch it pass. After leaving the church, people hurry to their cars, to the shops in the *bourg*, or to one another's houses without casting a backward glance. This pattern of behavior presents a striking contrast to the eagerness with which people watch funeral processions arrive at the church before the Mass begins. Although it was never explicitly stated in La Feuillée that one should not watch the procession to the cemetery, the obvious efforts made to avoid doing so may reveal the continuing influence of the nineteenth-century folk belief that "one must never stand at the window or on one's doorstep to watch a funeral pass; by doing this one gives the impression of mocking the deceased, of saying to him, 'You see, we remain here while you are leaving, going down there.' The deceased, provoked in this way, will always take revenge" (Le Braz 1928:1:297).

Changes in the Form of Funerals

Prior to 1972 the church in Brittany offered three differently priced categories of funeral ceremony (Lambert 1985:333–334). Funerary ritual thus provided an opportunity for the display of social class

---

24. Words and music for the "Kantik ar Baradoz" are published in La Villemarqué ([1839] 1963:514–518, XLIV). Words are also published in *Eskopti Kemper ha Leon* (1953:71–74).

distinctions, as indicated in the following description of classed funerals given by a La Feuillée woman in her late sixties:

> The third class was used infrequently, except perhaps for the poor *clochards* without any family, who didn't have a cent, because it was absolutely free. Everything was simple and bare, reduced to the absolute minimum. The first class was reserved for the very well-off families who could afford the price. There were two or three crosses instead of one, the chancel of the church was decorated with black draperies embroidered with silver, and the coffin was covered with the same type of cloth. The priest wore matching vestments. The ceremony and the music, all were elaborate. The second class was shorter and simpler.

The system of classed funerals came under particular criticism in the anticlerical and egalitarian Monts d'Arrée. In abolishing the distinctions between categories of funerary ritual, the church followed the more general trend toward the leveling of rigid class boundaries throughout Breton society during the 1960s.

In small rural communities such as La Feuillée, funerals continue to be the most public of rites of passage. In Breton urban centers such as Brest, however, funerals are often sparsely attended. This difference is related to the decreasing force of the face-to-face community in the urban setting. Low attendance at urban funerals is also a product of the same questioning of public ritual encountered among young people in La Feuillée. Rather than emphasizing obligations to the collectivity, the urban context provides scope for individual autonomy. Consequently, responses to death have become increasingly privatized. There has been a mutually reinforcing relationship between these social factors and the denial of death in urban Brittany. In urban areas, where people live relatively independently of their neighbors, they do not incur obligations to attend funerals for those in the *quartier*. It becomes unusual, rather than normal, to attend a funeral. Death ceases to be a familiar event and begins to be repressed. The anxiety evoked by contact with death leads to avoidance of funeral attendance. More and more, such reminders of death are excluded from the realm of everyday social interaction.

While levels of funeral attendance in La Feuillée and other rural communities remain high, one significant change has occurred in the form of rural funerals. This is the disappearance of the ceremony of condolences, during which all those present at the funeral embraced or shook hands with the close family of the deceased. In La Feuillée condolences generally took place at the graveside. Until the custom was discontinued in this parish in the late 1970s, all those present at a funeral would accompany the coffin to the cemetery. Condolences disappeared earlier in urban centers than in La Feuillée, and the practice is considered locally to be slightly old-fashioned. Although some people in La Feuillée regret the change, most maintain that condolences placed too much of a psychological strain on the bereaved family. The ceremony in the cemetery could easily last for an hour or longer if the funeral was large. Particularly difficult in inclement weather, condolences were physically exhausting for those overcome by grief after the sleepless nights of the wake, and it was emotionally traumatic to receive expressions of sympathy from the entire community.

The discontinuation of condolences is another aspect of the deritualization of death. Moreover, the loss of this custom provides further evidence for the privatization of bereavement. What was formerly a community event is now increasingly conceived of as an exclusively individual one. The public, external expression of emotion, both by the bereaved and by those who sympathize with them, has been devalued in favor of an interior, personal experience of grief.

Another change in folk tradition associated with funerals in La Feuillée relates to the distancing of the dead from the social world of the living and to the disenchantment of Breton worldview. Formerly in La Feuillée it was customary to "guard" the home of a deceased person throughout the funeral service. Some continue to observe this practice. Two women, usually trusted neighbors or distant family members, stay behind in the house after the mourners leave for the church. During the funeral they remove the sheets from the *lit de mort* and rearrange the room in which the wake was held so that it resumes its normal character. They clean and tidy the house after the crowd of visitors which has passed through in the preceding days. When the family returns home, all traces of the wake will be gone. Sacred space is reconverted into the realm of the everyday. The women left to guard the house refrain from shutting the front door from the time the coffin leaves until the family returns after the burial. Although the only explanation for this custom advanced in La Feuillée is that "it's a tradition," it would seem to be linked to the folk belief collected by Le Braz

(1928:1:298) that "the house must never be left alone during a funeral, otherwise the deceased whose corpse one believes to be accompanying to the cemetery will remain to guard the house." He records a story in which a dead woman was discovered by a passerby to have returned to her home during her own funeral after her family had left the house unoccupied with the door closed (1928: 1:298–301).

A number of families in La Feuillée continue to request neighbors to guard the house during the funeral of a relative. However, at some funerals in 1984, the women left to guard the house finished their tasks of cleaning and tidying and departed, shutting the door, in time to arrive at the church for the last part of the funeral service. As with the shortening of the wake, the perception that it is no longer necessary to guard the house throughout the funeral bespeaks a changing relationship between the living and the dead and a changed conception of the condition of the soul after death. Formerly the soul was considered to be "still there," and it was thus necessary to keep it from returning to resume the roles it had occupied during life. One had to "watch" the social space of the living to prevent its usurpation by the dead. This concern is no longer expressed. As many people in La Feuillée assert, "The dead do not return."

After the *Enterrement*: The *Café*

The final stage of the funeral is the burial, which completes the transition of the deceased from the social world of the living to the Anaon, or the community of the dead. Burial, as a rite of incorporation for the deceased, is paralleled by a rite of incorporation for the living, the *café*, which follows the funeral. The *café* is a small meal offered by the family of the deceased to their relatives, those who have journeyed from outside the commune to attend the funeral, those who have given Masses and services for the soul of the deceased, and those who have carried the coffin and flowers. The carpenter and grave digger are also invited. The *café* generally takes place in the restaurant of the Hôtel Rozec in the *bourg* of La Feuillée. As many as one hundred people may be present. The mourners are served bowls of hot coffee, wine, bread, crêpes, butter, and pâté. Toward the end of the *café*, the men present are offered a glass of cognac.

The *café* clearly falls into the category of rites of incorporation for mourners discussed by van Gennep in his analysis of funerary ritual: "Among rites of incorporation I shall first mention the meals shared after funerals and at commemoration celebrations. Their purpose is to reunite all the surviving members of the group with each other, and sometimes also with the deceased, in the same way that a chain which has been broken by the disappearance of one of its links must be rejoined" (1960:164–165). In La Feuillée the *café* does not function as a reunion with the deceased but as a reaffirmation of the social bonds among the living. It is the final phase of the liminal process inaugurated by the wake. The atmosphere during the *café* is one of warmth, both physical and psychological. Conversation gradually becomes animated, particularly toward the end of the *café*. Mme Rozec, the hotel owner, who knows the community well, often tries to seat the family and those closest to the deceased at some distance from those for whom the funeral represents more of a social occasion than a personal loss. In this way the mourners whose grief is the greatest are insulated to some extent from conversation that might strike them as inconsiderately banal or overly humorous.

Festive rites of incorporation for the living similar to the *café* in La Feuillée are a key feature of the tame response to death. Writing of death in the Middle Ages, Ariès observes that "mourning was more social than individual. . . . Condolence visits repaired the unity of the group and re-created the human warmth of holidays; the ceremonies surrounding burial also became a holiday from which joy was not absent, in which laughter was often quick to take the place of tears" (1982:582). In contemporary La Feuillée, the festive aspect of the *café* has come under criticism. For some the custom is "a scandal." They consider it disrespectful to the dead and to the bereaved "to hold a party right after the funeral." These criticisms, like those of condolences and wakes, reflect the current tendency to devalue public rituals expressing community rather than private responses to bereavement.[25] In spite of such senti-

---

25. The same process may be occurring in Basque funerary ritual. By the 1960s banquets following Basque funerals were being deemphasized. Fewer guests were invited and the meal offered was simplified. People approve of this trend, claiming that "drunkenness and revelry are out of place at what should be a solemn occasion" (Douglass 1969:49).

ments, funerals not followed by a *café* are rare in La Feuillée. Those who break with this tradition find themselves censured for stinginess: "The Prigent family didn't offer a *café*, and yet they certainly could have afforded it." Such comments stem from the fact that the *café*, like almost all social institutions in La Feuillée, serves on one level as a vehicle for reciprocity. One provides a *café* for those who have come from some distance to thank them for attending the funeral and to compensate them for the expense and inconvenience of the journey. Similarly, the *café* is literally a *pourboire*, or tip, for those who formed part of the temporary work group associated with the funeral: the carpenter, the gravedigger, and those who carried the coffin, cross, and flowers. It also reimburses those who have paid for Masses and services.

Rite of reciprocity on one level, rite of incorporation for the living on another, the *café* generates a sense of psychological relief, as mourners find themselves once again in the community of the living rather than on the margins of the world of the dead, as they were during the funeral ceremony. After the *café* one may return home to resume one's ordinary, nonritual activities. On many occasions, however, after the end of the "official" *café*, the men prolong the rite by visiting other bistros in the area to drink as a group. In the past, funerals presented a socially sanctioned opportunity for a drinking binge. It is recalled that after a funeral, "All the men from the *quartier* used to come home drunk!" One celebrated funeral is remembered locally as *friko* Fanch ar Riou, or Fanch Riou's wedding banquet, because the friends of the deceased, Fanch Riou, celebrated by drinking after the funeral as if it were a wedding.[26] The continuing high level of alcohol consumption at Breton funerals reveals the liminal condition of the participants in these rites of passage, which lends itself to transcendent experiences, including those generated by alcohol.

Those who attend the funeral Mass but not the *café* offered by the bereaved family participate in other, less formal, rites of incorporation. Small groups of men meet after the funeral to have a drink in the bar of the *bureau de tabac*, and women invite one another to their homes for afternoon coffee. A funeral gives people

---

26. This anecdote again underscores the folk association between funerals and weddings.

the chance to meet relatives and friends from villages in other parts of the commune to reinforce social ties and exchange news and information.

Conclusion

In La Feuillée death is marked by a sequence of rituals that can be interpreted in terms of the structural model for rites of passage developed by van Gennep (1960) and Turner (1969). The wake, as a rite of separation, distances the deceased from the social world of the living. The funeral, as a rite of transition, completes his or her transfer to the Anaon, or community of the dead. This process culminates with the physical act of burial. Following the burial the *café*, as a rite of incorporation for the living, enables the mourners symbolically to leave the ritual state and eases their return to "ordinary" time.

Throughout this sequence of rites, aesthetic operators such as flowers, fine linen sheets on the *lit de mort*, and music contribute to create a sense of the sacred, delimiting ritual space and time and setting them off from the everyday. During the wake and funeral, fluids function as important symbols of rebirth and regeneration for the deceased, whose condition is represented as "dry." Alcohol, in addition to serving this symbolic function (*pour arroser le mort*), also heightens a sense of *communitas* among the living. The use of holy water to bless the corpse recalls birth and baptism, earlier life-cycle transitions, and creates a structural equivalence between the state of the deceased and that of the newborn infant. Thus, Breton funerary ritual, like the death-related traditions of other cultures discussed by Bloch and Parry (1982), is ultimately regenerative. The dead person, like the infant, is incorporated into a new social category and a new phase of existence.

Comparisons between La Feuillée, Plouguerneau, and Brest reveal that the organization of funerals differs between urban centers and small rural communities. The most significant change in the urban setting has been the creation of funeral specialists, the *pompes funèbres*, in the context of the more general development of the division of labor in Breton society over the past forty years. Even in rural communes, specialization is apparent in the *toilette des morts*, now frequently performed by medical professionals rather than by neighbors of the deceased. As specialized personnel take on major roles in funerary ritual, death is progressively distanced from the experience of most other individuals.

The privatization of bereavement and the questioning or abandonment of funeral customs such as the wake and condolences have also contributed to the growing denial of death in Brittany. As individuals and families become more autonomous, community responses to bereavement are criticized. This rejection of public rituals associated with death has generated a distancing of death itself from everyday social life. To an increasing extent, in Brittany as in many other parts of Western society, the socialization process does not provide preparation for death and the emotions it provokes. Currently, for example, it is rare for children in La Feuillée to attend wakes.

The form of funerary ritual has been influenced by changes in Breton social organization, including the decreasing intensity of face-to-face social interaction, the growing emphasis on individual autonomy, and the increasing division of labor and occupational specialization. In Plouguerneau refusal to carry the cross at the head of one's nearest neighbor's funeral procession becomes possible, whereas in the past, informal social sanctions such as gossip or exclusion from networks of reciprocal aid would have made this kind of decision infeasible.

With the change from a stratified to a relatively egalitarian social system, religion in Brittany has become less authoritarian and ritualistic. The new Catholic liturgy for the dying stresses humanistic ethical values and a rational, intellectual approach to the faith. Concern for the welfare of the soul in the afterlife is no longer a major theme in the funeral Mass or in rites such as the *onction des malades*.

Closely related to the trend toward secularization in orthodox Catholicism is the waning of belief in less orthodox aspects of the supernatural. The survival of the soul after death and the ability of the dead to return to the social space occupied by the living are being called into question, as the shortening of wakes and the decreased importance of guarding the house during funerals suggest. These developments are linked to changing conceptions of the nature of the community in contemporary Brittany. In the past the world of the dead was believed to exist parallel to that of the living.

The dead remained important, if invisible, members of the community. Now its boundaries are being more narrowly drawn to exclude the Anaon. With the "disenchantment" of Breton worldview, the borders between the natural and supernatural domains are more and more rigidly defined. Likewise, death is progressively being removed to the margins of social reality.

4

Mourning and Masses for the Dead

Introduction

Until the 1960s, purgatory remained a reality within the Roman Catholic eschatological schema in Brittany. One of the *tableaux* used in teaching church doctrine at Breton missions up to World War II depicts the deliverance of souls from purgatory (fig. 7), a theme popular in religious iconography throughout the Catholic world from the seventeenth to the early twentieth century (Ariès 1982: 465). In the center of the *tableau* a church scene is painted. The faithful are kneeling devoutly before the altar, where the priest celebrates a Mass for the dead. Below those in prayer are the souls in purgatory being devoured by flames. On both sides of the purgatory scene appear angels dressed in flowing robes. One of them empties a golden chalice on the upstretched arms and faces of the souls in purgatory, while others raise purified souls, released from their suffering, to heaven. The symbolism of the *tableau* is evident: it is the prayers of the living which, like water, bring relief to those doing penance in the afterlife for their sins and hasten their departure from purgatory.

Although the message this image conveys is no longer a part of church doctrine, it continues to influence many middle-aged and elderly people, particularly in rural Brittany. Moreover, the concept that sins must be expiated after death through a period of punishment in purgatory remains the basis for the custom of offering Masses and services for the soul of a deceased person on the occasion of his or her funeral.

Masses and Services

It costs fifty francs (five dollars) to give, or *mettre,* a Mass, and ten francs (one dollar) for a service.[1] Ostensibly each Mass and service shortens the time that the deceased must spend in purgatory. Some people continue to give Masses and services with the intention of aiding the soul of the deceased. When asked what motivates people in their parish to give Masses and services, a couple in their seventies from the La Feuillée area responded, "In general, here it is the faith." Others disagree. As many point out, Masses and services are given even when neither the deceased nor those paying for the Mass are *croyants,* or believers. This paradox is well illustrated by the case of Eliane, a forty-three-year-old woman from the Monts d'Arrée who serves as a local official of the Parti Communiste Français. Eliane observes that she pays for a Mass or service as "a mark of sympathy. It's a social convention." However, Eliane is quick to point out the difference between herself and her eighty-year-old mother, who is *croyante* and who gives Masses and services for the sake of the soul of the deceased. "As for me, I don't believe very much," concedes Eliane, "but my mother, *she* believes."

The La Feuillée priest describes the ten-franc service as a "calling card." Both Masses and services perform this function, whether or not additional spiritual concerns motivate those who pay for them. As noted in Chapter 3, the list of those who have given Masses and services which is read at the funeral is a concrete manifestation of the networks of social relationships that surrounded the deceased and continue to be activated among the living.

The giving of Masses and services is not only an expression of personal emotion toward the deceased and the bereaved. Often it is also a social obligation. Annick, a sixty-five-year-old widow from Plouguerneau, and her forty-year-old neighbor defined in order of priority the categories of people who would be obligated to give a Mass and service after the death of a married person with no children:

---

1. Throughout, I use an exchange rate of ten francs to the dollar, which approximately reflects the rate during the time of my fieldwork.

1. husband or wife
2. parents
3. brothers and sisters
4. cousins
5. more distant relatives, such as aunts and uncles
6. friends, neighbors, and those who have some reciprocal obligation to the deceased

Formerly in Plouguerneau close relatives such as siblings marked their degree of relationship to the deceased by giving another kind of ceremony, the *octave*, which was more costly than the Mass and service. Now, however, *octaves* have been discontinued.

Social obligations to give Masses and services may be incurred in a variety of ways. Unusual aid extended by the deceased would obligate the person assisted to pay for a Mass and service. Such obligations are also generated by certain economic relationships. For example, in Plouguerneau, according to Annick, a tenant must give a Mass and service for his landlord. However, the obligation is not reciprocal. A landlord need not provide a Mass for his tenant, although on occasion he may do so, especially if the landlord-tenant relationship was supplemented by ties of friendship. As in Plouguerneau, *politesse* in La Feuillée requires that a tenant give a Mass and service for his or her landlord. Clearly, even though social class distinctions in rural Brittany are currently much less pronounced than in the past, the rules underlying the giving of services and Masses continue to reinforce existing hierarchical social relationships within local communities.

Most frequently obligations to give Masses and services result from the custom of giving them in itself. As Eliane, the Communist party official, remarks, "Here one likes to know who gave a service and who gave a Mass." This information is particularly important when the deceased is a member of one's own family, because at a later date, should a death occur in the giver's family, one must reciprocate. It is very important to reciprocate exactly. Should a person give a service for someone in one's own family, one reciprocates with a service, not a Mass or a service and a Mass. One seeks not only to avoid debts but to avoid putting others unnecessarily in one's debt.

Sometimes the elderly seek to reciprocate in advance for the Masses that they know will be given at their funeral. On a visit with Annick to her invalid aunt Eugénie in Plouguerneau, Eugénie insisted on thrusting a fifty-franc note into Annick's hand as they parted. The next day, while discussing the visit, Annick commented that she had been shocked by the deterioration of Eugénie's health. Then she reflected on the gift of fifty francs: "That's the price of one Mass. I think she gave me the money so that I wouldn't have any expenses for her after her death." From Annick's perspective, her aunt's gift was a form of "advance reciprocity." In another light, Eugénie's gift may be interpreted as an attempt to ensure that after she dies, Annick will not omit to pay for a Mass. Annick is now obligated to *rendre,* to return the gift, and one obvious way of doing so is to pay for a Mass. The Mass would have considerable importance for an elderly woman like Eugénie, who has been influenced throughout her life by a rigid interpretation of Catholic doctrine emphasizing sin and damnation. Salvation is probably an important preoccupation for Eugénie. In addition, it is also possible that she may want to avoid the embarrassment of having too few Masses and services given at her funeral. A funeral with few Masses and services, like a poorly attended funeral, is considered *triste* and a mark of inferior status within the community. Such are the funerals of *les pauvres,* the poor, who cannot afford to give Masses and services for others.

Until recently the list of names of those who paid for Masses and services was read from the pulpit at funerals in all Breton parishes.[2] The practice of reading the list has been discontinued in the churches at Grouannec and in the *bourg* of Plouguerneau, although

---

2. Writing of the Vannes region, Lambert (1985:206, 335) suggests that this custom did not become widespread until after World War II, when the clergy started to promote the giving of services and Masses for a broad range of kin and associates in order to raise funds for the church. In the Cornouaille the practice seems to have originated earlier. A nineteenth-century description of funerary ritual in this region states that the list of names of relatives, friends, and neighbors of the deceased who had paid for services was read aloud from the pulpit. It was not read at the funeral, however, but at High Mass on the following Sunday (Le Calvez 1888:49). The author notes that frequently as many as three hundred services could be requested after a single funeral. Moreover, he observes that while payment for services represents a financial burden for every family, "this very onerous custom is not about to disappear, since the clergy profit from it and the people are flattered by the announcement thus made from the high pulpit of the Masses and services which they have requested" (Le Calvez 1888:49).

it continues sporadically in the third church in the commune of Plouguerneau, at Lilia. Priests in Monts d'Arrée parishes continue to read the list for practically all funerals, except when explicitly requested not to do so by the family of the deceased. In both Plouguerneau and La Feuillée the list of names is given to the family of the deceased after the funeral. It is kept, carefully folded, in the drawer of an armoire and consulted at each subsequent funeral in the community, in order to determine whether or not an obligation to reciprocate has been incurred.

According to certain people in the Plouguerneau area, social pressure to reciprocate for Masses and services has decreased now that the list naming the givers is no longer read publicly. However, others claim that the number of Masses and services given in recent years has actually risen, which presents somewhat of a paradox, given the declining levels of religious practice over the same period. Discussing this situation in the Morbihan, Lambert (1985:335) concludes that the giving of Masses and services has increased since the church discontinued the practice of providing different classes of funerals. The number of Masses and services offered remains the only mark of distinction available in the funeral service to indicate the status of the deceased. An alternative explanation is suggested by Jacques, a thirty-eight-year-old school teacher in the Plouguerneau area. In Jacques's opinion, once a Mass or service has been given, friends and associates of the bereaved family consider themselves free from all further obligations. "After you've given a service, you don't have to do anything more," he explains. The monetary payment to the church which provides a "calling card" has replaced more active and time-consuming forms of support for the family of the deceased. With the generalization of wage labor and cash-based transactions since World War II, social relationships are increasingly mediated in economic terms. Fifty or sixty francs serves to meet one's obligations in the face of a death.

Jacques's observation also suggests that in contemporary Brittany, as in other parts of Euro-American culture, people are growing reluctant to come into direct contact with the bereaved. As Gorer ([1965] 1967) and Ariès (1982) point out, the bereaved in Western society are frequently socially ostracized. Grief is considered to be self-indulgent and its public expression is viewed as a sign of character weakness bordering on mental instability. No longer socialized to cope with death, friends of the bereaved refrain from contacting them, to avoid being caught up in what Gorer terms "a distasteful upsurge of emotion" ([1965] 1967:xxxii).

From Jacques's perspective the increased giving of Masses and services is related to the decreasing intimacy of face-to-face social relationships within Breton communities. However, from another point of view, the same phenomenon can be read as evidence for the continuing importance of death as a central theme in Breton culture. In communities like Plouguerneau and La Feuillée, death continues to provide a focus for the reaffirmation of reciprocal social networks, through the institution of Masses and services.

The number of Masses and services given in Plouguerneau has not dropped even though the givers are no longer publicly named. Increases in the fees charged by the diocese for these ceremonies may, however, cause a decline, both in Plouguerneau and the Monts d'Arrée. Fifty or sixty francs is a significant donation to the church, especially for agriculturalists and retired persons on pensions. An attractive pot of flowers can be bought for approximately the same amount of money, although large wreaths cost considerably more. Some think that the giving of Masses and services is declining in favor of offering flowers: "Now there are more flowers and fewer prayers." Others say that people give both. Flowers are simply added to the Mass and service for which one pays.

It is certain that flowers have become an increasingly important part of the funeral ceremony in Brittany since the early 1960s. To paraphrase Panofsky's (1964) distinction for tombstone art, flowers are a retrospective rather than a prospective symbol. They function within the context of the world of the living to highlight the aesthetic impact of funerary ritual. In contrast Masses and services refer prospectively to the afterlife, at least theoretically, in that they concern the welfare of the deceased's soul. However, such issues are deemphasized in contemporary Catholicism. Ethical conduct in the present world is given precedence over concern about salvation and damnation in the next. Death is portrayed as a prelude to reconciliation with the Dieu d'Amour rather than the inception of a period of penance for one's sins. The presence of flowers at funerals is more consistent with this new eschatological stance than with that of the church in pre-1960s Brittany.

In the La Feuillée area the anticlerical *rouges* consistently give flowers rather than Masses and services at funerals as a matter of principle, in order to avoid contributing directly to the church. In one village adjacent to La Feuillée that is renowned for its allegiance to the Communist party, a collection is made for each funeral. Neighbors contribute the amount of money that would otherwise be spent on a Mass or service, and this fund is used to buy a large wreath on behalf of the whole village. At funerals of Communists, even those who are not themselves *rouges* will often give flowers rather than Masses out of respect for the deceased's wishes and personal beliefs.

Formerly the Masses and services given at a funeral were performed by the priest in the parish of the deceased. As recently as the mid-1960s in Plouguerneau, the services were said as a group between seven and ten o'clock on the same morning as the *messe de huitaine*, a memorial service held one week after the funeral ceremony. One could pay for *petits services* and *grands services*, which varied in price and in the number of prayers offered. A *petit service*, costing five francs, consisted of three psalms, three Scripture readings, and three matins. Middle-aged people in Plouguerneau remember vividly the rapid monotone recitation of these services, which continued nonstop for hours. The present curé of Plouguerneau recalls, "You had to say them fast. You couldn't understand a thing, all you did was count. You had to count them all." He remembers being criticized for slowness by his superiors because he could complete only five *petits services* in half an hour. "You had to do them as rapidly as possible," he observes. Breton priest and author René Le Corre, who characterizes traditional Catholicism in Brittany as "blackmail of the living by the dead" (1982:42), describes with wry humor the services as they were formerly celebrated:

> Every day, or nearly every day, one used to sing the *petits services* from the Angelus before and during the Mass. . . . On Sunday, two *grands services* before High Mass. I still have a record (it is not all that old) on which one hears the vicar and the sacristan alternate: one cannot hear without laughing those nasal voices singing as quickly as possible the Latin psalms and matins for the dead. (The sacristan used to set aside his handkerchief and his tobacco pouch and get on with singing(?) those verses of which he understood nothing and which no one understood. But people didn't need to understand: the rite functioned by itself.)
>
> (1982:41)

Le Corre's final comment that "people didn't need to understand: the rite functioned by itself" underscores the ritualistic quality of pre–Vatican II Catholicism in Brittany.

In the La Feuillée area, Masses and services were said early in the morning on the days immediately following a funeral. The family, neighbors, and associates of the deceased were expected to be present. Now, however, in the Monts d'Arrée as in all other regions of Finistère, Masses and services are no longer performed before a congregation. Related to the overall decrease in regular church attendance in Brittany, this change is also a product of changes in the character of face-to-face social interaction in rural communities. An elderly couple from Loqueffret recalls that Masses and services were first performed privately by the priest in that parish in 1951. On this occasion the family of the deceased requested that the ceremonies be performed in private in order to spare their neighbors the inconvenience of attending church early on a weekday morning. As face-to-face contact within the *quartier* diminished following World War II, when families began to perform agricultural tasks without help from others in the neighborhood, it was perceived to be tactless to burden neighbors with unnecessary ritual obligations. The increased participation of rural people in the salaried labor force, which entailed new patterns of organizing time and thus made it difficult for many to attend church on several consecutive mornings following a funeral, was another factor contributing to the disappearance of publicly performed Masses and services.

The last priest to recite Masses and services publicly in the La Feuillée area died in 1983. It has become common for local curés to send a large proportion of their Masses and the money paid for them to overseas missionaries or to monasteries in France such as the Abbey of Landévennec, near Brest. Others are sent to priests in needy parishes of the diocese. In Plouguerneau, where until recently a family was not considered "respectable" unless it had supplied at least one son to the church, many families have uncles or cousins serving abroad as missionary priests. Before funerals in Plouguerneau the curé asks the family where they would like the Masses given for their deceased relative to be sent, and many request that the recipient be a family member in the clergy. In La

Feuillée the curé sends most of his Masses to a religious chapter in Paris that cares for orphaned boys.³

Since Masses and services are in most cases no longer performed publicly in the parish, doubts arise about whether they are actually celebrated at all. Despite assurances from the clergy that the ceremonies do indeed take place, many people express skepticism, with comments like, "Do you really believe that all those Masses are said?" The institution is perceived, particularly among the anticlerical in the La Feuillée area, as an ingenious money-making device perpetrated by the church. Notwithstanding these attitudes, people continue to give Masses and services, possibly because, in the final analysis, it does not matter whether they are said. Their most important role—that of demonstrating one's sympathy for the bereaved and one's ongoing reciprocal relationship with them—is fulfilled, regardless of where or even whether the ceremonies are performed. The lists of names of those who have paid for Masses and services, read aloud or typed and given to the bereaved family, may be viewed as a tangible embodiment and reaffirmation of the social networks within the community. These lists, by their very existence, are symbolic reminders that in spite of the rupture in the networks caused by a death, in spite of the "missing link" in the chain of social relationships, these relationships and the reciprocity that underlies them will continue to exist.⁴

The *Messe de Huitaine* and *Messe d'Anniversaire*

In addition to the Masses and services given by neighbors and associates of the deceased, in Plouguerneau and La Feuillée there are several other types of Masses for the dead. The most important of

---

3. In Plouguerneau, between January and July 1984, the curé sent 100 Masses to the chaplain of the old people's home in the commune; 100 to missions in Brazil; 120 to a priest working with psychologically disturbed young people in Morlaix; 100 to a teacher-priest; 100 to the curé's own uncle, who is also a cleric; and others to the chaplain of the Catholic lycée in Brest.

4. Describing death in Basque society, Douglass (1969:214–215) also underlines the importance of reciprocity in all aspects of funerary ritual. In Basque communities, as in Brittany, payments are made to the church at the funeral and anniversary Mass and are used to cover the cost of Masses or *nocturnos* (consisting of three

these are the *messe de huitaine* and the *messe d'anniversaire*, which are celebrated at intervals of one week and one year after a death. They serve both to perpetuate the memory of the deceased in the minds of the living and ritually to reinforce his or her entry into the social world of the dead.

The *messe de huitaine* and the *messe d'anniversaire* are offered by the family of the deceased. Like the funeral, these Masses are formal, public occasions. Likewise, mourning, discussed later in this chapter, is an institutionalized expression of an individual's status as bereaved. Grieving, the informal, unstructured and personal emotional response to bereavement, occurs both within and outside of these ritual contexts.[5] As Rosaldo (1984:192) argues, it is essential to avoid confusing grieving with the ritual process surrounding death. Sometimes mourning customs and rituals such as the *messe de huitaine* and the *messe d'anniversaire* coincide with and express the inner grief of the bereaved. At other times, as Rosaldo (1984:189) suggests, such "rituals . . . act as catalysts that precipitate processes whose unfolding occurs over subsequent months or even years." In Plouguerneau and La Feuillée the *messe de huitaine* and the *messe d'anniversaire* denote major landmarks in time after the death of a community member. These ceremonies can also mark emotional watersheds in the grieving process, at least for some of those people who have lost a loved one through death.

In order to understand the full significance of the *messe de huitaine* and the *messe d'anniversaire*, it is useful to consider them in the light of van Gennep's work and Hertz's classic (1907) study of sec-

---

psalms and the Lord's Prayer) for the soul of the deceased. The names of those who make such payments, together with the amounts of money contributed, are recorded by the sacristan in a notebook, which is given to the bereaved family. This list is then used by the family to calculate obligations at future deaths in the community. The funerary donations to the church are locally known as *artu emon*, meaning "to take and give." As in the Breton case, *artu emon* obligations arise from kinship or neighborhood ties with the deceased or the bereaved family, and the amount of the donation depends on the closeness of the relationship. In addition, formerly those who gave *artu emon* contributions were invited to a banquet offered by the family of the deceased after the funeral. Finally, as in Brittany, the numbers of contributions, particularly of the more costly *arimen onrak* donation (which includes a Mass and *nocturno* and corresponds to the Breton donation of a Mass and service), have increased dramatically since 1945 (Douglass 1969:37–40, 47). See Ott (1981:127) for a related description of Masses given in the French Basque region.

5. For discussion of the distinction between grief and mourning, see Kastenbaum (1977:242–244).

ondary burial. Basing his arguments primarily on data from Borneo, Hertz claims that rites involving secondary treatment of the corpse which are held at a prolonged interval after the initial burial function to confirm the incorporation of the deceased into the community of the dead. From this perspective, the funeral initiates a liminal period for the deceased during which the soul continues its transition to the otherworld. This process is not complete until the body has been exhumed and reburied (Hertz 1907). In the European context, secondary treatment of the corpse has been described in detail for rural Greece by Danforth (1982). There, as in Borneo, the state of the body upon exhumation is believed to parallel the state of the soul. Successful incorporation of the deceased into the world of the dead is not considered to have been achieved unless all the flesh has decayed, leaving only dried bones in the grave (Danforth 1982:48–51).

Recently Huntington and Metcalf (1979) have reexamined Hertz's model in relation to ethnographic materials from other parts of Indonesia published subsequent to his work. They suggest that Hertz's theory of secondary burial can be applied in cultural contexts where no secondary treatment of the corpse occurs, but where, nonetheless, rituals concerned with the deceased take place at intervals after the primary burial (1979:87–92). Huntington and Metcalf's position is in line with van Gennep's ideas on beliefs concerning a prolonged liminal period for the soul in societies that lack a tradition of secondary burial. He observes that in such contexts the transition period for the deceased from the community of the living to that of the dead is "sometimes subdivided into several parts, and . . . its extension is systematized in the form of commemorations (a week, two weeks, a month, forty days, a year, etc.) similar in nature to the rites of the anniversary of a wedding, of birth" (1960:149).

In Lower Brittany secondary treatment of the corpse was practiced throughout the nineteenth and early twentieth centuries. Ceremonies involving exhumation and transferral of bones to ossuaries, followed by the eventual reburial of bones from the ossuary in large common graves, were discontinued after World War I. These will be discussed more fully in Chapter 5. Less formalized types of secondary treatment, such as the exhumation and transferral of remains to special boxes, continued in certain regions until the 1950s (Croix and Roudaut 1984:215–216). At present, however, the prolonged passage of the deceased to the world of the dead and the termination of this passage are marked only symbolically, through the *messe de huitaine* and the *messe d'anniversaire*.

The *messe de huitaine* is held eight days after the funeral ceremony or on the Sunday closest to that date.[6] In La Feuillée the *messe de huitaine*, like the funeral itself, is an occasion for those who do not normally attend Mass to do so. Some undoubtedly attend because they believe their prayers will aid the soul of the deceased. Others attend out of respect for the memory of the deceased and to demonstrate solidarity with the bereaved family. Neighbors, friends, and relatives from both inside and outside the commune attend the *huitaine*. However, *messes de huitaine* are not as well attended as funerals.

As celebrated in La Feuillée, the *messe de huitaine* starts ten or fifteen minutes earlier than the Sunday morning Mass. During the first fifteen minutes the priest gives a short eulogy for the deceased, special prayers are offered on his or her behalf, there may be a Scripture reading, and several hymns are sung. Both the prayers and the hymns chosen by the priest for the *huitaine* solicit God's forgiveness and protection for the deceased, as well as for those present in the congregation. In this respect the ritual in La Feuillée echoes the older eschatological themes of traditional Catholicism in Brittany. Although well-versed in the Church's post–Vatican II theological stance, the La Feuillée priest, in his seventies, remains to some extent influenced by the Catholic teachings that shaped his own youth.

After the fifteen-minute *huitaine* the Mass is celebrated as usual, but it is dedicated to the deceased. Prior to the Communion, during his general prayer for the dead of the parish, the priest makes special mention of the person for whom the *huitaine* is being celebrated. Throughout the *messe de huitaine* in La Feuillée, the deceased is symbolically present. He or she is represented by the catafalque, near the door at the back of the church. The catafalque in La Feuillée is an ornately sculpted wooden platform on wheels,

---

6. Similar Masses exist in other parts of the Catholic world. For example, in the Basque region of Spain the *argia*, a Mass held on the Sunday following a death, corresponds in structure and role to the *huitaine* (see Douglass 1969:44–45).

approximately 2 meters long, 1.2 meters high, and 60 centimeters wide, surmounted by a wooden coffin-shaped box. Six tapers are affixed in holders around the sides of the catafalque. In the past the catafalque was used at funerals to transport the actual coffin and corpse within the church. At all other times the catafalque remained near the front of the church among the seats of the parishioners, to serve as a memento mori.

Unlike many catafalques in Brittany, the one in the church at La Feuillée is not decorated with macabre symbols.[7] Breton catafalques often bear painted and sculpted motives relating to death, such as skulls or crossbones. Some display inscriptions painted in black, reminding the viewer of the transitory nature of human life. On the catafalque in the church at Loqueffret, to the south of La Feuillée, a painted book is open at the words *skol ar marv*, school for death, referring to the role of the catafalque as a constant reminder of human mortality (see fig. 8).

In La Feuillée the purchase of modern pews precipitated the removal of the catafalque to the back corner of the church. The priest explains that there is no longer room for it at the front, since the new benches cannot be arranged around it as could the chairs they replace. On a deeper level, however, the change in position of the catafalque signals a change in worldview. One now has to make a conscious effort to see it, hidden in a corner of the unused portion of the church. The memento mori is no longer continually present with the worshiper. Nevertheless, in retaining the catafalque within the church, La Feuillée is an exception to the general trend in Brittany. In Plouguerneau and most other parishes the use of catafalques has been entirely abandoned, and these artifacts have been removed from the church building. Here again there is evidence for the increasing exclusion of death and its reminders from the social space of the living in contemporary Brittany.

Only at *messes de huitaine* and *messes d'anniversaire* in La Feuillée does the catafalque assume a prominent ritual role. During these Masses the tapers surrounding it are lit. A container filled with holy water is placed at the end of the catafalque and, just as they bless the coffin at funerals, the parishioners bless the catafalque as

---

7. For examples of macabre catafalques, see those illustrated by Croix (1981: Plates 170, 171, 173, 174).

they enter and leave the church. This action permits the mourners to meditate on the deceased and symbolically includes him or her as a participant in the ceremony.

The *messe de huitaine* in Plouguerneau appears less concerned with the deceased as a specific individual than in La Feuillée. This difference may be partly a result of the sizes of the two communities. It is more difficult for the priest to be on close terms with all his parishioners in a parish of 3,200 than in one of 600. In Plouguerneau the fifteen-minute *huitaine* prior to High Mass is often celebrated for two or three people at the same time if a number of closely spaced deaths have occurred in the community.

The form of the *messe de huitaine* in Plouguerneau also reveals a declining concern with death and the afterlife. Here the service consists entirely of hymns. There are no special prayers and no eulogy for the deceased, who is barely mentioned by name in the Mass that follows. The Mass is less marked by themes of salvation and prayer for reconciliation with God than it is in La Feuillée. This differing emphasis is a conscious choice on the part of the Plouguerneau priest, who is younger than his La Feuillée counterpart and has been more eager to adopt a progressive theological stance. He acknowledges that "the dead hold an important place" in the religious life of his parishioners, but he sees this as a negative, retrogressive phenomenon. He seeks to reorient their religious concerns away from the afterlife, toward what he considers to be rational ethical principles that can be applied in the present life. To this end he has deemphasized the significance of the *huitaine* by attaching it to the High Mass. His more traditional predecessor, who left the parish in 1982, had refused to celebrate *messes de huitaine* on Sundays. As one Plouguerneau Catholic notes, "That made people come to church twice, once for High Mass and once for their dead." On one level the present priest's decision to combine the *huitaine* and High Mass is a response to the constraints of wage labor, which now prevent many of his parishioners from attending Mass on days other than Sunday. However, the church has shown itself to be flexible in scheduling offices in a manner that fits with contemporary patterns of organizing time, through such practices as holding Masses on Saturday evenings. A similar accommodation could have been achieved in the case of the *huitaine*, by holding it on a weekday evening, for example. That this has not been done reflects the willingness of the post–Vatican II church and the current Plouguerneau priest to deemphasize rituals that imply connotations of damnation or suffering in the afterlife. In the larger context, therefore, the merging of the *huitaine* and High Mass that has occurred in both Plouguerneau and La Feuillée had the effect of promoting the deritualization of death. Through this process death is increasingly denied a special place in the cycle of activities of the living.

In Plouguerneau and La Feuillée, relatives and associates of the deceased continue to make special efforts to attend the *huitaine*. Those who were unable to attend the funeral will take particular care to attend the *huitaine* and to be seen there by the bereaved family, thus demonstrating that they have fulfilled their reciprocal obligations. In Plouguerneau the family and those who have come specifically for the *huitaine* join together after the High Mass at the grave of the deceased, which they bless with holy water.

There are a number of parallels between the *messe de huitaine* and the funeral Mass. First, both are attended by the same categories of relatives and associates of the deceased. Moreover, in La Feuillée (although not in Plouguerneau) the deceased is symbolically present, represented by the catafalque. Both ceremonies involve a similar use of holy water. Finally, both the funeral and the *huitaine* are followed by a rite of incorporation within the social world of the living. For the *huitaine* this rite involves reunion at the grave of the deceased and sometimes a meal for the bereaved family after the Mass. This meal corresponds to the *café* offered after the funeral.[8]

These parallels suggest that the *messe de huitaine* is analogous, in some senses, to a second funeral. The *huitaine* ritually reinforces the transfer of the deceased out of the community of the living and into the Anaon. Its timing, several days or one week after the funeral Mass, is fundamental for the understanding of the relationships between the social rituals of mourning and the personal, psychological process of grieving. Describing the experience of grief, many bereaved persons in Plouguerneau and La Feuillée comment that for several days after the death of a family member they sensed

---

8. Van Gennep (1960:164–165) draws attention to the parallel functions of meals following funerals and those associated with commemorative ceremonies as rites of incorporation for the living.

that individual's continued presence, particularly in places where he or she had spent considerable time, such as the family home. As one woman expressed it, after the death of her mother "it was as though she was there in the house with me all the time. Finally I had to tell her: 'Mother, this is not your place anymore. Leave me now.'" She continues, "They say that something, the soul, lingers on at first." From one perspective, the *messe de huitaine* can be seen as a social restatement of this interior dialogue between the bereaved and the deceased, in which the dead person is told, "This is not your place anymore." The ritual provides a formal, institutionalized occasion for loosening the emotional ties that link the living and the dead. It is important to stress that there is no necessary correspondence between the ritual and the grieving process. Although the *messe de huitaine* may make a public statement about this loosening of ties between the living and the dead, it does not always help assuage the grief of the survivors. However, like the funeral, the *messe de huitaine* can provide the occasion for catharsis, allowing the bereaved to express and share their grief.

In La Feuillée, where adherence to the church is low, the curé estimates that only two out of every ten families ask for the *messe de huitaine*. In Plouguerneau, however, it is said that "everyone, more or less," pays for this ceremony, "even those who don't practice regularly." The Plouguerneau curé suggests that although deep religious faith undoubtedly motivates many of those in his parish who request *huitaines*, others are more concerned about the opinion of their neighbors, the *qu'en-dira-t-on*. As he states, "Here people worry about what others in the community will think. 'What will people say about us if we don't pray for our dead?'" Similarly, a high proportion of Plouguerneau families request anniversary Masses, or *messes d'anniversaire*.

The *messe d'anniversaire* is offered by the family of the deceased on the first anniversary of the funeral. To an even greater extent than the *huitaine*, the *messe d'anniversaire* resembles a second funeral. It is almost as well attended as a funeral and, as at the funeral, Masses and services are given by the mourners for the soul of the deceased. The structural pattern of a rite of transition succeeded by a rite of incorporation, seen in the *huitaine* and the funeral, is repeated in the *messe d'anniversaire*, with the religious ceremony being followed by a family meal. In the Plouguerneau area the *messe d'anniversaire* is often announced, like the *huitaine* and the funeral, on the obituaries page of the local newspaper. Confirming the finality of the deceased's incorporation into the community of the dead, the *messe d'anniversaire* in contemporary Brittany corresponds to secondary burial in Indonesia (Hertz 1907; Huntington and Metcalf 1979) and to exhumation in rural Greece (Danforth 1982).[9]

Relative to Plouguerneau, the *messe d'anniversaire*, like the *huitaine*, is infrequently celebrated in La Feuillée. The lack of concern for these Masses in La Feuillée is linked to the anticlerical tradition of this parish. It is also related to its poverty. Both *messes d'anniversaire* and *huitaines* cost 150 francs. In the past the small farmers of this region were unable to pay for these ceremonies, and consequently the custom of requesting them was never firmly established. In wealthier Plouguerneau, however, the ignominy of "not praying for one's dead" stems in part from the implication that the family is too poor or too miserly to do so.

The approach of the *messe d'anniversaire* may signal a period of depression and renewed grief for the bereaved, as memories relating to the circumstances of the death are revived.[10] However, although the Mass evokes memories of the person who has died, it also separates that individual from the bereaved, at least in a public, formal sense, for the *messe d'anniversaire* is the final ritual obligation that family members owe the deceased. Here again, parallels with secondary treatment of the corpse in Greece are apparent. As Danforth (1982:56) observes, exhumation is the "last important rite that must be performed individually for a particular dead person by his surviving kin."

As in the case of the *messe de huitaine*, a complex interrelationship between the inner experience of grief and the public ritual exists for the *messe d'anniversaire*, which serves as another landmark in the grieving process. This interrelationship can be seen in the experience of Maryvonne, a woman in her mid-fifties from the La Feuillée area, whose mother died in 1980. Maryvonne notes that

---

9. Douglass (1969:211) advances a parallel interpretation of the *ogistie*, the Mass marking the first anniversary of death in the Basque country of Spain.

10. It is not just the first anniversary of a death which provokes such a response. In La Feuillée, during the month of February 1984, Marie-Thérèse became increasingly irritable and morose as the ninth anniversary of her husband's death drew near.

for the first year after her mother's death, she sensed that her mother continued to guide her and give her support. Her mother's guidance related particularly to those obligations which the living bear toward the deceased, such as burial and the *messes*. Significantly, Maryvonne describes her mother as a strong-willed and dominant woman, prone to organize and superintend the lives of her children. On her deathbed she insisted on giving Maryvonne instructions about the *veillée mortuaire:* where to find the best sheets, how to organize the room, and what china to use when serving the guests their coffee. These instructions continued, in a less direct manner, after her death. As Maryvonne explains, her family had plans to construct a *caveau,* or vault, below the monument at her mother's grave. This project was of special importance to her mother during the last year of her life; she mentioned it to Maryvonne practically each time they met. However, time passed and nothing was done. When Maryvonne's mother died, her coffin was placed temporarily in the *caveau* of a cousin, pending construction of a vault for Maryvonne's own family. Maryvonne made the arrangements for construction to begin, but because of a misunderstanding she neglected to sign the necessary request form and return it to the builder. Several months passed without the commencement of work on the *caveau*. Then one night Maryvonne had a dream in which she saw her mother's body lying on a shelf or trestle in a bare room. Maryvonne recalls,

> I dreamed there was a person dressed all in white, on a shelf, and she was laid out completely straight, and on a shelf. Then all of a sudden she fell! She fell from the shelf onto the floor. And I said to myself, "But why hurry? [i.e., to help her]. In any case she's dead. There's no reason to be afraid or to pick her up, she hasn't been hurt," because she was dead. And right after that I heard—uh, I don't know if you have ever heard a coffin being moved? But that certainly makes a strange noise of wood rubbing against stone. You've never noticed that noise? And so I heard the noise of the coffin that moved.

According to Maryvonne's interpretation of the dream, this was the sound of her mother's coffin attempting to move out of the cousin's *caveau*, signaling that it was time for Maryvonne to build a *caveau* of her own. The next morning Maryvonne made an appointment with the builder and completed the construction arrangements:

Eh ben! [Well!] The next morning, I can tell you, I phoned the man [who was supposed to construct the *caveau*]. "Are you planning, are you going to build the *caveau*?" "But no," he told me. "I'm waiting for your request form. I wouldn't have started," he told me. "I was waiting for the request form." Ah, it was right after that dream that I called him.

A second dream recounted by Maryvonne occurred shortly before the first anniversary of her mother's death. This dream concerned arrangements for the *messe d'anniversaire*. As Maryvonne explains, relations among her brothers and sisters at the time had deteriorated because of disputes over her parents' estate, and she did not want to organize the *messe d'anniversaire*, which would necessarily involve a family meal.

And another time, because we had some problems after the funeral—the estate had been divided, and there were other things, this and that. And they played some dirty tricks on me, to tell you the truth. And I said to myself—because here it's the custom to give a *messe d'anniversaire*—and I said to myself, "Why? After all that they did to me after the death of my mother . . ." I'm the fourth child. And I said to myself, "Why?" So I put a pot, a plant, on her tomb, and I had a Mass said for her at Châteauneuf. Discreetly, for my mother. And I said to myself, "I won't have a *messe d'anniversaire*," you see. And I was stubborn. I didn't want to give in either. Everyone was against me, and I didn't want to. I was upset. . . .

And one night I dreamed again, uh, my mother appeared to me again. She came again. And we started to make crêpes together. And at one point she said to me, "But my poor daughter, you don't have time to make crêpes. Tell Margit to make those crêpes for you," and then, "You don't have time to make crêpes like that." And my dream stopped there. But if I was upset before, afterward I was even more so. . . . And I asked Margit, my cousin, . . . to make some crêpes. And my mother knew, she used to buy her crêpes all the time from Margit.

The morning after this dream, Maryvonne felt herself capable of organizing the *messe d'anniversaire* and the family meal to follow it. She decided to invite fifteen family members to her home and asked Margit to provide a meal of crêpes. As with the *caveau*, Maryvonne's ambivalence—an inner conflict between her desire to avoid a potentially volatile family gathering and the necessity of performing her ritual obligations—was again resolved through projection. Maryvonne's inner psychological imperatives are symbolically externalized in the advice given by the dream apparition of her mother.

Significantly, Maryvonne notes that her mother has made no more "appearances" and given no more guidance since the *messe d'anniversaire*. In her view this is because "after the *messe d'anniversaire*, there's nothing more to be done. You can give a Mass from time to time if you want, but there are no more obligations." In a striking parallel to this Breton case, Danforth (1982:60) notes that frequently women in rural Greece report dreams in which deceased relatives implore them to perform the rite of exhumation. After exhumation the dead rarely appear in dreams, because like the *messe d'anniversaire*, this is the last ritual obligation they require from the living (Danforth 1982:135).

In actuality obligations toward the deceased do not entirely end with the *messe d'anniversaire*, but they change in character, becoming more generalized. Whereas the *messe d'anniversaire* involves one particular deceased person and his or her living family, subsequent obligations, such as celebration of the annual festival of the dead, Toussaint/Fête des Morts, involve the entire community of the living and juxtapose it to the entire community of the dead. At this festival, described in Chapter 8, each family honors all its deceased kin as a group.[11] In Plouguerneau there is a second type of collective Mass for the dead, the *messe pour tous les défunts*, or Mass for all souls, which is held at weekly intervals. The money paid to the church in Plouguerneau for the services offered for the deceased at funerals and *messes d'anniversaire* is used to pay for the *messe pour tous les défunts*. Held at six o'clock on Tuesday evenings, this Mass is well attended, particularly by middle-aged and elderly women from the Plouguerneau *bourg*, for whom it represents an important part of their weekly cycle of activities.

Mourning

According to van Gennep, mourning is a liminal period for the bereaved, which is entered through rites of separation and ended

---

11. Again, parallels with Greek death ritual are apparent. As Danforth (1982:56) points out, after exhumation has been performed, the only remaining obligation for the bereaved is to participate in the celebration of Soul Saturdays or All Souls' Days, which collectively honor the community dead.

through "rites of reintegration into society" (van Gennep 1960: 147). As he points out, in many cultures mourning, as a transitional period for the bereaved, parallels the transitional period required for the deceased to enter fully into the community of the dead. Frequently the termination of both these liminal periods coincides (van Gennep 1960:147). Danforth's (1982) work in Greece provides a clear example of this parallelism between mourning and the gradual entry of the deceased into the world of the dead. In rural Greece, as noted earlier, the rite of exhumation and secondary burial both ends the mourning period and confirms the final incorporation of the dead person into the otherworld. Similarly, until recently in Brittany the *messe d'anniversaire*, which functions in the same way as secondary burial, also served in many cases to close the period of *grand deuil*, or full mourning, for the bereaved.[12] Even today the *messe d'anniversaire* continues, at least for some people, to be a turning point in the grieving process. As one Plouguerneau widow remarked, "The first year is the worst. After the *messe d'anniversaire*, things begin to get better."

Before World War II, mourning customs were strictly observed throughout rural Brittany. The length of the mourning period varied according to the mourner's degree of relationship to the deceased. Mourning traditionally involved two phases, *grand deuil* and *demi-deuil*, half or partial mourning. In La Feuillée it is recalled that *grand deuil* was observed for one year after the death of a close relative such as a spouse, parent, sibling, child, grandparent, or grandchild, and for six months after the death of an aunt, uncle, or cousin.[13] During both *grand deuil* and *demi-deuil*, restrictions were placed on the clothing and behavior of the bereaved. Men and women alike were forbidden to dance during *grand deuil*. Men were expected to indicate their status as mourners by wearing a black armband and women were required to wear only black clothes. This obligation was not onerous for older married women, who wore the traditional costume of the region, which, aside from the

---

12. Likewise, among the Basques of Spain the *ogistie* terminates the period of official or public mourning, during which women from the deceased's household are required to burn candles on their *sepulterie* in the church during religious offices (Douglass 1969:211).

13. The period of full mourning for nuclear family members sometimes exceeded one year, especially after the death of a husband. The length of the period of *grand deuil* varied from place to place within Brittany.

apron, was black. However, mourning was a greater sacrifice for unmarried girls and younger women who had adopted urban styles of dress.[14] Some La Feuillée women remember dyeing their entire wardrobes black following the death of a relative. Headgear was the only exception to the requirement for black mourning clothes. During winter elderly women from La Feuillée and neighboring parishes wore a distinctive wool hood known locally as the *koef rous*. The *koef rous* was normally black, but those in mourning wore a *koef rous* made of white cloth. The ties of the white lace *coiffe* worn by La Feuillée women in summer were left hanging loose by those in mourning, rather than knotted in the usual fashion.

A succession of deaths in the same family created particularly difficult mourning obligations for teenage girls. One woman from the Monts d'Arrée, now in her seventies, recalls that as an adolescent, when she lost several relatives over a three year period, she wondered whether she would ever again be able to wear colored clothes or attend dances. However, others say that the sanction against dancing corresponded to their own interior feelings of grief: "We weren't allowed to dance, but we didn't *want* to dance anyway after losing a loved one."

Grand deuil was followed by a period of *demi-deuil*, during which bereaved women ceased to wear black but continued to wear clothes in dark colors such as gray, mauve, or navy blue. However, many widows and elderly women never resumed wearing colored clothes, preferring to wear black until the end of their lives. At present a number of elderly black-clad widows remain in both Plouguerneau and La Feuillée.

In addition to marking the liminal status of the bereaved, mourning restrictions as portrayed by traditional Catholicism in Brittany involved an element of sacrifice offered for the deceased on the part of the living. The bereaved would voluntarily suffer by giving up brightly colored clothes and avoiding joyous social occasions in order that God would shorten the sojourn of their dead kin in purgatory. It should be noted that the burden of this sacrifice fell upon

---

14. This generational difference suggests that clothing restrictions during mourning were less noticeable in Brittany in the nineteenth century than after World War I, when commercial clothes of varying colors began to be worn in rural areas.

women rather than men. The penitential aspect of mourning is particularly apparent in the *mantelet,* or mourning cape, which was worn only by women.

Prior to the 1950s the *mantelet,* a long black hooded cape made of heavy wool, was worn to the funeral, the *messe de huitaine,* and High Mass for several Sundays following the death of a close relative.[15] The hood partially covered the mourner's face and the cape extended almost to her ankles. A silver clasp held the cape together at the neck. In the Plouguerneau area, women wearing the *mantelet* were required to stand or to remain kneeling rather than to sit throughout the Mass and ceremonies for the dead. Plouguerneau women recall the difficulty of attending Mass in the heavy mourning cloak in hot weather. Before the Vatican II reforms, one had to fast from midnight on Saturday in order to receive Communion at Sunday morning Mass, and women would come to church after doing their farm chores, having eaten nothing since the previous evening. Under such conditions it was often a great strain to stand or kneel in the *mantelet* throughout the ninety-minute-long Mass, and frequently women in mourning would faint.

In contemporary Brittany, mourning in an institutionalized, formal sense has disappeared. The *mantelet* was abandoned in the Plouguerneau area in the mid-1950s, and slightly earlier in La Feuillée. The observance of *grand deuil* and *demi-deuil* remained general, however, until the early 1970s. The disappearance of mourning has been a complex process that cannot be assigned with accuracy to a single date. Rather, mourning customs have been discontinued at different rates in different areas and by different individuals, as several examples will illustrate.

A woman from the Plouguerneau area in her late fifties remembers that when her father died in 1955 she wore black for six months, including black stockings, coat, and shoes. When her mother died in 1981 no one in the family went into mourning. Another Plouguerneau woman of the same age says that in 1965 she was one of the last of her contemporaries to wear mourning for more than a year. In contrast, Marianne Penguilly, a sixty-three-year-old woman

---

15. Similar mourning capes are attested for the Léon at the end of the eighteenth century and possibly existed as early as the mid-sixteenth century (Croix 1981:960).

from the same community, wore black for the first year after her husband's death in 1982, as she had done after the deaths of her parents-in-law in 1971 and 1973. Marianne explains that she was brought up to observe mourning, and she could not ignore the custom on her husband's death. Moreover, she has found it difficult, after two and a half years, to come out of mourning, and she continues to wear dark-colored or mauve clothes. Asked whether she would have been criticized in the community for not observing mourning, Marianne replies that some women would likely have made "remarks," but that others undoubtedly condemned her just as forcefully for continuing to practice what they consider an outmoded tradition.

In the La Feuillée area, some claim that mourning disappeared around 1970. "When that started to fall by the wayside, it went fast," it is said. A woman in her sixties recalls that when her father died in 1962, she wore mourning for nine months. Her children, then aged nine and twelve, complained that it was "sad" to see her always dressed in black. At their insistence she did not wear a black coat to the funeral of her father-in-law, who died in 1974, although she did compromise by wearing a black skirt and blouse. "At that time we continued to observe mourning a little bit," she explains. After the death of her mother in 1983, she wore a navy blue suit to the funeral and did not make any changes to her wardrobe.

The role of the younger generation in providing a reason for suspending mourning customs appears to have been significant, reflecting a change in the orientation of Breton culture away from death and concern for the elderly toward an emphasis on youth. A number of women in both Plouguerneau and La Feuillée explain that they gave up mourning or changed from black to navy blue or mauve for the sake of children who were upset by the "sad" or "old" connotations of black clothes. These attitudes, which parallel those concerning the presence of children at wakes, also reflect the tendency in contemporary Brittany to shield children from death rather than socialize them to deal with it in a realistic fashion.

The decision to observe mourning is currently a matter of personal choice rather than something socially imposed. "One can wear anything to a funeral now," says a woman in her forties who frequently returns from the city of Quimper where she resides to her parents' home in La Feuillée. Nevertheless, even if they are not related to the deceased, many elderly Plouguerneau and La Feuillée women continue to wear navy or dark gray coats to funerals. It might be expected that practicing Catholics would adhere more closely to mourning traditions than would the anticlerical or those who do not attend Mass regularly. This is not necessarily the case, however, in La Feuillée. A woman in her late forties who was widowed in 1979 and who rarely attends Mass was strongly criticized by a dedicated Catholic of the same age because she had insisted, "unnecessarily," on observing both *grand deuil* and *demi-deuil*. Similarly, Annie Kervella, a sixty-nine-year-old La Feuillée widow who lost two brothers within six months of each other in 1983, added black clothing to her wardrobe during the first weeks following their deaths. Although she did not dress exclusively in black, she would wear a black sweater with a brown skirt, a black dress for certain social occasions, or a black scarf over her hair. A supporter of the Parti Communiste Français, Annie did not decide to wear a modified form of mourning on the basis of religious beliefs. Rather, she explains that she wore black to honor the memory of her brothers: "It is a question of respect for the dead." Exposure to urban milieus might also be expected to encourage the abandonment of mourning traditions. However, the situation is more complicated. Both Annie Kervella and the dedicated Catholic who considers mourning unnecessary lived for many years in urban centers.

There is a general consensus among contemporary Breton women that one's internal emotions of grief are now more significant than one's external appearance. States Anna Le Guen of Plouguerneau, explaining her decision to abandon black attire one month after her husband's death, "I don't need to wear black to prove that I am sad. My sadness is inside." Similarly, in a discussion of mourning with women from La Feuillée, one widow reflected, "That serves no purpose. It won't bring them back to life."

The majority of young people under thirty-five claim to see no reason to alter their style of dress or stop going to dances and social events after a family death. The advertising slogan of a clothing manufacturer, "La vie est trop courte pour s'habiller triste"—life is too short to dress sadly—suggests that contemporary attitudes toward personal attire are life- rather than death-oriented. Yet subtle details indicate that the liminal status of the mourner, although no longer socially demarcated or prescribed, continues to be marked on a personal level. Close examination of the wardrobes of recently bereaved middle-aged and elderly women in both Plouguerneau and La Feuillée reveals that many have simply substituted dark blue, gray, burgundy, or mauve—the colors of *demi-deuil*—for black clothes. After the meal on a day-trip of the La Feuillée *club du troisième âge*, several women discreetly refrained from dancing the local gavotte, explaining that they have not felt like dancing since the deaths of sisters or husbands. Likewise, for ten months after the sudden death of Jeannie Kervao, her mother and her twenty-five-year-old sister, Pascale, stayed away from *festoù-noz*, evenings of Breton music and dance popular in the Monts d'Arrée.

Despite these indications that mourning is still observed privately, it is no longer an institutionalized, public state. Failure to go into mourning is not subject to criticism through channels of social control such as gossip. Indeed, those who do observe some mourning traditions are as likely to be censured by their neighbors as those who do not. Like the hospitalization of the dying and the discontinuation of the wake in urban areas, the disappearance of mourning is an additional aspect of the distancing of death from everyday experience in contemporary Brittany. In the past, the presence of numerous black-clad women in both urban and rural communities provided a potent reminder of death among the living.

The abandonment of mourning is also related to the privatization of bereavement, the deritualization of death, and the internalization of emotion related to death. As bereavement becomes more a personal than a collective event, it becomes less important to make a public statement through one's attire about one's condition as a mourner. Moreover, post–Vatican II Catholicism in Brittany has deemphasized themes of purgatory and damnation, making it meaningless to observe mourning restrictions in a penitential spirit to hasten the salvation of deceased kin. Finally, it should be noted that the rejection by Breton women of ritual restrictions on clothing in favor of authentic, internal emotions of grief corresponds to Douglas's suggestion that ritual in contemporary Western culture is generally devalued because it is not conceived to provide a vehicle for the expression of authentic personal emotions: "The confirmed anti-ritualist mistrusts external expression. He values a man's inner convictions. . . . In rejecting ritual forms . . . it is the 'external' aspect which is disvalued" ([1970] 1978:74).

Conclusion

In rural Brittany several types of Masses may be offered for the souls of the dead, including Masses and services given on the occasion of a funeral and the commemorative *messe de huitaine* and *messe d'anniversaire*. The spiritual justification for requesting Masses has its roots in medieval Catholicism, which taught that the soul must do a period of penance in purgatory before achieving heaven's grace (Le Goff 1984). The prayers of the living, including services and Masses, were held to hasten the release of those suffering in purgatory. Even though this eschatological model is at present neither widely accepted nor an integral part of Catholic teaching in Brittany, the giving of Masses persists. Indeed, according to some, the number of Masses and services offered at funerals has actually increased since the 1950s.

The giving of Masses and services reinforces reciprocal ties among individuals in rural Brittany. Moreover, as the cash-based economy has come to dominate in the region, social relationships are also increasingly mediated in monetary terms. By paying fifty or sixty francs to the church for a Mass which serves as a calling card, people can avoid involvement in more emotionally stressful or time-consuming forms of support for the bereaved. This trend indicates that the isolation of the bereaved characteristic of other parts of Western culture is also developing in contemporary Brittany.

The *messe de huitaine* and *messe d'anniversaire* serve to commemorate the deceased and reaffirm his or her incorporation into the community of the dead. The *messe d'anniversaire* in particular corresponds to rituals of secondary burial documented elsewhere by Hertz (1907) and others (Danforth 1982; Huntington and Metcalf 1979). In Brittany the *messe d'anniversaire* is the final ritual obligation owed by the bereaved to specific deceased individuals. Prior to the early 1970s, when a formal period of mourning was generally observed, the *messe d'anniversaire* also marked the end of the year of *grand deuil* observed for a close family member. After the *messe d'anniversaire*, during the period of *demi-deuil*, the bereaved gradually emerged from their liminal status by exchanging black for mauve, navy blue, or gray clothing. The liminal period during which the deceased completed the transition to the world of the dead thus coincided with the liminal period during which the most severe social restrictions were placed upon the mourner.

Since the mid-1970s, institutionalized mourning has been discontinued in both urban and rural Brittany. Nevertheless, many people still observe some mourning traditions privately. The disappearance of formal, public mourning is thus part of a transition in the experience of bereavement. Although responses to bereavement have always involved both external, public, and interior, private, components, in present-day Brittany the balance between the two is shifting. Whereas bereavement in the past was predominantly a shared, community event, it is now becoming more of an exclusively personal and private one. The rejection of external mourning customs harmonizes with the contemporary valorization of inner emotions over external ritual form. This new definition of appropriate mourning behavior has contributed to the denial of death in Brittany. Formerly the presence in Breton communities of women dressed in black or men wearing black armbands over an extended period of time served as a powerful memento mori. Increasingly, however, in contemporary Brittany the idea of death and its reminders, such as mourning customs, are being distanced from the everyday world of the living.

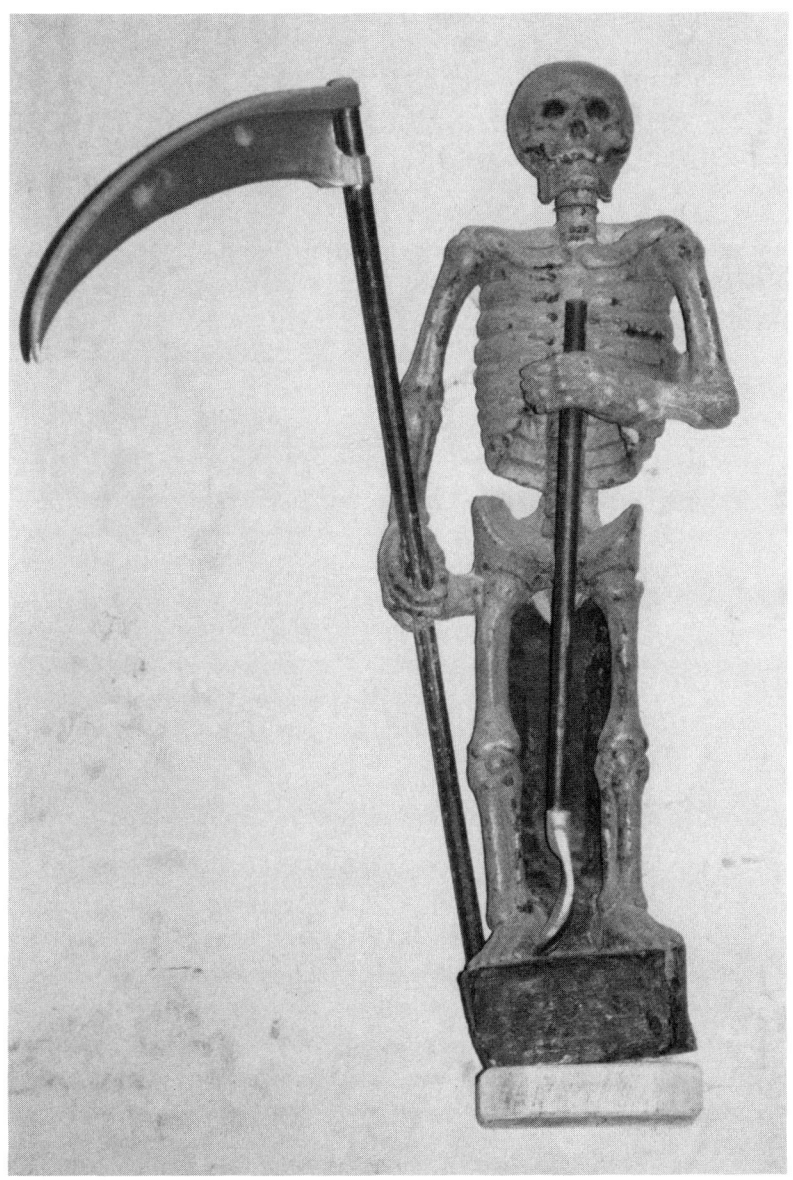

Fig. 1. Statue of the Ankou in the parish church at Ploumilliau, Finistère

Fig. 2. The *place* and *monument aux morts* in La Feuillée

Fig. 3. Elderly women, La Feuillée

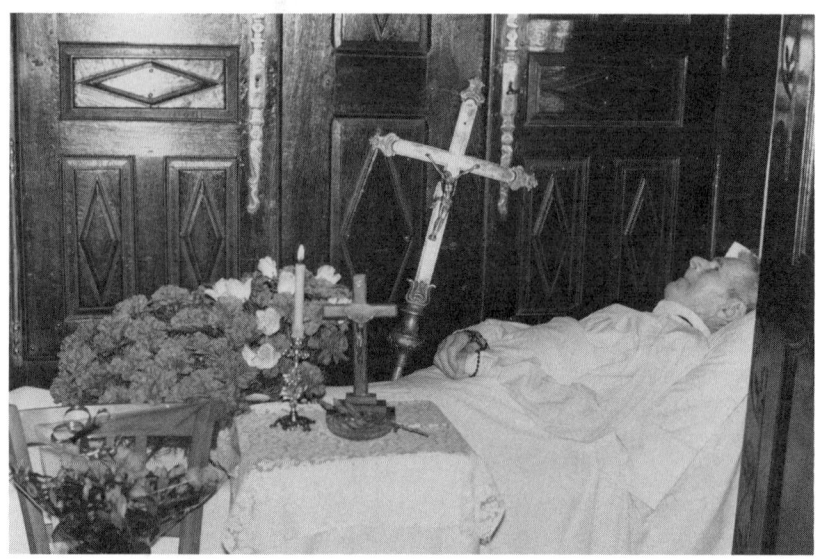

Fig. 4. The *lit de mort*. A sprig of boxwood is placed in the saucer of holy water next to the crucifix on the bedside table so that visitors may bless the deceased.

Fig. 5. Detail of tomb monument. A piece of boxwood is placed in the concave depression containing holy water, which is covered by a shell, symbol of immortality.

Fig. 6. Funeral procession, La Feuillée

Fig. 7. Mission *tableau:* Purgatory

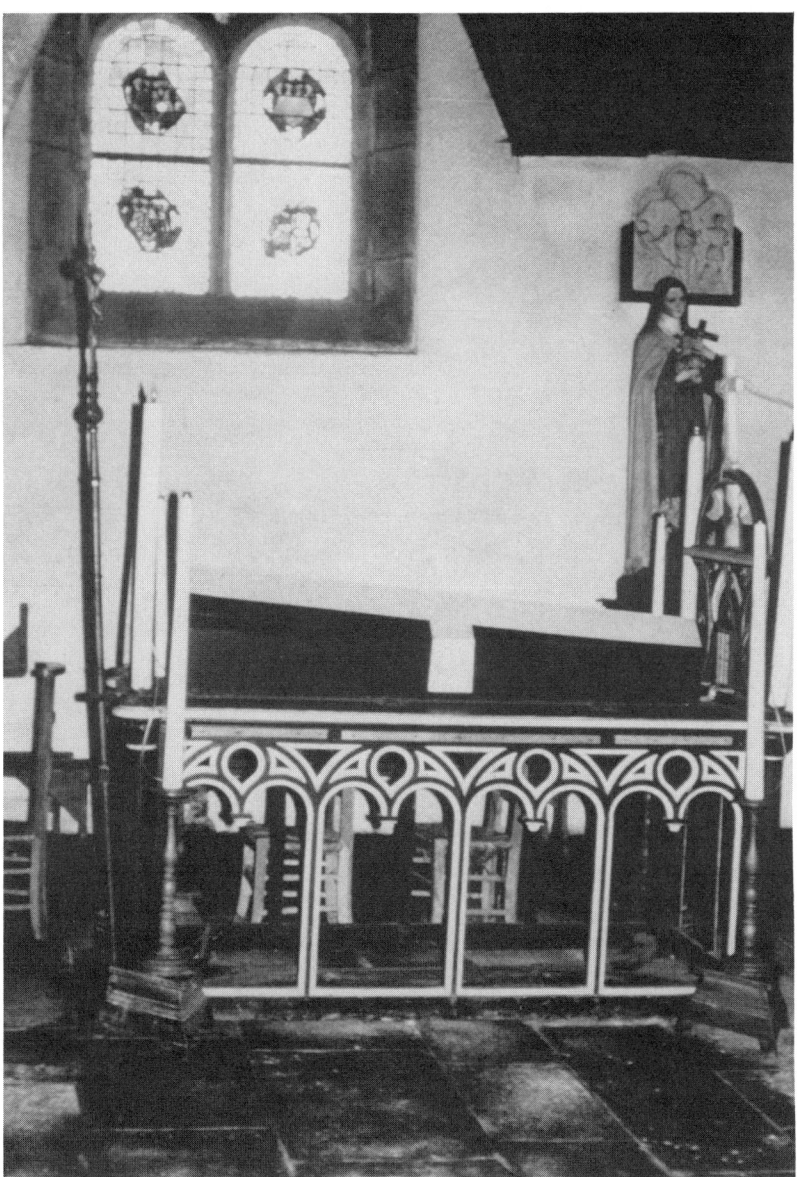

Fig. 8. The *catafalque* in the parish church at Loqueffret

Fig 9. Tomb monument. Note boxwood sprig in receptacle for holy water at lower right.

Fig. 10. Mission *tableau:* Deadly Sins

Fig. 11. Mission *tableau:* Death of a Sinner

Fig. 12. The procession with statues of the *petits saints*, *pardon de saint Michel*, Plouguerneau

Fig. 13. Prayer and benediction of the tombs after the Toussaint Mass, La Feuillée

Fig. 14. Preparing the cemetery for Toussaint, La Feuillée

Fig. 15. Flowers in the cemetery at Toussaint, La Feuillée

5

The Cemetery

Introduction

The rituals surrounding death are concerned with the transition of a deceased person from the world of the living to that of the dead. The cemetery represents the point of intersection between these two worlds. For rural Bretons the continuing existence of those who have died is localized in the cemetery. It is the place where the living can go to recover a measure of contact with the deceased.

The cemetery in La Feuillée is situated on a knoll in the outskirts of the *bourg*. From the large granite cross, or *calvaire*, in the center of the cemetery, one looks down on the *bourg* to the west, a cluster of houses dominated by the church spire. To the north, the windswept, rocky slopes of the Monts d'Arrée attract the eye. Here, as people in La Feuillée remark, at least they will have a beautiful view of the mountains once they are laid to rest.

The La Feuillée cemetery is arranged in neat rows of well-kept granite monuments. Between the tombs, the walkways are covered with white gravel that sparkles in the sunlight. All the tombs are oriented with their headstones facing west, except for one or two where priests are buried, which face east. Almost all the grave markers in La Feuillée, even those belonging to *rouge* families, bear religious symbols, such as bronze crosses or representations of the head of Christ. On some monuments photographs of those interred below are displayed, protected from the elements in china and glass frames. Other monuments bear small plaques inscribed with phrases such as *A notre père et grand-père*, "To our father and grandfather," or *A ma marraine*, "To my godmother" (see fig. 9). It is rare to see a monument that lacks some floral decoration, even during the winter. The tombs of young children are typically decorated with white flowers and statues of small angels, for baptized infants who die shortly after birth are said to go directly to heaven. In stark contrast to these infant memorials is a tombstone in the form of a roughly truncated granite column. According to the parish priest, this monument commemorates a Communist, whose impoverished spiritual existence, in exile from God, was similarly truncated at death.

Despite the importance of Masses and services, discussions about heaven, purgatory, and hell are unusual among people in Plouguerneau and La Feuillée. For the majority of people in the two communities these conceptions from traditional Catholicism now hold little meaning. Ideas about the afterlife are for the most part vague and poorly defined. The only vision of existence after death which people are willing to advance with any certainty is an extremely concrete and materialistic one: "On va dans nos tombes"—we go into our tombs, we go to the cemetery. The cemetery is conceived to be the place where the dead, in some sense, continue to "live." In talking to men and women from La Feuillée, one receives the impression that the dead in the cemetery are envisaged as maintaining a subterranean existence parallel to that in the above-ground community of the living. *Caveaux,* the cement-lined burial vaults that have become increasingly popular in Brittany over the past fifteen years, are frequently referred to, with ironic humor, as the *résidence secondaire,* or "second home," a phrase that usually means "holiday residence." *Caveaux* are also called "the home for afterward." People joke about installing television sets in their *caveaux* or building a *caveau* close to that of friends, so they will be able to play cards together in the afterlife on Saturday afternoons, "just as we do now."

Such comments, which underscore the continuing familiarity with death in rural Brittany, suggest that the dead are believed to exist in an ethically neutral state. They are neither damned, nor glorified in heaven. Rather, the body and soul remain together in the tomb. The widespread acceptance of this unorthodox, non-Catholic view of the afterlife could easily be attributed to the decline of religious faith in Brittany since the 1950s. Other evidence, however, indicates that this is a deeply rooted popular eschatological notion that has existed for hundreds of years alongside Catholic orthodoxy. According to Ariès, the belief that body and soul remain together in the tomb in a condition resembling sleep is central to the tame death of the early Middle Ages (1982:24). By the sixteenth and seventeenth centuries, particularly among the elite and wealthy classes, this representation of the afterlife began to give way to more orthodox beliefs that depicted postmortem existence as purely spiritual. Despite efforts on the part of the clergy to promote such an eschatological model, the tame view persisted in oral and popular tradition (Ariès 1982:267–268, 277). This conception combined belief in the survival of the *homo totus*, or whole man with body and soul united, and the representation of the afterlife as a rather indefinite state of repose. Ariès documents this attitude in a number of cultural contexts postdating the Middle Ages, most notably in nineteenth-century America (1982:449). Likewise, it is found in contemporary rural Brittany. However, whereas Ariès would regard the Breton view of the dead as evidence for the survival of an archaic *mentalité*, I suggest that such a conception of the afterlife is linked to features of social organization and lifestyle which contemporary communities like La Feuillée continue to share with those of earlier periods.

Perhaps the most important social characteristic shared by communities in present-day Brittany and others in which Ariès's tame vision of the afterlife predominates is the relative importance assigned to the individual and the collectivity. For Ariès, it is the increasing consciousness of individual identity, personality, and autonomy during the sixteenth and seventeenth centuries that led to the acceptance of the dualism of body and spirit and gave rise to the notion that only the soul, as "the crystallization of being, the individuality itself," survived after death (1982:293). On this basis it is possible to argue that belief in a strictly spiritual afterlife will be emphasized in social contexts where individualism is highly developed. Conversely, the separation of body and soul is unlikely to be a central eschatological theme where the group is given precedence and social controls are inflexible. Until recently, rural Breton society shared these latter characteristics. Therefore, it is not surprising that the depiction of the deceased as *homo totus* at rest in the tomb is frequently evoked in Plouguerneau and La Feuillée.

Social change in Brittany since World War II has, however, influenced eschatological beliefs. In turn, changing ideas about the afterlife are reflected in the appearance of cemeteries. The transformation of the Breton cemetery over the course of the twentieth century provides evidence for the increasing importance assigned to the individual in Breton culture and also for the disappearance of the tame death.

The Breton Cemetery through Time

The tame response to death is accompanied by an "unconcerned familiarity with the places and artifacts of burial" (Ariès 1982:29). In Brittany this attitude of familiarity toward the cemetery is clearly apparent during the sixteenth and early seventeenth centuries. The historians Croix and Roudaut cite numerous documents attesting to the use of cemeteries in both Upper and Lower Brittany at this period as public meeting places and markets. Cemeteries also provided open areas for dances and sporting events. Moreover, livestock was pastured freely among the graves (Croix 1981:1095–1100; Croix and Roudaut 1984:54–56). Ariès (1982:63–71) shows that cemeteries in other parts of Europe during the medieval and early modern periods served similar social functions. In Brittany the cemetery continued its role as public square and meeting place into the twentieth century. Le Braz (1928:1:xlviii) records that in rural Breton parishes the town clerk, or *embanner*, made public announcements in the cemetery each week following High Mass. The cemetery also provided a place for young people to meet during courting (Le Braz 1928:1:xlvii–xlviii). A Breton song still remembered by people in La Feuillée begins with a description of a young man who comes to meet his sweetheart who waits for him sitting on the cemetery wall.

In contemporary rural Breton communities the cemetery remains a familiar place. La Feuillée women frequently set out on afternoon or evening walks to the cemetery knowing they will encounter friends or neighbors there. In other Monts d'Arrée parishes, where the cemetery is located around the church in the center of the *bourg*, those living nearby often lean on the cemetery wall, chatting with friends who are cleaning tombs or watering the flowers on their family graves.

The cemetery in rural Brittany thus continues to serve as a "forum, public square and mall" as it did in other regions in earlier periods (Ariès 1982:64). Nevertheless, attitudes toward graves and funerary architecture in Brittany have changed dramatically since the sixteenth century. No longer is it acceptable for animals to graze in the graveyard. Indeed, in La Feuillée, the few recent occasions when cows inadvertently strayed through the cemetery gates are remembered as desecrations. In contemporary Brittany the cemetery, although familiar, is a sacred place. Moreover, the anonymity that characterized the graves of all but the elite in Brittany from the Middle Ages to the late nineteenth century has given way to an emphasis on personal identity, through the construction of permanent and elaborate monuments to the deceased as individuals and to the dead of individual families.

From the late seventeenth to the early twentieth century, most parishes in Lower Brittany had an ossuary or charnel house. Periodically, as the cemetery became overcrowded, bones were exhumed from individual graves and transferred to the ossuary. The ritual accompanying this transfer gave parish priests the opportunity to preach on the themes of death, Judgment, and damnation. Similar ceremonies were held to transfer bones to a communal grave in the cemetery when the ossuary itself became full. These secondary burial practices were discontinued after World War I, although many ossuaries continued to house bones until after 1945 (Croix 1981:1100–1105; Croix and Roudaut 1984:212–216).

The use of ossuaries and communal graves meant that prior to the early twentieth century, an individual's burial site remained intact for only a few years. Thus grave markers, except for those of the wealthy, were generally simple and impermanent. The identity of the individual was dissolved as the flesh decayed, and in the ossuary and communal grave his or her bones mingled with those of the collective dead. The ossuary therefore reflects the relative importance of group membership over individual autonomy in traditional Breton society.

By the late nineteenth century, however, a movement toward more individualistic treatment of the dead had started to develop in Brittany. Bones were still stored in ossuaries, but the skull was often kept separate and housed in a small wooden box with a heartshaped opening at the front and peaked covers like the roof of a house. Information about the deceased, such as names and dates of birth and death, was inscribed on the outside of the box. As Ariès describes this trend, "The Breton family, moved by a modern concern for personalizing the tomb, abandoned the traditional anonymity of the charnel in favor of a sort of individual miniature ossuary, the 'skull box'" (1982:60–61). Skull boxes were stored in the ossuary or the church. Even today visitors to the cathedral at Saint-Pol-de-Léon can see a number of such boxes, most dating from the nineteenth and early twentieth centuries.[1]

Although some ossuaries in rural Breton parishes are simple structures abutting the church, others, such as those at Saint-Thégonnec, Ploudiry, and Guimiliau, are elaborate buildings rivaling churches in their artistic embellishment. The ossuary was an important feature of the *enclos paroissial*, or parish enclosure, constructed in these and other Breton communities during the seventeenth century. The *enclos* consisted of a wall around the parish church and cemetery, within which were also housed the ossuary and an elaborate *calvaire*. The *enclos* with its ossuary represents the peak of ecclesiastical architecture in Brittany and bears witness to the importance of religion and death in Breton culture of the period (Debidour 1979:110–117; Waquet 1960:143–146). Often the ossuary was decorated with macabre inscriptions and memento mori, such as death's-heads, crossbones, and representations of the Ankou. The ossuary in Lannédern, south of La Feuillée, bears the words *cogita mori, respice finem*, "think of dying, look to the end." Since World War II, however, as macabre themes have been increasingly distanced from the mainstream of Breton Catholicism, the ossuary has fallen into disuse. By 1961 only twenty ossuaries continued to hold bones, and by 1984 bones remained in only three (Croix and Roudaut 1984:215–216). The ossuary has been transformed from a structure reserved for the dead to one dedicated to the interests of the living. Many have been cleaned out and converted into chapels, sacristies, or catechism classrooms, or simply abandoned. Those in communities with *enclos paroissiaux*, which attract large numbers of tourists, now serve as museums or gift shops.

Over the course of the twentieth century, with the increasing emphasis on the individual in Breton culture and the concomitant

---

1. Contrary to Ariès, Croix (1981:1104) notes several examples of skull boxes antedating the nineteenth century and suggests that special treatment of the skull may date at least to the sixteenth century in Brittany. However, the evidence he presents suggests that even if they were known earlier, skull boxes probably did not become widely used until the nineteenth century.

abandonment of collective burial practices, individual and family tombs and monuments have become progressively more elaborate. This trend reflects both the influence of a growing consciousness of individual identity, and the development of the romantic cult of the dead documented by Ariès for nineteenth-century Europe. As Ariès demonstrates, the importance accorded to cemeteries and tombs, beginning in the late eighteenth century among the wealthy and spreading to the lower classes throughout the nineteenth century, was linked to the romantic sensibility, which refused to accept separation from loved family members. It was during this period that affectivity began to be channeled toward a few significant individuals within the nuclear family rather than diffused over a wider group (Ariès 1982:472). The death of a loved one thus became increasingly difficult to tolerate. The romantic approach to death is typified by desire for reunion with deceased kin, and death is frequently portrayed in this period as a prelude to such a reunion (Ariès 1982:452). As the cemeteries in Plouguerneau and La Feuillée reveal, contemporary responses to death in rural Brittany combine the tame approach to death with the romantic perspective defined by Ariès.

Monuments for the Dead

In Plouguerneau and La Feuillée it is often the death of a family member which motivates the construction of a funerary monument, particularly when death occurs suddenly or when the deceased is a young person. After twenty-two-year-old Jeannie Kervao was killed while crossing the highway in La Feuillée, her family constructed both a *caveau* and a costly monument. A similar case is recounted by Louise Creac'h, the wife of a monument builder in the Monts d'Arrée. A local farmer was caught in his hay baler and died from the ensuing injuries. After the accident his wife commissioned a monument costing 30,000 francs or approximately $3,000. "It's the only thing I can give to him now," she explained. According to Louise, this widow and many other people perceive the monument as a gift for the deceased. They commission monuments because they feel "the need to offer something to the dead." The monument symbolizes one's respect for the deceased and demonstrates that one "hasn't forgotten them."

The inability to accept the death of a beloved relative, which is characteristic of the romantic response to death, is clearly a motive for the construction of tomb monuments. Visiting the tomb where her parents and brother are buried, a La Feuillée woman explains that for the living, some quality of the deceased is embedded in the monument: "It's the only thing that remains to us, their monument. We looked after them during their illnesses; we will never forget them." As Ariès (1982:541–547) shows, such sentiments are equally central to both secular and Catholic versions of the romantic cult of the dead. In La Feuillée the importance of perpetuating the memory of the deceased is affirmed by those who attend Mass regularly and by those who do not, by Catholics and Communists alike. "There are no political divisions in the *culte des morts*," observes Louise Creac'h. The desire to build an appropriate monument for the dead in one's family transcends religion.

Between World War I and the 1950s, the dominant type of funerary marker in the cemeteries at both Plouguerneau and La Feuillée was constructed of unpolished gray Kersanton granite, procured from local Breton quarries near Brest. Impoverished families, "whose relatives had died in the poorhouse," could buy wooden markers or cheaply produced wrought-iron crosses. These had been the most common types of grave markers during the nineteenth century (Le Calvez 1888:50). Wrought-iron crosses have not been manufactured since the early 1950s, and wooden crosses have also virtually disappeared from contemporary cemeteries. Many of the Kersanton granite monuments were cruciform. They were carved to resemble a tree trunk, with projecting knobs that evoked an image of newly severed branches. These crosses are known as *kroaziou ar vosenn*, or "crosses of the pestilence." They are said to be adapted from the large *calvaires* erected in the Léon during the seventeenth century, apparently on the occasion of a plague. The *kroaziou ar vosenn* were hand-sculpted, as were the attached figures of Christ in granite or white marble. After the Kersanton quarries closed at the end of the 1940s, unpolished monuments in the La Feuillée area were produced from local blue-gray Huelgoat granite. However, by 1950, granite-cutting machines had been introduced, putting an end to manual craftsmanship, at least in areas near urban centers. Mechanization enabled relatively inexpensive production of large, highly polished granite monuments. The majority of these are composed of a rectangular granite slab, almost flush to the ground, flanked by two slightly narrower slabs and a vertical headstone. The square or rectangular headstone averages between eighty and one hundred centimeters in height. Cruciform monuments have declined in popularity over the past twenty-five years, possibly as a result of the waning influence of Catholicism in Breton society.

The granite used for tombstone construction in contemporary Breton cemeteries is frequently imported from as far away as Norway, Finland, and Africa. Hues vary from black to gray to salmon pink. Depending on size and the type of granite used, the cost of a monument varies between 12,000 and 40,000 francs or approximately $1,200 to $4,000. It is clear that a funerary monument is a significant investment, especially if accompanied by the construction of a *caveau*. These cement-lined burial vaults with space for up to twelve coffins cost a minimum of 5,500 to 6,500 francs, approximately $550 to $650.

Caveaux have become popular in rural Brittany since the mid-1950s. According to Jean-Philippe, a monument builder in the Plouguerneau area, 10 percent of the tombs in most cemeteries in northern Finistère have *caveaux*. This figure is true for La Feuillée, where 41 of the 467 tombs in the cemetery have *caveaux*. The first *caveau* in the La Feuillée cemetery was built during the 1920s, but like the second, built thirty years later, it was the idiosyncratic whim of a relatively wealthy family in the parish. Most of the *caveaux* in La Feuillée were built during the 1970s and early 1980s. Yann Marc'h, the retired municipal employee who formerly served as grave digger in La Feuillée, states that many more families than the 41 who have already done so would like to build *caveaux*, but they have been unable to because of the close spacing of plots in the cemetery. The lack of space between plots both impedes construction and makes it impossible to maneuver a coffin into position for placement in the *caveau* at burial. Moreover, the topsoil in the La Feuillée cemetery is shallow and rocky, precluding the use of a mechanical excavator. The excavation for the vault must be done by hand, which adds to construction costs.

The construction of increasingly elaborate funerary monuments and *caveaux* over the past fifteen years has been made possible by the penetration of the consumer economy into rural Brittany, bringing increased opportunities for wage labor, and by the extension of both government and bank credit. As in other regions of Europe, in

Brittany since World War II, the material goods once exclusively associated with the wealthy elite have become more and more accessible to those from other social classes.[2] Attractive tomb monuments and *caveaux*, like new houses and cars, are now generally affordable in Brittany. Moreover, like other items of material culture, tombs have come to serve as markers of newly acquired social status.[3] That it is considered important to legitimate one's social position through investment in a tomb, and not just through other types of conspicuous consumption, attests to the continuing centrality of death in Breton culture.

The desire to validate family status through a display of wealth in the cemetery is particularly pronounced in communities along the coastal rim of the Léon. In Plouguerneau, for example, over 90 percent of the tombs in two of the three parish cemeteries have *caveaux*. Jean-Philippe attributes the popularity of *caveaux* in this region to an overriding ethos of *orgueil*, or pride. He notes that in the economic boom of the 1960s and early 1970s there were strong social pressures in Plouguerneau to compete with one's neighbors in acquiring "modern" items of material culture: "When one person bought a television, everyone else had to have the same thing, or preferably a better model." This spirit of rivalry existed on all levels—with respect to homes, furniture, tomb monuments, and *caveaux*. On visits to the cemetery many Plouguerneau women estimate with ease the cost of monuments and compare their own with those of neighbors and acquaintances in the community. Jean-Philippe claims that the height of the era of *orgueil* has passed. It was most marked among those now nearing their seventies. "The young people don't think that way anymore," he observes.

Although funerary architecture functions in one sense as a symbol of social status in the community, it is not necessarily those families who consider themselves to be the community elite, nor the wealthiest families, who affirm their social position through the construction of *caveaux* or elaborate monuments. The Pierres and

---

2. See Colclough (1971:216–217), Hutson (1971:57–58, 63, 66–67), Silverman (1975:220, 224), and Weingrod and Morin (1971:313) for other French and Italian examples of this process.

3. Brandes (1981:185–186) documents a similar process in Andalusia, where the cemetery has become a focus for the display of status distinctions and newly acquired wealth on All Saints' Day.

the Le Gralls, two couples from La Feuillée in their late sixties and early seventies, have built *caveaux* side by side in the parish cemetery. They commissioned large, modern, colored granite monuments on which their family names are inscribed in gold letters. As yet there have been no burials in these *caveaux*; they have been prepared in advance. The two couples are close friends, and their social positions in La Feuillée are structurally similar. Both migrated into the commune from Plonévez-du-Faou, located to the south in the *pays* Dardoup, a flatter, more fertile region than the Monts d'Arrée which has its own traditions of costume, dance, and music. The Le Gralls and the Pierres earned their living as small tenant farmers and are considered slightly "rustic" by some of the other retired people in the community who have not spent their working lives on the land. Only in their retirement have these two couples achieved a certain measure of independence and financial security. The Le Gralls bought a small parcel of land on which they built a new house. The Pierres refurbished an older residence. Shortly afterward both couples had *caveaux* and funerary monuments constructed. Their *caveaux* and monuments are a symbolic statement of "arrival" in the community: the achievement of landowner status and the establishment of ties in La Feuillée that will extend to their children's generation. One of the Pierres' daughters is married to the most successful carpenter in La Feuillée. Her children attend the communal school, and the family is securely rooted in La Feuillée. The Le Gralls' children do not live in the commune. However, two of their three sons return frequently for vacations and would like to build holiday residences in La Feuillée. The Le Gralls speculate that at least one of their sons will, like themselves, eventually spend his retirement in the community. For both the Pierres and the Le Gralls, the *caveau* represents an investment in the future. It is not only the place where they will be buried but also the final resting place for at least some of their children and grandchildren, who are committed to a future connected with La Feuillée.

Kinship and Burial

Yann Marc'h, the former grave digger in La Feuillée, notes that it is no longer possible to gauge the relative wealth of families from the parish by visiting the cemetery. In the past, he says, it was possible to do so, but now "everyone can afford an attractive monument." Whereas the earliest *caveaux* built in La Feuillée belonged to the wealthy, now "even the poor deprive themselves of other things in order to pay for a decent tomb." The Plouguerneau grave digger agrees that there is no longer a difference between the graves of the rich and the poor. As he remarks with wry humor, "Everyone is rich now."

The popularity of *caveaux* is related not only to their role as status markers but also to the romantic sensibility that, for Ariès, underlies the nineteenth-century and present-day cult of cemeteries and tombs in France. With space for six, nine, or twelve coffins, the *caveau* facilitates the reunion of a family group in death. As people in La Feuillée explain, "There one can reunite the whole family." It should be noted that it is not in fact necessary to build a *caveau* to accomplish this goal. Ordinary earth graves also lend themselves to multiple burials. If the grave has been excavated deeply enough for the first burial, other coffins may be superimposed on the first as it disintegrates.[4] However, the *caveau* promises a more permanent family reunion, both because its cement lining retards physical decomposition and because *caveaux* are usually built on cemetery plots leased from the commune "in perpetuity."

The popularity of *caveaux* in contemporary Brittany reveals the fusion of two distinct attitudes. The first is the idea of the survival of the *homo totus* after death in an afterlife of repose localized in the tomb. The second is the romantic desire to reunite loved ones in death. In his All Saints' Day sermon, the La Feuillée priest evokes a vision of life after death which echoes the concerns of his congregation for reunion with their kin: "Thus let us hope that despite our frailty, God will take into account our efforts and our good will, so that when we have departed from this earth, we will find ourselves together again, in the same shelter." The priest undoubtedly envisages this reunion as a spiritual one and intends his reference to

---

4. According to the local understanding of French law in Plouguerneau and La Feuillée, however, a five-year interval is required for hygienic reasons between burials in the same earth grave, unless the coffins previously interred are zinc-lined. This restriction creates difficulties for families who wish to reopen their earth tomb in the event of a succession of closely spaced deaths. Because the restriction does not apply to *caveaux*, it has contributed to the growing preference for this kind of tomb.

"the same shelter" metaphorically. Although the concept of reunion in this metaphorical sense is accepted on one level by his parishioners, they also conceive of the reunion with deceased relatives in a very material sense. More surely than in heaven, it is in the tomb, particularly in the *caveau*, that one will rejoin beloved family members after death.[5]

While reunion of the family dead is frequently voiced as the justification for *caveau* construction, certain features of the *caveau* suggest that it is not the ideal solution to the problem of grouping together deceased kin. There are only a limited number of spaces in the *caveau*. The maximum number is twelve, and many contain only six. Therefore, in frequent instances certain family members must be excluded. Bitter arguments may develop over the question of who has the right to be buried in a particular *caveau*. The question of who will be buried where and with whom is a critical issue regardless of whether the family possesses a *caveau* or an ordinary earth tomb, but it takes on special significance in the case of the *caveau*. Since decomposition is retarded in the sealed environment of the vault, the *caveau* is not reusable as is the earth tomb. Once the *caveau* has been filled, new space for further burials is created at a very slow rate.

Although the *caveau* is envisaged as the last resting place for the "entire family," its space limitations pose problems concerning the definition of the kin group. In the Plouguerneau area there are arrangements whereby each person in a family who wants to have the right to be buried in a particular *caveau* must contribute a share of the construction costs or reimburse the original owner for his or her *place*. Such arrangements do not occur in the La Feuillée area, where, according to one *caveau* builder, normally a single individual or couple decides to have the *caveau* constructed and pays for it. The rest of the family has the right to be buried there without making a contribution. Often retired parents or grandparents pay for the *caveau*, since they are likely to have fewer financial obligations than younger couples with houses to buy, children to educate, and farms or businesses to manage.

---

5. The belief that families will be reunited in the afterlife is also common in Basque culture (Douglass 1969:81). However, at least in the Spanish Basque country, such sentiments are not expressed through attachment to family grave sites (Douglass 1969:73).

The question of who will be buried where and with whom is closely related to problems of inheritance. In families with numerous children it is obvious that not all members of the sibling group along with their spouses and children can be buried in the same tomb, whether it be a *caveau* or an ordinary earth grave. On the basis of several genealogies including information on burials collected in both Plouguerneau and the La Feuillée area, some generalizations can be offered about the solutions that are worked out for this problem.

In both regions unmarried children of any age are usually buried in their parents' tomb. The situation becomes more complex with married children. In some cases in the Plouguerneau area, the child who succeeds to his or her parents' farm and continues to live with his or her spouse and children in the parents' home succeeds to the family *caveau* or tomb. Children who marry off their parents' land onto the family farm of their spouse and into their in-laws' homes are likely to be buried in their in-laws' family tomb, rather than with their family of origin. In both the Plouguerneau and La Feuillée regions it is rare for husbands and wives to be buried separately.

For the purpose of inheritance, tombs are considered *biens de la terre,* or immovable property, and they are grouped with items such as the family home and land. Both the French civil code and a local cultural preference for egalitarian inheritance decree that each child in a family is entitled to an equal share of the parents' estate. However, there is a difference between succession and inheritance.[6] Although in some cases only one child succeeds to, or takes over, the *biens de la terre,* all those in a sibling group must receive their inheritance portion. The child who succeeds to the family home and farm must therefore provide monetary compensation for his or her siblings equal to the value of their shares in the immovable property. In some Plouguerneau families the same reasoning applies to *caveaux*. The child who takes over the *caveau* must pay his or her siblings for the right to use their *places*.

Often only the child who succeeds to the family farm remains in the Plouguerneau region, as the other children leave to find work

---

6. See Segalen (1985:79–115) for a more complete analysis of inheritance patterns in Lower Brittany, which emphasizes the distinction between inheritance and succession.

off the land in urban centers. It is then logical and practical that he or she take over the tomb and be responsible for its upkeep. The issue becomes less clearly defined when two or more siblings remain. In such cases, the *biens de la terre* are often divided, with one parcel of land going to one child, the house to another, and a second parcel of land to a third. Under these circumstances the child who remains in the family house or takes charge of the parents in their old age generally will have the strongest claim to the right to be buried, along with spouse and children, in the family tomb.[7]

It is more difficult to discover how decisions are made about the question of "who will be buried with whom" in the La Feuillée area than in Plouguerneau. Inheritance is a less vital issue in La Feuillée, since the land is only marginally productive and has ceased to be an important economic resource. Moreover, the rate of population turnover has been higher than in Plouguerneau, with steady emigration from the Monts d'Arrée since the late nineteenth century, and later immigration from the regions neighboring to the north and south. Many immigrant families have not been established in La Feuillée long enough to pass down tombs over generations. In families whose offspring have been dispersed in the *exode rural*, often only one child remains in the parish or returns on retirement. This person will be responsible for the upkeep of the family tomb and will have the right to be buried in it, regardless of whether he or she has continued to farm the family land.

Finally, there seems to be a slight uxorilocal tendency in burial patterns, at least in the La Feuillée area, if for no other reason than that women take responsibility for the tomb, and they, rather than their husbands, think and make decisions about burials.

The genealogy of a La Feuillée family (chart 1) illustrates some of the burial patterns characteristic of the Monts d'Arrée. *Ego* Thérèse Philipot is from Brennilis, the commune adjacent to La Feuillée on the southeast. She is now seventy-two years old and is married to Roger Trebern, seventy-seven, who was born in La Feuillée. Roger, an only son, inherited both the Trebern farm and the family tomb in La Feuillée, where he and Thérèse will be buried. Roger and his wife lived in Quimper, where he worked as a customs official, but they returned each weekend to La Feuillée and have re-

---

7. Usually the same child who takes over the family house looks after the elderly parents.

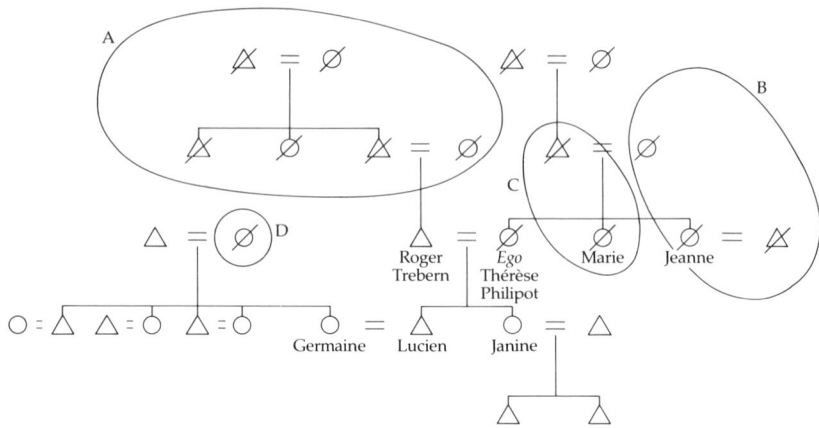

Chart 1. Trebern-Philipot family tombs (groups of individuals buried together are circled).

tired there. They have remained more closely tied to La Feuillée than to Brennilis, where Thérèse's married sister, Jeanne, and her mother lived. Thérèse has had a *caveau* built in La Feuillée in the Trebern family plot, where Roger's parents and paternal grandparents, aunt, and uncle were buried (A). Note that the two unmarried children were interred with their parents. All of these remains were exhumed before the building of the *caveau* and placed in a small reliquary for reburial after construction was completed. Thérèse intends to have her mother, sister, and brother-in-law exhumed from the tomb where they are buried in Brennilis (B). Their remains will also be placed in a reliquary for reburial in the Trebern *caveau*. Thérèse greatly regrets that she will not be able to do the same for her father's body and that of her other sister, Marie, who died in infancy. Both were buried in an earth tomb in Brennilis (C) with many others of her father's family. Exhumation and transfer is no longer feasible, for it is now impossible to distinguish the remains of one individual from those of another in this tomb.

Thérèse and Roger Trebern have two children: a married daughter, Janine, and a married son, Lucien. Lucien lives in Huelgoat with his wife Germaine. Germaine's parents constructed a *caveau* in Brennilis, where her mother is buried, and Lucien and Germaine will also be buried there (D). Germaine has three other married siblings, but all of them live in Paris and will not be buried in their parents' *caveau*. In the Trebern family it is the daughter, Janine, who has taken over her grandparents' farmhouse in La Feuillée, which she has restored as a weekend home for visits to the commune from Quimper, where she now lives. Similarly, Janine will also succeed to the Trebern family tomb.

The exhumation and reburial of relatives which Thérèse has planned is by no means unusual. A number of other La Feuillée and Plouguerneau families have had the bodies of relatives who were initially interred elsewhere exhumed and returned to family tombs in their native commune. It is particularly important to do so if no family members who can maintain the tomb live in the community where the deceased was originally buried. Such is the case with another elderly La Feuillée resident, Anne-Marie Ploneis, whose married daughter lived in Lorient. The daughter died and was buried there, as was her husband, who committed suicide shortly afterward. Their children have left Lorient, and no other relatives live in that city. Thus, Anne-Marie has recently had the bodies of her daughter and son-in-law exhumed and returned to La Feuillée for burial in the tomb where her own husband is interred and where she herself will be buried. Similarly, in the La Feuillée area there are several families whose unmarried sons died while working temporarily in Canada or the United States. These families have gone to great expense to have the bodies shipped back for burial in their natal commune. Like the *retour au pays* of émigrés from La Feuillée on retirement, the practice of returning those who die elsewhere for burial in the parish bears witness to the prevalence of the romantic response to death in contemporary Brittany. As Ariès (1982:523) points out, the "union of birth and death, of the native soil and the burial ground, is one of the favorite themes of the romantic era."

Caveaux and *Maisons*

The *caveau* is frequently described in both Plouguerneau and La Feuillée as "the last home for the entire family." It is the *maison* or *petite maison*, little home, waiting to receive the family after death. The large number of *caveaux* in the cemeteries at Plouguerneau assumes special significance when viewed in the light of house construction in this commune. With 28.2 percent of its principal residences constructed since 1962, the canton of Lannilis, which includes the commune of Plouguerneau, has a high proportion of new housing relative to other rural cantons in the department of Finistère. The casual observer in Plouguerneau is struck by the number of well-landscaped modern houses. Conversations among Plouguerneau women are filled with frequent allusions to young couples who have built new homes, *maisons neuves*, in one of the *quartiers* of the commune. With the emphasis on the residential autonomy of the nuclear family which has developed since the 1950s, the *maison neuve* is regarded as a virtual prerequisite for the establishment of a family. Although many newly married couples, particularly agriculturalists, do live with their parents, at least on a temporary basis, this arrangement is not considered desirable.[8] Young couples make every effort to construct a house of their own, even if it is on part of their parents' land which has been ceded as an advance on their inheritance portion. There appears to be a symbolic link between the desire to build a *maison* in which to house the family during life and the desire to construct a parallel *maison*, the *caveau*, for the family in the community of the dead.

Despite the symbolic parallels between *caveaux* and *maisons neuves*, it should be noted that the *maison neuve* is intended primarily to house a single two-generation nuclear family, while the *caveau* is prepared in order to reunite an extended kin group spanning three or more generations. In part, this difference reflects the fact that *caveaux* are frequently constructed by people of middle age or older who define "family" in terms of children, grandchildren, and great-grandchildren, whereas *maisons neuves* are built by younger people at the beginning of family formation. As Pierrette, the wife of a monument builder in Morlaix, explains, retired couples often choose to build a nine- or twelve-place *caveau* with the rationale that "maybe the grandchildren will be buried here too."

Among the elderly there is a close association between preparation of homes for retirement and construction of *caveaux*. Describing her husband's clients, Pierrette observes that many are people of fifty or sixty years of age who have retired and started to think about their tomb, jokingly referred to as their *maison secondaire*.

---

8. The proverb "Mieux vaut un petit chez-soi qu'un grand chez-les-autres" (Better a little place of one's own than a big place that belongs to other people), which is well known in Plouguerneau, expresses the high value placed on separate accommodation for individual nuclear families.

Jean-Philippe, the monument builder from the Plouguerneau area, caters to a similar clientele: "They have their homes, so they build their *caveaux*." As in La Feuillée, those who return *au pays* on retirement to Plouguerneau first build the home, then consider the *caveau*.

Further parallels between the *maison* and the tomb exist with respect to the role of women. Unlike men, women are concerned with things interior: the decoration of the home and the running of the household. Just as, on the occasion of a death, a woman from the family decides what type of fabric should be used to line the interior of the coffin, so too do women make decisions about the type of funerary monument to buy and about the feasibility of building a *caveau*. According to Pierrette, the tomb is like a piece of household furniture, which the woman in a married couple would choose. For both types of purchases she claims, "Men don't care. They would more likely be the ones to choose a car." Similarly, Louise Creac'h, the wife of the monument builder in Huelgoat, explains that while the purchase of a piece of agricultural machinery is "the husband's domain," tombs, like houses, are a feminine responsibility, and it is left to women to make decisions.[9] Even if a couple comes to choose their monument together, the wife has the final word, and she picks the type of granite from which the monument will be constructed. Jean-Philippe notes that women generally come alone to commission a tomb, rarely in the company of their husbands: "They have agreed between husband and wife that they will have something built, but it is the wife who decides." This separation of roles is reflected in women's discourse concerning tombs. It is always, "I have built a *caveau*" or "I have had my monument repaired," and never "My husband commissioned the *caveau*." When men talk about funerary architecture, which is less frequent, they are more likely to use "we," "our tomb," or phrases such as "my wife had the *caveau* built."

Tame Death or Death Denied

Although it is frequently a death in the family which motivates monument construction, many of the *caveaux* and funerary monu-

---

9. "Les tombes sont comme pour les maisons. Les hommes les laissent choisir." A similar extension of women's roles from the household to the graveyard is described by Brandes (1981:182) for Andalusia. See Chapter 8, note 6, below.

ments in Breton cemeteries are built well in advance of the time when they will be needed. The preparation of one's tomb in advance implies acknowledgment of the inevitability of death. Jean-Philippe, in the Plouguerneau area, estimates that half his clients commission a monument years before their own death or that of a close family member. He explains, "Here people accept death easily, and building your *caveau* in advance is part of the preparation for death." Moreover, building one's own tomb allows one to exert some degree of personal control over the future, even beyond the moment of death. At least one aspect of death, which is ultimately an uncontrollable biological fact, is tamed. One can determine the location and appearance of one's final resting place and thus in some sense "know where one is going."

Whereas the construction of funerary monuments in advance attests to the continuing familiarity with death in Plouguerneau and La Feuillée, the emphasis placed by contemporary Bretons on retarding the physical decomposition of the body through *caveau* burial suggests that the denial of death is developing in the region. The desire to prevent the disintegration of the body after death is frequently cited as a reason for the construction of *caveaux*. An employee of the *pompes funèbres* in Brest comments, "People build *caveaux* because they want to keep the material remains." Likewise, Jean-Philippe explains that the popularity of *caveaux* derives partly from their prevention of *pourriture,* or decay. In his view, people feel it is preferable to be buried in a *caveau* than to "go into the earth." Just as the moment of death has been distanced by relegating it to the social space of the institution, and contact with the dead body has been decreased through delegation of the *toilette des morts* to specialized personnel, so too is the reality of bodily decay after death becoming unacceptable in contemporary Brittany. People often claim that *caveaux* are "cleaner" than earth tombs. As the material environment of everyday life in rural Brittany has become "cleaner" over the past thirty years, with the installation of running water and sanitary facilities and with ameliorations such as the paving of barn floors, the desire for a clean habitat for the dead has also been created. The concern to make the tomb clean seems to be part of a general effort to avoid contact with such categories of the natural world as dirt, earth, and manure. This trend is itself closely associated with the "sterilization" of death, or the repression of its grosser aspects, including the sufferings of the dying, which are now less evident since they take place in a hospital.

The contemporary distaste for physical decomposition after death in Brittany is radically different from the traditional tame response to death, which accepted decay and the accompanying dissolution of individual identity as a positive process (Ariès 1982: 554). Although it is disappearing in Brittany, such a perspective has been maintained in other regions of Europe. In present-day Greece, for example, where exhumation and secondary burial are performed, the failure of a body to decompose is considered a disturbing indicator that the soul of the deceased is not at rest, owing either to the improper performance of burial rites or to sins committed by the dead person during life (Danforth 1982:50). Likewise, in Portugal those whose bodies do not decay are held to be either saints or unredeemed sinners (Pina-Cabral 1986:230–233).

In rural Brittany the response to *caveaux* and the retardation of decomposition varies, even among people of the same generation. The traditional positive view of decomposition has not disappeared. Discussions with La Feuillée women reveal the complexity of the pattern of continuity and change which characterizes attitudes toward *caveaux*. Seventy-five-year-old Joséphine Kerouac is strongly opposed to *caveau* burial. A self-proclaimed "pillar of the church," she states with finality that "when one is dead, one is dead." In her opinion the process of decay is inevitable, whether or not one is buried in a *caveau*, and it is not something to be feared. She says that she would rather decay quickly in the earth than over a long period of time in a *caveau*. Describing a recent visit to the earth tomb where her mother, sister, and two husbands are buried, she remarks that she found a finger bone protruding from the gravel around the monument. "And I knew that it must have belonged to one of them, perhaps my mother or my sister." She is not disconcerted by the prospect of the dissolution of individual identity represented by the body's decay. Whether the bone belonged to her mother, her sister, or one of her husbands is of no significance. She herself will ultimately decompose and her body will intermingle with theirs in a generalized mixture of earth and bones, distinguished from that in neighboring tombs by virtue only of the kinship bonds that unite the deceased. "No, I wouldn't buy a *caveau*," Joséphine says. "For me, it doesn't matter. I would rather be buried directly in the earth, where in ten or fifteen years there will be nothing left."

Joséphine Kerouac was married to a naval officer and accompanied him to posts in Toulon and Brest. When he retired they opened a small grocery store in Brest, and she continues to divide her time between La Feuillée and Brest, where she passes the winter months every year. It might be expected that a woman with this extensive urban experience would hold opinions closer to the denial of death, and that she would have been attracted to the concept of the *caveau*. That she is not is particularly noteworthy, for she is comfortably well-off and could easily afford to build one. However, Joséphine's readiness to accept the body's decay is related to her religious faith and to her belief in a spiritual afterlife.

But the rejection of *caveaux* is also shared by those who are not practicing Catholics. Like Joséphine, Annie Kervella and Cécile, two strongly anticlerical *rouge* women from La Feuillée in their early sixties assert that they do not want to be buried in a *caveau*. Cécile has resisted the advice of her married children, who want her to build one. Both women express the opinion that it is somehow unnatural for the body, "sealed in its own juices," to decay slowly in a vault. As Annie explains, she would prefer to "return naturally to the earth." For her this image of decay is less repugnant than that of the body trapped in the *caveau* with the by-products of its own decomposition. She graphically describes a reddish substance she claims to have seen seeping out from around *caveaux* in the La Feuillée cemetery, the "juice" of the corpses which cannot be absorbed into the ground through the cement walls of the *caveau*.

As these examples show, distaste for *caveaux*, combined with the tame acceptance of decomposition after death, is not uniquely characteristic of either Catholics or Communists in La Feuillée. Likewise, many devout Catholics and confirmed *rouges* have built *caveaux* and are in favor of the practice. Thus, it would be overly simplistic to correlate the tame attitude toward decomposition solely with religious belief. Moreover, since many people reject *caveaux* despite their widespread use it is clear that overemphasis on the denial response ignores the complexity of contemporary patterns of transformation and persistence in Breton attitudes toward death.

Relocation of Cemeteries

For rural Bretons the cemetery provides a privileged meeting ground between the living and the dead. This is especially true in parishes where the cemetery remains in its original location around the church, centrally placed in the *bourg*. In his introduction to the 1928 edition of *La légende de la mort*, Le Braz describes the traditional importance of the cemetery in Breton communities. Noting that "elsewhere, for reasons of hygiene, there is a tendency to locate sepulchers farther and farther away from the village," he observes that in Brittany

> such enterprises are regarded as pure profanation. To exile the dead from the immediate neighborhood of the church, is that not, in some sense, to make them die a second death, by cutting them off from communion with their close friends and family, in whose work and deeds they no doubt continue to be interested? Moreover, but for some rare exceptions, everywhere the cemetery occupies the center of the *bourg*. In fact, it is the essential feature of the town, and its vital node. The houses surrounding the cemetery seem to be gathered there only to keep it company.
> (1928:1:xlvi–xlvii)

In La Feuillée the cemetery was removed from the churchyard in 1918, an early date relative to other communities in the region. In most of the Breton parishes where the cemetery has been moved from the center of the *bourg*, this change has been made since 1960. Overcrowding is the principal reason for the relocation of cemeteries. With the growing desire for *caveaux* and permanent monuments to families and individuals, the space in small rural cemeteries is rapidly filled. Many plots are now granted "in perpetuity" or leased to families for a thirty-year period with the possibility of renewal. For this reason the reuse of tomb sites, which was feasible when bones were exhumed to be stored in ossuaries, is now virtually impossible.

Although on one level pragmatic considerations of space underlie cemetery relocation, on another level the removal of cemeteries from town centers reflects a rigidification of the boundary between the community of the living and that of the dead. The dead are no longer located, both literally and figuratively, at the center of community activity. While many people, especially middle-aged and elderly women, continue to make frequent visits to their family tombs, it is no longer necessary to pass by the cemetery in the course of one's daily routine, when one goes to the post office or to the bakery, for example. In many communities, the space formerly occupied by the cemetery has been turned to uses that derive from the changing interests of the living: widened roads, parking lots, or landscaped open space. In the words of a thirty-five-year-old woman from a commune adjacent to La Feuillée where plans are underway for relocation of the cemetery, "It will be better not to have the cemetery around the church. There will be more room for taking wedding photos."[10]

Despite such opinions, the relocation of cemeteries has not been universally greeted with enthusiasm in rural Brittany. The traditional acceptance of proximity with the dead coexists alongside new attitudes resembling the denial of death. In communities in the La Feuillée area there has been resistance to using relocated cemeteries. There are two cemeteries currently in use in Huelgoat, for example, and it is felt that the newer of these, located two kilometers from the *bourg*, is "out of the way" and "too far to walk." People fear that the tombs will consequently be neglected. Similar opinions are voiced in Berrien, where a new cemetery outside the *bourg* was opened in 1983. By mid-1984 only two plots had been purchased there, owing to the distance of the cemetery from the town and people's desire to be buried in the old cemetery where other family members are interred.

Alternatives to Burial

As resistance to cemetery relocation indicates, the maintenance of ongoing relationships with the deceased remains of central importance in Breton culture. The significance of these relationships is also reflected in the generally negative response to cremation and to the donation of organs for medical research or transplants. The thousand-member Société des Crématistes de Bretagne is currently

---

10. Segalen (1985:326) notes that in Saint-Jean-Trolimon in the *pays* Bigouden, "little by little, the tombs are being moved from the churchyard, where they have rested since time immemorial. The graves are making room for a parking lot."

lobbying for funding to construct a crematorium at Carhaix, approximately thirty kilometers south of La Feuillée. They claim that cremation is unpopular at present because of the high cost of transporting coffin and corpse to the nearest crematorium, in the Paris suburbs, and suggest that once a local facility has been constructed, people will quickly come to accept cremation as an alternative to burial.

However, the current disapproval of cremation stems from deeper causes unconcerned with economics. Cremation contradicts the idea of preservation of the *homo totus* in the *caveau* or tomb. Once the body is destroyed by fire, nothing remains of it below the monument that the family visits in the cemetery. Ashes are not sufficient to meet the desire expressed by many Bretons to retain direct, physical contact with the deceased. While it is accepted that the body will decompose, either inside or outside the *caveau*, this process is more or less gradual. With cremation, however, it is abrupt, brutal, and irrevocable. It is also likely that the church's former rigid opposition to cremation continues to influence opinions on this subject. Prior to 1963 the Catholic hierarchy condemned cremation, in part because it posed a logical contradiction to the doctrine of physical resurrection at the Last Judgment. Moreover, for some people in rural Brittany the fires of the crematorium are too close a symbolic parallel to the fires of hell and purgatory evoked in the recent past through the sermons of parish priests.

It is possible that cremation will slowly gain acceptance in Brittany, particularly as cemeteries in urban areas become more crowded. Attitudes may also be changing across generations. In a discussion with Marie-Jeanne Kerjouan, a sixty-four-year-old woman from Plouguerneau, and her three daughters, aged forty-four, forty-one, and thirty-two, each of the younger women said that she would prefer to be cremated. Marie-Jeanne, in contrast, was not in favor of cremation; she felt that "what is done now is fine." A remark made by one of the Kerjouan daughters underscores the primary difficulty most Breton families find in accepting cremation: "It is harder on the living than for the dead person himself."

Donation of the body to medicine presents a similar void for the bereaved, because, like cremation, it destroys the possibility of a continuing relationship with the deceased. A La Feuillée woman explains that her relatives in Brest were shaken by the decision of their father, a doctor, to leave his body for medical research. A memorial Mass was held instead of a funeral, and a plaque bearing his name was placed on the family monument in the cemetery; but these rituals appeared hollow without the physical presence of the deceased. The family faces the annual celebration of All Saints' Day with difficulty, for while they would like to place flowers for their father on the tomb, the gesture is meaningless, since his body is not there.

Conclusion

Tombs, monuments, and burial patterns in Brittany provide a clear indication of both change and continuity in responses to death. As in the past, the Breton cemetery today is envisaged as the locus for the continued existence of the dead. In Plouguerneau and La Feuillée body and soul are conceived to remain together in an afterlife of repose in the tomb. This vision of postmortem existence, like that in the medieval world described by Ariès, is intimately linked to a social setting in which the collectivity is emphasized over the development of individual personality and autonomy. Over the course of the twentieth century, however, the growing importance of individualism in Breton culture is evident in changing forms of funerary architecture. Burials have become progressively less anonymous, with the abandonment of ossuaries, the use of skull boxes, and since World War II, the increasing elaboration of individual and family tomb monuments for people of all social classes. This trend is associated with the generalization of the romantic response to death, typified by the inability to accept separation from beloved relatives. The importance placed on reuniting the kin group after death in the tomb or *caveau* represents the contemporary expression of this perspective in Brittany. Likewise, the rejection of cremation stems from the desire of the bereaved to perpetuate contact with the loved one as *homo totus* after death.

Certain developments since 1945, such as the relocation of cemeteries and the popularity of *caveau* burial, which retards bodily decomposition, indicate a distancing of death. However, change has not exclusively taken the direction of denial. The current importance of funerary architecture as a marker of social status is a case in point. Status symbols serve no purpose unless they are highly visible. Clearly the cemetery continues to be visited as a familiar place, at least in rural communities like Plouguerneau and La Feuillée. Death and the community of the dead have obviously not been entirely excluded from the social world of the living. Moreover, the practice of building one's *caveau* and tomb monument in advance indicates a continuing acceptance of death.

Discussing Zonabend's (1973) study of a rural cemetery in contemporary Burgundy, Ariès recognizes a fusion of the tame and romantic responses to death in this setting: "It is as if the romantic model has been grafted onto the archaic" (1982:555). The same conclusion applies to Plouguerneau and La Feuillée. In each community the cemetery bears witness to the intermingling of the denial response with the tame death and to the continuing importance of the romantic cult of the dead.

6

Religion and Death I
Orthodox Models and Local Interpretations

After spending fifteen months during the mid-1970s on the island of Houat, off the south Breton coast, French ethnographer Paul Jorion concluded that "there are other sources of religion and they certainly appear more prominently in other parts of the world, but in Houat and in Brittany in general those aspects of the common Roman Catholic creed which deal with the dying and the dead have taken a considerable extension" (1982:275). This "extension" of Catholic concepts about death is the focus of this chapter and the next. The influence of the Catholic church in shaping and defining Breton responses to death can be understood only from a historical perspective. Therefore, it is important to begin with a discussion of pre- or non-Christian local religious traditions relating to death which have become closely associated with orthodox Catholicism in Brittany. Some of these have analogues in other Celtic regions of Europe. The contribution of these folk practices and beliefs to the importance of death as a theme in Breton culture is assessed. Next the impact of Catholicism is considered, starting with the Breton missions of the seventeenth century. In Chapter 7 the social and political role of the church in nineteenth- and twentieth-century Brittany is discussed. Chapter 7 concludes with a survey of contemporary eschatological beliefs and an analysis of the changing relationships in Brittany between religion, social structure, and attitudes toward death.

Catholicism and Popular Belief

In the face of the contemporary trend toward secularization, Breton priest and author René Le Corre observes that the church's rituals for the dead are the ones that have retained the greatest popular support in Brittany: "Religion for the dead is the religion which has survived best today, and it is that which preceded the Catholic faith" (1982:41). As Le Corre's statement implies, it is possible to interpret the importance of death in Breton religion and culture as a "survival" of pre-Christian, Celtic traditions. Indeed, as historians Croix and Roudaut point out, this hypothesis of a Christian overlay incompletely covering a "pagan" cultural base has become the accepted model for many folklorists working with Breton material (1984:37). This view was shared by Le Braz and van Gennep, among others.[1]

One of the foundations for the hypothesis of Celtic survivals in Breton eschatological traditions is the concept of hell as a cold place—*an ifern yen*, "cold hell." Breton folklore collected during the nineteenth century includes frequent references to souls that suffer from glacial cold in the afterlife. Le Braz (1928:2:30–35), for example, records a legend in which a young man aids the soul of his dead friend by accompanying it during three nights of penance at the bottom of a freezing pond. In other legends the dead return to the homes of the living, where, since they are always cold, they "seek constantly to steal across to the hearth" (Le Braz 1928:2:22). The presence of the phrase *ifern yen* in Breton hymns, plays, and poetry dating from the fifteenth, sixteenth, and seventeenth centuries indicates that the nineteenth-century Breton representation of hell as cold is derived from an earlier tradition (Le Menn 1979). An inscription dating from 1619 on the ossuary at La Martyre cautions the living to repent of their sins and to beware of hell's cold:

> *An Maru, han Barñ, han Ifferñ yEN*
> Death, Judgment, and cold hell,—
> *Pan ho soing dEN ez dle crENaff:*
> When man meditates on these things, he must tremble:
> *Foll eu na preder è SperET,*
> He whose spirit does not reflect is foolish,
> *GuelET ez eu rET decEDaff.*
> Given that it is necessary to die.
>
> (quoted in Le Menn 1979:24)

---

1. See van Gennep (1946:658, 800–802). In this connection it is important to note that the concept of cultural unity among those areas of Europe where Celtic languages have been spoken in modern times—Ireland, Scotland, Wales, Cornwall, Brittany, and the Isle of Man—has been challenged by McDonald (1986).

According to van Gennep, the Breton depiction of hell as a cold place is part of a tradition of folk belief which may be of Celtic origin (1946:800). In contrast, Croix and Roudaut (1984:80) have argued that the Breton adjective *yen* does not exclusively mean "cold." Rather, the same word connotes "cruel," "evil," "hard-hearted," and "perfidious." They conclude that the importance of the theme of the cold hell and its Celtic origins has been exaggerated in studies of Breton folklore because of this mistranslation. In their view cold was only one of the possible torments in hell as conceived of by Bretons during the seventeenth century and not its essential quality. This conclusion is supported by the frequent allusions to hell as a place of fire and flames in the same texts that refer to its frigid quality (Croix 1981:1057; Croix and Roudaut 1984:80).

A slightly different position in this debate is adopted by literary historian and philologist Gwennole Le Menn. Analyzing the depiction of the otherworld in middle Breton texts, Le Menn concludes that while the word *yen* may signify "cruel" or "hard-hearted," "it is difficult to restrict *yen* only to the sense of 'cruel.' The presence of ice and frost is too often mentioned" (1979:33). Moreover, he notes that the conception of hell as a cold place is also found in medieval Welsh poetry. Le Menn posits that the Breton vision of hell with its alternation between extremes of cold and heat, which has parallels in texts recounting the lives of the Irish saints, represents a "marriage of the Christian hell with the Celtic hell" (1979:30).

While the image of hell as a cold place can certainly be detected in Breton oral and literary traditions from the nineteenth century and earlier, it is unlikely that this eschatological conception is uniquely Breton or Celtic. Hell is associated with ice and cold in several non-Celtic cultural contexts. A well-known example is Dante's *Inferno*, in which the lowest part of the last circle of hell is depicted as a lake of ice (Dante 1971:264–268, canto 32).

In addition to the concept of the cold hell, a second element of Breton death-related folklore is thought to have Celtic origins. This is the Ankou, or personification of death. References to the Ankou exist as early as the fifteenth century and possibly earlier if an undated marginal gloss can be considered contemporary to the ninth-century Latin text it accompanies (Le Menn 1979:8–9). The geographical distribution of iconographic representations of the Ankou provides good evidence for Celtic associations. With one exception, all known depictions of the Ankou come from the historically Breton-speaking Lower Brittany. The single exception is found in the border area of Upper Brittany, close to the Breton-speaking zone (Croix and Roudaut 1984:83). Of even greater significance is existence of figures parallel to the Ankou in the folklore of other Celtic regions: the *angheu* in Wales and the *ankow* in Cornwall (Croix and Roudaut 1984:85). Whereas nineteenth-century iconography portrays the Ankou with a scythe, fifteenth- and sixteenth-century sources arm him with an arrow, pick, dart, or javelin.[2] Sometimes the Ankou is depicted with a hammer, mallet, or staff, suggesting a possible relationship with Sucellos, the Celtic God of Death, one of whose attributes is also a mallet (Le Menn 1979:19–23; see also Croix 1981:1065–1067). This link is tenuous, however, since no known representations that arm the Ankou with a mallet predate the nineteenth century (Croix 1981:1066–1067). Moreover, despite indications that the Ankou may have Celtic origins, it should be noted that death is frequently depicted elsewhere in Europe from at least as early as the fifteenth century in the form of similar personae.[3]

In Brittany sculptured depictions of the Ankou are frequently part of the exterior ornamentation of ecclesiastical edifices, such as the ossuaries at Ploudiry, Landivisiau, La Roche-Maurice, and Brasparts, and the churches at Noyal-Pontivy, Bulat-Pestivien, and Lannédern. The holy water font at the main entrance to the church at La Martyre is surmounted by a sculpted figure of the Ankou. The extent to which this unorthodox element from popular traditions concerning the supernatural was integrated into official Catholicism in Brittany can be seen in the church of Saint-Mathieu in Morlaix and in the Trégor parish of Ploumilliau, where statues of

---

2. It has been argued that the scythe, whose blade points outward, to the left, rather than inward, to the right, may be an element borrowed from other European traditions, probably in the seventeenth century (Le Menn 1979:18–19).

3. For examples of iconographic representations of Ankou-like figures dating from this period, see, among others, Eichenberg (1983:19, 20, 25), Holbein ([1538] 1947), Mâle (1958:94, 141), and Tenenti (1952). In Croix's opinion, however, the Breton Ankou differs from these more classic European representations of death: "Here we are far from the traditional image of the horseman-reaper, the harvester, or even that of the hunter armed with bow and arrow. This Death [the Ankou] has been considerably modified for the local [Breton] climate, or else it derives from an independent tradition" (1981:1065).

the Ankou were erected, alongside those of the Catholic saints, in the church interior. According to Croix and Roudaut, such examples of syncretism prove the existence of a symbiotic relationship between Breton culture and the Catholic church prior to the 1960s. This relationship flourished as a result of their shared sensibility to the theme of death. Thus, through time the rites of the church in Brittany were able to coexist with "anterior practices much less orthodox in spirit" (Croix and Roudaut 1984:209).

The consciousness of the pre-Christian religious traditions of their ancestors is never far from contemporary Breton Catholics. Several of the saints credited with the conversion of Brittany are reputed to have come from the British Isles.[4] These legendary figures, such as Saint Ronan, Saint Pol Aurelian, and Saint Samson, are immortalized in the Breton *Buhez ar Sent*, or Lives of the Saints. This book was often the only one owned in rural households during the nineteenth century (Le Gallo 1980:65). Even now many middle-aged people in La Feuillée and Plouguerneau recall reading a chapter of the *Buhez ar Sent* at nightly family gatherings in the pre-television era.

The pre-Catholic past is also present in the landscape in the form of menhirs, dolmens, and tumuli. Christian symbols have been added to some of these monuments, like the menhir at the entrance to Grouanec in Plouguerneau, which is surmounted by a cross (Le Scouëzic and Masson 1983:132–133). These "pagan roots" and their assimilation to Christianity are recalled by the faithful of La Feuillée on the festival of Saint Houardon, a seventh-century Breton saint. In the small twelfth-century stone chapel in the *bourg* of La Feuillée, the congregation sings the "Cantique de saint Houardon," which includes the following lines:

> *Devant toi, le druide antique*
> Before you, the ancient druid
> *Abandonne sa forêt*
> Abandons his forest,

---

4. Although the Armorican peninsula was probably initially exposed to Christianity during Roman times, the religion spread slowly to rural areas. Both the character and intensity of adherence to Christianity in this region were altered significantly by the influx of immigrants from the British Isles under the leadership of religious figures, the Breton saints, during the sixth century A.D. (Chadwick 1969:238–291).

> *Et sur le dolmen celtique*
> And on the Celtic dolmen
> *La croix du Christ apparaît*
> The cross of Christ appears.
> (Diocèse de Quimper, 1975)

Notwithstanding its inaccurate ascription of the dolmen, most likely erected by earlier Neolithic populations in Brittany, to the Celts, this hymn reflects the popular recognition that Catholicism is not an indigenous Breton religion.

The symbiosis that Croix and Roudaut point to between Catholic and pre- or non-Christian religious traditions in Brittany can clearly be seen in the local consensus in La Feuillée on the meaning of the terms *croyant* and *croyance*, believer and belief. These terms are used to refer to belief both in the tenets of orthodox Catholicism and in phenomena which, from the church's point of view, fall under the rubric of superstition, such as ghosts, witchcraft, and premonitory experiences. These less orthodox aspects of the supernatural will be discussed in greater detail in Chapter 9. Here it is important simply to reaffirm what was mentioned in Chapter 1, that from the believer's perspective the distinction between popular or folk religion and Catholicism may be of little relevance. Freeman (1978:120–122) underlines this point, observing that in Spain and other European contexts religion frequently involves strong personal faith in facets of the supernatural which lack official church sanction.

Calendrical Festivals

The fusion of Catholic and pre- or non-Christian elements in Breton religion is particularly evident in three calendrical festivals celebrated in La Feuillée, all of which are associated with the dead. The first of these, Toussaint, or All Saints' Day, discussed more fully in Chapter 8, coincides with the festival of Samhain, November 1, celebrated in Celtic areas of the British Isles until the early twentieth century. Samhain marked the beginning of the winter season prior to the adoption of the Julian calendar in Ireland and other Celtic regions (MacNeill 1962:1, van Gennep 1953:2810). Van Gennep speculates that the survival of the festival in France may have facilitated the acceptance of the Catholic Toussaint and Fête des Morts (All Souls' Day, November 2) during the Carolingian period. He cautions, though, that documents attesting to the continuity of pre-Christian rituals associated with November 1 are lacking for the period between the sixth and thirteenth centuries (van Gennep 1953:2810). Bonfires were one of the characteristic elements of Samhain celebrations in Celtic areas of the British Isles. Van Gennep (1953:2810–2811) cites only two cases of bonfires associated with Toussaint in France and suggests that this absence of evidence does not favor the hypothesis of a linkage between the two festivals. However, a possible connection involving fire not noted by van Gennep may be found in Breton Toussaint customs of the nineteenth century. Le Braz records that on the night of November 1, when the souls of the family dead were believed to return to the homes of their living relatives, "The fire is kept burning in the hearth by an enormous log, the log for the dead (*kef ann Anaon*)" (1928:2:80).

In La Feuillée Toussaint is the most important annual festival. It surpasses Christmas, Easter, and the New Year in terms of the level of preparation for the festival, the excitement it generates, and the numbers of people who return to the commune for the holiday. Whereas thirty-five or forty people attend Mass at Christmas and Easter, almost ten times as many attend on November 1. As a local schoolteacher comments, "Toussaint is the real family and religious celebration of the year. Christmas and Easter are religious festivals because *monsieur le curé* says they are festivals, and it is necessary therefore to do something, to go to Mass." That Toussaint is primarily a festival of popular, rather than official, religion is further indicated by the fact that it is the only one of the church's celebrations which does not alienate the anticlerical, who say that it is "for the dead, not really a religious festival."

There are two other calendrical festivals celebrated in Brittany that are not Celtic in origin but which unite Catholic and non-Christian elements in a process Delumeau (1977:166–167) has termed "folklorization." The first of these is the festival of Saint John the Baptist (*la Saint-Jean*). Celebrated on June 24, this festival falls close to the longest day of the year. For this reason many researchers during the nineteenth and early twentieth centuries postulated that it was related to pre-Christian summer solstice rites.

Van Gennep (1949:1734, 1896–1899, 1929–1931) systematically disputes that connection. Nevertheless, he cites numerous customs associated with this festival indicating that June 23 and 24 were traditionally considered to have an exceptional, almost magical potency, that could be both auspicious or dangerous. In many parts of France, plants collected on June 24, as well as the dew that fell on this day, were held to possess a special power. Likewise, it was thought to be a propitious day for the discovery of treasure (van Gennep 1949:1734–1735, 1963). Although the early church forbade the association of any Christian saint with the "theory of lucky and unlucky days" known to the Romans, van Gennep suggests that the folk, "however, have conserved this theory to our times" (1949: 1734, 2001).

Formerly throughout Brittany, as in certain other regions of France, St. John's festival was marked by bonfires on the evening of June 23. In van Gennep's view this custom is not related to veneration for Saint John. Rather, it represents the addition to the saint's festival of a practice foreign to Christianity (1949:1743, 2082–2084). In Brittany, as in other regions of France, the post-Tridentine church attempted to co-opt the festival and control its popular, "superstitious" aspects (Delumeau 1977:177–178). Until recently in La Feuillée and many other Breton communities, the Saint John's eve bonfire, or *tantad*, was lit by the parish priest, a representative of orthodox Catholicism.

According to Breton folk tradition, the festival of Saint John was, like Toussaint, a time when the Anaon was believed to draw especially close to the world of the living (van Gennep 1949:1730). After the living members of the community dispersed, it was said that the spirits of their ancestors returned to warm themselves around the embers of the *tantad*. Prayers were recited around the fire and stones thrown into its midst or placed beside it for the returning souls to use as seats (Le Braz 1928:2:72–74). Plouguerneau residents recall that nine rocks were placed in a circle around the perimeter of the *tantad*, although it is not specifically stated that these were provided for the dead.[5] The association between Saint John's

---

5. The custom of providing stones for the spirits to use as seats is recorded as early as the seventeenth century (Le Braz 1928:2:73–74). In Plouguerneau it is also remembered that when the Saint John *tantad* was burning low, two types of plants were passed through the flames. One of these, *armoise* (artemisia), was then passed

Day and the dead is also recognized in the Spanish Basque country, where Masses for the souls are offered at this festival (Douglass 1969:68, 79).

Many communities in interior Brittany continue to light their *tantad*, either on Saint John's eve or on the night of the festival itself. This tradition is particularly important in La Feuillée, since Saint John is the patron saint of the parish, and the annual *pardon*, or saint's day festival, is held on the following day. Formerly bonfires were lit in every *quartier* of the parish on the night before the festival. In 1983, however, only the *bourg* and one other *quartier*, Ruguellou, prepared fires. Ruguellou residents note with pride that the custom has continued uninterrupted in the *quartier*, "even during the Occupation." Despite the small crowd present, several people danced the local *gavotte des montagnes* to tape-recorded music around the *tantad*.

It is remembered in Ruguellou that in previous generations, ashes left over from the Saint John's eve fire were collected and mixed with soil in the village gardens, "for good luck and to make things grow." This practice was also known in Plouguerneau. Similarly, in Ireland cinders from bonfires prepared at the festival of Saint John were also spread in the fields to ensure an abundant crop (Haddon 1893:359). Le Braz (1928:2:75) notes that in parts of the Kernev the ashes of the *tantad* were collected and sold by auction. The buyer was said to be protected from death throughout the coming year. At Carnac, in southern Brittany, charcoal and ashes were conserved from these fires to protect both people and livestock from misfortune (Le Braz 1928:2:75n). A woman from Ruguellou recalls a parallel practice: her grandmother made a point of keeping a piece of charcoal from the *tantad* in a niche at the back of her chimney in order to ward off thunder. It is perhaps signifi-

---

over the eyes to ensure good eyesight. The other, *orpin* (stonecrop), was passed over the lower back in order to prevent back pain. One or both of these plants was known in Plouguerneau as *louzaouenn Sant Yann*, "Saint John's herb." Elsewhere in Brittany, related practices were denounced by members of the clerical hierarchy as "superstitious" during the seventeenth century (Croix 1981:1196). Another folk belief recorded by Le Braz (1928:2:74) concerning *louzaouenn Sant Yann* is not recalled in Plouguerneau. According to Le Braz, the herb was passed through the flames of the *tantad* nine times and then taken home, where it was placed in an upright position behind a piece of furniture such as the armoire. If the top of the plant bent down as it dried out, this was taken as a sign that the person who had gathered it would die during the coming year. All these customs concerning herbs are linked to the auspicious quality popularly attributed to June 23 and 24.

cant that salt was kept in that same place in most rural Breton households prior to World War II, to protect it from moisture. The Saint John's eve charcoal and salt possess similar symbolic significance as tokens of fertility (Jones 1923). It is probable that the protective and regenerative power of ashes and charcoal from the *tantad* derives from the association between the fire and the souls of the dead.

The third religious festival that provides evidence for the assimilation of unorthodox practices into Catholicism is Rameaux, or Palm Sunday. According to van Gennep, the rites associated with Rameaux are the product of convergence between Catholic and popular traditions (1947:1159). As noted in Chapter 3, those who attend Mass on Rameaux bring sprigs of boxwood to be blessed. Pieces of the plant are later placed in the home. Until recently, in La Feuillée and the surrounding district a branch of blessed boxwood was also placed in every grainfield to ensure a good harvest, as well as in stables and farm outbuildings for "good luck." In 1983 at least one elderly woman from La Feuillée continued to hang a sprig of blessed boxwood in the stables of her son's farm. Others from the Monts d'Arrée place boxwood twigs in their gardens. In addition, it remains current practice to make a pilgrimage to the cemetery, where small branches of the blessed plant are placed on the family tombs or stuck into the ground beside them.

Ostensibly the custom of blessing boxwood branches at Rameaux commemorates the palm fronds strewn in Christ's path on his entry to Jerusalem one week before the Crucifixion. Yet this does not explain why the plant is placed in fields and stables. Several features of the Rameaux ritual suggest that it is an agrarian festival celebrating the renewal of vegetation in the spring that has been integrated into Catholic tradition. In the first place, boxwood is evergreen and thus symbolic of regeneration and the continuity of life. In the second place, the festival falls at the beginning of the growing season. A proverb collected in La Feuillée makes an explicit link between Rameaux and the harvest, at the other end of the agricultural cycle:

> *Pa vez brav da venniget ar beuz*
> When the weather is fine for the blessing of the boxwood,
> *e vez brav da zaspugn an eost*
> It will be fine for the harvest.

As the elderly in La Feuillée recall, in the past the boxwood was blessed outdoors, at Saint Houardon's chapel. During the ceremony the congregation would observe carefully the direction from which the wind was blowing. The direction was taken as a prognosticator for the weather throughout the coming growing season: the weather would be good if the wind was blowing from the peaks of the Monts d'Arrée, but if it came from the west, a poor season was indicated.[6] This belief is clearly linked to the practice of placing boxwood in the grainfields to ensure a good harvest. Another feature of the ritual which implies a connection with fertility and increase is the traditional emphasis on having numerous children present at the Rameaux Mass. Finally, as noted in Chapter 3, the placing of the blessed boxwood in the cemetery and its use at *veillées mortuaires* suggest a concern with immortality and the regeneration of the dead.

In La Feuillée the curé is clearly aware of the unorthodox quality of the faith which motivates his parishioners to participate in the church's ritual at Rameaux. Remarking that attendance at Mass is always high at Rameaux, he explains, "They come in order to get divine protection. The boxwood is like a good-luck charm." Similarly, a woman from the parish observes, "They go for the boxwood. At base, they are believers." Once again the ambiguity of the concept of belief is underlined. Another strongly Catholic La Feuillée woman expresses disdain for those who rarely attend Mass but do so on Rameaux for the sake of the boxwood, or who request their churchgoing neighbors to bring them a sprig of the blessed plant: "For people like that, half Christian, half pagan, the little bit of boxwood is all there is to religion."

The dead have an important place in the celebration of Rameaux at La Feuillée. Those who for some reason, such as illness or absence from the parish, were unable to clean their family tombs at Toussaint do so for Rameaux. On the afternoon of the festival many small groups of people can be seen visiting the cemetery to place boxwood on the tombs. In certain parishes, such as neighboring Loqueffret, the Rameaux Mass itself terminates with a procession to the cemetery. This tradition of honoring the dead at Rameaux is not unique to Brittany, however. As Zonabend (1980:

---

6. Similar beliefs are noted by Lambert (1985:33) for the Morbihan.

218) points out, Rameaux rivals Toussaint as a festival of the dead in Burgundy. This observation holds true as well for Normandy. There, in addition to placing boxwood on the tombs, families decorate them with flowers.[7]

Comparisons between Brittany and other regions of northern France thus reveal a similar unorthodox, non-Christian concern for the dead embedded within Catholicism. Zonabend quotes a priest from Burgundy who complains: "For me, this whole region has never been Christianized; they are ancient Gauls. Look at Catholicism—it's a religion of life, and here there is nothing but the cult of the dead. . . . Even Rameaux has become the festival of the dead. They put the branches on the tombs. The church is full only for that festival and for Toussaint and for funerals" (1980:220). What, then, makes Brittany unique? Croix and Roudaut argue that the special intensity and success of the symbiosis between the church and Breton folk religion, as well as the longevity of this relationship, set the region apart from its neighbors. Whereas other regions shook off the domination of the church much earlier as a result of dissatisfaction with its emphasis on death, in Brittany this very feature struck a harmonious cultural chord, at least until the mid-twentieth century (Croix and Roudaut 1984:208–209, 217–218). Moreover, Croix and Roudaut argue that the history of the church in Brittany is more than a regional nuance in the history of French Catholicism in general: here "the faithful maintain a real cultural autonomy, at least in the realm of death" (Croix and Roudaut 1984:222).

Folk Rituals for the Dying

For Croix and Roudaut, the "autonomy" of Breton Catholicism is most clearly apparent in the proliferation of ossuaries and the elaboration of rites associated with them in Lower Brittany (1984:58). It is also evident in Breton folk rituals to aid the dying. Unlike the Catholic rite of extreme unction, which was directed toward the salvation of the dying person's soul, these rites sought to relieve

---

7. See also Gueusquin-Barbichon (1981), and van Gennep (1947:1188–1192), who notes that the custom of placing foliage blessed at Rameaux on tombs is recorded from several regions of France but is not widespread.

the physical agony of death and to shorten the process of dying (Croix 1981:944–946; Croix and Roudaut 1984:38–41). Significantly, the same types of concerns that inspired such rites during the nineteenth century and earlier periods persist in contemporary Brittany. For Marie-Thérèse and many other elderly people in La Feuillée, the process of dying itself is a greater source of anxiety than the possibility of an afterlife in which divine Judgment might condemn one's soul to eternal suffering.

Several of the Breton rites to aid the dying described by nineteenth-century folklorists do not make use of Catholic symbols. These rites have parallels in other regions of Europe, and they probably derive from pre- or non-Christian folk religious traditions. Other related rituals depend for their efficacy upon access to places, personages, objects, or prayers established as sacred by the Catholic church.

From a man living in the vicinity of Scaër, Le Braz records that "when a dying person has too much difficulty in passing over to the other side, there is an infallible means of abridging his agony: that is to get him out of bed and make him place his bare feet on the bare earth. No sooner does he make contact with the earth than the influences that held his life in the balance will be broken" (1928:1:101). An identical practice is reported from nineteenth-century Scotland, where it was held that one could not die so long as one rested on a bed with a pillow or quilt containing the feathers of wild birds. The same belief is recorded from Ireland and Cornwall (Le Braz 1928:1:101n). Christiansen (1946:25–26) cites its existence in Scandinavia, Germany, and Russia and suggests that the idea that feathers of certain birds prolong the agony of dying may be a later addition to the belief in the efficacy of contact with a bare earth floor, which was probably known in Roman times.

A second folk practice to aid the dying which bears no overlay of Catholicism was reported from Quelven, in Morbihan (Le Braz 1928:1:101n, see also Croix 1981:921–922; Croix and Roudaut 1984:39). Here a circular granite stone, known as the *mel beniguet* or *mell benniget*, "blessed mallet," was placed on the head of a dying person to shorten his or her suffering. The custom of breaking a spindle over the head of a person experiencing a difficult death, which existed in Scotland at the same period, may be related to the *mel beniguet* (Le Braz 1928:1:101n).

Other rites to assist the dying differ from the two just described only in that they incorporate elements of the sacred as defined by orthodox Catholicism. M. Le Grall, aged seventy-two, remembers that when he lived next to the chapel at Quilliou in Plonévez-du-Faou as a boy, he frequently saw people come to the chapel to practice what he describes as a form of "supernatural euthanasia." He explains, "At that time there were no painkillers, and there was no money for medical help. If it was obvious that someone was going to die, it was better that they die quickly." When the agony was prolonged, a neighbor of the sick person would be sent to light a candle in the chapel at Quilliou. No special prayers were required, and no saint's aid was invoked; the act of lighting the candle was sufficient in itself. After lighting the candle, the neighbor would remain in the chapel for a time, then extinguish the candle and return home. "And by the next day the person would have died," M. Le Grall recalls. Similarly, he recounts that Saint Diboan, whose statue was housed in the chapel of Saint Clair at Plonévez-du Faou, was invoked in that chapel when people in the area were suffering their final agony, or in the rich metaphorical idiom of the local Breton, "plowing their last furrow" (*ober e dalaroù*).

According to one tradition, Saint Diboan was believed to ease the pain of the dying. His name means "without pain." Le Braz records that near Gourin "they go for the dying to the chapel of Saint Min. . . . In this chapel there is a statue of Saint Diboan" (1928:1:101). There, however, a form of divination was practiced to discover whether or not the dying person would live (Le Braz 1928:1:102). In other areas, such as the vicinity of Kergloff, Masses were offered to Saint Diboan after a death, to ease the sufferings of the soul of the deceased in purgatory. It should be noted that Saint Diboan, as one of the many local saints in Brittany, is only marginal to Catholic orthodoxy.

Other practices involved recourse to more central figures in the Catholic supernatural hierarchy. An informant from Plouénan provided Le Braz with the following description of a rite performed for the dying in the Léon:

> When a person is gravely ill and without hope of a cure, ten young girls from the neighborhood make a procession to the closest chapel of the Virgin to ask Christ, through the intercession of His Mother, that the sick person be delivered from his agony without delay. Nine

of these young girls walk as a group, each one carrying a rosary, and they repeat the prayers without stopping all along the way. They are forbidden to exchange a single word, either among themselves or with any passerby. Only the tenth girl, who follows them at some distance, is allowed to answer the questions of those who, on seeing this procession pass by, wish to know for whom it has been organized.

(1928:1:100)[8]

Le Braz offers another example in which gestures and objects decreed sacred by the church are co-opted to unorthodox ends. Describing the entourage of a dying person, he notes: "One generally does not wait until he has rendered his last breath or totally lost consciousness before lighting at his bedside a 'blessed candle'; and as soon as he enters his final agony, the sign of the cross is traced above his face with this candle. This is done, it is said, to facilitate the separation of body and soul" (1928:1:100). In other words, this ritual was performed to abridge the dying person's suffering.

A conversation with Alice Laot, a middle-aged woman in the La Feuillée area, reveals the persistence of the attitude underlying the rites described above, an attitude that certainly predates the collectors of the nineteenth century who recorded these customs to aid the dying. The hallmark of this attitude is a solicitude to shorten the physical agony of the moribund by using elements of Catholicism in ways that differ widely from the church's intentions. Alice, who runs a small farm in an isolated village, described how her mother lingered in a coma for a week before her death. A neighbor suggested to Alice that the curé be summoned. The curé performed the rite of extreme unction. Yet, dissatisfied, Alice exclaims contemptuously, "She didn't die any more quickly; she suffered just as long." In her view the ritual was ineffective, for it did not hasten the death of her mother or ease her physical pain. The meaning ascribed to the ritual by Alice and her neighbor diverges sharply from that recognized by the church.

One could argue that the rites to aid the passage of the dying—along with other aspects of Breton religion, such as the proliferation of sacred fountains with curative properties—are Christianized versions of earlier institutions. Alternatively, one might hypothesize that at least certain such customs developed well after Catholicism

---

8. See Croix and Roudaut (1984:38–39) and Croix (1981:944–945) for discussion of comparable *neuvaines* and rites involving Saint Diboan.

had been implanted in Brittany, perhaps as the expression of a worldview that remained constant over time despite the introduction of a new faith. However, one can only speculate about such questions, because the strong symbiotic interpenetration of folk and official religious traditions in Brittany makes it difficult to distinguish Catholic elements from those that are pre- or non-Christian.[9] In the words of Croix and Roudaut, "Death at the heart of Breton culture, death at the heart of Breton Catholicism, and religion in Brittany particularly well embedded in everyday life: these are the terms of a particularly solid and coherent triptych" (1984:11). In order to understand how the Catholic vision of death and definition of the sacred gained such acceptance in Brittany, it is essential to survey the history of the Breton missions.

The Missions

Throughout Catholic Europe from the mid-1500s, the Council of Trent set in motion a program of reform aimed at regularizing religious practice, "purifying" religion of its "superstitious" elements, and educating the rural masses in the articles of the faith (Bossy 1970; Delumeau 1977). In Brittany the effects of the Counter-Reformation did not make themselves felt until the mid-seventeenth century. It was at this period that a large-scale campaign of missions took shape throughout both rural and urban sectors of the region. The broad outlines of the impact of the Counter-Reformation on the religious life of European Catholics have been traced by Delumeau (1977), who argues that prior to the reforms initiated by the Council of Trent, the average Catholic in Europe had only a limited understanding of the faith. In Delumeau's view it was not until the Counter-Reformation that the rural European peasantry and urban proletariat were effectively Christianized (Delumeau 1977:161). Concurring with this point of view, Croix (1981) and Croix and Roudaut (1984) have delineated the process of Christianization as it occurred in Brittany.

As Delumeau points out, traveling missionaries were ubiquitous in Catholic Europe during the Tridentine period, and it was in France that these "itinerant messengers of the faith worked most

9. See Croix and Roudaut (1984:208–209).

zealously and above all most methodically" (Delumeau 1977:189). Within France the effects of the Counter-Reformation missions were greater and more long-lasting in Brittany than elsewhere. This success is partly the result of idiosyncratic factors, such as the peculiar dynamism of some of the early Breton missionaries. Moreover, Lower Brittany in particular was especially well preadapted to the new discourse of the seventeenth-century church, centered as it was on death. The new style of predication emphasized fear of damnation and the torments of hell, whereas promise of salvation had tempered preaching on eschatological themes in earlier periods (Croix 1981:1241; Croix and Roudaut 1984:91).

The missions of the seventeenth century represented a campaign by the church in Brittany to impose its own definition of the sacred and to ensure that the sacred was respected. In so doing, the church sought to expand its control over rural Breton society. Prior to this period, Catholicism in Brittany had been "a religion of liberty," imposing minimal constraints on the behavior of the faithful and requiring little instruction in the articles of the faith (Croix and Roudaut 1984:101). Laxity on the part of the laity and the clergy, including the drunkenness and sexual promiscuity of clerics, although denounced by the church hierarchy, was largely tolerated (Croix 1981:1162–1168).[10] The discourse of the sixteenth-century church in Brittany, as in other regions of France, was concerned with death but did not focus undue attention on themes of mortality and damnation; nor did it seek to terrorize (Croix 1981:1177).

Like their counterparts elsewhere in Europe, sixteenth-century Bretons of the rural and popular classes were only superficially Catholic (Delumeau 1977:161). Levels of church attendance were low and comportment in church differed little from that in secular settings such as the tavern. Drunkenness and fighting were not uncommon during religious offices, and while the priest celebrated Mass, those in the congregation used the occasion to conduct business affairs, eat, or converse with acquaintances. Dancing regularly

---

10. The weakness of the pre-Tridentine clergy was by no means unique to Brittany. Delumeau (1977:154–161) points out that drunkenness, concubinage, and ignorance of Catholic doctrines were endemic among priests throughout Europe prior to the Counter-Reformation, particularly in rural areas. These problems were augmented by the widespread failure of priests to reside in the parishes to which they had been assigned.

took place in the church at festivals, and on certain occasions, including Toussaint, it was common practice for the faithful to spend the night in the church, talking and playing games (Croix 1981:940, 1179–1183).[11]

As in other Catholic regions of Europe, in Brittany the teachings of the Counter-Reformation church were calculated to enhance religious spirituality as well as to enforce respect for ritual and for the role of the priest (Delumeau 1977:161, 179, 189, 194–199). In the context of the Breton missions, the clergy campaigned to close taverns and shops on Sundays and holidays in order to generate respect for the Mass. Such efforts met with resistance from the rural masses, who valued church rituals but did not share the same conception of the sacred as the predominantly urban ecclesiastical authorities who had been influenced by the Counter-Reformation. To increase the authority of parish priests, the clerical hierarchy sought to widen the gap between clergy and laity. New prohibitions were introduced preventing priests from becoming godparents and thus involving themselves with lay persons through relationships of fictive kinship (Croix 1981:940, 1179–1183, 1192–1193, 1198).

The seventeenth century missions added a new dimension of fear to the preexisting familiarity with death in Brittany. The church manipulated fear of death and damnation in a form of psychological coercion to enforce the post-Tridentine model of correct religious comportment. Seventeenth-century preaching differs from that of the previous century in that the theme of death is reinforced, particularly through fear. Hell is depicted in more graphic, realistic terms, and the prospect of damnation is not tempered by that of salvation. A new insistence on the imminence of death appears in inscriptions on ecclesiastical monuments, as well as in predication. Although these changes distinguish sixteenth-century from seventeenth-century church discourse throughout France, Breton culture was particularly receptive to the new emphasis on death (Croix 1981:1183–1186; Delumeau 1977:193).

During the seventeenth century the church's efforts in Brittany to define and elevate the sacred domain are apparent in the increased numbers of orders to repair dilapidated church buildings,

---

11. Parallel practices existed throughout Catholic Europe at this period, as Delumeau (1977:197) points out.

emanating from pastoral visits at this period. Likewise, the enclosure of cemeteries and the construction of ossuaries were attempts by the church to enhance the sacred status of the dead and to cast relationships with them in terms of a new idiom of respect (Croix 1981:1095–1105, 1192).

Seeking to extend its authority, the seventeenth-century church embarked on a program of moral reformation which focused on dancing and pre- or extramarital sexual activity. These sins were frequently depicted in the missions as leading to certain damnation. The church's condemnation extended to all collective festivities not directly under its control. The moral program of the missions was accompanied by a strong emphasis on religious education (Croix 1981:1194–1195, 1200–1202; Croix and Roudaut 1984:92, 94–98).

Under the direction of the most influential early missionary, the Jesuit Maunoir, catechism classes were given prominence both within the context of missions and in the normal course of parish affairs. The sacraments of confession, Communion and marriage were to be denied to those not knowing their catechism, as was the right to be a godparent. Learning the catechism required a level of effort and discipline which at first provoked discontent among the faithful. To make religious education more attractive, Maunoir instituted a system of prizes for the best students (Croix 1981: 1206–1211; Croix and Roudaut 1984:100–103). The importance of catechism class has continued to be an integral feature of Breton religious practice to the present. Many middle-aged and older people in Plouguerneau and La Feuillée recall with pride the prizes they won as children in catechism class. In the present generation it is still considered important for children to learn their catechism and to "take their Communions" even if they cease to attend Mass once the period of instruction has been completed. As Croix and Roudaut (1984:102) assert, from Maunoir's time, "To learn one's catechism was henceforth to mean something in Brittany."

In addition to the catechism, hymns were developed as an alternative means of instruction, all the more potent because they required active participation by the faithful. The thirty-nine "Canticou spirituel" composed at this period by an associate of Maunoir continued to be used until after World War II. In Breton rather than Latin, and hence understandable, these texts were additionally appealing in that they were set to the music of seventeenth-century popular songs (Croix 1981:1202–1204; Croix and Roudaut 1984: 98–100).

With the exception of Michel Le Nobletz, the earliest and in some ways least effective Breton missionary, all of the early missionaries were Jesuits. After 1650 the Capuchins began to conduct some missions, and the Lazarists worked in the Trégor following 1674. These last two orders, however, were never as influential as were the Jesuits under Maunoir's leadership (Croix and Roudaut 1984:112).

The early missionary Michel Le Nobletz merits some discussion in the context of the present study, on account of his connections to the community of Plouguerneau. Le Nobletz was born in 1577, the son of a noble family in the Plouguerneau hamlet of Kerodern. He trained for the priesthood in Bordeaux and Agen, and was ordained in Paris in 1607. After spending a year as a hermit near the chapel at Saint-Michel on the coast at Plouguerneau, Le Nobletz started to preach as a missionary more or less independently in the Trégor in 1608, as well as in Plouguerneau, at Landerneau, and especially on the islands of Ouessant, Molène, and Batz, off the northwest Breton coast. After 1614 he began to conduct missions in Cornouaille, notably at Douarnenez, where he stayed between 1617 and 1639. Following this period he returned to the Léon, where he worked in Le Conquet, near Brest, until his death in 1652. Le Nobletz worked alone, never traveling with more than one companion. These early efforts, carried out in isolation until approximately 1630, and for the most part in larger centers rather than in the countryside, had limited impact (Croix 1981:1212; Croix and Roudaut 1984:93, 112–113). Moreover, Le Nobletz's mysticism hindered the effectiveness of his preaching on the popular level (Croix 1981:1230; Croix and Roudaut 1984:129).

The tradition of small-scale missions was carried on after 1640 by Julien Maunoir at the beginning of his career. However, in 1650, Maunoir started to organize teams of priests to assist him with his missionary work. These priests, who soon numbered roughly a thousand, served in their regular parishes while not engaged in the missionary enterprise. Thus, the spirit of the missions and their goals were perpetuated outside the actual context of the mission (Croix 1981:1214–1215; Croix and Roudaut 1984:114). Maunoir himself was an efficient organizer and an indefatigable preacher.

In the forty-three years prior to his death in 1683, he conducted 439 missions. This effort touched almost all the parishes of Cornouaille, as well as many in the Léon, Trégor, and the western part of the diocese of Vannes. He made frequent visits to the parish of Plouguerneau in honor of his predecessor, Le Nobletz (Croix and Roudaut 1984:113). Maunoir's energy makes the efforts of other contemporary missionaries pale by comparison, and in part explains why the seventeenth-century missionizing activity of the church was to have a greater and more lasting impact in Lower Brittany than in Upper Brittany and other regions of France (Croix 1981:1215–1217; Croix and Roudaut 1984:119). In Upper Brittany the principal missionary work was carried out by the Lazarists, who conducted only sixty-two missions during a fifty-six year period starting in 1645. Similarly, the founder of the Montfort Fathers, Grignion de Montfort, who worked in Upper Brittany between 1706 and 1710, conducted only twenty-six missions in a highly localized area (Croix and Roudaut 1984:137, 141).

The success of Maunoir's missions also stems from the fact that Maunoir, born in a non-Breton-speaking region, on the border between Upper Brittany and Normandy, took the trouble to learn the language of those to whom his preaching was directed. He thus set a precedent for later missionaries working in Lower Brittany: all those unable to speak Breton were required to master the language. This use of the local language is an additional reason for the greater influence of the missions in Lower Brittany relative to other areas of France (Croix 1981:1220; Croix and Roudaut 1984:120).

Not only did Maunoir realize the importance of preaching in Breton, but he also understood the need to tailor the content of his predication to the local cultural milieu. Although one of the goals of the missions was to purge Breton religion of its "superstitious," non-Christian elements, certain of these provided tools for effectively communicating the church's message. Maunoir sometimes interpreted church doctrines in ways that bordered on the unorthodox, to gain the acceptance of his auditors (Croix and Roudaut 1984:119). Following the precedent set by Le Nobletz, Maunoir attracted a following by the promise of miraculous cures. His preoccupation with the power and artifices of the devil, an important theme in his sermons, resonated with his listeners, who shared similar concerns. In some communities the missionaries were even believed to be sorcerers or werewolves, so closely did their methods and speech resemble those of such unorthodox folk representatives of the supernatural (Croix 1981:1221–1222; Croix and Roudaut 1984:122). It was, however, the importance of the related themes of death and concern for the dead in Brittany which provided the missionaries with their greatest local asset. Taking account of the important position of the Anaon in Breton culture, Maunoir made the welfare of the souls central to his predication. His biographer, Boschet, writes: "Long experience had taught the Father that the Bretons were not only good friends but also good relatives, and this tenderness of feeling did not end with the death of those whom closeness of blood or a reasonable fondness had bound them to love" (Boschet, quoted in Croix 1981:1232). Boschet's statement applies equally well to relationships between the living and the dead in twentieth-century Brittany, as will be seen in Chapter 8.

Maunoir skillfully organized his three-week missions so that the central focus of the last day was the Communion for the dead. In this way he was able to maintain an intensity of enthusiasm and a high level of attendance to the end of his stay in each parish. By consecrating the final Communion to the dead, Maunoir realized that more people would seek to receive the sacrament and its prerequisite of confession (Croix and Roudaut 1984:131–132). Like Le Nobletz, Maunoir wrote his sermons with the assumption that the most effective subjects for touching his audience and securing conversions were those relating to death and the afterlife. In order to reinforce the immediacy of these themes, Le Nobletz had made dramatic gestures with startling "special effects," such as presenting a skull wearing a blond wig styled in the latest fashion to a repentant noble as a memento mori. Likewise, Maunoir gave graphic descriptions of the torments of hell which are reputed to have reduced his audience to tears (Croix 1981:1231–1233; Croix and Roudaut 1984:130–131).

The use of visual images, the *taolennoù* or *tableaux*, added to the force of such predication. First developed by Le Nobletz and refined by Maunoir, the *tableaux* were to become a central feature of religious instruction within the context of missions in Brittany for the next three hundred years. Painted on pieces of sheepskin approximately fifty by ninety centimeters in size, Le Nobletz's early *tableaux* are highly mystical in their symbolism and difficult to interpret. Intended for use with only a few spectators at a time, they are filled with numerous small, complex figures. The difficulty of explaining these *tableaux* to a mass audience prevented Maunoir from relying on them to any great extent (Croix 1981:1222, 1224). However, it was probably he who introduced the classic set of *tableaux* that served as the model for those used into the twentieth century. These classic *tableaux*, examples of which date from the eighteenth century, were probably adapted from books of pious images known as the *Miroirs des âmes*, or Mirrors of the Souls, which were popular at the end of the Middle Ages (Croix and Roudaut 1984:187).

Like Le Nobletz's earliest *tableaux*, the later series emphasized the representation of sin, death, and hell over a more optimistic eschatological vision. The *tableaux* were part of a program of predication promoting "salvation through fear" (Croix and Roudaut 1984: 191). In one series of *tableaux* widely used during the nineteenth and early twentieth centuries, the devil appears in ten of the twelve images. The theme of death recurs in two of these same twelve *tableaux* and in two of another series of four portraying the end of the world (Croix and Roudaut 1984:192).

The *tableaux* used in the twentieth century are painted on rectangular canvas scrolls, with approximate dimensions of one and a half by three meters. They were designed to be suspended in the church during the mission. The intense colors of the oils in which the large, clearly visible images are painted adds to their potency, which Breton author Pierre-Jakez Hélias vividly evokes in recalling a mission from his childhood:

> The words of the preaching went through our heads in one ear and out the other without leaving a trace. . . . But the *tableaux*, they were something else. Hard as we tried to shut our eyes tight, our eyelids were no sooner joined than they would spring open again, and the successive images of our destiny would strike us like so many punches, the most terrible being the first. That night and during yet a good many more, these images were multiplied in vivid, stirring nightmares, of which nothing remained at dawn but the smell of sweat and the desire for contrition.
>
> (1975:144)

The series of twelve *tableaux* modeled on the medieval *Miroirs des âmes* portrays the inner state of the sinner through the device of a heart surmounted by the head of a man or woman. Within the heart seven animals are depicted, each symbolizing one of the deadly sins (see fig. 10). The pig represents gluttony; the goat, lust; the viper, envy; and the peacock, pride. These *tableaux* evoke repentance, the process of conversion, and the state of the righteous soul. Other images in this series document the possibility of relapse into sin and its consequences: death, Judgment, and hell. A second possibility, that of perseverance in righteousness, is also represented. Nevertheless, even in those *tableaux* concerned with the life and death of the righteous person, the danger posed by the devil remains omnipresent. In the final *tableau*, depicting purgatory and paradise—the destiny of the righteous after death—purgatory occupies the greater space on the canvas (Croix and Roudaut 1984:187–188).

Indeed, the torments of hell and purgatory are always more graphically depicted than the pleasures of heaven. The *tableaux* representing hell are replete with flames, demons, and serpents. Likewise, in a twentieth-century *tableau* depicting the death of a sinner, one devil confronts the dying man with a book inscribed with the records of his misdeeds, while another demon pulls him by the leg into the waiting fires. A woman dressed in red—obviously of dubious morals—blocks the figures of the priest and guardian angel, who are incapable of saving the sinner at this late hour (see fig. 11). The companion *tableau* showing the death of a righteous man is, by contrast, lackluster. The moribund recites his rosary before the priest. Gray-clad, sober family members pray at the bedside as a pallid guardian angel motions the devil, here only marginally visible in the corner of the *tableau*, to keep his distance. Similarly, in the *tableau* that portrays the Last Judgment it is the fate of the damned, pushed by demons with pitchforks into the flames of hell, which catches the eye, rather than that of the elect.

Certain of the later *tableaux* contain elements of political commentary, such as one dated 1939, in which the figures of Marx, Lenin, Trotsky, Stalin, and Hitler appear in hell.[12] Another, dating from the 1920s, condemns a worker carrying a red flag on which

---

12. For the church, the alliance between Germany and Russia signed by Hitler and Stalin linked the forces of "atheist Bolshevik materialism" and "Nazi neo-paganism" against the "Christian West" (Lambert 1985:187).

the words *Ni Dieu ni maître,* "Neither God nor master," are inscribed (Croix and Roudaut 1984:204).

Although the seventeenth-century missions in Lower Brittany did not achieve their immediate goal of eliminating drunkenness, witchcraft, "superstitions," and dance, they did have a long-term effect on the Breton clergy, including both missionaries and parish priests. Partly as a result of Maunoir's efforts to include regular parish priests in his missionary teams, a lasting missionizing spirit was generated among those who preached on the local level (Croix 1981:1214–1215; Croix and Roudaut 1984:167–168, 173). This missionary approach remained characteristic of the Breton clergy until the mid-twentieth century. Moreover, the respect for the authority of the priest and for the sacred as defined by the clergy which was inculcated among lay people in Brittany through the missions also persisted (Croix 1981:1243). These attitudes were reinforced by the more recent missions, which retained Maunoir's typical methods of predication based on the use of *tableaux,* instruction in the catechism, and insistence on the theme of death (Croix and Roudaut 1984:175). Such preaching was on occasion carried to excess: the diocesan archives describe the case of a Plouguerneau woman so overcome with despair after attending a mission in that parish in 1836 that she committed suicide by throwing herself into her kitchen fire (Le Gallo 1980:1035).

Twentieth-Century Missions

In the twentieth century the Jesuits, Capuchins, Montfort Fathers, and Oblates of Mary Immaculate were the orders that, together with the parish clergy, conducted the majority of missions in Lower Brittany. In theory, a mission of three weeks' duration was required by the diocesan headquarters every ten years in each parish of Finistère. As recently as 1946, thirty-six parishes, or one in nine, hosted a mission. The hiatus caused by World War II appears not to have affected the level of missionary activity, for a comparable number of parishes—thirty—received missions in 1937 (Croix and Roudaut 1984:185–186). In a rural milieu with few entertainments, the missionary priests filled an almost theatrical function (Croix and Roudaut 1984:191). As people in Plouguerneau and La Feuillée recall, the prospect of a mission in one's parish was a "real event."

Many middle-aged and older people in both Plouguerneau and the La Feuillée area have vivid memories of the mission *tableaux*. These souvenirs are tinged with a mixture of fear and humor. Significantly, the figure most frequently alluded to in conversations about the *tableaux* is "the devil with his horns." This is an image now regarded as quaint and faintly humorous, suggesting continuity with earlier attitudes: as Croix and Roudaut (1984:49) note in reference to the sixteenth century, "the devil . . . makes one afraid, indisputably, but he also makes one laugh, or at least smile."[13]

An elderly couple in Lilia, on the Plouguerneau coast, recount that the woman whose face surmounted the heart in the series of *tableaux* portraying the inner states of the soul was nicknamed Marjonig, or Little Mary-Anne (fig. 10). In their childhood homes the chimneypiece and the box bed, or *lit clos*, were decorated with pictures resembling the *tableaux*. Their dreams, like those of Hélias, were haunted with these images. Such pictures were probably purchased as souvenirs of a mission, in the same way as one could purchase a small booklet by Abbé Balanant, a renowned missionary, with reproductions of the *tableaux* and an interpretive text in Breton (Balanant 1899). Images similar to the *tableaux* were also used in catechism instruction probably as late as the 1960s in certain poor, isolated parishes. Published in the format of a large book known as the *Catéchisme en images* or as a set of cards approximately sixty by forty-five centimeters, such devices were used in other parts of metropolitan France as well as in Brittany.

Even the young have been marked by the eschatological vision popularized by the missions. A twenty-four-year-old La Feuillée man claims to have seen *tableau*-like pictures, particularly those of the devil and hell, in his own catechism class. So does a woman in her early thirties from Landéda, in the Plouguerneau area. A thirty-two-year-old woman from Plouguerneau recalls seeing *tableaux* from the "Mirrors of the Souls" series. Another woman, aged

---

13. In Breton folk tradition the devil is often given diminutive names that suggest a rather affectionate, mocking familiarity, such as Polic (Little Paul), or Cornik (Little Horned One). He is frequently portrayed in legends as a rather slow-witted individual, easily tricked into letting escape the souls he seeks to ensnare. See, for example, Le Braz (1928:2:312–315). This popular image of the devil contrasts with the more frightening one advanced in the teachings of the post-Tridentine church (Croix 1981:1074).

twenty-four, whose family lives in the heart of the strongly Catholic Léon, remembers that her parents owned a picture similar to the mission *tableaux* in which the devil was graphically depicted. After her childhood misdemeanors, her grandmother would point to the picture of the devil and admonish her, "Don't be like *that!*" The young woman still retains the memory of this picture and the emotions of horror and repugnance it evoked for her at the time.

Despite the humorous reaction that some of the images from the *tableaux* now provoke and the amazement expressed about the dramatic changes in the church's discourse over the past thirty years, the dominant theme of discussions with contemporary Bretons about the missions are fear and death. Even priests remark that "it used to be a religion of terror. It was high time for a change."

Discussing a mission from her youth in Kernilis, near Plouguerneau, fifty-seven-year-old Louise Vaillant recalls that one day was set aside for the deceased, "to encourage people to think about death." The congregation was told by the officiating priest: "You have only to listen closely and you will hear your dead relatives asking you for your prayers at the mission." Similarly, Croix and Roudaut (1984:192) describe a mission held at Lampaul-Ploudalmézeau, also in the Plouguerneau area, in 1946, at which a model tomb was set up in the chancel of the church during the days leading up to the day reserved for the dead. That day itself was typically marked by the recitation of the names of those who had died in the parish since the preceding mission, followed by a benediction of the tombs and a sermon on eschatological themes delivered in the cemetery (Croix and Roudaut 1984:192). A sister of Louise Vaillant from Kernilis, Léonie Ronvel, remembers that at the end of each mission, it was said that *le bon Dieu* would choose one very pious person from the parish, who would die and go directly to heaven. This was considered to be one of the *grâces,* or indulgences, connected to the mission. Léonie recalls that in 1944 an aunt whom she remembers as a very devoted Catholic died directly after a mission in her parish. "She was very, very religious. I used to think she was saintly. The only songs she sang were hymns, and she talked about God all the time." Léonie speculates that it was her aunt who became the recipient of the mission's *grâce* on that occasion.

Plouguerneau residents remember that missions in their parish were often held after the harvest, in October, when farmers were free to absent themselves from work in the fields. The mission consisted of three week-long sessions. One week was devoted to the children of the parish. The two adult sessions enabled family members to alternate between household or farm work and attendance at the mission. The rigor of the predication is particularly well remembered. A different missionary was assigned to preach on each of the three eschatological themes of heaven, hell, and purgatory. Not surprisingly, hell was the most vividly portrayed, with the aid of *tableaux* showing "the devil with his horns and his fork." As Corentine, a seventy-year-old Plouguerneau seamstress recalls, "People were more frightened in those days. That's why they were more religious."

A reserve of fear continues to motivate religious behavior in Plouguerneau, particularly among the elderly. Annick, a widow in her mid-sixties, reminisces that "at the missions, they used to tell us to pray for the souls in purgatory." The parish priest suggests that the number of Masses given for the dead in contemporary Plouguerneau, as well as the importance placed on *huitaines* and *messes d'anniversaire*, is partly a by-product of such predication and the fear it induced.

Missions continued to be held in Plouguerneau up to the early 1960s. However, after the mid-1950s, the "classic" style of mission developed by Maunoir, with *tableaux*, Communion for the dead, and numerous, lengthy sermons, was discontinued. The general trend at this period involved a move away from the earlier *foi du charbonnier*, or unreflective faith, toward a more intellectual approach to religion and a greater concern with defining a Catholic role in the processes of economic development and social change that began following World War II. This spirit is reflected in the formation of the Jeunesse Agricole Chrétienne and in related forms of Action Catholique. The last missions were organized around the formation of small discussion groups, which could continue to meet and become involved in the Catholic social movement after the mission was over.

In La Feuillée, where the level of religious adherence has historically been low relative to that of Plouguerneau, the last mission took place in 1926. Prior to that the most recent mission in this parish had been held in 1899, after a gap of twenty-three years (*Semaine Religieuse* 1899:716–717). The 1926 mission is remembered for the "violence" of the preaching of the père Yvon and his assistant, the père Tugdual, who conducted the event, and for the *tableaux* with their representations of "the devil with his pitchfork. Certainly, it was frightening!" The mission climaxed with a procession throughout the *bourg* of La Feuillée, in which the men of the parish carried the huge wooden statue of Christ on the cross which is now housed in the parish church. In several *quartiers* small booths representing the stations of the cross were set up, and the procession traced the *via crucis*. This mission left a permanent marker on the landscape of the parish—significantly, in the cemetery, through the erection of the large granite *calvaire* that overlooks the tombs on either side and the town below. Some households in La Feuillée still display crucifixes bought as souvenirs at the mission of 1926 or at the one held in neighboring Botmeur in 1933.

The conclusion of the mission of 1926 in La Feuillée was celebrated with a large bonfire. Each *quartier* was required to supply a certain amount of wood, symbolizing the sins of its inhabitants, which were to be purified through the fire. Apparently, however, not all of the parish's sins were burned. The report of the mission in the diocesan newsletter notes with pride that 681 women, 371 men, and 116 children in this parish of 1,591 souls received Communion (*Semaine Religieuse* 1926:346). One wonders about the other 423 inhabitants, many of them men with undoubtedly left-wing and republican sympathies.

The history of the missions has also left an imprint on folk tradition. In Plouguerneau, on the coast at Saint-Michel near the small chapel where Michel Le Nobletz is reputed to have lived as a hermit, a rock formation with a chairlike depression is said to be the place where he would sit and meditate, gazing out to sea. Close by, the elderly remember the point at which a stream used to emerge between the rocks. Here Le Nobletz apparently procured his drinking water. In the past, water from this stream was sought for its curative qualities, and those with foot ailments would come there to bathe their feet.

In La Feuillée too, the missions have contributed to folklore that continues to be transmitted to succeeding generations. Among the most potent images of the *tableaux* is that of "the two roads," one of which leads to paradise and the other to the torments of hell. One of Le Nobletz's early *tableaux* depicts the different roads that the righteous and the sinner follow through life (Croix 1981:1225–1227,

Plate 187). This theme was taken up again during the nineteenth century and in a mission *tableau* commissioned in 1936 (Croix and Roudaut 1984:175; Croix 1981:Plate 194). The nineteenth-century *tableau* shows a winding, narrow path leading uphill to heaven at the summit of a mountain in the center of the picture. It traverses a series of steps marked with words naming the Christian virtues, including obedience, humility, frugality, and work. To the right and left of the mountain, the other road—broad, flat, and easy to follow—divides into two branches. Each leads to the same destination, hell, where the travelers are greeted by demons bearing pitchforks. In a striking example of continuity, a La Feuillée grandmother commented in 1984 that every night at bedtime, her three-year-old granddaughter demands to hear the "story of the two roads": "Every night it has to be the same thing. I can't change it the slightest bit. I tell her about the narrow, difficult road that leads to heaven and the wide, easy one that ends up in hell."

Conclusion

Over time, Catholicism in Brittany has acquired a distinctive character through its association with unorthodox popular religious traditions concerning death. Some of these traditions, such as belief in the Ankou and the depiction of hell as a cold place, may be Celtic in origin, although they also have analogues in non-Celtic regions of Europe. The symbiotic relationship between Catholicism and folk religion in Brittany is further illustrated by popular nineteenth-century rites to ease the suffering of the dying, which manipulated Catholic symbols in an unorthodox fashion. In contemporary Brittany as in the past, the three most important calendrical festivals are Toussaint, Rameaux, and the festival of Saint John the Baptist. All of these celebrations combine Catholic with non-Christian elements, and all three are associated with the dead.

As the folk-religious traditions discussed in this chapter indicate, Breton culture during the seventeenth century was particularly receptive to the predication of the post-Tridentine church, which centered on death and the afterlife. Partly for this reason, the missionary efforts that began during the seventeenth century made a lasting impression in this region. In Brittany, as in other parts of Catholic Europe, the Counter-Reformation discourse on death and damnation provided a weapon that enabled the church to enforce its program of reform. With the missions the church introduced a new element of fear into Breton Catholicism, particularly with respect to hell (Croix 1981:1251–1252).

The work of Le Nobletz and Maunoir provided the foundation for an ongoing program of missions in Brittany which endured until the mid-twentieth century. Interviews with people from contemporary Plouguerneau and La Feuillée show that a reserve of fear concerning the afterlife and a preoccupation with death remain, particularly among the elderly, as a legacy of the missions. By elaborating on a preexisting cultural theme, Catholicism, through the missions, consolidated and heightened the importance of death as a central concern in Breton society.[14]

In Brittany and throughout Catholic Europe, the Counter-Reformation introduced discipline and conformity into religious practice by insisting on religious instruction, regular attendance at Mass, and the importance of receiving the sacraments. Moreover, by campaigning against the community-based popular rituals that had typified medieval Catholicism, the Counter-Reformation attempted to enforce an individual rather than a communal pattern of religious response (Bossy 1970:62). As the following chapter suggests, in Brittany this effort was only partially successful. Neither did the post-Tridentine church in Brittany succeed in eradicating earlier systems of folk eschatology. Instead it relied on them to increase support for its own agenda. However, as Bossy (1970) has argued for Europe more generally and as Croix (1981) suggests specifically for Brittany, the Counter-Reformation created a climate of discipline among the rural masses and submission to a definition of orthodox behavior determined by external representatives of dominant classes and institutions. In so doing, post-Tridentine Catholicism, like its Protestant counterpart, helped to bring about the change in *mentalités* which was a necessary precondition for the development of capitalist society (Bossy 1970:70; Croix 1981:1252–1253; Schneider forthcoming).

---

14. The Spanish Basque country is another European region where death has been shown to be a predominant cultural theme. There its importance is likewise seen as a result of the continued reliance by the church on post-Tridentine styles of predication, which emphasize death, damnation, and the afterlife (Douglass 1969: 209). Elsewhere in Spain, missions similar to those in Brittany fostered fear of a wrathful God well into the twentieth century (Christian 1972:98; 1981:264).

7

Religion and Death II
Faith and Anticlericalism in the Nineteenth and Twentieth Centuries

Starting with the seventeenth-century missions of Le Nobletz and Maunoir, the church in Brittany was able to maintain the same eschatological discourse with little variation over a three-hundred-year period. We have seen that the importance accorded by Catholicism to death reinforced the Breton cultural preoccupation with this theme. The interplay between traditional Catholicism and responses to death in Brittany is examined further in this chapter, with a focus on the relationships between the church and community identity, as well as on the social power of the clergy and the anticlericalism it provoked. Local variations in responses to Catholicism are also discussed, along with contemporary patterns of religious observance and present-day beliefs about the afterlife in Plouguerneau and La Feuillée.

Da Feiz Hon Tadoù Kozh— The Faith of Our Forefathers

In his comprehensive study of changing patterns of religious practice and belief in Limerzel, a community in the Morbihan, Yves Lambert (1985) outlines the main principles of traditional Catholicism in this region. Although Limerzel is located in Upper Brittany, many of Lambert's observations apply equally well to the situation in Lower Brittany. According to Lambert, prior to the 1950s Breton Catholicism was primarily oriented toward the afterlife. The church taught the necessity of saving one's soul and avoiding eternal damnation. Liturgy, ritual, and catechism instruction emphasized the idea of sin. A sense of guilt was instilled among the faithful and reinforced by the depiction of God as an omnipotent, omniscient

Judge who punishes those who break His laws. The clergy manipulated fear of hell and purgatory as a moral sanction. The doctrine of the Fall portrayed the human condition as sinful. Only through observing the church's commandments, receiving the sacraments, and resigning to suffering during one's earthly life could one expect to achieve salvation after death. The universe was conceived to be the battleground between God and Satan, and the division between good and evil was believed to extend from the moral domain to the social and political fields (Lambert 1985: 355-356).

As Lambert observes, this was a religion of fear. However, it also offered reassurance, through the absolution obtained after confession, the possibility of accumulating indulgences to shorten one's penance in purgatory, and the opportunity of soliciting the intercession of the saints or the Virgin Mary in times of trouble (Lambert 1985:356). Moreover, although the Catholicism of this period was directed toward the otherworld, it also offered the faithful the promise of success in the present life by teaching that God aids the righteous (Lambert 1985:218). Finally, the church was able to account for the existence of evil through the doctrine that tragedies are sent by God to chastise, and ultimately redeem, those who suffer; future happiness would compensate for poverty and suffering in the present life (Lambert 1985:356-357).

Lambert's study underlines the ritualistic character of Catholicism in Brittany through the 1950s. The church emphasized that the observance of specific rites was necessary for salvation. These included regular attendance at Sunday Mass, recitation of the rosary, and abstinence from meat on Friday. Catechism instruction was also ritualistic, consisting of a set number of questions and responses to be memorized. In all aspects of ritual, "rigorous execution counted for more than the inner state of mind" (Lambert 1985:68). The fact that religious observances were conducted primarily in Latin both added to their ritualistic character and hindered comprehension for the majority of parishioners.

Use of Latin also contributed to the elevation of the sacred above the everyday realm of the believer. This distinction was reinforced through the size and architectural elaboration of the church and the richness of ecclesiastical material culture, including the crosses, chalice, monstrance, and ornaments used during religious celebrations. The high social status of the clergy, together with their education, special dress, and celibate lifestyle, also increased the distance between the sacred world of the church and the profane one of the congregation (Lambert 1985:68). A concomitant of this separation was the establishment of a hierarchy of obedience, both within the church and between the clergy and the laity, which was maintained partly through the church's insistence on a strict moral code (Lambert 1985:69). The clergy represented their role as indispensable to the orderly functioning of society, for without religion, morality was inconceivable (Lambert 1985:85).

As in the Limerzel depicted by Lambert, the nightly family prayers, the tradition of crossing oneself each time one passed a roadside *calvaire,* and the importance of regular attendance at Mass demonstrate the ubiquitous influence of religion in daily life up to the mid-1950s in Plouguerneau and, to a lesser extent, La Feuillée. Even the bread that was a staple of the rural diet served also as a token of the faith. Before cutting into a new loaf, one would trace the sign of the cross on its underside with the tip of the knife. This rite is still observed today in certain households. Thoughts of death and the afterlife were equally omnipresent. At New Year's, a festival generally associated with happiness and new beginnings, the traditional greeting in La Feuillée contains a reminder of the hereafter:

> *Bloavezh mat a souhetañ deoc'h*
> Happy New Year I wish to you:
> *Yec'hed ha prosperité*
> Health and prosperity,
> *Hag ar baradoz da fin ho puhez*
> And paradise at the end of your life.[1]

According to the religious instruction that boys and girls in the parish received, the "end" could be imminent. Learning their catechism, children repeated the phrase "We know not the day nor the hour [i.e., of our death]." A La Feuillée woman in her fifties recalls the words of an elderly neighbor which echo the catechism refrain:

> *Bezañ prest atav da rentañ un ene vat da Zoué*
> Always be ready to render a pure soul to God.

---

1. Numerous La Feuillée residents over the age of fifty remember greeting their neighbors with this formula on New Year's Day during their childhood.

She comments, "That is really true. One must be ready to die at any time, because one doesn't know when one will die." Similarly, a fifty-eight-year-old Breton priest remembers that evening prayers in his home included one to Saint Joseph, patron of *ar marv mat*, "the good death." "Life was shorter and more precarious in those days," he reflects. "You spent more time preparing for your death."

Although the predication of the church was centered on the otherworld, its rituals performed important this-worldly social roles. Prior to the 1960s, Sunday Mass in most rural Breton communities represented the major social gathering of the week. It is remembered that "we used to point with scorn at people who did not attend Mass." In the past, the Sunday High Mass was one of the few occasions on which practically the entire community assembled in the same place. For this reason it lent itself to the publication of newsworthy events. As noted previously, the town crier, or *embanner*, would announce information of importance on the church steps or in the cemetery following the religious service. The Mass also provided the community with a forum in which its social categories could be displayed. In Plouguerneau, for example, certain elite families had their own reserved seats in the church. Among these were the local nobles, the de Poulpiquets, who had the right to a lifetime place in the raised gallery area of the church. The mayor and his deputies had special seats in the chancel next to the curé. Gender differences were also expressed through seating arrangements, with men occupying a block of seats at the front right-hand side of the church and women sitting on the left and at the back. Although men and women increasingly tend to sit together in the Plouguerneau church, especially married couples with young children, these gender-specific seating patterns are maintained to some extent.

As recently as the late 1960s, attendance at Mass in Plouguerneau was almost universal. Those from farms recall that family members would alternate each week, some attending the Low Mass at 8:30 A.M. and others the High Mass at 10:30 A.M. Those who attended the earlier service would return to do the basic farm chores. The others, who ostensibly had the day off, were expected to return to church for vespers later in the afternoon. Sunday, the only day of rest, was given over to religion: "All our Sundays, ruined with *le petit Jésus!*" remarks one woman, with humorously irreverent hindsight.

The church represented practically the only source of recreational activities in rural Brittany before the 1960s. Attendance at Sunday Mass or vespers provided the opportunity to meet friends in the cafés or bistros near the church and to do one's shopping in the *bourg*. Likewise, the annual parish patron saint's festival, or *pardon*, was an important social event, particularly for the young. In Brittany, as in the southern European contexts described in Christian (1972), Freeman (1968), and Riegelhaupt (1973), such festivals gave the parish an opportunity to reaffirm its distinctive identity in opposition to neighboring communities.

In pre-World War II Brittany, religion was also the most important vehicle for the expression and display of aesthetic emotions, through the architecture and ornamental embellishment of the church, through its music and processions, and through the popular artistic displays it encouraged at festivals such as the Fête-Dieu, Corpus Christi day, when roadways were decorated with designs made of flower petals (Lambert 1985:36, 227).

Together with its other temporal functions, the Catholicism of the past provided Bretons with a source of supernatural patronage in times of difficulty. Saint Anne, the mother of the Virgin Mary, and Saint Yves, patron of lawyers, are traditionally the two most important Breton saints. Even today, the shrines of Saint Anne d'Auray in Morbihan and Saint Anne la Palud in southern Finistère remain sites of large annual pilgrimages. Older fishing boats in the coastal hamlets at Plouguerneau often bear a small statue of the Virgin, placing their owners under her protection. Assistance from a saint entails reciprocity, and the interior walls of many Breton churches are decorated with votive plaques expressing thanks to the local patron saint for such things as cures, the safe return of family members from war, and the birth of healthy children. The chapel of Saint Margaret in Collorec, twenty-five kilometers south of La Feuillée, was an object of special pilgrimage for women, because Saint Margaret is the patroness of women in childbirth. At the *pardon* of Saint Margaret, those women troubled by sterility were counseled to follow the procession around the chapel to enhance their likelihood of becoming pregnant. As recently as the 1950s, women experiencing a difficult pregnancy would promise Saint Margaret to attend her *pardon* should their pregnancy terminate successfully.

Social Influence of the Church

The traditional social power of the Breton clergy has been compared to that of the church in Ireland and Poland or in pre-1960s Quebec (Croix and Roudaut 1984:222). In rural areas, challenges to clerical ideology were rare. The political message of the clergy, based on the idea that all temporal power is ordained by God, was one of submission to civic and familial authorities (Croix and Roudaut 1984:200–201). The interests of the curé in maintaining the status quo in society were often closely related to those of the local nobility and the upper peasantry, or *juloded*, as this class was known in the Léon (Croix and Roudaut 1984:197–198). A Breton prayer attributed to the *juloded* expresses the concerns of this class to maintain a God-given social order:

> Ha lavarom bremañ eur bater hag eun ave
> And let us now say a Pater and an Ave
> Da c'houlenn ar c'hras
> To ask for the grace:
> D'ar paour da baouraad
> That the poor get poorer,
> D'ar pinvidig da binvidikaad
> That the rich get richer,
> Ha da bep hini da chom en e renk
> And that each one stays in his rank.
> (Le Gallo 1980:82–83)

In the Léon the boundary between spiritual and temporal power was extremely poorly defined. The clergy was able to maintain its social power because of the parishioners' interest in death and fear of the afterlife (Croix and Roudaut 1984:211, 222). As Le Gallo (1980:1031–1032) points out: "Clerical despotism was inseparable from a predication in which the most frequent resort was terror, in particular that of the Last Judgment." It is remembered in Plouguerneau that local priests frequently exerted their control through the women of the parish, who attended confession regularly and could thus be coerced to bring their menfolk under the church's authority through fear that absolution would be withheld.

The relationships between religion and social class were especially evident in Plouguerneau. Religious observances in the parish served as the occasion for the manifestation of class distinctions. These were most apparent in the system of classed weddings and funerals. However, wealthy Plouguerneau families were also entitled to seats of honor in the church, and certain of the banners and statues carried in the parish processions were reserved for those sufficiently affluent to own the local costume and to contribute a substantial sum of money to the church for the honor of participating in the procession. Those chosen to carry these statues and banners were named during the High Mass, along with the sums of money they had donated. The *pardon de saint Michel*, held in Plouguerneau at the end of June, provided a further opportunity for the conspicuous display of wealth. This *pardon* features a procession in which the *petits saints* are carried. These are polychrome wood statues of saints approximately forty-five centimeters high, which are attached to the end of three-meter-long poles (see fig. 12). Until the 1960s, the right to carry each of the twenty *petits saints* was sold to the highest bidder. Certain saints were bought year after year by the same families in a spirit of competition, with people paying a high price to carry a particular saint simply in order to prove that they were rich enough to do so. Other buyers were motivated by the desire for the patronage of a specific saint. The owner of the local bus company, for example, would buy the right to carry Saint Christopher every year.

While the style and content of its predication were the same in the Monts d'Arrée as in the Léon, the church was less successful at maintaining its position of social dominance in the former area. This was partly because of the poverty of the region, which was dominated by small independent landholders. Here there were few noble families and no *juloded* to uphold the power of the church. Poverty and historical factors in the Monts d'Arrée also encouraged the development of a tradition of egalitarianism and independence, which opposed the church's hierarchical ideology. The ability of the parish curé to serve as a broker with the outside world, and his tendency to favor supporters of the church in such transactions, is remembered with resentment in the Monts d'Arrée. A La

Feuillée mother in her seventies recalls that when her son left home to work in Paris for the first time, in the late 1950s, he did not receive the position he had initially hoped for with a major bank because the letter of reference he had requested from the parish priest cast doubts on his character, stating that "although his mother is a good Catholic, the father is not."

The social power of the clergy in Brittany prior to the 1960s was reflected in the success of the church at imposing its moral code upon the rural population. The moral program of the church was particularly rigorous with respect to sexuality. As Lambert points out, the church's stand on sexuality was in large measure a reflection of the social and economic realities of peasant household-based agricultural production (1985:138, 140). In such a system there was no place for divorce. Likewise, unwed mothers and illegitimate children were a burden on the household. Thus, the church emphasized chastity prior to marriage, stigmatized illegitimacy, and refused the sacraments to those who divorced. Within marriage, sexual activity not exclusively directed toward procreation was condemned. On occasion during the early twentieth century, absolution was refused to couples practicing birth control through coitus interruptus (Lambert 1985:133–135). As late as 1962, in parts of Brittany, there remained a high correlation between cantonal levels of religious practice and levels of fecundity (Lambert 1985:137).

Traditional Catholicism generated feelings of guilt and ambivalence with respect to sexuality which have not entirely disappeared in contemporary Plouguerneau and La Feuillée. Sixty-five-year-old Annick clearly recalls terrifying sermons at missions in Plouguerneau, when priests harangued the women in the congregation, exhorting them to have large families: "You must do your conjugal duty. Have children! Women who don't do their conjugal duty won't go to heaven!" Although Annick herself had only two children, many women felt morally obligated to have large families. While families of ten and twelve children, common up to the present generation, are now rare, some women in contemporary Plouguerneau continue to express a moral condemnation of birth control methods which has earlier origins than Pope John Paul II's pronouncements on this issue. The insistence of the missionaries on the necessity of performing the "conjugal duty" contrasted with their strict condemnation of sex outside of or prior to marriage. Guilt concerning sexual activity was induced through the confessional. As a neighbor of Annick recalls, with a certain bitterness, priests frequently refused absolution at confession, claiming, "There is something you haven't confessed! Come back tomorrow."

The advantages of numerous children for the agricultural household are clear: in addition to supplying labor, children were expected to support their parents during illness and old age. Nonetheless, the desire to avoid excessive subdivision of the family property provided a motive for limiting family size and led to conflicts with the church. A high rate of celibacy acted to minimize problems related to inheritance and property division (Lambert 1985:136, 140). Celibacy was indirectly encouraged by the church, both through the depiction of sexuality as sinful and through the provision of opportunities for religious vocations.

Many women from the Léon recount that they were strongly urged to become nuns by the local curé or by the sisters placed in charge of Catholic schools. Léonie Ronvel, in her early fifties, from Kernilis, recalls that after her confirmation, at age twelve, the sisters who taught her at school encouraged her to join their order. "Didn't you hear a voice inside you, telling you something at the moment of your confirmation?" she was asked. Not being of a mystical nature, Léonie maintained that she had heard nothing, and after a period of soul-searching decided that she did not have a vocation. However, the influence of the nuns continued to make her feel guilty and uneasy with respect to sexual relationships or the prospect of marriage. Now, middle-aged and childless, she regrets that she never married. Likewise, many of her contemporaries who entered religious orders are now abandoning the cloister.

The church's stance on sexuality was reinforced through fear invoked by a discourse stressing death, the Last Judgment, and the possibility of damnation. One can interpret this clerical campaign to curb extramarital sexuality and encourage high levels of fecundity as an attempt to conserve existing social institutions in Brittany and, in so doing, to maintain the church's position of social dominance. By promoting fecundity the clergy was able to ensure the reproduction of the peasant household-based agricultural system. Keeping the peasant family large also kept it relatively powerless. Large numbers of children limited the wealth of peasant families and prevented them from accumulating property over successive generations through judicious marriage alliances between single heirs.

To maintain the traditional agrarian social order—a goal the clergy shared with other elite groups in Brittany prior to World War II—the church also sought to control the influx of modernizing influences from metropolitan France. Books and newspapers or magazines expressing Socialist or Communist views were condemned from the pulpit as *influences mauvaises* (Lambert 1985:160). The clergy encouraged the use of Breton, a policy that worked to insulate the rural milieu from outside ideas that might have challenged both the church and other social and political authorities. Innovations such as film and radio were initially denounced by the clergy, as were the first steps toward agricultural mechanization and installation of modern household conveniences. All represented a threat to the clerical control of rural Breton society (Lambert 1985:113–115). The most intense of the church's campaigns against external influences was, however, waged against modern couple-dances, which were introduced during the 1920s. For the clergy these dances were an especially potent symbol of the threat to the traditional rural social order because of their sexual implications.

From Maunoir's time, the church in Brittany had adopted a position against *assemblées nocturnes* and the activities to which these were supposed to give rise, including dancing (Croix and Roudaut 1984:165). This position was to harden during the nineteenth and early twentieth centuries (Le Gallo 1980:1008). Plouguerneau women in their mid-sixties recall returning home from confession in tears because absolution had been refused them for dancing. Damnation threatened should they die unexpectedly without absolution. Likewise, in La Feuillée, after nearly sixty years, impressions of the priests who conducted the mission of 1926 remain clear: "The people who were leading the mission, they were madmen! All they could say was *kof à kof.*" The Breton words *kof à kof*, meaning "stomach to stomach," were used to describe the couple dances of the era.

The late 1940s marked the appearance of *dames en noir,* or "ladies in black," in various Breton parishes. One such apparition was frequently sighted in the La Feuillée area between the railway station at Locmaria-Berrien and the *bourg* of Poullaouen, a community noted as much for its anticlericalism as for its devotion to music and dancing. The "lady in black" was seen on a number of occasions, always in the same place, on evenings when dances were scheduled in Poullaouen. The young people had to face the fearful prospect of passing the "lady in black" on their way to the dance. After some time, a man with more courage than most of his peers attacked the so-called apparition, only to find that it was a baker from Locmaria in disguise. He had been paid by the local priest to "haunt" the road in order to discourage attendance at dances. By staging such apparitions, the clergy were able to use traditional fears of the supernatural to counterbalance the attraction of the new dances which, together with other aspects of modern popular culture, were invading the Breton countryside in the aftermath of World War II.

At times the emotions repressed by the church's campaign against sexuality and dancing appear to have surfaced within the church itself. One Plouguerneau woman claims she was dragged onto the ferris wheel at a local fair by the parish vicar, who was "locked up in the presbytery for a week afterward." Another story is told about a nun in the parish who was made pregnant by a priest. Both were swiftly removed from their offices and transferred to other parishes. Whether or not these stories are apocryphal is less important than the fact that they exist. Perversely, the church's former fervor with respect to sexual issues invites continuing speculation about possible sexual activities indulged in by the clergy themselves. As one La Feuillée man comments, "They make love too, whenever they get the chance!"

Contrasting Religious Traditions: The Léon and the Monts d'Arrée

As noted in Chapter 1, important differences in dialect, folk traditions, and politico-religious *mentalités* distinguish the Léon from the Kernev side of the Monts d'Arrée. The Léon has long been nicknamed "the land of the priests." This epithet has a strong basis in fact. As early as the seventeenth century, the average number of priests per parish in the Léon, at ten, was higher than in other dioceses throughout Brittany and France as a whole (Croix and Roudaut 1984:104). During the nineteenth century, 60 percent of the priests ordained in the diocese of Quimper and Léon came from the Léon, although this region accounted for only 43 percent of the diocesan population (Le Gallo 1980:83). Plouguerneau boasts a particularly large number of ordinations. Between 1803 and 1964 this parish contributed a hundred new priests to the ecclesiastical hierarchy. By way of contrast, the much larger and more prosperous parish of Fouesnant in the southern Kernev produced only two priests over the same period (Le Gallo 1980:83). In 1984 there remained thirty-eight living priests who were born in Plouguerneau, including one newly ordained. There are no living priests from La Feuillée. The most recent ordination from that parish took place in 1931. Plouguerneau represents a special case, even for the highly religious Léon. As the birthplace of both Michel Le Nobletz and Monseigneur de Poulpiquet, bishop of the diocese between 1824 and 1840, who strongly encouraged the recruitment of new vocations, Plouguerneau was "in some ways condemned to militant piety" (Le Gallo 1980:83).

Support for the church in the Léon was almost universal. It is said that "before the war [World War II], there wasn't a household in the Léon where you wouldn't find *le bon Dieu.*" In contrast, other regions of Lower Brittany, particularly the Trégor and the Kernev, never experienced the same unconditional acceptance of the moral program or the social power of the church. Many priests ordained from the Léon were unwilling to accept pastoral appointments in these regions, considering them "a land of exile." According to Le Gallo (1980:85–86), "The folklore of the presbyteries has conserved the memory of one priest who, unhappy at having been stationed in a parish on the Cornouaille [Kernev] side of the Monts d'Arrée, used to climb to the summit of Roc'h Trévézel to contemplate the saintly Léon extended at his feet, and begged the Lord to bring him as soon as possible into the Promised Land." Since the Roc'h Trévézel is located within the boundaries of La Feuillée, it could well have been this nineteenth-century priest's parish of exile.

In the past, clerical posts in the Carhaix area as well as in the Monts d'Arrée were held to be particularly undesirable, owing to the isolation and poverty of these regions as well as the *sauvage,* independent character of their inhabitants. Thus, the ratio of priests to population in these areas was low, at least according to early nineteenth-century sources, which probably document the continuation of an earlier trend. Moreover, many of the parishes in the Monts d'Arrée were populous and geographically extensive, making it hard for the understaffed clergy to respond to the needs of all their parishioners. These problems were compounded by the difficult terrain and inclement weather of the Monts d'Arrée, where fogs and heavy winter snowfalls are not unusual (Le Gallo 1980: 115–122). In addition to the physical difficulties and discomforts of running a parish in the Monts d'Arrée, the clergy objected to the festive nature of the local inhabitants and their openness to outside influences that represented a challenge to church doctrine (Le Gallo 1980:115, 1010). Parishes in the Monts d'Arrée were frequently without priests. The few resident clergy in the area were often of "mediocre quality," having been sent to the Monts d'Arrée as a punishment for misdemeanors committed in other parishes or because of character failings considered unacceptable in more "respectable" regions (Le Gallo 1980:121).

By the late nineteenth century the foundations for a strong tradition of anticlericalism had been laid in the Monts d'Arrée (Siegfried 1913:176–180). Contributing factors to this trend included the poor quality and inadequate number of priests in the region, the church's negative reaction to laws passed to strengthen the secular schools under Jules Ferry between 1879 and 1889, and the growing perception that the Communist and Socialist parties provided viable alternatives to right-wing, church-supported political representatives. Moreover, by the turn of the century, the secular state rather than the church was increasingly perceived in the Monts d'Arrée as a vehicle for social mobility. Many from the region escaped rural poverty by training to become civil servants or schoolteachers in the state school system. Indeed, if the Léon chose the church as the channel for the social advancement of its sons and daughters, the Monts d'Arrée chose the *école laïque*. La Feuillée provides a particularly striking example of this process. A supplementary course instituted in the La Feuillée state school enabled students to complete their secondary school degree without leaving the commune. This program was so successful that La Feuillée is reputed to have produced by the mid-twentieth century more certified teachers relative to its population than any other commune in France. During the interwar years many of these teachers and their families were alienated from the church because of its campaign against the *skol an diaoul,* or school of the devil, as the state education system came to be known.

Significantly, although Protestantism enjoyed little success in Brittany, one of the few regions where small Protestant inroads were made was the Monts d'Arrée. Protestant chapels were founded in the early twentieth century in both Poullaouen and La Feuillée, but the evangelizing efforts of their pastors made little lasting impact on these communities.

Rouges and *Blancs:* Contemporary Anticlericalism in La Feuillée

The anticlerical reaction provoked by the former social power of the clergy remains a characteristic feature of worldview in the Monts d'Arrée to this day. The anticlericalism of this region is basically linked to a perception that the church is aligned with the interests of the rich. The rejection of the church for its association with wealth and property does not necessarily imply a rejection of the idea of the divine. As one anticlerical La Feuillée woman explains, she believes that there is a God, but He is unrelated to the teachings of the church. She complains that "the curés are always too close to their money." As an example, she notes with resentment that she was asked to pay 350 francs for her mother's funeral Mass in addition to the 300 francs collected for Masses and services. It is the fees charged for rites of passage and the curé's annual *quêtes,* or door-to-door collections, which provoke the greatest criticism of the church in La Feuillée. During one week in May 1984, for example, there were four funerals in the community, two of which were held on the same afternoon. Despite the unseasonably cold weather, the curé did not turn on the heating system in the church, apparently to save money on gas bills. The congregation who sat in the damp, cold church commented later that the priest had amassed a goodly sum of money that week with the four funerals and their associated Masses and services. "This curé is just stingy," they complained. "He could have afforded to heat the church! Three hundred and fifty francs for the funeral Mass now! He certainly made his million this week!"[2]

2. Weber (1976:358) provides analogous examples of anticlericalism provoked throughout France during the late nineteenth century as a result of the fees charged by the clergy for performing funerary rituals.

The church's annual *quêtes* are another source of resentment. These were more onerous in the past, and those who criticize the contemporary *quêtes* do so partly in memory of childhood poverty and the difficulties experienced by parents and grandparents. In La Feuillée there were formerly three annual *quêtes:* the *quête de la moisson,* when the priest and sacristan collected grain from each household after the harvest; the *kest an Anaon,* or collection for the souls on the eve of Toussaint; and the *quête du beurre,* or butter collection before the *pardon* on June 23. The grain collected in the autumn was kept by the priest for his personal use or sold, as was the butter collected for the *pardon,* to raise money for the needs of the church. Explaining the bitterness with which the poor gave up their hard-won agricultural produce, an eighty-six-year-old woman recalls: "We used to think the whole harvest was going to the curé and the sacristan, little by little."

The *kest an Anaon* was discontinued in the 1960s, but both the *quête de la moisson* and the *quête du beurre* remain. Now, however, cash donations rather than contributions in kind are solicited. The curé himself visits each household for the autumn *quête,* and two women are delegated from each *quartier* in the parish for the *quête du beurre.* Households generally give between twenty and fifty francs at each collection. At the 1984 *quête du beurre,* 4,812 francs were raised. That same year the curé began his *quête de la moisson* in August, a month earlier than the traditional date, before the harvest had even been started and barely a month after the *quête du beurre.* It was rumored that the priest had changed the timing of the *quête* in order to take advantage of the fact that many émigrés from La Feuillée return to the parish in August for their summer vacations. This provoked the accusation that "the curé runs after money." While the *quêtes* are considered unjust, even by certain people who attend Mass regularly, local norms of generosity and unwillingness to be considered stingy make it difficult to refuse to contribute. However, according to supporters of the church, a number of households donate nothing, particularly in one hamlet they nickname "the village of the red devils" because of the *rouge* tendencies of its residents.

In a region where material well-being has traditionally depended on manual labor, the curés with their *quêtes* are seen as parasites who live by usurping the property of others. Commenting that priests could easily find paying jobs and support themselves without *quêtes*, one La Feuillée man contends: "They're just ordinary people like everyone else. And in addition, they're well educated." Education is commonly held to be a passport to lucrative employment, therefore it is considered immoral and lazy for priests to rely on collections for their support. Moreover, the fact that priests in the past were often the most educated people in the rural milieu made them an object of suspicion. They were accused of using their instruction to maintain themselves in positions of power, through both natural and supernatural channels. La Feuillée residents claim that "in the past, the curés used to lead the people by the nose."

The collections taken at Mass and at funeral services, like the *quêtes*, spark criticism of the clergy. Not all parishes have retained the custom of taking a collection at funerals, but in La Feuillée the priest justifies it: "Otherwise, the church would never receive anything, because people only attend Mass for *enterrements*." At special festivals such as the *pardon*, the priest often announces the use to which the collection money will be directed, such as to purchase new pews or to pay the church's heating bills. These announcements lead to comments like, "Why can't he pay for his own gas? We have to pay for ours. And he must have paid for the pews in the church five times over!" A particularly revealing criticism followed a collection made for the Catholic university at Angers: "The people there are rich. Nothing but the rich. Why is money taken from the poor to be given to rich people like that?"

Anticlerical sentiments in the Monts d'Arrée are most frequently voiced by those who define themselves as *rouge*, in opposition to the *blancs*, or supporters of the church. To some extent society in the Monts d'Arrée is organized around the cleavage between *rouges* and *blancs*. Yet these opposing categories do not have simply religious significance. Explains one man from the region, "Here religion is not just religion. There is a whole series of things that are connected to it." Religious practice is a means of classifying others. If a person attends Mass regularly, he or she will also likely vote *à droite*, for the political right. Moreover, the *blancs* are considered to be *les riches*. In contrast, the *rouges* are expected to vote for left-wing candidates and are represented as being the poorer members of the community.

Support for the Parti Communiste Français (PCF) gained ground in the Monts d'Arrée during the Resistance activities of World War II. The Resistance movement was especially strong in Berrien and Scrignac, the communes directly to the east of La Feuillée. While not all of the *résistants* were Communists, sympathizers of this party were dominant in the movement and its leadership. The assassination of Abbé Perrot, a priest in the Monts d'Arrée parish of Scrignac, by *résistants* in 1943 did much to polarize *rouge-blanc* animosity. Perrot, an ardent Breton nationalist, had been suspected of collaboration with the Germans, who had promised to create an autonomous Breton state. Forty years later the *blancs* of Scrignac, along with clergy and autonomists from elsewhere in Brittany, continue to attend an annual service commemorating the death of Perrot.

In the political realignment following World War II, former Resistance chiefs with Communist affiliations emerged as the new political leaders in the Monts d'Arrée. Municipal councils in the region have been dominated by PCF members from 1945 to the early 1980s. Over time the resistance has taken on the function of an "origin myth," sanctioning the Communist monopoly of political power in the Monts d'Arrée (Le Guirriec 1984; 1986:222).[3] Religious and political attitudes in the area have been passed down from father to son and are emblematic of individual and family identity. They may also have direct economic ramifications. Prior to the municipal elections of 1983, the commune of Huelgoat was led by a Communist mayor who had held office for thirty-eight years. Those without PCF membership cards reputedly found it difficult to obtain employment in municipally funded enterprises, such as the *maison de retraite*. Conversely, in the recent past a chicken abattoir in Plounéour-Ménez, a Léonard commune directly across the Monts d'Arrée from La Feuillée, is said to have refused to hire persons who had not been baptized.[4]

In addition to signaling left- and right-wing political affiliations,

---

3. Kertzer describes a parallel use of the Resistance (*Resistenza*) as a "sacred symbol" that serves as a "mythical charter of its moral superiority" by the Italian Communist party (Kertzer 1980:160; see also 31, 35, 157–162).

4. Le Guirriec (1986:225–229) draws a distinction between the orthodox communism of the national-level PCF and the "local communism" of the Monts d'Arrée which is preoccupied with issues arising from the regional social milieu—primarily the opposition between rich and poor agriculturalists. This distinction presents an interesting parallel to that between orthodox and local or folk Catholicism.

the terms *rouge* and *blanc* also denote, at least to some extent, two opposed lifestyles and systems of values. *Rouges* and *blancs* typically hold different opinions about death and the rituals surrounding it, as well as different eschatological beliefs.

For certain *blancs*, Catholicism, Breton identity, and respect for the dead, *le culte des morts*, are symbolically linked in opposition to what are perceived to be the antithetical values of the French Republic. This attitude bears the imprint of the ultramontane ideology of the nineteenth- and early twentieth-century church in France. Jean-Marie Trellu, a *blanc* from Loqueffret, south of La Feuillée, interprets the removal of cemeteries from around the church as a conspiracy on the part of the French state to undermine the heart of Catholic Breton culture, the ongoing relationship between the living and the dead. The Decree of Prairial Year XII, a law requiring removal of cemeteries from urban areas and *bourgs* for hygienic reasons, was passed, although not enforced, throughout France in 1804 (Ariès 1982:516–520). Although this regulation pertained to all parts of the country, Jean-Marie Trellu believes that its effects were particularly unjust in Brittany because of the more highly developed sense of respect for the dead in this region. He blames a former *rouge* mayor of the commune, a representative of the secular state, for the removal of the cemetery from the churchyard in Loqueffret during the 1950s.[5]

Many *blancs* feel that they possess a privileged, insider's understanding of the church, commenting, for example, that nonpracticing families will frequently take Communion at the funerals of relatives because "it looks good." The *blancs*, in contrast, argue that one should not take Communion unless one has first been to confession and received absolution.

The *rouges* take pride in similar symbols of their identity. Accustomed to being in the position of the poor or less powerful segment of society, they have developed a type of "reverse snobbery." A *rouge* member of a folk music group from a community south of the Monts d'Arrée remarks that the streetlights are always left on late in the *bourg* on nights when *blanc* groups have meetings or fes-

---

5. Significantly, nineteenth-century writers from other regions of France were similarly critical of the Decree of Prairial Year XII, interpreting it as an attack on Catholicism by the Republic (Ariès 1982:545–546).

tivals. Yet they never remain lighted for events sponsored by the *rouges*. "That doesn't matter," a fellow *rouge* responded. "We can see just as well in the dark!" In a related spirit, a *rouge* woman from the La Feuillée area observed that church attendance is not necessarily correlated with ethical conduct. In her view the *blancs* who attend Mass regularly are often those of least moral repute, "people who would seize any opportunity to stab you in the back." She concludes that they attend church frequently because they need to be pardoned for their many sins.

The *rouge* ethic of pride in spite of poverty continues to be transmitted to the younger generation. At the high school in Huelgoat a teenage girl from a bourgeois, churchgoing family, whose father owns a local business, made a derogatory remark about the way some of her classmates dressed. The daughter of a local PCF official retorted: "We can't all afford to dress the way we'd like to. Some of us wear what we have and make do."

Despite the ideological positions held by both groups, in La Feuillée it is not true that all *blancs* are richer than all *rouges*. Some supporters of the church come from poor families and have eked out a living working small parcels of marginally productive land. Similarly, certain *rouges* have made careers as civil servants or schoolteachers and have returned to La Feuillée on retirement with comfortable pensions. The economic discrepancy between the two groups appears to be more a symbolic than a substantive issue at present, at least in La Feuillée. Nevertheless, certain upwardly mobile *blancs* who have managed to leave the land and succeed in white-collar careers have greater social pretensions than their *rouge* counterparts. This tendency is evident in their style of dress, the furnishings of their houses, and the manner in which they entertain guests. Such people also consider themselves superior to those who have continued to pursue an agricultural lifestyle, especially *rouge* agriculturalists. One *blanc* woman, a former shopkeeper, categorizes all those who live in "the village of the red devils" as "savages," referring to their supposed lack of social graces, their politico-religious affiliation, and the fact that they make their living from the land.

Although *rouge* and *blanc* milieus are divided by radical differences in attitudes, social interaction in La Feuillée crosscuts the boundary between these two groups, while still preserving its existence. The animosity of the *rouges* is directed primarily at the rather vague categories of *les gros*—the rich—or *les capitalistes*, and at the church as an institution rather than at specific churchgoing individuals. Moreover, *rouges* and *blancs* alike share certain ethical values. Foremost among these is "simplicity," a character trait that refers to a person's openness and his or her willingness to interact socially without standing on ceremony or demanding the conventions of politesse accorded to *les messieurs* or *les grandes dames*. Furthermore, many *blancs* who attend Mass regularly complain to the same extent as the *rouges* about *quêtes* and the greediness of the curé. Conversely, the same *rouges* who berate the inherent laziness of the clergy readily concede that it is "sad" to see a parish left without a resident priest.

The La Feuillée priest is clearly aware of the ambivalent attitudes toward religion shared by many of his *rouge* parishioners. He remarks that "attendance at Mass doesn't say anything to them. They just let it slide. And yet they seem to have some kind of a faith. They are glad to have a priest here, to have religious services for their dead. The priest is very well accepted in the parish, but beyond that, *bien sûr*, they are negligent with respect to their religious practice."

As in the Portuguese case documented by Riegelhaupt (1984), in La Feuillée anticlericalism involves antagonism toward priestly authority and the refusal to practice religion in the fashion deemed appropriate by the church, but it does not necessarily imply the rejection of Christianity. This distinction is clear in one woman's comment that "people here believe in God, but not in the church." Many of the residents of the parish characterize themselves as "believers but not practicing Catholics." As one young La Feuillée woman contends, "There is not a single unbeliever in the commune. We have all been baptized and all of us have taken our Communions. People here are believers at heart." A Huelgoat woman echoes these sentiments, disputing the suggestion that many people from her parish are dedicated Communists: "I doubt that there are many true Communists in the Huelgoat area. Everyone has been brought up in the Christian tradition. Our generation and our children. Perhaps their children will not be. At base, people here are Christian. They believe in religion a little bit all the same, because they were raised in a Catholic milieu."

Eliane, an officer of the PCF committee in Huelgoat, maintains that it is not impossible to overcome the ideological contradictions between Communism and Catholicism: "To be truly Christian is to be Communist." Disharmony between the two philosophies arises, she believes, because "the *capitalistes* do not follow Christ's teachings," even though they may be strong supporters of the church. When asked whether she feels that the region is anticlerical, Eliane replies, "No, because, you see, in the face of death, we are believers at heart."

Nonreligious Funerals

Death and the rituals that surround it are the ultimate test of the strength of a person's anticlerical convictions. Whether through force of habit or a lingering belief that "maybe there is something" in Catholic doctrine, many *rouge* families choose religious funerals over the option of a civil burial.

The alternative to a Catholic funeral, the civil burial is a simple graveside ceremony. Mourners gather in the cemetery where a short speech or eulogy for the deceased is delivered, generally by a secular official such as a municipal councilor or the mayor of the commune. Civil burials, like religious funerals, are well attended. Even when the traditional ceremony has been rejected, attendance remains a reciprocal obligation that overrides politico-religious differences for the neighbors and associates of the deceased. Moreover, in La Feuillée it is noted that greater numbers of flowers are given for civil than for religious funerals. Unable to pay for Masses and services, the mourners seek an alternative expression of solidarity with the bereaved. At the end of the graveside eulogy, those present file past the coffin to pay their last respects to the deceased, throwing a handful of earth into the grave. This gesture recalls the blessing of the corpse with holy water at religious funerals. Earth, while lacking the regenerative significance of holy water, is a powerful Communist symbol, as the title of a local PCF weekly paper for agriculturalists, *La Terre*, indicates. At certain *rouge* civil burials, red roses are thrown on top of the coffin rather than earth. The significance of the color is self-evident.

According to their vision of reality, the *rouges* are the simple working people of the earth who have no need of the elaborate rituals of the church. As Pierrot, a *rouge* from La Feuillée scornfully states, "Religious funerals are worth nothing. The deceased would be better off going directly to the cemetery than having a bit of water thrown on top of him in the church." Significantly, Pierrot claims to be one of the few people in the commune who would insist on a civil funeral. While the majority of people in La Feuillée do not attend church, in Pierrot's view, "they have too much faith. The minute anything goes wrong, they run for the priest. It happens every time. At base, they believe."

In La Feuillée only one civil burial was performed between July 1983 and August 1984. Several others, numbering six or seven in total, took place in the neighboring communes. Even a longtime Communist municipal councilor and founder of the Resistance in the Monts d'Arrée, a generally acknowledged "enemy of the church" who had himself frequently officiated at civil burials, received a Catholic funeral. This ceremony, which sparked a great deal of social commentary, was in fact a compromise. After the priest performed a funeral Mass in the church, the blessing of the coffin took place exclusively in the cemetery, where a local Communist mayor delivered a eulogy. Many *rouge* comrades of the deceased attended only the second, secular section of the ritual. Some people contend that the funeral "should never have passed through the church." The deceased, Michel Quiviger, "would have turned over in his coffin had he known." Many blamed Michel's wife for requesting a religious service without regard for the convictions of her husband. Others recounted that Michel himself had stipulated that he should be buried according to Catholic ritual. Recalling the civil burial of Michel's sister some time earlier, a former neighbor of the family relates that Michel was very distressed. "That won't do, that just won't do," he apparently reiterated at the time. "We are not animals, after all."

Michel Quiviger's comment reveals the principal reason for the general aversion to civil burials, among both *rouges* and supporters of the church. To be buried civilly is to be buried like an animal. Many people echo this assertion, in both Plouguerneau and La Feuillée. A nonreligious funeral is *triste*, sad. It is equated with "burying a cat or a farm animal, like burying a dog." It is considered "too abrupt to go directly from the house to the cemetery, as if one were burying a beast."

These attitudes, which correspond to similar ones recorded by Lambert (1985:379) from the Morbihan, support Ariès's assertion that "the ritualization of death is a special aspect of the total strategy of man against nature" (Ariès 1982:604). Death, like birth and reproduction, is essentially a biological fact, common to all living creatures, human and animal alike. These natural occurrences are threatening, for they highlight the similarities among humans and other "baser" forms of life. They must therefore be brought safely into the domain of the cultural and given meaning. From the Breton perspective, the death of a human individual should not be a trivial event like the death of an animal. The funeral ritual makes death a cultural event and imbues it with significance. In contemporary Brittany the civil funeral is not generally conceived to possess the symbolic power of the Catholic Mass to elevate death from the natural to the cultural realm.[6]

At birth, Catholic ritual demarcates the boundary between nature and culture through baptism. Formerly the ceremony of churching or purification for new mothers, current in Brittany until the 1940s, performed the same symbolic role. Likewise sexuality is brought into the domain of the cultural through marriage. It is significant that consensual unions without marriage and failure to baptize children are characterized by some people in Plouguerneau and La Feuillée in the same way as civil funerals: "That is the way animals live."

For devoted Catholics, civil funerals are distressing because of the God-less worldview they imply. As one La Feuillée woman says, "Those who do not have the faith, who are buried civilly, they believe that after death that's the end, one is just thrown into the hole like a dog." Similarly, a Plouguerneau Catholic recounts the story of a woman from the commune who contracted cancer, ostensibly as a result of using contraceptive pills. Refusing to follow her doctor's advice, she remained on the pill and died within a year, leaving a husband and two young children. Her civil funeral was *triste:* "She had no religion and was buried like an animal." The details of this case may be partly the invention of local gossip. If this story is an item of folklore, it is not without significance, es-

---

6. Likewise, in northern Spain, William Christian (1972:139) was told: "Those who do not die in the grace of God die like animals."

pecially because the woman's death is attributed to contraceptive use. The puritanical tradition of the missions, the former insistence of the clergy on the moral imperative of women to perform their "conjugal duty," and the papal directives of the 1980s make birth control a particularly sensitive issue in Plouguerneau. It is therefore not surprising to see logical connections drawn among the use of contraceptives, death as implied divine retribution, and burial "without religion." It should be noted that civil burials in Plouguerneau are rare and are generally requested by people who were not born in the commune. One young woman from the Plouguerneau area now living in the Monts d'Arrée observed that she had never heard of the existence of nonreligious funerals before moving away from the Léon.

While practicing Catholics express an aversion to civil burials on the grounds of their faith, others choose a religious funeral "because it looks better." It is a more fitting tribute of respect for the dead than a civil funeral. As one La Feuillée woman expresses it, "The funeral should be the last honor for the deceased." The La Feuillée priest understands such concerns, reassuring the bereaved family on the eve of a funeral that "I will do my best tomorrow to make the ceremony dignified."

Although the Catholic funeral may no longer meet the needs of all contemporary Bretons, it still retains a greater symbolic coherence and power than the civil burial. Moreover, there exists at present no third option for those lapsed Catholics, atheists, or committed anticlericals who nevertheless wish to mark their passing in an honorable manner. For this reason the funeral Mass will likely remain for some time disproportionately important in Brittany relative to actual levels of religious practice. The Catholic rites of passage endure because *rouges* and *blancs* alike continue to feel the need for ceremonies with which to mark life-cycle transitions. The traumatic quality of death makes this need especially strong in the case of funerals. As Lambert (1985:365) observes, the fact that civil weddings have gained greater acceptance than civil burials indicates that for Bretons, death has remained more closely linked to the sacred: "And what could underline the extraordinary character of this ultimate event better than the sacred?"

The position adopted by many *rouges* on religious funerals is expressed by a retired schoolteacher in La Feuillée who has made her family promise to give her a Catholic funeral. She reasons that "I was baptized and married in church, and my death can pass through the church as well." This attitude is deplored by deeply committed, progressive Catholics who take an intellectual approach to the faith. In their view the value of the Catholic rites of passage has been debased because they have become customary. They resent the current situation, in which Christians and unbelievers alike are buried in the same way because of the lack of emotionally satisfying ritual alternatives. In the opinion of one priest in the Monts d'Arrée, "The Communists should die as they have lived. If someone has been an enemy of the church all his life, why should he be buried by the church? It's hypocrisy." Moreover, he notes that people are mistaken if they believe that the Catholic funeral ritual has some inherent efficacy for saving the soul of an unbeliever. The *rouges* tend to be more flexible in reconciling the contradictions between practice and political ideology. Explains one Communist party worker, with respect to funerals, "One is not Communist in all situations."

The persistence of support for Catholic funerals even among the *rouges* represents an instance of what Croix and Roudaut (1984:224) have termed "the rarity of radical questioning of the clerical model." In their view anticlericalism remains a "counter-church" which, rather than erecting revolutionary new structures of thought, operates within the structures previously established by the church itself. As the current lack of alternative, non-Catholic patterns of funerary ritual indicates, the clerical model continues to dominate worldview in contemporary Brittany.

Changing Patterns of Catholicism in Brittany

If the clerical model remains unchallenged, what is the nature of contemporary Catholicism in Brittany? In order to answer this question it is necessary to look at changing ideas concerning religious practice, age- and gender-based differences in religious adherence, contemporary beliefs about the afterlife, and the effects of church reforms introduced after the Second Vatican Council of 1962–1965.

Levels of Religious Practice

Throughout Brittany the proportion of practicing Catholics, the number of priests ordained, and the extent to which the church intervenes directly in social life have decreased dramatically over the past twenty years (Croix and Roudaut 1984:223; Lambert 1985). Formerly priests from Brittany occupied posts in parishes throughout France and her colonies (Le Bras 1955:81-82). Now, however, Breton priests serving as missionaries overseas are being called to return home. In 1984 a summer conference was held for overseas missionaries originally from the diocese of Quimper in order to draw their attention to the shortage of priests in the diocese and to encourage their return. Not surprisingly, Plouguerneau is one of the few parishes in Brittany that has recently produced new clerical vocations, with one ordination in 1984 and a second scheduled for 1985.

Until the 1960s each Breton parish had its own priest, and the level of religious practice in the region was significantly higher than elsewhere in France. During the late 1950s and early 1960s, in 117 of the 215 Breton cantons at least 50 percent of the adult population regularly attended Mass. The percentage of practicing Catholics at this period dropped below 20 percent in only 11 cantons. In 1957, 17.6 percent of men and 29.8 percent of women between twenty-five and forty-four years of age attended Mass on a weekly basis in the city of Brest. By comparison, in Paris during 1954 only 5.6 percent of men and 8.9 percent of women in this age category attended religious services regularly (Croix and Roudaut 1984:200). Assuming that Limerzel, the Morbihan parish studied intensively by Lambert, is a representative case, levels of regular religious practice in Brittany have fallen by approximately 50 percent since the 1960s (Lambert 1985:245).

The abandonment of the church in Brittany follows a trend that occurred earlier in other regions of France. The post-Tridentine emphasis on death alienated the majority of church adherents in France during the eighteenth century, except in regions such as Brittany, where the fixation on death corresponded to parallel concerns in the local cultural milieu (Croix and Roudaut 1984:217). The rejection of Catholicism by Bretons after the mid-twentieth century is thus intimately linked to their rejection of death (Croix and Roudaut 1984:217–218). Not only did this change in worldview come later in Brittany, but it also occurred with greater rapidity.

Referring to the drop in church attendance, one hears comments like, "People never used to miss Mass the way they do now, *mon Dieu*, no! Now those who go to church are singled out and criticized. And before, it was the reverse!" Priest and author René Le Corre describes the transition thus: "In the past, life in Brittany was oriented toward death and the hereafter. Now it is oriented toward the present moment, making money, having children, building one's home, buying a car" (pers. com. June 27, 1984). In his view the new, present-oriented *mentalité*—which he describes as hedonistic—is a product of the influx of the capitalist market economy. He finds its influence particularly disturbing in the Léon. Formerly the "country of the good death," this region has become, in his opinion, one of the most materialistic in France. Even if people in the Léon continue to attend Mass, he believes that "the heart has gone out of it."

In Plouguerneau the curé estimates that of the 3,200 Catholics who live in the *bourg*, 900 to 1,000 attend Mass on a regular basis. At approximately 30 percent, this remains higher than the national average: 24 percent of Catholics in 1984 (Lambert 1985:245).[7] Yet it must be remembered that the religious tenacity of Plouguerneau is regarded, even by observers within the church, as a "special case." Even here, the curé notes, the majority of his congregation is elderly. With the exception of a few whose faith he describes as solid, there are no twenty- to thirty-five-year-olds who attend Mass regularly. As recently as the 1960s, weekly Masses were held in each of the five chapels in the parish as well as at the churches in Lilia, Grouanec, and the *bourg*. Now only the churches and the Chapelle de Saint-Michel, by the coast, are used every Sunday.

Sunday is no longer given over exclusively to religion. It is reserved as a day for family outings and recreation. Sometimes farmers go so far as to undertake major agricultural work on a Sunday, particularly if there is a crop to be brought in and bad weather threatens. In Plouguerneau it is said that "the *paysans* don't bother

---

7. As noted in Chapter 1, the commune of Plouguerneau includes three parishes: Lilia, Grouanec, and the *bourg* of Plouguerneau itself. The curé's comment refers only to the latter.

to go to Mass much any more. Only those from the *bourg* still attend." Nevertheless, the demand for religious funerals, Masses and services, and *huitaines* and *anniversaires* remains almost universal. The number of church weddings has dropped in recent years, as more young couples tend to live together without formal marriage (Grignon 1983). To a lesser extent, observance of children's rites of passage such as baptism, confirmation, and the *communion solennelle* has also diminished, although these rituals continue to remain important. In part the continued adherence to ceremonies involving children may derive from respect for the grandparent generation or a desire to avoid family controversy. A twenty-four-year-old Plouguerneau mother explains that she has recently had her eighteen-month-old son baptized even though she and her husband never attend church "except for funerals, *huitaines*, and *anniversaires*." The child was baptized primarily for his grandmother's sake and also because, as his parents reasoned, "We have both been baptized, so why not him?"

While the drop in religious practice in Plouguerneau may be dramatic relative to its former level, the parish remains extremely *pratiquant*, or religiously observant, compared with those in the Monts d'Arrée. There are daily Masses in the main church in the *bourg* of Plouguerneau, and two Masses are held there on Sunday, in addition to the regular weekly observances in the churches at Grouanec, Lilia, and the chapel at Saint-Michel. In contrast, there are only two weekly services in La Feuillée. Approximately 25 of the parish's 627 inhabitants attend Mass on a regular basis. In neighboring Botmeur, with a population of 180, the number of those who attend regularly has dropped to 3 or 4. As of 1984 the communes of Berrien, Scrignac, Botmeur, and Lannédern lacked resident priests. The curé of nearby Loqueffret died in that year, and the parish remained for several months without a priest, although the office of the bishop had promised a replacement. Similarly, further south, in the parish of Saint-Hernin, near Carhaix, there was no full-time priest, and the congregation was made up of only 15 or 20 faithful.

According to Le Corre, the decline in religious practice has not been restricted to rural areas. The urban parishes, too, have in his words "disintegrated" over the last ten years. He notes with ironic humor the comment of a fellow cleric, in charge of a parish in Brest:

"Only people who ride the bus come to Mass now." These are the elderly and the very young. The elderly attend out of habit and because they seek solace in religion in the face of imminent death. The very young attend because they are interested in their confirmation and *communion solennelle*. Those who fall between these two age categories, "who drive their own cars," have other interests and find other activities with which to occupy their Sunday mornings (Le Corre, pers. com. June 27, 1984). Despite this priest's pessimism, it is important to recognize that the urban centers of Quimper and Brest are also the setting for a new, revitalized Catholicism, which features study groups where young people and those who take a reflective approach to the faith can meet for discussion, in the tradition of programs sponsored by Action Catholique. However, this revitalization represents a minority movement, within both the church and the larger society.

Religion and the Young

As Le Corre notes, the *communion solennelle* acts as an incentive for children to attend Mass. The *communion solennelle* is actually the culmination of two earlier ritual episodes. Children receive their first Communion, or *petite communion*, at the age of nine. At ten or eleven they are confirmed, and at eleven or twelve they make their *communion solennelle*. During the three-year period between the *petite communion* and the *communion solennelle*, they are expected to attend catechism class and Mass regularly. Yet most, if not all, children cease to attend church as soon as they have made their *communion solennelle*. As the Plouguerneau curé wryly notes, there are practically no children over the age of thirteen at Mass. Although it no longer serves as it did in the past as the ritual transition between childhood and young adulthood, the *communion solennelle* is an important festive occasion in a child's life. Both boys and girls dress in a long, surplice-like white robe for the ceremony, and girls, like nuns, wear a veil covering their hair. It is rare to see a family photo collection that lacks the stereotypical portrait of each child on the day of his or her *communion solennelle*, complete with white costume and demure smile.

The *communion solennelle* is also an occasion for children to receive presents from their godparents and other family members. Since the 1970s these gifts have become increasingly more elaborate and expensive, including tape recorders, record players, and electronic calculators. A child thus has fairly strong incentives to remain in catechism class until the entire process leading up to the *communion solennelle* is completed. As one woman in La Feuillée remarks, "Now children do their *communion* only for the presents and a fancy meal afterward. When it's all over, they never set foot in the church again!" The same type of comment can be heard in Plouguerneau, where many twelve-year-olds freely assert that they will not attend Mass after their *communion solennelle*. In their teens, as part of a general adolescent defiance of parental values, even some who attend private Catholic schools openly mock religion. Others claim that one does not need to practice regularly in order to be a believer and to live according to Catholic ethical norms.

Religion can be a controversial issue in families where the younger generation has ceased to practice while the older family members continue to do so. Deeply religious mothers in both Plouguerneau and the Monts d'Arrée express concern over their children who have stopped attending Mass after marrying nonpracticing spouses. In one family from the Plouguerneau area, twenty-three-year-old Marc Vaillant disputes his father's claim that Christ's Resurrection is proof of the veracity of the Christian faith: "All religions are equally good," he contends. "How can we say the Catholic church is true and the others are not?" A cousin of Marc's, also in his early twenties, suggests that television and other influences from the outside world have weakened the church's hold on the young. In his view liberty is a central value for those under thirty. The desire to live independent of all constraints, which reflects the growth of individualism in Brittany, leads the young to reject the yoke of the church: "Three-quarters of an hour in church each week is just too much."

Although the younger generation in the Vaillant family no longer attend Mass, they feel that they have been marked by their early exposure to religion. As Marc explains, "Even if we are no longer practicing Catholics, something remains." They cannot detach themselves from certain attitudes and patterns of behavior which derive from Catholicism. In particular they consider that they have retained a strong respect for the church's rituals in the face of death, which Marc suggests is generally true of other young people who have left the faith: "All the prejudices against the church are left aside in the case of a death." Although the young rarely attend Mass, they temporarily ignore their atheistic or anticlerical sentiments to attend the funerals of friends or family members. This respect extends to the bereaved and to the dead themselves. Thus, the Strollad ar Vro Bagan, a Plouguerneau-based Breton-language theater troupe composed primarily of people in their twenties and thirties, contributed to pay for a Mass at the funeral of the father of one of the group's members, even though they had recently produced a strongly anticlerical play about the life of Michel Le Nobletz.

Gender and Religion

In all parts of France the decline in religious practice proceeded more rapidly among men than women (Le Bras 1955:80). Rural Brittany is no exception to this more general trend. Of the congregation present at any given Mass in Plouguerneau, roughly two-thirds are women and one-third men. Similarly, in La Feuillée women greatly outnumber men as practicing Catholics. In 1984 only five men from the parish could be said to be regularly practicing Catholics, and two of these were over seventy years of age. One of the younger men in this group is a relative newcomer from Brest who has married into a La Feuillée family. Another is from a family who came to the Monts d'Arrée approximately fifteen years ago from the Léon. It is rare to hear a male voice, other than that of the curé, singing during the Mass.

While he recognizes that the loss of faith is more marked among the men in his parish than among the women, the curé of La Feuillée believes that "even for the men, there is something there." Although they seem to be indifferent to religion most of the time, he notes that they attend Mass in large numbers for those ceremonies which are important to them: the commemorative Masses on November 11 and May 8, marking the ends of the two world wars; the funerals of other men; and to some extent Toussaint. The curé observes that men frequently go alone to visit their family tombs after following the cortege to the cemetery at the end of a funeral. For men more than women, he believes, religious practice is inextricably linked to the idea of death. Their tendency to overlook other aspects of the faith and to ignore rituals other than those concerned with death owes, he suggests, to the perception in Breton society that religion is primarily a women's responsibility.[8] Unlike politics, which belongs in the male domain of the external world, religion is associated with the interior, female realm of family and household affairs. For this reason priests tend to be alienated from their male parishioners, who see them as sexually ambiguous. Their celibacy calls into question their ability to function as "real men." Yet, while they presumably have no sexual power, they have more social power than most working men. As in the Spanish contexts described by Brandes (1980:177–204), Christian (1972:152), and Gilmore (1984), in Brittany anticlerical folklore focuses on this paradox, expressing both the sexually ambivalent position of the priest and male hostility to his social and religious authority. A number of Breton folklore items imply that priests are in fact oversexed, despite their theoretical chastity. The stories told in Plouguerneau about priests seducing young girls have already been mentioned. A Plouguerneau woman joked that "all priests should be castrated!" Similarly, one curé in the Monts d'Arrée is the butt of male humor for his name, which means "ten penises" in the local folk idiom. "He doesn't even need one and yet he has ten!" it is said.

The ambiguous sexual identity of the priest is clearly apparent when he participates in sexually mixed social gatherings such as meetings of the *club du troisième âge*. Here there is an unofficial segregation of the sexes. Men sit together to drink their afternoon coffee at "men's tables" on one side of the room, while women sit together at "women's tables" along the opposite wall. When the curé is present, his indecision about which group to join is patently obvious, and if not directed specifically by a third party to a "men's table," he will often end up among a party of sympathetic, churchgoing women.

The alienation of the priest from his male parishioners has also been noted elsewhere in Brittany. On the island of Houat, the priest is perceived as "very much a creature of the land, along with the women and children" (Jorion 1982:278). Unlike other Houat men, who are constantly exposed to danger at sea owing to their

---

8. Likewise, in the Spanish communities studied by Brandes (1980:182–188) and Christian (1972:134), men leave responsibility for the spiritual domain to their women relatives.

occupation as fishermen, the priest knows nothing of the courage men need to face death alone by drowning. Jorion's analysis of the importance of religion for men in Houat echoes that offered by the curé of La Feuillée: "as far as the fishermen are concerned, religion has much to do with dying" (Jorion 1982:275).

Changing Conceptions of Catholicism and Community

The decline in attendance at Mass which has occurred in Brittany since the 1950s is partially a result of changing religious beliefs. However, it is equally a product of changing concepts of the community and its relationship to the individual. In the past the High Mass was the only meeting place for the entire parish. Particularly in the Léon, church attendance provided one of the few opportunities for recreation. Now, however, new recreational activities have displaced the role of the Mass as a diversion. Television has reinforced the decrease in neighborhood social interaction. New patterns of agricultural production permitted by mechanization have made work as well as leisure a more individualistic activity. Increasingly, both the need and the desire for participation in the larger community represented by the parish church are being counterbalanced by a *chacun chez soi* mentality. At the same time, new notions of community that encompass persons and places outside the borders of the parish are developing. The contraction of the family and the decline of neighborhood *entraide* have been paralleled by the expansion of the social universe to the national and international levels, through increased travel opportunities, increased exposure to the mass media and increased education. Sentiments of local identity remain strong in rural Breton communities (Badone 1987). Nevertheless, the church is no longer the unique focus for their expression. Other activities have supplanted religious practice as vehicles for expressing and reaffirming community membership. There are now new institutions that provide alternatives to church membership for those who seek identity and *communitas* within a larger social group. These include local sports teams, parent-teacher associations, and organizations dedicated to the preservation and revival of Breton culture.

As Lambert (1985:336) points out, the church has lost most of its former social functions. The boundaries of the church and those of the community no longer coincide. In part this displacement explains the decrease in the number of children who are baptized and the generally longer interval between birth and baptism in contemporary Brittany relative to the past. Baptism no longer represents the necessary precondition for entry into the human community, for the church and the body social are no longer defined as one and the same.

A young woman from Coat-Meal, approximately fifteen kilometers south of Plouguerneau, recalls that fifteen years ago, when she was a child, "everyone" in her parish attended Mass. Now, she says, such a situation is "unimaginable." She describes the gulf that separates the elderly from the younger generation in Coat-Meal: "The elderly complain that they no longer know the young people of the commune." Many old people regret that the younger generation does not attend Mass. Yet surprisingly, their complaint does not stem from a concern for the spiritual welfare of the young: "The elderly say, 'If only the young people would attend Mass, then at least we would have a chance to *see* them. It doesn't matter whether they believe or not.'" For the older generation, attendance at Mass is a demonstration of "belonging," of one's continued participation in the parish community. Those who attend Mass are "seen," and thus known. In the past, religious observances provided the occasion for the community to display itself to itself. The class- and gender-linked seating arrangements in the church made manifest the salient distinctions among social categories. In this way, these distinctions were perpetuated, and the community was reassured of its continuing existence.

The Effects of Vatican II

To some extent the reduced levels of religious practice in contemporary Brittany are also related to popular reaction against liturgical and doctrinal changes instituted in the 1960s by the Second Vatican Council. These changes sought to promote a more intellectual and less ritualistic approach to the faith. They included the discontinuation of the Latin Mass, the adoption of regular street clothes for nuns and priests, and the removal of the altar to the center of the chancel, where the priest celebrates Mass facing his congregation rather than with his back turned at the far end of the apse. In La Feuillée the change in the position of the altar is recalled as having been "traumatic" for certain parishioners.[9] The changes were introduced slowly over a two-year period. Still, some complain that "too many concessions were made too quickly." People were shocked at first to see priests in ordinary clothes. In the Plouguerneau area likewise, a man in his late fifties explains, "We no longer had any respect for priests and nuns, because they looked just like everyone else." Many regret the passing of the Gregorian music and the accompanying Latin liturgy. The La Feuillée curé notes with humor that a woman from the parish who practiced regularly prior to Vatican II now complains that she "doesn't understand anything of the Mass" since it has been translated from Latin to French. She speaks French fluently and has never studied Latin, but she knew the responses for the Latin Mass by rote.

While the curé of La Feuillée, like many of his colleagues, agrees that the Latin Mass was more aesthetically pleasing, he nevertheless believes that "we must keep up with the times." In his view the congregation should understand the meaning of the words they sing and the rituals in which they participate. He interprets the rejection of the use of French as part of a refusal to accept the demystification of religion. "The use of Latin has nothing to do with one's faith," he asserts. At present, there is one retired couple living in La Feuillée who openly express support for Archbishop Marcel Lefebvre and his *intégriste* campaign to reinstate the pre–Vatican II liturgy. Although this couple is not originally from La Feuillée, others who are of local origin hold similar convictions about the liturgy, although they do not share Lefebvre's conservative political ideas. As one La Feuillée woman comments, the reforms instituted after Vatican II did not succeed in keeping the young people in the church, and they alienated many of its more traditional supporters such as herself. Another woman in her mid-forties from the Plouguerneau area echoes these sentiments: "People are saying that the priests have abandoned *le bon Dieu*." She explains that although she still considers herself a Catholic, she no longer attends Mass: "It's not what I was taught when I was

---

9. Ironically, when the old altar rails that formerly separated the nave of the church from the chancel were removed, they were stored for some time in an empty room of the secular *école laïque*.

young. They don't preach the same things anymore. How is one supposed to know what to believe?"

In Plouguerneau the discontinuation of time-honored rituals has produced both resentment and doubts about the immutability of the tenets of the faith. Changes in the form of the Fête-Dieu, or Corpus Christi, celebrations have been particularly unsettling for older Plouguerneau residents. Until the 1960s this festival was marked by a procession around the *bourg*. Housefronts were decorated with sheets bearing painted motives and religious symbols. Designs were made on the pavement of the roadways with grease paint and flowers. People regret the loss of these customs. The procession was maintained in attenuated form up to 1983, with those children from the parish who had recently made their *petite communion* walking between the church and the Catholic school for boys, a distance of three blocks. Banners were carried and the monstrance, an ornate gilt holder for the Sacred Host, was elevated by the priest during the procession. In 1983, however, the newly appointed curé announced that there would be no outdoor procession. As a compromise, to placate the anticipated criticism of his congregation, a small procession within the church was organized with the children carrying lighted tapers around the periphery of the nave. Despite this token effort many of the older parishioners were angered and perturbed by the change, voicing comments like, "That's the end of everything now. A new curé—no more processions!" It was feared that the priest would make a similar attempt to discontinue the *pardon* procession, which had already been shortened, losing much of its earlier aesthetic appeal.

Throughout Europe processions are an important element of Catholic folk tradition, which has become a target for reform by progressive priests (Brandes 1976; Riegelhaupt 1973). As Riegelhaupt (1984:101) has pointed out, a strong sense of attachment to collective religious expressions persists in rural Europe, despite the efforts of the post-Tridentine church to replace these with a faith based on individual salvation. In promoting individual responses to religion at the expense of processions, Vatican II is simply completing the work of the Counter-Reformation.[10]

---

10. For the Breton context, Croix (1981:1194) observes that during the period of the missions, the clergy had difficulty persuading parishioners to participate in pro-

The Plouguerneau Fête-Dieu procession was valued both aesthetically and as a symbol of community identity. Its discontinuation is disturbing to the faithful because it ruptures a link with the parish's religious traditions and with their own personal memories of the past. Other innovations strike more directly at the core of belief. "I think it is the priests themselves who are changing the faith," comments Anna Le Guen from Plouguerneau, looking at her son's catechism workbooks.[11] She finds it incomprehensible that he learned only one prayer in two years of catechism instruction: "I had to teach him the Hail Mary and other prayers myself. All they do is play with coloring books and cut and paste."

As Croix and Roudaut (1984:217) observe, one of the principal areas toward which the post–Vatican II reforms of the church in Brittany have been directed is the representation of death. Ossuaries have been emptied of their bones and the use of macabre catafalques has been discontinued in all but the poorest regions of interior Brittany, which have been the last to experience the influence of the outside world (Croix and Roudaut 1984:223). Similarly, in predication the insistence on death, Judgment, and damnation has been replaced by an effort to represent God as a loving Father. "I think there used to be another *bon Dieu*," muses Anna Le Guen. At her son's recent confirmation the curé referred constantly to the Holy Spirit and to the God of Love. "When I was young," she recalls, "we never heard anything about them." For her, religion was formerly associated with fear, inspired principally by the ritual of confession. In La Feuillée one hears similar incredulous comments: "Religion used to make everyone feel guilty. And now they talk all the time about the Dieu d'Amour." A nursing sister at the *centre hospitalier* in Morlaix makes a related observation about changes in funerary discourse. Prior to Vatican II, she notes, the priest would emphasize the negative aspects of death, such as sin and suffering

---

cessions. This would suggest a certain initial reluctance to adopt the forms of communal ritual sanctioned by the post-Tridentine church. However, it may be hypothesized that when other opportunities for collective ritual, such as dancing in church at saints' day festivals, were prohibited by the missionaries, the faithful transferred their support to processions, and as a consequence their centrality in Breton popular religious life may have been dramatically increased.

11. This comment is strikingly similar to those heard by Brandes in rural Spain, where he was told that the priests "themselves are taking religion away from us" (Brandes 1976:23).

in the afterlife. Now the positive aspects are stressed: reconciliation with God and reunion with one's kin. She welcomes such changes, but others find it difficult to make the conceptual shift between two apparently opposed doctrines, asking questions like, "Why did the church say you had to do certain things that it now ignores? How can you believe that what they used to say was true, if it has changed now, and how can we be sure that what they tell us now is true?" The growing number of priests and nuns abandoning their vocations in contemporary Brittany lends confirmation to such doubts.

Croix and Roudaut suggest that the popular fascination with death in Brittany slowed the church's efforts to eliminate certain aspects of the macabre from its rituals. However, they maintain that since the 1960s, "the clerical culture that death had cemented for so long is breaking up before our very eyes with an astonishing rapidity: religion has changed profoundly since Vatican II, and the few recent steps backward will change nothing with respect to the detachment of numerous confused believers" (1984:218).

In Plouguerneau the support of the laity exceeds that of the clergy for certain death-related institutions. One of these is the *services de continuation,* monthly Masses held in memory of all those who have died in the parish over the preceding year. *Services de continuation* are celebrated on the first Friday of every month at 7:15 A.M. Families pay sixty francs annually to have their deceased relatives named in the prayer offered at the *services de continuation* for the salvation of their souls. Plouguerneau is one of the few Breton communities where *services de continuation* have not yet been abolished. The current priest would like to phase out these Masses, and he is grateful when families neglect the tradition of their own accord. In his view the *services de continuation* represent "the vestiges of a religious education that was too rigid, that placed too much importance on the wrath of God, on a terrifying, authoritarian God." He sees the *services de continuation* as an attempt to engage God in a type of reciprocity: "It is necessary to offer something to God in order that the souls may leave purgatory." One offers money and prayers to the church and sacrifices one's comfort by attending Mass at an hour when many remain in bed, so that God may shorten the sufferings of one's relatives in the afterlife.

Despite the efforts of the present curé to discourage his parishioners from requesting *services de continuation,* for many in the group of mourners who attend these early morning Masses, the prayers offered for the deceased continue to be meaningful. Moreover, the monthly gathering generates a sense of *communitas* among the bereaved, all of whom share similar experiences of grief.

The conversion of extreme unction into the *onction des malades,* discussed in Chapter 3, provides another example of a post–Vatican II modification in death ritual which has not been universally accepted or understood. In La Feuillée a *blanc* woman recalls that in the past, priests placed a great deal of importance on the ritual of extreme unction, threatening to withhold a religious funeral if they were not summoned to administer this sacrament. "Now," she comments, "you never hear that so-and-so has received the last rites." While the church seeks to displace the sacrament from the moment of death, many of the faithful continue to believe that the presence of the priest at the bedside of the dying is essential. Moreover, the families of the ill and elderly frequently wish to avoid confronting the sick person with a priest before it is absolutely necessary, "at the last moment." This concern leads to misunderstandings and conflict between priest and parishioners. The Plouguerneau curé recalls one recent incident in which the family of a man who had been seriously ill for months waited until the afternoon of his death before requesting the *onction des malades.* The priest, who was busy with other affairs, was delayed and did not arrive until after the invalid had died. The family berated the priest for not making the effort to come more quickly, but he responded that they should have requested the sacraments months earlier, when the dying man would have been capable of participating actively in the ritual.

Despite the church's efforts since Vatican II to eradicate the legacy of the missions in Brittany, fear and a sense of death's potential imminence still mark the religious experience of many Bretons. Even in the Monts d'Arrée, where levels of church attendance are now extremely low, vestiges of anxiety induced by religion remain. "People have a lot of fear here," reflects a middle-aged woman from the La Feuillée area. A man in his sixties recalls that his father, who never attended church and never prayed at any other time, would always pray during thunderstorms. The relationship between religion and fear of death is clearly apparent. For many people, especially the elderly, the image of God as a vengeful Judge also remains current. "*Le bon Dieu* doesn't want people to have happiness in the world," remarks one elderly La Feuillée woman. Another, bedridden and going blind, attributes her physical disabilites to divine retribution for her sins. Similarly, eighty-six-year-old Marie-Thérèse, tired of living alone, of being unable to walk any distance outside the house, and of a myriad other major and minor ailments, asks, "What have I done to *le bon Dieu* that he has given me so much sorrow?"

To some extent the traditional interpretation of tragedy as divine retribution is being replaced by a "disenchanted" outlook, according to which God is not conceived to intervene directly in the personal lives of individuals. Seventy-five-year-old Amélie Le Hir, who has lived in La Feuillée since her teenage years, recalls that her mother was tormented by guilt because she was unable to fulfill a vow she had made to give one of her eleven children to the church as a nun or priest. None of her children wanted to assume a vocation, and her anticlerical husband was strongly opposed to the idea. The issue came to a climax with the death of her youngest son, an extremely intelligent and attractive boy, whom the local curé had wanted to send to a seminary school. Because of M. Le Hir's opposition the child remained at home, but at the age of eleven he contracted meningitis and died. Amélie's mother was convinced that God had taken her son in revenge. When she became paralyzed at the end of her life, she interpreted her illness as another punishment for breaking her vow. For a long time Amélie shared her mother's perspective. Now, however, the difficulties of life during World War II, personal tragedies, and exposure to new ideas from the outside world have changed Amélie's point of view. While still *croyante et catholique,* she no longer believes in a vengeful God.

Like Amélie Le Hir, other older people in La Feuillée have altered their ideas about retribution. However, traditional ideas about God's vengeance continue to influence one of Amélie's young neighbors, twenty-eight-year-old Bernard Broc'h. Of Léonard background, Bernard was always more devout than most men in La Feuillée. Then, after one of his four-month-old twin sons died unexpectedly of sudden infant death syndrome, Bernard started attending Mass regularly every week. He was deeply troubled because the baby had died unbaptized. Steps were taken by the family immediately to arrange for the baptism of the surviving son. People in the community note Bernard's increased church attendance and ask one another, "What can be going on in his mind?" It is as though he is trying to do penance for the unknown sin that provoked a wrathful God to take his child.

Contemporary Eschatological Beliefs

Pasion digwener
Death's agonies on Friday,
Marv disadorn
Dead on Saturday,
Interet disul
Buried on Sunday,
Baradoz sur
Sure of paradise.

Told by Joséphine Kerouac of La Feuillée, this proverb was also recorded in the nineteenth century (Le Braz 1928:1:92). It reflects a secure faith, in which the proper observance of ritual ensures salvation in the afterlife. Likewise, in Plouguerneau it is recalled that salvation was held to be certain if one participated at least once in the annual Rogation Day processions to each of the parish chapels. Now, however, life, death, and religion have become more complicated. The Rogation processions have been discontinued since the 1960s. As for paradise, the elderly remark rather wistfully, "We would be happy to believe that there is such a place."

Few continue to envisage existence after death in terms of the tripartite structure of heaven, purgatory, and hell depicted until recently in the mission *tableaux*. Not surprisingly, most of those who express a continuing belief in hell come from strongly Catholic backgrounds in the Léon or are themselves clerics. For some people the concept of hell is a logical correlate of the ideas of heaven and divine justice. They reason that God could not be just with respect to the righteous if the evildoers of the world were left unpunished. Thus, a curé from a Léonard parish on the north slopes of the Monts d'Arrée argues that if hell does not exist, the Nazi murderers of the Holocaust will no more be held accountable for their actions than will upright and charitable citizens who support the moral teachings of the church. This priest's attitude is shared by a forty-five-year-old woman from another Léonard parish close to Brest. Remarking on the recent death of a particularly unscrupulous relative, she observes: "If all they taught us in the past about the afterlife is true, he will have something to answer for."

A less extreme position is adopted by Rose Abgrall, a woman in her sixties from a deeply religious family in Plouguerneau. She is now unsure whether hell exists, although in the past she believed in it because of the teachings of the missions. She still feels that the existence of hell is logically necessary if God is to be considered truly just. Nevertheless, Rose reasons, "If there is a hell, there cannot be many people in it, for if God is really a God of Love, how could he damn people? Life on earth is so difficult, and each person has a cross to bear. Why should there be suffering after death as well?" Her brother remarks that their family does not often think about hell, because as good Catholics they do not believe that they are in danger of damnation. Besides, "the priests themselves have told us that it doesn't exist." Commenting on the changing emphasis of Catholic predication since Vatican II, Rose's husband observes with humor, "Now there aren't any more fires in hell. They've installed central heating! The road to heaven used to be rocky and difficult. Now it has been paved and they're going to take us there by car!" These joking remarks draw a parallel between the changing view of the afterlife and transformations in the material environment in rural Brittany over the past thirty years.

Speaking of the eschatological beliefs of his clients, Jacques, the funerary monument builder from the Plouguerneau area, states: "They do not think about the afterlife anymore, about either hell or purgatory, as in the time of the missions. Those past a certain age who are still believers are certain they will go to heaven. Thus, they don't think about hell at all. And the young prefer not to think about it either." In Jacques's view the afterlife continues to have significance only insofar as it represents the ultimate reunion of the family.

As noted in Chapter 5, the emphasis on reunion with kin after death is a product of the romantic pattern in which affectivity is channeled primarily toward members of the nuclear family. The *espoir de se revoir,* or hope for reunion, a common theme in funeral sermons, is shared by Catholics in both Plouguerneau and La Feuillée. For some, however, the representation of the afterlife as reunion makes it difficult to accept the choice of their family members who no longer adhere to the church. They fear an irrevocable separation after death. Marianne Penguilly, a Plouguerneau widow in her sixties, is a devout Catholic for whom heaven, purgatory, and hell remain meaningful concepts. She is deeply troubled because her sons no longer attend church. As she explains, "They tell us that everything is beautiful in paradise, but how can parents be happy there if their children are not with them?" She has concluded that this is an irresolvable mystery. To her mind it is inconceivable that one's nature should be so completely changed after death that one could not remember one's children or know that they are suffering in hell.

A slightly less literal acceptance of traditional Catholic doctrine marks the attitude of eighty-two-year-old Marguerite Prévost from La Feuillée. She does not believe in the physical resurrection but suggests that "we will all see one another again one day [i.e., after death]." In Marguerite's opinion there must be a God and life after death, if only because this is believed by many well-educated people such as priests and bishops. "We don't know anything about it," she maintains, "but we know that there is something." This "something," in her view, includes some form of recompense for those who have lived an ethical life, but no purgatory or hell. For the evil "there is nothing after death." Masses and services cannot help the soul: "It is the way one has lived one's life that matters," Marguerite asserts.

Others in La Feuillée agree that if existence continues after death, its quality will depend on one's moral conduct during life. However, as two anticlerical women point out, those who attend Mass regularly do not deserve privileged access to paradise, for supporters of the church are not necessarily the most ethical people in the community. As such comments illustrate, certain *rouges* accept the idea of God as a supreme and just moral authority while rejecting the church's claim to represent Him. This attitude is expressed by Yvette, a seventy-eight-year-old La Feuillée widow, who professes that she believes in God, "but not in everything the curés say." Although Yvette thinks there is an afterlife, in her view it will be totally different from existence on earth. Yvette no longer believes in the physical resurrection nor in damnation, although she remembers vividly the pictures of hell with its flames from catechism class: "And everyone believed," she exclaims, with amazement at her own former credulity.

Even the *blancs* in La Feuillée have difficulty accepting the literal interpretation of hell. Most share the curé's opinion that hell is a metaphor for the psychological and spiritual suffering of separation from God. One woman, who has a violent and unemployed alcoholic son, makes the revealing statement that "hell is life right here." Despite the large number of Masses and services given by both *rouges* and *blancs* at funerals in La Feuillée, people from both groups laugh at the suggestion that these reflect a belief in purgatory.

Many people in La Feuillée feel that existence ends definitively with death: "No one has ever returned from the other side to tell us what is there. Therefore, the conclusion is that there must be nothing." Many *rouges* argue that if God existed, he would intervene to prevent the injustices and tragedies of human life. As one young woman, a *rouge* member of the municipal council in a Monts d'Arrée commune, observes, occasionally the existence of beauty and order in nature makes her believe that there is a creative organizing force. "Sometimes I say to myself, even so, things are well made; nature is well made. And that gives me the idea that maybe there is something." Yet, paradoxically, it is the contradictory realization that in many ways things are not "well made"—that children are born handicapped, that people die needlessly in wars and famines, and that the social order is often unjust—which prevents her from being able intellectually to believe in God. Despite her unbelief, she notes that on an emotional level, "when things have gotten really bad, when I've been truly beside myself, I've found myself saying a prayer."

It is frequently suggested that belief in the afterlife and an interest in religion develop late in life, in response to the inevitability of death. The son of an elderly woman from La Feuillée remarks, "The older people get, the greater their tendency to believe. When you are young, you don't think about death or give a damn about the Eternal Father and all His saints." Nevertheless, many elderly people in La Feuillée, like Marie-Thérèse, assert that "once you are dead, it's all finished—*echu tout*. You go into the coffin and you decompose. Eaten by the worms. And to think that everyone finishes the same way."[12] For some of the elderly, death is welcomed as a release from the physical sufferings of old age: "Once you are dead, you feel no more pain." Such comments do not imply a belief in any kind of life after death and certainly preclude the possibility of torment in hell.

In the Plouguerneau area many of the middle-aged who continue to identify themselves as Catholic, who are politically conservative and who attend Mass regularly, have now abandoned belief in divine retribution in the afterlife. As one woman in her fifties explains, "Our generation no longer believes in hell or purgatory. Everyone will go to heaven." Another slightly older woman says with resentment that "in the past, the priests lied to us. They told us hell existed." She conceives of God as the force "that makes the wheat grow every year at the same season, and that makes the tides rise and fall." After death "we will all be angels, all the same, but we won't be able to recognize one another." Another forty-year-old woman from Plouguerneau holds contradictory notions about the afterlife. "Dead is dead. I have never believed in the hereafter," she affirms. However, she states with equal adamancy that "everyone will go to the same place, to paradise." Sixty-five-year-old Annick, who rarely misses Mass, claims that after death there is nothing but decay: "Eaten by the crabs or eaten by the worms, it's all the same thing." Yet she also believes that now, everyone goes to paradise: "Tout an dud a ya d'ar Baradoz." Purgatory for Annick is "here on earth. We cannot believe that there is a hell. In the past, yes, people believed that there was a hell with demons and pitchforks and fire. But there is no hell any longer."

Even the elderly, who might be expected to adhere more closely to the doctrines of the missions, share a similar lack of certainty. According to Lisette, a seventy-five-year-old *paysanne* from Grouanec, "It's a mystery. We all go to the same place after we die; we don't move after we are buried." Although Lisette won several prizes in catechism class as a girl and still reads the Scripture les-

---

12. This highly material, earthy conception of the condition of the body after death has a long history in Brittany. The comment of a rural priest writing in 1617 parallels those made by present-day La Feuillée residents: "We do not know where or when death can take us, we are but dust and nourishment for the worms" (Recteur d'Izé, quoted in Croix and Roudaut 1984:91).

sons at the Mass in Grouanec, she does not believe in hell. Her sister, slightly younger, is undecided on the issue. She says a prayer each night before going to sleep. "That way I am safe," she explains, referring to the possibility that she might die during the night. In Lilia a couple in their mid-seventies concede that "we do not believe as much as we used to." While they continue to believe in the existence of God and are confident that "there is something after death," they no longer believe in hell or purgatory. "In the past," they recall, "the priests made purgatory sound almost as bad as hell. We used to pray a lot so that the souls could be released from purgatory."

Intergenerational differences and continuities with respect to eschatological beliefs stand out in sharp relief in the Kerjouan family from Plouguerneau. Marie-Jeanne Kerjouan, aged sixty-four, was born to a family of poor farmers in Grouanec. She moved to the *bourg* of Plouguerneau when she married the parish sacristan, who also serves as the grave digger. A regularly practicing Catholic, Marie-Jeanne says that she believes in God "by tradition, even though, privately, I ask questions. I do have doubts, but I believe just the same." Her conception of God as the Dieu d'Amour who pardons sin precludes the idea of hell. Purgatory is "here on earth." There is no physical resurrection in the afterlife: "That is something more surreal, spiritual. You prepare your heaven during your life, by living for others. It's a spiritual state rather than a place."

Marie-Jeanne's eldest daughter, Jeannette, aged forty-four, lives in Brest, where she works as a high-school teacher. "There are moments in my life when I believe in God more than at other times," she notes. "But is it the same God we learned about as children? Everywhere, all over the world, people believe in something. They hope and search and there are no solutions." While she "would like to believe in the afterlife, it is difficult to believe, truthfully." She definitely does not believe in hell or purgatory. Jeannette attends Mass regularly, partly out of habit, partly out of conviction, partly because of her desire "to belong to a community. Life doesn't have any sense in isolation." For the same reason she has become the teachers' union representative for her school. Her combination of faith and concern for social issues reflects the influence of Action Catholique.

Maryse, the second Kerjouan sister, aged forty-one, also works in Brest, as an accountant. She is a highly practical woman who rarely engages in philosophical speculation. When asked about the afterlife, she responds, "I don't know what to think. It's more important to be concerned with the present world." However, she rejects the rigidly hierarchical vision of heaven, purgatory, and hell put forward by the church in her youth. "Each religion strives for God," she concludes, "and they are all equally valuable. But since I was raised a Catholic, I will stay in the church."

The youngest daughter in the Kerjouan family, Monique, is a high-school teacher in Brest, like Jeannette. Monique claims that she is rarely troubled by the question of whether or not God exists, "because I know I will never find an answer. The great minds of the world have not found one, so why should I?" She contends that there is nothing after death. Heaven, purgatory, and hell are "artificial constructs dating from the Middle Ages, to force people to behave in a certain fashion, to maintain the status quo. There is no reason that they should exist now. Even the priests don't talk about them anymore." Although she never attends Mass, Monique feels that she remains influenced by her upbringing in a Catholic milieu, explaining that "the moral aspect will always be with me."

M. Kerjouan is much less willing than his wife and daughters to discuss religious issues. Like many men, he is reticent and prefers to leave such matters to *les femmes*. He expresses his opinions solely on a humorous level, observing that "you cannot go to hell anymore. There is no more room there, and the devil doesn't have enough money to build a new one!"

As the differences of opinion within the Kerjouan family suggest, both age and gender may influence an individual's ideas about eschatology. Like the youngest Kerjouan daughter, many people under thirty-five are not practicing Catholics. One thirty-three-year-old social worker from the Plouguerneau area remarks that since the age of nine she has never believed in the afterlife or the Last Judgment. Yet she has vivid recollections of the *tableaux* used in catechism class depicting these concepts. Similarly, the secretary at the town hall in La Feuillée, thirty-five-year-old Odille, remembers learning the standard answers by rote in catechism class to questions concerning the afterlife. "'What is hell?' 'What is purgatory?' Those were the stupid questions of the catechism," she recalls. "We used to hurry over them." Intellectually she does not believe in life after death, but emotionally she sometimes feels that "it's senseless that everything should stop all of a sudden like that." The social worker agrees: "It's hard to imagine that life is going to come to a stop." Such a perspective is shared by a man in his early twenties from Brest who spends weekends with his family in a converted farmhouse in La Feuillée. In his view "something" continues after death, otherwise existence would be futile, "too stupid." However, he does not subscribe to the traditional Catholic conception of the afterlife.

Other young people reject even these intimations of postmortem existence. Despite his Catholic upbringing, twenty-three-year-old Marc Vaillant concludes that "it is pleasant to think that there might be life after death, but that sort of thing is just self-deception." Likewise, his cousin maintains that even should God exist, human minds are incapable of understanding His nature or of penetrating the mysteries of death. To a large extent, these young men espouse a naturalistic, scientific view of the world. They believe in the theory of evolution, yet they also observe that the concept of God can be accommodated in such an explanatory model of the universe as a "first cause."

Increased exposure both to the outside world and to the positivist perspective of Western science, through the education system and the mass media, has cast doubt on many elements of traditional Catholic doctrine. Talking with his mother about the idea of the Last Judgment, a ten-year-old from Plouguerneau remarked that "everyone who has ever lived is supposed to be gathered together in a field at the same time. But it would have to be a huge field! And what about all the different languages? How would people understand one another?" Similar questions were raised by two elderly women in La Feuillée during a conversation on the same subject: "Think of all the millions of people who have died all over the world since the beginning of time! Where could they all be put?"

The loss of belief in hell undermines the foundation of Catholic ethical teachings. One priest notes, "Without hell, the whole structure falls apart." A nun concurs, suggesting that the conception of sin no longer exists. In her view the uncertainties associated with moral relativism provide the basis for the belief that "everyone goes to heaven now." Damnation becomes unimaginable. Opinions are divided concerning this loss of the moral absolutes, which, enforced by fear, marked the religion of the past. A *rouge* woman in her late thirties from La Feuillée observes that belief in hell used to check socially unacceptable behavior. In her opinion, fear of hell extended to encompass fear of all established authorities, including curé and *gendarmes* alike. It is the loss of this fear which lies behind contemporary elevated crime and divorce levels, she maintains: "One no longer fears, and it's a good thing, but a bad thing too at the same time." Surprisingly, this woman's views coincide with those of M. Vaillant, a much older and more politically conservative Catholic from the Léon. He too suggests that not just the authority of the church but all social authority is currently being rejected. In his opinion, "a little bit of fear wasn't such a bad thing." Like the legal penalties imposed for criminal actions, the fear instilled by the missions operated as a deterrent, he believes.

In general it is agreed that the church no longer provides widely accepted behavioral standards. Says one La Feuillée Catholic: "People don't listen to what the church says about morality anymore. Just look at the examples of birth control and living together before marriage." Yet a psychiatrist who was born in the Plouguerneau area disagrees. In his opinion, "the comportment of people in Brittany has remained Christian," and despite the dramatic decline in church adherence, the Breton ethos and worldview continue to be marked by the influence of Catholicism.

The transformation of eschatological beliefs in Brittany has occurred with a dramatic rapidity. As Le Corre states, "Thirty years ago everyone believed in hell and purgatory, without question." Asked how those who formerly believed could adopt a radically new conception of the world without becoming schizophrenic, he responds, "Like the Third World peoples who have just recently been exposed to Western culture, they adapt" (pers. com. June 27, 1984). Once-frightening eschatological images are now being transformed into historical curiosities. A large nineteenth-century oil painting of purgatory hanging above one of the side altars in the church at Plouguerneau was restored in 1984. After years of neglect, the flames of purgatory are once again a luminous red and the lines of anguish have been redrawn on the faces of the souls doing penance. Paradoxically, the Plouguerneau curé, a strong supporter of the Vatican II innovations, is unperturbed by this seemingly retrograde resuscitation of an outmoded vision of the afterlife. He concurred with the desire of his parishioners to restore the painting, as a historical artifact rather than as a symbol inspiring belief. The curé explains, "People wanted to see it restored as they remembered it from the past. Personally," he continues, "I doubt if they are even consciously aware of the content of the painting."

Alternatives to Catholicism

The religious changes that have taken place in Brittany since the 1960s can easily be conceptualized in terms of decline. Church attendance has dropped, and the extent of adherence to church doctrines appears also to have decreased. However, it is equally important to think in terms of growth and development. Are new spiritual alternatives to Catholicism being created in Brittany? What is emerging to fill the religious vacuum left in the church's wake?

Levels of formal religious practice are only a partial and imperfect indicator of actual religious faith. Contemporary Bretons may be rejecting the formal structure of the church without rejecting Christianity. Now as in the past, this is certainly the case among the *rouges* in the Monts d'Arrée, who perceive the church to be connected with alien political and class interests. As Freeman (1978) has suggested for Spain, faith and religious experience in Brittany may be turning into private rather than public matters. Opportunities to watch Mass on television clearly provide a context for new forms of private observance, although few people in Plouguerneau and La Feuillée express much interest in televised religious services. When discussing religion, many people in both the Léon and the Monts d'Arrée describe themselves as *croyant, mais pas pratiquant,* or non-practicing believers. Such comments reveal much about the character of contemporary, privatized religious faith.

For the most part those who have ceased to be practicing Catholics have not joined other formal religious organizations in Brittany. Although the Protestant chapel founded in La Feuillée before World War I sparked some temporary interest, the efforts of the pastors who ministered there left no permanent impression on the spiritual landscape of the commune. Over the long term, people in La Feuillée have remained Catholic rather than adopting an alternative form of Christianity. They may be lapsed and anticlerical Catholics, but they have nevertheless remained within the structures of the "clerical model," even while rebelling against it. It seems impossible for most people from both Plouguerneau and the Monts d'Arrée to conceive of religion in other than Catholic terms. For the elderly and middle-aged, at least, one may be for or against Catholicism, but rarely independent of it. The tenacity of Catholicism can be seen in the negative responses evoked by door-to-door evangelical campaigns by the Jehovah's Witnesses. As one sixty-year-old Plouguerneau *paysanne* confesses, the Jehovah's Witnesses have caused her to doubt, particularly because she agrees with their argument that the money collected by the church for Masses and services is not well used. Nonetheless, she concludes, "I've been Catholic all my life. I'm too old to change my religion now."

Despite the reluctance of older people to adopt alternative forms of spirituality, many of the young display a strong interest in the occult sciences, reincarnation, vegetarianism, parapsychology, and astrology. Rosicrucianism has attracted a small following, and yoga is especially popular. The Breton cultural revival of the 1970s spurred an ongoing interest in ancient Celtic forms of spiritual awareness. At least to some degree, these movements are able to respond to the emotional needs of those facing death or bereavement. Pascale, the twenty-five-year-old sister of Jeannie Kervao from La Feuillée, for example, seeks to interpret Jeannie's death in the light of yoga philosophy as "the beginning of a new existence, not the end, senselessly, like that." This perspective offers some consolation for herself and her mother, neither of whom are practicing Catholics. Pascale values yoga both as a philosophical system and as exercise. Moreover, in her view yoga provides the type of transcendent experience which is lacking in Catholic ritual: "In yoga you rise above your problems and enter into communion with the group."[13]

Perhaps the real contemporary alternatives to Catholicism in

---

13. Writing of northern Portugal, Pina-Cabral (1986:191–196, 212–213) has observed a similar recent growth of interest in parapsychology and other nontraditional forms of spirituality, especially in urban areas.

Brittany are not to be found in the religious domain. At the conclusion of his study of religion in Limerzel, Lambert suggests that the Catholic system of meaning is being replaced by a view of the world in which the dominant principle that structures reality in a meaningful fashion is the search for immediate happiness and material well-being. Worldview has thus become present-oriented rather than directed toward a future existence (Lambert 1985: 372–374).

Ironically, the church in Brittany is itself to some extent responsible for the introduction of this secular worldview, with its emphasis on material success. During the 1920s, realizing that social change was inevitable, the church sought to exert its influence on the process of modernization through the Action Catholique social programs. In Brittany the Jeunesse Agricole Chrétienne (JAC) branch of this movement was particularly influential. From its inception in 1929 to the late 1950s, the JAC attracted a large following of young people, especially in the Léon. It sponsored recreational events, discussion groups, and theatrical productions which encouraged personal development and self-expression. Moreover, the JAC introduced a new climate of agricultural modernization by presenting a scientific vision of farming. Through the JAC, professional training for agriculturalists was promoted and information about technical developments was disseminated. Many of the most successful Breton farmers and leaders of agricultural syndicates from the 1960s through the 1980s are former active members of the JAC. By encouraging discussion of rural problems and by creating an extralocal network of social relationships for young people from peasant backgrounds, the JAC provided the organizational groundwork for the development of the syndicates that were to bring about radical changes in the organization of agriculture in Brittany during the 1960s. The syndicates promoted intensive market-oriented production, as well as creating cooperatives that cut prices for supplies and gave agriculturalists a measure of control over the marketing of their produce (Berger 1972:90–95, 195–200; Lambert 1985:119–126).

Paradoxically, the JAC helped to create the new social-structural conditions that have undermined the church in Brittany. The agricultural modernization promoted by the JAC has led to a decrease in reciprocal assistance at the local level. This in turn is linked to declining intensity of face-to-face social interaction within neighborhoods and has facilitated the expression of an individualistic perspective. The emphasis on individual autonomy characteristic of contemporary Breton society is also partly the product of the JAC's efforts to instill a new sense of self-worth among rural youth. The organization sought to encourage personal decision making through its study sessions and discussion groups, which were organized around the principle of *voir, juger, agir* (see, judge, act). Such a program was diametrically opposed to the church's traditional insistence on obedience to authoritarian precepts. In the sphere of religion, the JAC began to deemphasize ritual in favor of ethics and an inner, personal religious commitment (Lambert 1985:123–124). Ultimately, then, although intended to maintain the allegiance of the rural milieu to the church, the JAC in Brittany helped to generate a secular vision of society.

The outlines of the process of rationalization, Weber's "disenchantment of the world," are clearly delineated in the transformation of Breton Catholicism over the twentieth century. The dynamics of this complex process are analyzed further in Chapter 9, focusing on aspects of the supernatural which fall outside the scope of orthodox Catholicism.

Conclusion

Before the 1960s, the rituals of the church played a central part in affirming the identity of the parish community in rural Brittany. Within that community, the clergy exercised considerable social and political power. Although clerical authority provoked a strong anticlerical reaction in the Monts d'Arrée, even in this region no coherent alternative religious structures to Catholicism were developed. The absence of alternatives is particularly apparent in the domain of funerary ritual. Despite the opposition to the church voiced by many *rouges*, the clergy continues to provide the only acceptable ritual mediation of the passage from the community of the living to that of the dead. Civil burials, which lack a Catholic ceremony, are regarded by most people, including the anticlerical, as emotionally unsatisfying. They are not considered a fitting demonstration of respect for the deceased, and they fail to elevate death from the biological level to set it within the framework of a cultural system of significance.

Dramatic changes have taken place in Breton Catholicism over the past forty years. This period has seen the opening of rural Brittany to new influences from the larger society through the media, prolonged schooling, contact with émigrés who have left to work in metropolitan France, and greater opportunities for travel (Lambert 1985:237–238). With Bretons receiving further education, greater material advantages, and exposure to the competing, scientific, interpretation of reality, the church's ability to coerce obedience has diminished (Lambert 1985:358). Whereas the necessity of attending Sunday Mass was unquestioned up to the 1950s by the majority of people in most regions of Brittany, now, in the 1980s, only a minority attend Mass on a regular basis. As previously noted, this development is partly the result of changes in face-to-face social interaction on the local level. Networks of kin, friends, and colleagues are no longer exclusively bounded by the parish (Lambert 1985:239, 241). One no longer needs to attend Mass to see and to be seen, to reaffirm one's social status, or to discover important news about community events. In addition, as opportunities for recreation multiply, new types of leisure activities compete with those offered by the church.

In post–Vatican II Catholicism, as Lambert emphasizes, the sacred has moved closer to the profane. The priest no longer represents a quasi-supernatural figure, set apart from the congregation by his role, social standing, superior education, and attire. Lay readers have been granted an active role in the Mass, and the use of French rather than Latin has made ritual more accessible to the general public (Lambert 1985:253). All of these changes have given contemporary Catholicism a more intellectual, "disenchanted," and less ritualistic character. The traditional emphasis on mortal sin and divine punishment for transgressing the commandments of God or the church has been replaced by a new concern for ethical conduct, which stresses principles such as charity and universal goodwill (Lambert 1985:326). The threat of hell and purgatory is no longer used by the clergy to compel moral behavior, and God is increasingly portrayed as a relatively distant God of Love rather than an omniscient Judge who intervenes regularly in human affairs. No longer able to impose itself through fear, Catholicism now seeks to attract the faithful by depicting itself as the ultimate route to individual self-fulfillment (Lambert 1985:283, 357–358).

In William Christian's terms, post–Vatican II Catholicism has ceased to be a vertical system, stressing the role of the saints and the dead as mediators between man and God. Now egalitarian relationships of brotherly love are emphasized, and "other people are the intermediaries on the path to God" (Christian 1972:183). Although retained in contemporary Catholicism, the concept of the afterlife no longer occupies a central role in the church's predication. In Brittany, as in the rural Spanish context that Christian describes, salvation has become "the by-product of the good life, not its goal" (Christian 1972:183). The new Catholicism is more a religion of transcendent humanism than one oriented toward salvation in the other world (Lambert 1985:358). In Ariès's view the decline of belief in an afterlife is partly responsible for the development of the denial of death in Western society (1982:573, 576). The idea of death is repressed because of the terrifying prospect of the void upon which it opens. However, conversations in Plouguerneau and La Feuillée suggest that committed Catholics do not necessarily confront death more easily than those who lack religious faith. As the curé of La Feuillée remarks with unusual candor, "Everyone wants to live as long as possible. In the last analysis, death is a great mystery for everyone, even for believers."

The changes that have occurred in Breton Catholicism may be characterized in general terms as the replacement of an authoritarian, divinely sanctioned system of morality by a humanistic ethical code, which has been accompanied by a deemphasis of ritual. These transformations have been precipitated by changes in Breton social organization and have also contributed to reinforce those changes. Over time, religion, social structure, and attitudes toward death in Brittany have been closely interdependent domains. The history of the missions demonstrates that the preoccupation with death typical of traditional Breton culture, although undoubtedly derived in part from pre- or non-Christian folk beliefs (some of which may be Celtic in origin), was shaped to a large extent by the Catholic church through its insistence on sin, divine retribution, hell, and purgatory. From the seventeenth to the mid-twentieth century the church used fear of death and damnation to maintain a moral system which in itself was the prerequisite for the reproduction of a rigidly hierarchical, authoritarian social order dominated by the clergy and landed proprietors. Anticlerical reactions developed in those areas where this social order was weakest, like the

Monts d'Arrée, a region of small, independent landholdings with few noble families or wealthy landed proprietors. During the interwar period the church-sanctioned stratified social order began to undergo transformation in other regions, including the Léon and the Morbihan. However, radical changes did not occur until the 1950s. At this period land lost its traditional importance as the primary means of production, and economic development opened new opportunities for wage labor outside the agricultural sector. With mechanization, agriculture itself became less labor-intensive, reducing the need for a pool of landless agricultural workers, which the church's encouragement of large families indirectly sustained. Paradoxically, while trying to maintain its position of social dominance through the JAC, the church helped to create the necessary preconditions for structural transformation.

Since the disappearance of the traditional social order the moral code and eschatological system on which it was based have also been largely abandoned. With its new emphasis on humanistic ethics and self-fulfillment, the church has dropped its former concern for the afterlife. In Brittany, as elsewhere in the Catholic world, death no longer plays a central role in predication. The this-worldly focus of religion parallels the present orientation of contemporary Breton society at large.

8

The Living and the Dead

Breton culture of the nineteenth and early twentieth centuries was characterized by the close association of the world of the living and that of the souls, *les êtres d'outre-tombe* (Le Braz 1928:1:lv; 2:21). In contemporary Brittany the gap between these two domains has widened. Nevertheless, for many people in Plouguerneau and La Feuillée it remains important to maintain ongoing relationships with the deceased. Despite the growing tendency to exclude death from the realm of everyday life, in subtle ways beliefs about the proximity of the spirit world continue to parallel those of earlier periods.

The Anaon

In nineteenth-century Brittany the distance between the domains occupied by the living and the dead was barely perceptible, for to a large extent they interpenetrated: "No sooner is the coffin nailed shut than you encounter the dead person again, one minute later, leaning on his garden fence. If death is a voyage, the return trip in any case follows quickly upon the departure. . . . Hence, the dead come to life again, in the final analysis, in the same places where they have always lived" (Le Braz 1928:1:lvi–lvii). Although the physical space occupied by the living and the dead was the same, they were separated by the dimension of time: "As long as it is day, the earth belongs to the living; come night, it belongs to the dead. Respectable people try to be asleep with their doors closed at the hour of the revenants. One should never stay outside needlessly after sundown" (Le Braz 1928:2:24).

Aspects of this folk belief are reflected in contemporary attitudes toward the night. Many La Feuillée women have a vaguely defined fear of being outside at night. For this reason they often refuse invitations that require travel after dark, even by car within the commune: "I don't like the night, you know." This comportment is not restricted to the elderly. Some women in their forties share such sentiments, although teenagers and those under thirty tend to be more adventurous and willingly drive miles at night to dance at the nearest disco boîte.

The elderly and the middle-aged are acutely sensitive to abnormalities in their environment at night. Strange sounds around the house are listened to attentively, and a light noticed outside where no lights are usually seen provokes unease. Dusk is marked by an almost obsessive shuttering of windows, as each household turns on its lights and closes itself in on itself. The heavy wooden shutters seal out wind and cold and protect those inside from the casual gaze of passersby. However, they also seem to fulfill a deeper, unspoken need to exclude the night and whatever supernatural beings might be lurking in its shadows.

Many elderly people in La Feuillée take care to lock their doors after sunset. As one seventy-four-year-old woman explained, "You know, I am timid in the evenings. If you come to visit me after seven o'clock, call from the window, otherwise I won't open the door." While such caution may to some extent be justified by anxiety about threats from the living rather than the dead, crime is virtually nonexistent in La Feuillée. Moreover, some people explicitly state that it is not criminals who make them anxious. Recalling her elderly mother who died in 1980, a La Feuillée woman in her early seventies explains, "Those beliefs about the dead who returned to the earth used to be so strong that my mother was troubled by them to the end of her life. When she had to stay alone in her house at night, she used to tell me: 'I'm afraid at night. Not of the living—I don't even think about burglars—but I am afraid of the dead.'"

The desire to shut out the night and the beings to whom it belongs takes on added significance in the light of the folk belief that the dead seek to return to their former homes after dark. According to Le Braz's nineteenth-century informants, one should never sweep the house after sunset. If it is necessary to do so, the dust and debris should be swept toward the hearth and burned or left in a pile next to the fire until morning. On no account, however, should it be swept out of the house: "One would risk sweeping out, along with the dust, the souls of the deceased, who at that hour often obtain permission to return to their former homes" (Le Braz 1928:2:23).

During the nineteenth century, sweeping after dark was known as *scuba an anaoun*, "sweeping the dead" (Sébillot 1904:136). Some elderly people in contemporary Brittany continue to refrain from sweeping the house at night. The prohibition against sweeping after dark is almost universally known by women over forty, but mention of it often provokes half-embarrassed laughter at the superstitious nature of people in the past. Few women will readily state that it was the souls of the dead whom one sought to avoid sweeping out of the house. Other justifications for the belief are advanced: that one would cause all the happiness in the household to depart, for example, or that one would sweep away all the money earned during the day. A deeply Catholic family from Plouguerneau recounts that sweeping after dark would cause the household to lose all its indulgences, condemning its members to a longer stay in purgatory after their deaths. When an elderly grandmother and her middle-aged nieces in La Feuillée were asked about this custom, the younger women said that sweeping at night was prohibited because women who did their housework by dark were not clean and orderly. The older woman was reluctant to respond, but finally stated, "It was said that you would see someone running around the house." Asked if this "someone" was a revenant, she agreed, but quickly added, "That was one of those things that wasn't true."

Yet despite this disclaimer and the laughter which frequently greets discussions about sweeping after dark, more subtle signs suggest that private belief in the return of the souls by night exists alongside the skepticism often voiced in public conversations, particularly those with people from outside the Monts d'Arrée. Seventy-four-year-old Joséphine Kérouac lives in the house she inherited from her mother in the center of the *bourg*. It is a large house, where her mother lived for many years and operated a café. In one frank conversation Joséphine confided that when she awakes at night, she often has the feeling that her mother is present in the house with her. She senses that she is not alone. Joséphine's comment is significant because it raises the possibility that the embarrassed laughter about sweeping the house at night masks similar experiences, about which most people are unwilling to speak.

According to another folk belief collected by Le Braz, the dead, who are always cold, are attracted to the hearth when they return to their former homes. They seek to warm themselves, resting on any object they find close to the fire. For this reason the trivet, an iron tripod used for holding cooking vessels over the fire, should always be removed after use. Were the trivet left in place, the returning souls might sit on it and burn themselves. A nineteenth-century Breton proverb encapsulates this belief:

> *Pa chomm ann trebe war an tan*
> When the trivet is over the fire,
> *Ann Anaon paour a ve en poan*
> The poor souls are in pain.
> (Le Braz 1928:2:22)

While this proverb is still recognized by elderly and middle-aged people in the La Feuillée region, it is no longer spontaneously quoted. In households where a wood fire continues to be used for cooking or as a source of heat, the trivet is generally placed to one side of the flames or hung up on a nail in the chimney when not in use. However, this is now done more through force of habit than through conscious reference to the proverb and folk belief.

A vision of the dead returning to warm themselves at the hearth of their former household is poignantly presented in the legend "Les deux vieux arbres," collected by Le Braz (1928:2:46–55). In this narrative an elderly couple are condemned after their deaths to do penance for their sins in the form of beech trees close to their farm, which has been inherited by their son. On the way to the mill one summer evening, the son is surprised to hear voices coming from the beech trees overhanging his path:

> The first of the two trees, the one on the right, was saying: "I think you are cold, Maharit. You are trembling in all your limbs." And the second tree, on the left, replied, shivering: "Yes, Jelvestr, I am frozen, truly frozen, to the marrow. Each time night falls it is like this; the cold penetrates me like a second death. Luckily, tonight they are making crêpes at our son's place; there will be a good fire, and as soon as he and his wife are in bed we will have our turn to go and warm ourselves by the embers."
> (1928:2:49)

That night the trees move slowly but inexorably toward the farmhouse. Crossing the threshold, the old couple reassume human form. As during life, they sit next to the hearth, warming themselves until the clock strikes midnight and ends their brief respite from penance.[1]

Although not always visible, the Anaon were considered an omnipresent component of the social and natural environment in nineteenth-century Brittany. Should one see small patches of dry ground on a wet roadway during a rainstorm, one could be sure that the souls were serving their penance in these places (Le Braz 1928:2:26). Departing from a household after a visit, one did not omit to take one's leave of its deceased as well as its living occupants, with the phrase "Bennoz Doue war gement hini a zo êt da Anaon on deuz an ti-me" (God's blessing upon all those from this house who have gone to the Anaon). Similarly, out of respect for the Anaon, the name of a deceased person was never mentioned in conversation without the accompanying formula *Doué d'he bardono*, "God pardon him" (Le Braz 1928:2:21–22, 26). Although increasingly rare, this phrase may still be heard among Breton speakers.

Up to the mid-twentieth century, folk tradition went so far as to include the dead at weddings, the most joyful and life-oriented of rites of passage. A Mass or service for the souls of the deceased in the families of both the bride and groom was customarily held directly before or after the marriage ceremony. In this way the family dead were symbolically included in the celebration. As one La Feuillée woman explains, describing her wedding in 1933, "They rang the wedding bells, and right afterward they were ringing the death knell." This practice gradually disappeared, just prior to World War II, as families initially rescheduled the Mass for the dead to the Sunday following the wedding and then discontinued the ceremony altogether. The decline of this custom reflects the progressive exclusion of the Anaon over the last forty years from the world of the living.

The distancing of the dead from the community of the living in contemporary Brittany is partly a product of the process of secu-

---

1. Related folk beliefs about returning souls who warm themselves at the hearths of the living have been collected from Gaelic Ireland (Deeney 1900:5–6).

larization or rationalization which Weber terms "disenchantment." The supernatural, in both its non-Christian and orthodox Catholic manifestations, is no longer believed to permeate the natural world. Legends like "Les deux vieux arbres" are no longer told. Contemporary sophisticated audiences would have difficulty crediting such concrete manifestations by the dead. Nevertheless, the sense of a continuing relationship with the dead remains an integral part of Breton worldview in ways that recall aspects of earlier folk belief. This connection is apparent in the experience of Joséphine Kerouac, whose nightly impression of her mother's presence in the family home is reminiscent of the nineteenth-century belief in the return of the souls to their former dwellings after dark. Other examples provide additional evidence that the dead continue, in some degree at least, to coexist in the realm of the living.

Thoughts of deceased relatives come to mind for many people in Plouguerneau and La Feuillée when they are doing things that the dead used to do, such as routine household chores. Two unmarried sisters in their sixties from La Feuillée, living together in the home they occupied with their mother until her death five years earlier, frequently find themselves remarking to one another, "Look, *maman* would have done that this way." They note that it is hard sometimes not to believe that she is still in the house with them, sitting in her favorite chair. Whereas many bereaved people in North America discard items of household furniture or decoration evoking strong memories of a dead relative, in La Feuillée and Plouguerneau such mementos are preserved with care. As one middle-aged woman from Plouguerneau comments, "I live with my dead. Their pictures are up on my kitchen wall. It is more important to have the photos of the dead on display than those of the living. You have your living family with you, but for the dead all you have is the photo." She feels as close to her mother eighteen months after her death as they were during her life but explains that the nature of their relationship has changed.

Visits to the Cemetery

Although memories of the dead are evoked in the family home, visits to the cemetery are the most important form of ongoing communication or communion with the deceased. According to Ariès, the cemetery emerged in Europe in the nineteenth century as the privileged meeting ground between the living and the dead (1982:525–526). It was during the romantic era that the "cult of the dead," with its emphasis on perpetuating the memory of the deceased and immortalizing them through tomb monuments, became "the great popular religion of France" (Ariès 1982:543). Although initially promoted by positivist philosophers, the idea of the cult of the dead was adopted by the church, and reverence for the deceased came to be viewed as an integral doctrine of Catholicism (Ariès 1982:545).

In contemporary Plouguerneau and La Feuillée the romantic perspective continues to influence eschatological beliefs and ideas about the cemetery. As noted in Chapters 5 and 7, inasmuch as the dead are conceived to maintain some sort of existence after death, they are largely considered to do so in the tomb. This idea that the dead "live" in the cemetery underlies the importance of visits to the family tomb. Mothers and grandmothers frequently take small children with them on walks to the cemetery, visiting first one monument, then that of another relative. These pilgrimages are described in terms similar to those used when talking about paying a call to a living family member: "Now we'll go and see your godfather, and afterward we'll visit Grandpa."[2]

Visits to the tomb provide special consolation for widows and the newly bereaved. A woman from the Monts d'Arrée who has recently lost a grandson remarks that each time she goes to the *bourg*, whether to see friends or to do her shopping, she finds herself in the cemetery at the boy's tomb, without having consciously decided to go there. "It is as if something pulled me like a magnet," she explains. Similar sentiments are expressed by a La Feuillée widow in her late sixties, who recalls that she visited her husband's grave daily throughout the first year following his death. "It made me feel less as though I had abandoned him," she says. Speaking of her own deceased husband, Joséphine Kerouac provides a particularly revealing description of the type of silent dialogue between the living and the dead which such visits permit: "I tell him about all that is happening to me and what is going on in the com-

---

2. Identical phrases are used to describe visits to graves in Andalusia (Brandes 1981:182).

mune. 'Listen there, Henri, did you hear that? The hunting season has started and the men are going out on the mountain with their dogs.'" Through such communion, close ties are maintained between the Anaon and the living who walk above them.

In general, women in Plouguerneau and La Feuillée visit the cemetery more frequently than men. Just as the women in a family keep account of genealogical connections and maintain contact with distant relatives, so too do women assure that relationships endure between living and dead kin.[3] Kinship is the domain of women, and if there are women in a family capable of looking after the tombs of their relatives, men rarely do the task. Nevertheless, widowers may take over this responsibility, visiting and caring for the tombs of their deceased wives. One La Feuillée widower in his seventies divides his time between his home in the commune and that of a married daughter in Algeria. He notes that he visits his wife's grave frequently when he is in La Feuillée: "Every time I pass by the cemetery I have to stop." Before leaving for Algeria he makes a special visit to the cemetery, "for one needs to say goodbye."

While most people in Plouguerneau and La Feuillée accept that visits to the cemetery are psychologically beneficial for the bereaved—"that alleviates one's grief"—certain women who visit the graveyard too often are criticized. One Plouguerneau woman whose mother died suddenly has had great difficulty accepting her death and visits the cemetery twice daily. As a neighbor states, "People are saying she's gone a bit crazy."

The majority of those who visit the cemetery on a regular basis are elderly or middle-aged people. This may reflect the growing denial of death among the young. One florist in the La Feuillée area remarks that most of the flowers she sells for tomb decorations are bought by "little grandmothers." In her view, "the young people forget their families." Her use of the phrase "their families" rather than "their dead" is significant. It suggests that for the young, the dead, like distant relatives with whom little contact is maintained, are gradually being excluded from that category of people recognized as kin. It should be remembered, however, that the comport-

---

3. Likewise, Andalusian women both foster ties among living kin and, by caring for and visiting graves, perpetuate the links between the living and the dead (Brandes 1981:182).

ment of contemporary young people is likely to change as they grow older. Today's eighteen-year-olds who do not visit the cemetery may do so frequently when they reach fifty or sixty years of age. In addition, for certain young people, particularly those who have experienced the death of a close family member, the tradition of visiting the family tomb continues to be meaningful. In La Feuillée, one of these is Pascale Kervao, the twenty-five-year-old sister of Jeannie, whose sudden death at twenty-two has radically altered the lives of all those in her family. Pascale lives in Brest, where she teaches primary school. She returns to visit her family in La Feuillée each weekend and on Wednesdays, when school is closed in the afternoon. Upon her arrival her first concern is to visit her sister's tomb, often making the five-minute walk to the cemetery in the rain or as dusk falls. Similarly, on Sundays before returning to Brest, the solitary ritual is repeated. Another young woman in La Feuillée visits the tomb of her godmother, who died recently. Like many older women, this eighteen-year-old makes a visit each time she passes the cemetery, arranging flowers or tidying up around the tomb.

In Plouguerneau the close association between Catholicism and the cult of the dead is reflected by the fact that many people visit the cemetery after the weekly High Mass, either individually or with their families. Visits after Mass are a custom that developed when the cemetery was located around the church. While the Sunday morning Mass in La Feuillée is also followed by pilgrimages to the cemetery, the low level of church attendance in this parish makes the Mass a less important occasion for visits. In La Feuillée the cemetery is likely to be more frequented on Sunday afternoons, when it becomes a stopping point for groups of women on afternoon walks. Others, especially the recently bereaved, tend to visit alone, slipping in and out of the cemetery at the end of the afternoon, after most other visitors have returned home. On summer evenings, too, it is rare to pass by the cemetery without seeing several people tending the flowers on the graves of their kin.

All of the major calendrical festivals are marked in the cemetery. The main annual celebrations for the dead are, of course, Toussaint and the Fête des Morts (All Saints' Day and All Souls' Day), on November 1 and 2. Visits to the cemetery are also made in association with more personal annual events, such as the birthday of the deceased or the anniversary of death. Monument builders note that sales of commemorative plaques, artificial flowers, and other tomb ornaments increase at Christmas and Easter, as well as Mother's Day and Father's Day. At such times the decorations purchased for the tomb and the flowers placed on it are symbolic gifts for the deceased which serve to include them in the festivities shared by the living. For the same reason many families in La Feuillée put special bouquets on their tombs for the *pardon*, or patron saint's day celebration, explaining that "it is the *pardon* for the dead, too." This gesture has special significance since the patron of the parish is Saint John the Baptist, whose festival has historically been linked to the dead in Breton folk tradition.

The marking of calendar festivals by visiting the cemetery and offering flowers to the dead eases the rupture of separation caused by death. Since the deceased are in some sense "still there" in the cemetery, death does not radically truncate relations with them. Personal rituals and family traditions established during the lifetime of the deceased may still be honored. Seven years after the death of her husband, seventy-two-year-old Yvonne Robert continues to take a pot of lilies of the valley to his tomb in the La Feuillée cemetery on May 1. In many parts of France on this date, the *fête des muguets*, lilies of the valley are exchanged as good luck symbols, in a custom dating from the end of the nineteenth century (van Gennep 1949:1444–1445). M. Robert used to buy lilies of the valley each year for everyone in the household; now Yvonne buys them for his grave.

Summer vacation is another annual period of frequent visits to the cemetery in both Plouguerneau and La Feuillée. Many people from these communities who have been dispersed in the *exode rural* return for holidays in July and August. At this time ties are renewed with relatives, both living and dead. The visit to the tomb is an important feature of the return to the countryside for numerous families. Many elderly people living in *quartiers* in La Feuillée at some distance from the *bourg* have difficulty walking to the cemetery, and they take advantage of the presence of sons and daughters with cars to make a visit to the family tomb. One family, on vacation in La Feuillée from Paris, made a special day-long trip to Vannes, on the south Breton coast, in order to visit the grave of in-laws buried there.

In Brittany, as in the Châtillonais community studied by Zonabend (1980), flowers function as symbolic mediators in the relationship between the living and the dead. The flowers placed on tombs in Plouguerneau and La Feuillée vary with the seasons. Pots of begonias, sheltered from the weather in garden sheds, are encouraged to bloom in early spring for transfer to the cemetery. Summer offers the widest choice of cut flowers. If the weather is not excessively dry, flowers will last longer in this season than during the winter, when they are threatened by wind and frost. Artificial flowers of cloth or plastic are frequently purchased during the winter months. Since they do not need to be watered or replaced, artificial flowers circumvent the need for frequent visits to the cemetery. For this reason, as some La Feuillée women suggest, their increasing popularity may indicate a diminishing of the concern to maintain ongoing relationships with the dead.

Dreams and Prayers

The visit to the tomb represents an effort on the part of the living to seek out the dead and to establish communion with them. Dreams, in contrast, are interpreted in rural Brittany as one of the ways in which the dead attempt to communicate with the living. As noted in Chapter 4, this is the interpretation made by Maryvonne, whose deceased mother appeared to her in dreams throughout the first year after her death, giving instructions concerning the construction of a *caveau* and the organization of the *messe d'anniversaire*. Although Maryvonne herself would probably not conceptualize her experience in this way, from a psychoanalytic perspective these apparitions may be viewed as symbolic projections of Maryvonne's internal feelings of guilt about unfulfilled ritual obligations to her dead mother. A second incident recounted by Maryvonne also involves a dream that functioned as a medium for communication across the boundary between the world of the living and the Anaon.

Approximately ten years ago, a close friend of Maryvonne's was gravely ill. She had been hospitalized and Maryvonne intended to pay her a visit. However, she changed her mind on learning that her friend was in a coma and would neither recognize visitors nor derive any pleasure from their presence. Maryvonne depended on a mutual acquaintance, a mechanic from her friend's village who worked at the garage next door to Maryvonne's home, for news about the sick woman's progress. It was on a Friday that she learned from this man that her friend was in a coma. On Saturday and Sunday the garage was closed, so Maryvonne received no further news. Sunday evening Maryvonne had a dream that featured the road between Couzanet, the hamlet where her friend lived, and the *bourg* of Loqueffret, to the south. The road winds between two small hills. In her dream Maryvonne saw an ornate gold cross, like those carried at the head of funeral processions, making its way along this road. The morning after her dream, when the garage next door opened, Maryvonne's first concern was to inquire about her friend's health. Surprised, the mechanic burst out, "But didn't you know, my poor woman? She died on Saturday night, and the funeral is this morning at ten o'clock." Maryvonne had just enough time to prepare herself for the funeral, which was held in the church at Loqueffret. The funeral procession followed the same route she had seen in her dream, between the two small hills on the road from Couzanet. As Maryvonne explained, the dream had been a sign from her friend, a message telling of her death:

> And I had been thinking hard, and I was sad on Saturday evening and all day Sunday. And I had been saying to myself, "But why? They haven't gotten in touch with me" [i.e., no one from her friend's family had contacted Maryvonne to let her know whether her friend had died, or to tell her to come to the wake]. I was thinking about her a lot, you see. And it was her spirit. As soon as she died, she made that sign. And it was her spirit, without a doubt, that—that in the form of a dream or something, I don't know what—that gave me the sign. At least, me, I call that having a vision. It isn't [a dream]; for me it's stronger than a dream, you see.[4]

For Maryvonne, dreams are signs whereby the mute dead can make their needs and desires known to the living. Experiences like Maryvonne's are not restricted to the middle-aged and the elderly, although only a small minority in any age group will speak readily about such dreams. One young woman from La Feuillée who is currently completing high school in Brest frequently dreams of her deceased grandfather. Disturbed by these dreams, she confided in

---

4. The belief that ghosts indicate the direction that their funeral procession will take is a widespread motif in European folklore (Thompson 1955–1958: Motif E530.1.7, ghost light indicates route funeral will take).

her mother, who counseled her that "if a dead person appears in your dreams, it is because he needs your prayers." The girl now prays for her grandfather each time she sees him in a dream. Paradoxically, she notes, neither she nor her family are particularly religious: "We don't go to church all that much, only for the big occasions like weddings and funerals." Clearly, prayers for the dead and a concern for their welfare can exist outside of orthodox Catholicism.

Prayer is conceived in one sense as a means whereby the living can help to improve the condition of the deceased in the otherworld. In another sense, prayer provides the living with a medium through which they can communicate with the dead. Eighty-six-year-old Marie-Thérèse from La Feuillée lost her husband in 1975, when he died suddenly after a heart attack. Nine years later she confides that she thinks of him each day. "Every day, every day. One doesn't forget. And every night I say a prayer before going to bed." Marie-Thérèse rarely attends Mass and she describes herself as "neither for nor against religion." When asked about her view of the afterlife, she claims that "there is nothing, just the tomb." Yet her unorthodox form of prayer enables her to maintain contact with the husband she has lost. In a parallel fashion many people describe visits to the cemetery as "going to say a prayer." Standing quietly in front of the grave marker, the visitor appears lost in meditation. While some people cross themselves before turning away, this type of prayer is not an appeal to God or His intercessors in the Catholic sense of the term "prayer." Rather, it is a way of speaking to the dead. As one woman explains, "When I stand there in front of the tomb, I think of my father and my mother. I say to them, 'I hope that you are happy, there where you are now. You certainly merit happiness. I ask your forgiveness if I have ever done you harm. I have the faith that I will find you again someday.'"

Prayer thus offers a means of communication with the dead on a private and personal level. The giving of Masses for their souls, in contrast, is an institutionalized and public gesture. As Ariès (1982: 462–463) points out, the church responded to the development of the romantic sensibility by advocating its devotions for the souls in purgatory as an outlet for the growing popular desire to maintain ongoing relationships with deceased loved ones. In Plouguerneau and La Feuillée the church's rituals continue to be requested to aid the dead. Many people, particularly devout Catholics, believe that it is necessary to pay for a Mass for those dead persons who appear in one's dreams. Odette, the forty-year-old niece of Joséphine Kerouac, dreams often about her deceased father. Odette's parents were both in a serious car accident when she was seventeen. Her mother died immediately, but her father lingered as an invalid for eighteen months. Odette has dreamed of him many times since his death. Her dreams are always the same. She sees her father as he was during life, "well dressed, in a suit, but very thin, as though he were suffering." She adds, "They say that when you dream of a dead person, he needs a Mass." Odette's aunt, Joséphine, reacts to dreams of her own mother in a similar way: "Every time I dream about her, the next day, you can be sure, she has a Mass." Significantly, Joséphine's mother left both of her daughters specific instructions to give frequent Masses for her soul.

Masses, costing fifty francs, may be requested from the parish curé at any time. As mentioned earlier with respect to *services de continuation*, paying for a Mass may be likened to sacrifice. For those who request a Mass after dreaming of a deceased relative, however, the symbolic offering is made not to God but to the deceased individual, through the channel of the church, so that one's dreams will no longer be troubled with his or her presence. The existence of this type of supernatural transaction underscores the ambivalence and conflicting emotions that frequently characterize relationships with the dead. Although one loved one's deceased relatives and continues to do so, one wants them to remain among the dead. Perhaps it would be more accurate to state that one seeks to define and delimit the contexts in which interaction between the living and the dead is appropriate. One such institutionalized context is the annual celebration of Toussaint and the Fête des Morts.

Toussaint and the Fête des Morts

Throughout the Catholic world Toussaint, or All Saints' Day (November 1), is the festival of the saints, those among the deceased who have already ascended to heaven. The Fête des Morts, or All Souls' Day (November 2), is the festival of all the other dead, including those in purgatory and hell. In contemporary Brittany, as in many other Catholic regions, these two festivals have been largely fused into a single celebration on November 1. The Fête des Morts retains little of its separate identity partly because, unlike Toussaint, it is not a national public holiday. In many Breton parishes the distinction between the saints and the dead in general is maintained by the celebration of two separate religious services on November 1. In Plouguerneau, for instance, a "Mass for the saints" is held on the morning of that day, while "vespers for the dead" are held in the afternoon. In La Feuillée, however, the priest is also responsible for a second parish, neighboring Botmeur. Since it is impossible to celebrate two Masses in both of these communities, he offers one in each, alternating biennially between morning and afternoon.

By nine o'clock on the morning of November 1, the cemetery in La Feuillée is already a center of activity. Many of those visiting their family tombs are in a hurry to return to the *bourg* in time to find a seat in church for the Mass that begins at ten-thirty. Whereas the average Sunday morning Mass attracts perhaps twenty faithful, on Toussaint the church is full to overflowing. Extra benches must be placed near the back door to accommodate the three hundred or more people in the congregation. Many of those present are returned emigrants from Paris and other cities. Others, from the commune, are not practicing Catholics, and at least one-third are men. For many men and Communists, Toussaint is the single annual religious festival that merits attendance at church. As one man states, "This is a celebration that can exist independently of the Catholic faith."

The *glas*, or death knell that is rung at funerals, also announces the Toussaint Mass. Throughout the service the priest stresses themes of hope, trust in God's pardon, and eternal life. His sermon seeks to overcome the contradiction between the human desire to live forever and the fact of physical death: "A celebration for the dead. Why celebrate for the dead? *Eh bien*, very simply, because they are *living*. You who are assembled here in this church, you have the faith that all does not end here below. That, happily, there is a life waiting for us, where we will no longer know pain, suffering, trials; where all will be joy." Toward the end of the Mass a prayer is offered for the parish dead, and those from La Feuillée who have died in the previous year are listed by name. The ceremony ends with a procession of the entire congregation to the cemetery. Along the route, the congregation sings the "Kantik ar Baradoz." Formerly the "Gwerz ar Garnel," or Song of the Ossuary, was sung on this occasion. In the latter hymn the spirits of the dead tell the living of their sufferings in the afterlife:

> We have lived on the earth, just like you,
> We talked, walked, drank, and ate,
> And now here is the state to which we have been reduced;
> After having been buried we are but fodder for the worms.
>
> . . . .
>
> If you ask where our souls have gone,
> They are in purgatory, still far from heaven.
> They are in the fire that burns, to finish paying the debt
> That they contracted on earth to the true God.
>
> (Le Braz 1928:2:76–77, verses 6 and 9)

In the aftermath of the Vatican II reforms, however, the La Feuillée priest considers that such a graphic description of decay and torment presents too horrific and depressing a vision of the afterlife. As with many other changes in Catholic ritual since the mid-1960s, the discontinuation of the use of the "Gwerz ar Garnel" both reflects and encourages the contemporary Breton movement away from direct confrontation with death.

At Toussaint, as at funerals, the procession to the cemetery is led by the cross and the priest. The honor of carrying the cross at this celebration is given to one of the few practicing Catholic men in the community. Another is chosen to carry a container filled with holy water, which the priest will use to bless the tombs. A number of the women recognized as "pillars of the church," who know the words of the "Kantik ar Baradoz" and can be counted on to sing, follow closely after the cross at the head of the procession. Those who attend Mass less regularly stay close to the rear. Upon arrival in the cemetery the procession halts at the central cross, where the priest offers a short prayer (see fig. 13). Repeating the gesture of blessing seen at both funerals and wakes, he sprinkles holy water in all directions in a general benediction for the dead. At this point the ceremony is complete, and the congregation disperses, each family to its own tombs.

A much simpler celebration takes place on November 2. Again the *glas* sounds prior to the Mass, at nine in the morning. Less than one-third of those present on the preceding day, and very few men, attend the All Souls' Day Service. The catafalque, symbolizing the collective parish dead, is surrounded by lighted tapers at the back of the church, and it is blessed by the faithful with holy water, as at a *messe de huitaine*. After the mass the cemetery is again visited, but there is no procession. People go alone or in groups of two or three.

Preparations for Toussaint begin as early as three weeks prior to the festival. Weeds must be uprooted from around the tombs and monuments must be scrubbed, using a powdered cleanser and brushes or scouring pads to remove dirt and lichen growth. Some older tombs are marked by a rectangular enclosure of rough-cut granite slabs, within which the ground is covered by white quartz pebbles. These pebbles must be painstakingly removed, soaked in cleanser, dried and replaced. New polished granite monuments require less care, but even these must be wiped with a damp cloth. People repaint the gold letters of their family names on tombstones. This is the period of greatest demand for the services of monument builders, as families who plan to build a *caveau* or to erect a new monument frequently wish to have the work completed in time for Toussaint. After the death of Jeannie Kervao in September 1983, her family commissioned a *caveau* and a new granite monument. The construction was finished in time for her body to be transferred to the *caveau* at the end of October.

Preparations for Toussaint reach a peak of intensity during the last week of October. At this time the cemetery in La Feuillée bustles with the activities of the living. Especially if the weather is good, groups of women from the *bourg* make the cemetery the object of their afternoon walk, in order to see how work there is progressing and to exchange greetings with acquaintances. During these days of preparation, the social atmosphere in the cemetery is not always one of heavy seriousness. Conversations recall those heard on the town square or in the shops of the *bourg*. Talk is not restricted to the subject of the dead, although reminiscences frequently allude to deceased family members and friends.

On a sunny afternoon in late October 1983, while weeding around a poorly kept grave, eighty-two-year-old Angèle Kerriou, one of the most lively members of the La Feuillée *club du troisième âge*, remarked to her companions that this was the resting place of a bachelor uncle who no longer had any close family to maintain his tomb. "That's an uncle of mine there," she observed, "the godson of my father. How he used to make us laugh, that one—eh, Marie?" Here the emotions are ones of enduring fondness. Yet other tombs evoke more painful memories. Cleaning the tomb of her husband, a widow in her mid-fifties confided that she experiences an almost physical sensation of grief. "I feel it in there," she explained, motioning to her chest and abdomen. Her husband had committed suicide five years earlier, at age fifty-two. As she commented, "There are some days when you just don't want to do anything. You just don't know how you're going to keep on living."

Toussaint is often described as a depressing time of year, particularly for the recently bereaved. Although it is difficult in some cases to come to the cemetery to clean the tombs, these preparations also have a cathartic effect. Grief is evoked, but through its expression, the force of the emotion is dissipated. "Ultimately," many people from La Feuillée affirm, "one is comforted."

In many cases the women in a family share the cleaning of tombs, each having responsibility for one or more.[5] Frequently an older woman will "give" a tomb she formerly cared for to a younger niece or daughter-in-law who is more adept at reaching and cleaning the high parts of the monument. It is rare to see men working alone in the cemetery.[6] Women are by far the majority, although married couples may come to do the preparations together, particularly if there is heavy work to be done. Often two sisters will clean their tombs together. The *aides-ménagères*, home helpers for elderly invalids, have extra duties as Toussaint approaches, for they are often requested by their clients to ensure that the tomb is "made presentable." Some people make an effort to clean and

---

5. Similarly, Segalen (1985:363) observes that in the *pays* Bigouden, cleaning tombs for Toussaint is a task performed together by women kin.

6. Writing of Andalusia, Brandes (1981:182–183) also notes that cleaning graves for All Saints' Day is considered to be the responsibility of women rather than men: "In daily life . . . women take care of the physical needs of their families, including cleaning and decorating the house. On All Saints' Day this role is transferred to family gravesites, where women scrub and sweep tombstones and adorn them with candles and flowers" (1981:182). Since cleaning and arranging flowers are "household work," they are thought to be inappropriate masculine activities.

decorate the tombs of former friends or neighbors whose families have entirely died out or moved from the region. As one woman explains, "It's sad when there is no one to clean a tomb and it gets abandoned." Abandoned tombs are a sign that the dead buried there have passed out of living memory. They have died a second death through being forgotten.

Three days before Toussaint all cleaning work in the cemetery must be terminated, in order that the municipal workmen may begin their task of spreading fresh white gravel in the walkways around the tombs (see fig. 14). On the final day of cleaning, a flurry of activity in the cemetery calls to mind the ambience of a North American department store on the last day of shopping before Christmas. As with Christmas, there is also an economic aspect to the celebration of Toussaint. Whereas at Christmas money is spent on gifts for the living, at Toussaint it is used to purchase gifts for the dead. The objects exchanged in this symbolic transaction are flowers.[7] In the cemetery at La Feuillée there is hardly a tomb that does not bear at least one pot of flowers on November 1. However, flowers are not placed on *caveaux* "prepared in advance," where no one has yet been interred. This implies that there is something more than mere decoration involved in this custom. Flowers are an offering to the deceased and a homage to them.

Some people in La Feuillée severely criticize the "wasting of millions of francs on the cemetery" at Toussaint, claiming that people ignore the needs of their living relatives while spending to excess on flowers for the dead. Others suggest that Toussaint is nothing but a "flower contest," motivated by pride and rivalry among neighbors, to see who will have the best-decorated tomb. "All it does is give business to the florist shops." Despite such criticism, most people conclude that flowers are bought primarily "for the dead." As Marguerite Prévost conceded, after complaining about the high cost of chrysanthemums, "But fifty or sixty francs, that's not really too much to spend on the dead once a year."

Regardless of the motivation for purchasing flowers at Toussaint, florist shops clearly benefit from this custom. As Toussaint approaches, florists in Huelgoat and Morlaix carry special stocks of

---

7. The role of flowers in symbolic transactions between the living and the dead elsewhere in France has been stressed by Zonabend (1980:89-90).

potted chrysanthemums, azaleas, cyclamen, and heather, ranging in price from 50 to 150 francs. Commercially produced posters in the florists' windows remind customers of Toussaint well in advance and urge them to order their flowers ahead of time. In Brest the *hypermarchés* (combined grocery and department stores) offer a large selection of plants at bargain prices—*moins chers*. On a more modest scale, the grocery store in La Feuillée temporarily turns into a flower shop, as the grocer orders a shipment of chrysanthemums for the needs of her customers. When these plants arrive, the town square comes alive with people carrying chrysanthemums in crates, pushing wheelbarrows full of the brightly colored flowers, or arranging them carefully in the trunks of cars.

Some avid gardeners in La Feuillée and Plouguerneau circumvent the necessity to spend money on flowers by growing their own chrysanthemums. This can be a complicated process. Cuttings must be made from plants with flowers of the desired hue, and these must be coaxed along carefully, so that they will bloom exactly on time for Toussaint, neither too early in the season nor too late. Those who grow their own plants use these not only as symbolic offerings for the dead but also in exchanges with the living, giving some away or selling them to friends for their tombs.

The influx of cash to rural areas since World War II has made it possible to spend more on flowers for Toussaint. Earlier in the century there was less emphasis on decorating the tombs. Some of the more devout Catholics complain that at present one sees "more flowers and less faith" than in the past. One deeply religious La Feuillée widow in her late seventies says with pride that she has never bought flowers for her husband's grave in the seven years since his death. She decorates it simply, with flowers culled from her garden. The money she would otherwise spend is used to pay for Masses for her husband's soul. "You can never be sure whether your loved ones are in heaven or purgatory," she explains. "If he is already in heaven, the prayers will help someone else's soul."

The eve of Toussaint is marked by a day-long pilgrimage to the cemetery, with people bringing pots of flowers to place on their tombs. The plants are arranged with a concern for their aesthetic impact. Colors of flowers are matched or contrasted to the colors of the granite monuments. Orange-pink chrysanthemums are placed on a pink granite tomb; white flowers, on a black monument. Plants are placed so that their colors and sizes harmonize and create a balanced effect. Matching pots of flowers are often symmetrically placed around a tomb.

Late autumn weather is uncertain in Brittany, and many people recall years when the flowers in the cemetery for Toussaint were frozen or blown over in heavy winds and ruined by rain. Even when the weather is mild, it is only a matter of days before the expensive flowers wilt and die. It is considered shameful to leave dead plants on one's family tomb, and once the flowers have withered they are almost immediately removed. Like the floral decorations created for Portuguese *festas* described by Salvador (1981), the flowers placed in Breton cemeteries for Toussaint are "ephemeral art." Artificial flowers, although practical, are shunned at Toussaint. According to two elderly La Feuillée sisters, "Even if plastic flowers do last a long time, it would be better to have nothing on the tomb!" Flowers are meant to fade. They are, like human life itself, ephemeral, and this is part of the correct order of things.

On November 1 and 2, and for as long as the flowers last, the cemetery becomes the object of aesthetic appreciation, with its sparkling polished monuments, glittering white gravel, and multicolored floral decorations (see fig. 15). People walk through the cemetery to admire the flowers and to talk about those buried beneath them. Although this holiday is dedicated to the dead, it is not exclusively a sorrowful occasion. In some ways the festival seems more marked by practical concerns—which cleanser is most effective for removing lichen from granite, which flowers will best withstand the cold—than by grief. Perhaps grief is channeled into physical activity: the production of an aesthetically attractive memorial to one's dead. The preparations for Toussaint, particularly the washing of the tombs, have an almost ritual quality. They provide an institutionalized context for thinking and talking about the dead, and a creative outlet for sorrow. In this respect, Toussaint in Brittany presents a striking contrast to the North American Halloween, where the familiar reality of death is excluded, and the dead themselves are present only in the terrifying images of horror films and the comic representations of costume parties.

Toussaint as Family Reunion

The cemetery at Toussaint is both a *lieu de prières*, a "place of prayer" or communication between the living and the dead, and a *lieu de rencontre*, a "meeting place" for the living. The population of

La Feuillée nearly doubles over this holiday, as families return for several days from cities as far away as Paris, or even Marseille and Toulon. For many of these émigrés Toussaint provides the reason for their single annual visit to the parish. Those from Brest and more local centers, who can visit frequently, pass through their natal commune more briefly. For all, however, the cemetery is the focal point of their journey. As such it becomes a meeting place where paths are crossed with distant cousins or acquaintances not seen for many years. Here "one is reunited with people. Everyone comes." It is "the occasion to see friends from school, those of one's own age." In one such encounter, when two former schoolmates from La Feuillée exchanged addresses, they discovered that without knowing it both had been living for some time in the same Paris suburb, only minutes apart. Through this type of meeting, connections are revived and promises made to exchange visits. For some this potential for the renewal of old friendships is the most important aspect of Toussaint.

Writing of Plodémet, in southern Finistère, Edgar Morin (1970: 44) points out that in the aftermath of the *exode rural*, Toussaint has assumed new symbolic significance as a festival of family reunion. In La Feuillée as well, the tomb represents the point of contact for widely dispersed relatives. Meetings with kin are especially likely to occur after the Mass and procession to the cemetery, for following the priest's benediction each family visits it own tombs. Here relatives are embraced and invitations extended to "come for an aperitif." Describing the value of Toussaint, one forty-nine-year-old woman who returns from the Paris region to La Feuillée for the festival explains, "We get to meet one another again. We have a big family. Here the family counts." For others Toussaint "permits people to see one another. We find ourselves as a family again." It enables one "to maintain family ties" and to "keep in contact with the family." Such reunions not only "help to preserve the family spirit," but they also aid the bereaved "to get over their grief." Without Toussaint, it is claimed that relatives would see one another less frequently, and there would consequently "be less comfort for those who have lost someone." Conversely, this can be a difficult period for the bereaved who lack family support. It is not a time to be left alone.

If Toussaint is a festival of the family, it expresses the romantic conception of this institution by reuniting both living and dead kin. In the words of one La Feuillée woman, the holiday "allows us to find the family again, the family in general, the living and the dead. That creates a link." Without being morbid, family gatherings at Toussaint are the occasion to reminisce about deceased relatives. As a young mother explained, children learn about their ancestors at Toussaint. "We talk to the children about their great-grandparents. That way they learn what they were like." The grave monument with its inscribed names and dates provides a tangible link with family history. A grandfather visiting the cemetery with two grandchildren under ten years of age pointed out the grave where three generations of their family are buried. The memory of the ancestors is carefully cultivated. "We honor the memory," states a forty-year-old woman. "One must not forget that if we are here today, it is thanks to them."

Above all else, Toussaint is a day of remembering. People express the view that the dead continue to exist as long as they are not forgotten by the living.[8] As one woman observes, "I find that they still live with us. It is a comfort to find them again in the cemetery." Placing flowers on the tomb is a way of telling the dead "that we haven't forgotten them." It is for this reason that undecorated graves are regarded as *triste:* "If there are no flowers on a tomb, people think, 'Their relatives could have spared a thought for them, after all!'" Visiting and decorating the tomb are described as "a tradition. We don't forget people." The dead are "those we have loved. We must continue to think of them." The festival "brings us closer to our dead." At least "once a year, one can pass a day or several hours with them." Perhaps the most revealing comment, from a man and his wife in their sixties, projects the self with its desire for immortality beyong the grave: "We ourselves would not like to be forgotten."

The idea that the dead live on if they are remembered is embodied in the *prière prônale,* or prayer from the pulpit, offered for the souls at the Toussaint Mass. Formerly the *prière prônale* was a list read by the priest of the names of all the deceased in the parish

---

8. In this connection it is interesting to note the resemblance between *ankou,* one of the Breton words for death, and *ankounac'haat,* a Breton verb meaning "to forget." One might speculate that there is an etymological link between the two words, and hence a semantic connection between death and the condition of being forgotten.

who remained within living memory. Families registered their dead on the prayer list for a small sum. In La Feuillée prior to the mid 1920s, the entire list was read every Sunday at High Mass, in addition to being read at Toussaint. More recently the list was divided into four parts, with a different part read at each weekly Mass, so that the entire prayer would be offered once each month. In this way the dead were granted a prominent place in the weekly liturgical celebrations. The practice of citing individual deceased persons by name in the *prière prônale* was discontinued in La Feuillée around 1940. At present the prayer is read only at Toussaint, and it has been abbreviated to contain only family names, although the full names of those people who died since the previous Toussaint are read in a separate list. For families registered on the *prière prônale*, both the husband's surname and the wife's maiden name are listed. Thus, the priest reads a litany of names such as *famille* Riou-Creac'h, *famille* Laurent-Coat, *famille* Kergoat-Grall. During the weekly High Mass he offers a general prayer for the dead, in which allusion is made to the *prière prônale:* "Let us pray for those who are registered on the *prière prônale* and for all those who repose in the cemetery at La Feuillée." Because the latter category includes the former, people question the efficacy of paying five francs to have their family names placed on the *prière prônale.* Nevertheless, 134 families did so in the commune of La Feuillée at Toussaint in 1983. This surprisingly large number for a *rouge* and anticlerical parish suggests that entrenched politico-religious views are suspended in the face of an even more deeply rooted loyalty to the dead.

Like other preparations for Toussaint, registering the family names on the parish *prière prônale* is done by women in La Feuillée. One fifty-five-year-old woman observed that this used to be her mother's responsibility. She inherited the task after her mother's death in 1981, even though she is a strong supporter of the PCF. The tenacity of the tradition is also witnessed by the fact that several families registered on the La Feuillée *prière prônale* no longer live in the commune. Yet their roots and their dead are in La Feuillée, and these are the object of a special pilgrimage at Toussaint.

Although in La Feuillée the only deceased whose names are cited individually at the Toussaint Mass are those who died during the preceding year, in the neighboring communes of Scrignac,

Loqueffret, and Plounéour-Ménez the *prière prônale* continues to include individual names, grouped by family. In Loqueffret the list is typed and posted in the church, although in 1984 it was at least one year out of date, and with the death of the parish curé that same year, the *prière prônale* was likely to be discontinued. In Plouguerneau the *prière prônale* no longer exists. Obviously, the *prière prônale* can be lengthy, but according to the curé of Plounéour-Ménez, who continues to read individual names in the Toussaint prayer, "Being in church does not bore people that day. They like to hear the names of their dead." It is as if, according to some mystical union of signifier and signified, the very act of pronouncing the names of the dead somehow renews their life. By invoking them by name, one ensures that they have not passed irrevocably into the realm of the forgotten.

The *prière prônale* has its origins in the diptych tablets read during the Gallican Mass of the early Middle Ages prior to the introduction of the Roman liturgy in Charlemagne's time. The diptychs listed the names of both living and dead persons, including prominent ecclesiastics, benefactors of the church, saints, and deceased members of the congregation. Thus, these lists symbolized the unity of the social worlds of the living and the dead within the context of the Christian community (Ariès 1982:148–149). Reflecting the tame response to death, the diptych lists also emphasized a collective vision of the afterlife over a concern for individual destiny (Ariès 1982:151). After the introduction of the Roman Mass, the reading of the diptych lists was abandoned. However, the tradition persisted in the form of a prayer read from the pulpit (*prière prônale* or *prière du prône*) after the conclusion of the main part of the Mass, following the sermon and parish announcements (Ariès 1977:156; 1982:156). In contemporary Brittany the *prière prônale*, now reserved for Toussaint, does not include the names of living community members. The barriers dividing the world of the living from that of the dead are much more clearly defined than they were in pre-Carolingian times. Nevertheless, the fact that the *prière prônale* is read at all indicates a rapprochement between these two domains, at least on the occasion of Toussaint. Moreover, the yearly reading of the *prière prônale* symbolically reconstructs the community of the dead among the living by naming its members. In this way, like the diptychs of the early Middle Ages, the *prière prônale* continues to present a conception of the afterlife which emphasizes collective destiny.

For many people the evocation of the dead at Toussaint is a difficult experience. In the La Feuillée area it is nonetheless generally agreed that celebration of Toussaint is a valuable tradition. "If we didn't have Toussaint," people say "we would forget the dead." It is noted that the festival is especially difficult after a recent death, but as time goes on "one finds a reason," and "it gives pleasure to visit the tomb." A seventy-five-year-old widow whose husband was killed in a car accident in 1983 says of going to the cemetery, "When I have too much grief, I am comforted. It eases the pain to visit the tomb." Many comment that it is good to have a day set aside for the dead, "even if one thinks about them on other days, all the time." Without a specific festival, says a forty-year-old woman, one would tend to avoid visiting the cemetery, maintaining the tombs, and thinking about the dead. However, since "there is a set day, one has to do it, out of duty first, and later out of desire. It is good to remember the dead, not to be indifferent to them." Moreover, for those living at a distance from the rural cemeteries where their relatives are buried, "one is too far away and too busy" most of the time, and Toussaint provides an annual occasion when it is possible to visit the tombs. Finally, as one seventy-two-year-old man suggests, Toussaint reminds the living that they too are mortal. In his view it is important to retain such memento mori: "One feels a bit of sadness, but we are all called to follow the same route."

The most ambivalent and critical reactions to the festival come from the young. Those under thirty-five are more willing than people in their parents' generation to discuss the role of guilt as a motive for observing Toussaint. As a couple in their thirties explains, visiting the family tomb enables one "to have a clear conscience, to some extent. It's like saying to the dead, 'We haven't forgotten you.'" In their view guilt toward the deceased is often augmented by guilt induced by the living, for in certain families the older members become hurt and angry if young people do not visit the tombs of their ancestors on Toussaint. External psychological pressure is also exerted by others in the community outside the family, who may use gossip as a sanction against failure to visit and maintain the tombs of relatives.

The bitter comment of a twenty-six-year-old woman indicates that some young people perceive a certain hypocrisy in the celebration of Toussaint: "The bouquets of flowers don't serve any useful purpose. Three-quarters of the people just put them there to have a clear conscience. It's not right to come one day of the year and to forget the rest of the time." Another woman, aged twenty-four, echoes these sentiments, asking, "What's the use of thinking about the dead on only one day of the year?" This criticism is repeated by older persons as well. Complaining that Toussaint has become an overly commercialized celebration, one fifty-six-year-old man contends, "When one has loved one's family deeply, it is better to come and clean the tomb from time to time, rather than to set aside a special day."

Despite the devaluation of ritual which such statements express, respect for Toussaint is viewed by many in Plouguerneau and La Feuillée as an integral component of Breton identity. "Here we keep the memory of the dead," it is said. Although the festival is observed throughout France and in other Catholic countries, the manner in which it is marked is considered locally to be "special in Brittany." Historians Croix and Roudaut (1984:218) concur, suggesting that Toussaint in Brittany has retained a unique character even though death is no longer accorded a central place in Breton Catholicism. Bretons claim that in other parts of France, "once someone dies, that's it, he is ignored." Whereas in Brittany, they maintain, "we have the cult of the dead." While such comments provide insight into emic perceptions about the importance of the dead in Breton culture, it is difficult to assess their accuracy in the absence of detailed ethnographic studies of Toussaint celebrations elsewhere in France.

The Return of the Dead at Toussaint

Part of the distinctiveness of Toussaint in Brittany, at least in the past, may derive from the associations between this festival and the Celtic Samhain, which also took place on November 1. Samhain, like Toussaint, was believed to be a time when the spirit world was particularly close to the world of the living. Numerous parallels exist between Breton customs and popular beliefs concerning Toussaint and those from other Celtic regions.

Writing of Ireland in the mid-nineteenth century, Lady Wilde

(1973:140) reports the belief that revenants appear on the eve of All Saints' Day, or Samhain. Similarly, according to Rhŷs (1901: 2:226, 457), in Wales spirits were said to roam freely on All Saints' Eve and All Saints' Day, and these nights were also propitious for sighting fairies, supernatural figures closely connected in European folk belief with the souls of the dead, as Christiansen (1946:93–94) has observed. In nineteenth-century Ireland the dead were believed to visit the homes of their living friends on the night of All Saints' Day, where they would install themselves next to the hearth (Curtin 1895:157). Le Braz (1928:2:82) records the belief from the same era in Brittany that the dead returned to warm themselves on the night of Toussaint in their former abodes. According to Cambry, writing in 1799 about Finistère, "They say that on the eve of All Souls' Day there are more souls in each house than there are grains of sand in the sea and on the shore" ([1836] 1979:173). For the comfort of the dead, the fire was kept burning in the hearth throughout the night. In certain regions a special meal of cider, buttermilk, and fresh crêpes was also provided for the souls on this night (Le Braz 1928:2:79–80). This custom is similar to the tradition of preparing food for the dead at memorial feasts held on All Saints' Day and other occasions which Christiansen (1946:43–60) records from Scandinavia. In the late eighteenth century, Cambry ([1836] 1979:346) notes that Toussaint meals for the dead exist only in *quelques cantons reculés,* and a century later Le Braz describes the custom as "becoming exceedingly rare" (1928:2:79n). Nevertheless, one woman in her early fifties from Plounéour-Ménez, in the Léon directly across the Monts d'Arrée from La Feuillée, remembers hearing her father recount that certain families in the parish used to leave a loaf of bread on the table for the returning souls on the night of Toussaint. It was necessary to take the first slice from this bread, because the dead were reputed to be very considerate guests, who would be too embarrassed to partake of a loaf not already cut open.

Many elderly people in La Feuillée recall that in their youth the spirits were said to be abroad on both the eve of Toussaint and the night of November 1–2. A woman in her mid-seventies reminisces that "it used to be said that the last to die in the family would appear" on the eve of Toussaint. People would go to bed early on this night to avoid the returning dead. Farm animals were given their *fiskoan*, or evening snack, at eight o'clock rather than the usual ten or ten-thirty. It was a somber evening, when no social gatherings were held and no work done. Two variants of a traditional Breton rhyme from La Feuillée express a stern warning to the living against the dangers of keeping late hours on this day:

> *Gouel an Hollsent a zo warc'hoazh*
> The festival of All Saints is tomorrow;
> *N'eo ket poent echuiñ c'hoazh?*
> Is it not time to finish (work) now?

> *N'eo ket aet an dud*
> Are people not gone
> *Da gousket c'hoazh?*
> To sleep yet?
> *Gouel an Hollsent a zo warc'hoazh*
> The festival of All Saints is tomorrow.

When the second version of this rhyme was quoted to Marie-Thérèse and an elderly friend from La Feuillée, they recounted the story of a woman who disregarded its warning and continued to work, spinning her wool past midnight on the eve of Toussaint. Mocking the rhyme, she replied, "Let Toussaint come when it will. I will finish my spindle." Little did she know that she would never finish it. She died that night, punished for having failed to honor the saints and their festival.[9] Although both Marie-Thérèse and her friend regard this legend as true, they take care to distance it from themselves with the qualifying statement, "That's much older than we are." However, belief in the proximity of the spirit world, although rarely alluded to directly, persists at Toussaint.

Speaking of her childhood in Scrignac, Jacqueline Milin, a woman in her fifties now living in La Feuillée, remembers that "it used to be said that one should not stay out late on Toussaint." Despite this belief, her grandmother decided one year to visit neighbors late in the day on Toussaint to request their help with the upcoming harvest of turnips. As she walked along the road to her neighbor's house, she heard the sound of weeping. Distressed, she looked

---

9. Compare this legend with "L'histoire du forgeron," recorded by Le Braz (1928:1:132–135), in which a blacksmith dies after working later than the moment of the Elevation of the Host at the midnight Mass on Christmas eve.

around, but there was no living being in sight. The crying came from the Anaon. Jacqueline recalls that in the past everyone was at home by five o'clock on Toussaint. Even now, she herself becomes uneasy if she stays out late on that day. When she goes to visit her father's grave in Scrignac on Toussaint she always makes an effort to leave early in order to be home before dusk.

A Breton priest in his mid-forties from a community in the Monts d'Arrée recalls that in his youth, Toussaint and the Fête des Morts were much more serious festivals than they are at present. "People would not have dreamed of playing cards on the afternoon of Toussaint as they do now," he notes. The souls of the dead among the living were said to be "as numerous as the blades of grass in the fields" on that day. In his parish the faithful used to circle the church in a procession to obtain indulgences for their dead throughout the afternoon of the Fête des Morts. Similarly, in the Vannes region, Lambert notes that on the Fête des Morts an indulgence of three hundred days was offered for the souls in purgatory each time one entered the church to recite the Pater, Ave, and Gloria six times. Many people would reenter the church by the side door as soon as they had exited from the front, in order to increase the number of indulgences earned (Lambert 1985:43). In La Feuillée the *glas* was formerly rung on Toussaint from vespers in mid-afternoon to the Angelus at 7:00 P.M. This practice, described as "lugubrious" by those who remember it, was discontinued after World War II.

Le Braz records that in nineteenth-century Brittany the dead were believed to attend vespers on All Souls' Day along with the living (1928:2:83). In La Feuillée the dead were said to circle the church throughout the night on the eve of this festival in order to gain indulgences shortening their time in purgatory. According to popular belief, one should not mourn the dead to excess, for on this annual procession they were forced to carry each tear shed for them by the living. To cry for one's dead therefore served only to increase their burden. A La Feuillée woman now in her sixties remembers hearing this admonition as late as the mid-1940s.[10]

---

10. In "La jeune fille de Coray," Le Braz (1928:2:99–102) documents a related belief that the dead are forced to carry heavy buckets containing the tears shed for them by the living on a nightly procession in the parish church.

In a number of Breton communities during the late nineteenth century, groups of people went door to door after dark on the night of Toussaint collecting money to pay for Masses for the dead and singing the "Complainte des âmes," a melancholy hymn describing the sad state of the souls in purgatory (Pérennès 1925:8). Contrasting the situation of the living "at ease in their beds" with that of their dead relatives, who suffer "fire above and fire below," the singers urged the living to awake and pray for the Anaon.

> It is Jesus who has sent us
> To wake you if you are asleep,
> To wake you from your first slumber
> So that you may pray to God for the souls.
>
> You are in your bed at ease;
> The poor souls are in pain.
> You are stretched out comfortably in your bed;
> The poor souls are in distress.
>
> . . . .
>
> Perhaps your father and mother
> Are there in purgatory in the blazing fire;
> Perhaps your brother and sister
> Are there in the blazing fire of purgatory!
>
> They are there,
> Fire above and fire below,
> Fire above and fire below,
> Crying, imploring your prayers.
>
> By those whom we have nourished
> We have been abandoned now, when we need them.
> Pray, o relatives and friends,
> For our children will not!
>
> . . . .
>
> Get up! Jump from your bed,
> Jump with bare feet to the floor,
> As long as you are not ill
> Or already surprised by death!
>
> (Le Braz 1928:2:80–82,
> verses 2, 3, 6, 7, 8, 10)

As an observer of this custom wrote, "One would need to have been woken with a start in a box bed on some isolated farm by this dolorous song in order to know the extent of the intense melancholy, the poignant and primitive sadness of the hymns of death from Lower Brittany" (Le Braz 1928:2:80n). Le Braz notes that the singers circulating through their neighborhoods are said to feel the cold breath of the crowd of souls following on their heels and to hear the souls' footsteps crushing the dry leaves in the roads behind them (1928:2:82). A parallel belief from nineteenth-century Ireland holds that one should never turn one's head to look behind if one hears the sound of footsteps in the background on the eve of Samhain. The footsteps are those of the dead, and if caught in their regard, one will die (Wilde 1973:140).

In the "Complainte des âmes," the singers speak for the dead. Their voices become those of the souls as they urge the sleeping to awake:

> Pray, relatives and friends,
> For *our* children do not
> Pray, relatives and friends,
> For *our* children are ungrateful.
> (Le Braz 1928:2:82,
> verse 9; my emphasis)

Although the custom of door-to-door singing of hymns for the souls did not exist in La Feuillée, at least within living memory, the annual *kest an Anaon*, or "collection for the souls" made on the eve of Toussaint, continued until the 1960s. In every *quartier* two men were chosen to visit each household, soliciting contributions of money or grain for the church. Many people in La Feuillée recall that the *kest an Anaon* was nicknamed the *kest ar gwin*, or wine collection, because the men collecting would be served a glass of wine at each household they visited. As a consequence, they frequently returned home from the collection in a state somewhat less than sober. The custom of offering drink to those singing the "Complainte des âmes" and making the Toussaint collection is attested from other rural Breton parishes (Pérennès 1925:8). In La Feuillée the priest assigned to the parish in the early 1960s tried to augment contributions to the *kest an Anaon* by publishing a list of the sums donated by each family in the community. In so doing he hoped to generate interhousehold rivalry, encouraging people to give more than their neighbors. However, the men chosen for the *kest* decided that this was unfair manipulation and refused to carry out the collection. Following this incident the *kest an Anaon* was discontinued.[11]

In the contemporary Breton celebration of Toussaint, the pre-Catholic merges with the post-Catholic. As van Gennep has suggested, in losing the connotation of a festival strictly reserved for the commemoration of the Catholic saints, Toussaint has practically become a secular ritual: "One would almost be tempted to say that in European Christianity, prehistoric and classical beliefs have cast off the Christian mantle that cloaked them over many centuries, to take on a character more social than religious, to the point where atheists and even anticlericals would consider it wrong not to go and commemorate their dead" (1953:2809). Certainly, as the attitudes of people in La Feuillée demonstrate, Toussaint is not perceived to be solely, or even primarily, a Christian celebration. A young woman from a Communist family points out, "It's religious, but it's also a custom." Like many others, she visits the cemetery but does not attend Mass on Toussaint. Similarly, her mother proclaims the idea of a festival for the dead "magnificent." In her view it is not a church holiday in the same sense as other festivals, like Easter. Believers and unbelievers alike bring flowers to their tombs, and even the graves of those who have received civil burials are decorated.

In the final analysis, celebration of Toussaint, like the Catholic funeral ceremony, appeals to a need for ritual demarcation of the boundary between nature and culture. It is part of the symbolic overlay that brings the natural facts of death and decay into the cultural domain. Speaking of the festival, a La Feuillée woman explains, "If you don't do anything, you are, in effect, just like the beasts." This echoes the attitude toward civil burials. Death requires its rituals, and in the absence of others, those of the Catholic church are retained.

11. The door-to-door singing of the "Complainte des âmes" and soliciting of the *kest an Anaon* also resemble contemporary North American Halloween customs, in which children dressed as ghosts make a door-to-door collection.

Secular Festivals for the Dead

In addition to Toussaint and the Fête des Morts, the dead—or a particular category of souls—are honored on two other annual occasions, November 11 and May 8. These dates commemorate respectively the armistice concluding World War I and the Liberation of France from German occupation in 1945. Those killed in the two world wars and in the Resistance are remembered at these times. While both November 11 and May 8 are public holidays and are essentially secular occasions, they are also marked by religious observances. In contrast to the usual sparse Sunday Mass attendance, congregations of approximately one hundred attend Mass in La Feuillée on these holidays. Half of those present are men, which reflects the fact that the military is largely a male domain. War widows and the wives of war veterans also attend these ceremonies, even though many of these women, like the veterans themselves, are *rouges*.

In La Feuillée there are two separate components to the November 11 and May 8 celebrations. First the mayor and councilors decorate the *monument aux morts* in the town square with floral wreaths. Then follows a religious ceremony, which culminates in the priest's blessing the monument with holy water. It is on these holidays that political animosities between *rouge* and *blanc* factions in the community rise to the surface. A number of *rouges*, including the mayor and most of his council, boycotted the November 11 Mass in 1983. On May 8, 1984, one of the veterans decorated by the municipality for service during the Algerian war, a prominent Communist, refused to attend the Mass. Conversely, the La Feuillée priest is conspicuously absent during the civil placement of the wreaths. In Plouguerneau, however, both priest and mayor officiate jointly in a single service at the *monument aux morts*. Significantly, the monument in this parish is located directly adjacent to the church, whereas in La Feuillée they are separated by a five-minute walk. Secular and sacred authority are less in conflict in the pious Léon than in the anticlerical Monts d'Arrée.

Both November 11 and May 8 are emotionally charged events in the Monts d'Arrée, for they rekindle old memories and partisan rivalries, especially those associated with the Resistance. The interpersonal and ideological loyalties forged at that period provide the basis for the continued Communist and Socialist strength in the region to this day. The dead have their role to play in the legitimation of political authority. By honoring them and invoking their memory, contemporary politicians identify themselves as direct successors to those values and struggles of the Resistance and the French Republic which the dead represent.

Conclusion

Folk traditions collected from Brittany during the nineteenth century reflect a culture in which there were few barriers dividing the world of the living from that of the dead. In contemporary Brittany it remains important to maintain close ongoing relationships with the deceased. Dreams and prayer are conceived to be media of communications between the living and the dead. The cemetery, which came to be viewed during the romantic era as the principal site for communion with the dead, continues to serve this role in Plouguerneau and La Feuillée. The dead are perpetuated in the memory of the living through visits to the tomb. As Ariès contends, this cult of the dead is not restricted exclusively to Catholicism. Indeed, he claims that its popularity has increased with the decline of the church, since the only form of postmortem existence which remains credible is one provided for the dead in the memory and imagination of the living (1982:541, 543).

In Brittany as in other parts of France, the cult of the dead is honored annually at Toussaint. Derived in part from the Celtic Samhain, Toussaint was traditionally a time when the natural and supernatural domains interpenetrated. This interpenetration continues at Toussaint in contemporary Brittany through the *prière prônale*, which evokes the presence of the Anaon among the living, and through the offering of flowers as gifts for the deceased. The festival predates Christianity, and because of its ability to attract the agnostic and the anticlerical, its importance has not diminished despite the contemporary movement away from the church in Breton society. Indeed, as a result of the *exode rural*, Toussaint has assumed new symbolic significance as a rite of family reunion. In line with the romantic representation of the family, the festival reunites both living and dead kin.

Remembered by individual families, the dead are also present among the living in the public realm of the state. Secular festivals on May 8 and November 11 commemorate those who lost their lives during the two world wars and the Resistance. Through these ceremonies the dead provide continuing legitimation for the state and for contemporary political activity.

Certain factors suggest that the gap between the social worlds of the living and the dead is widening. Many people under thirty-five are critical of the traditional observance of Toussaint, and persons in this age group tend to visit the cemetery less frequently than older people. Nevertheless, as a form of civil religion and personal spirituality, the cult of the dead continues to hold meaning throughout contemporary Breton society.

9

Death and the Supernatural

Introduction

In contemporary Brittany, as in the past, the religious perspective includes both the tenets of orthodox Catholicism and faith in aspects of the supernatural which fall outside the domain of the church. Ideas about destiny, revenants, sorcery, witchcraft, magical healing, and *intersignes* (omens of death) all form part of a system of popular belief which, like the more established doctrines of Christianity, provides points of reference whereby the believer can situate his or her personal experience in a meaningful fashion.

The terms "faith" and "belief" are used in the La Feuillée area to refer both to Catholicism and non-Catholic aspects of the supernatural. The verb *croire,* to believe, used in connection with the church, is also used when speaking about such things as *intersignes* and revenants. Similarly, those who believe in these unorthodox supernatural phenomena are, like devout Catholics, described as *croyants,* or believers. The same logical process underlies both types of faith. Moreover, as observed in Chapter 6, many rituals associated with popular beliefs about the supernatural make use of Catholic gestures or symbols in non-Catholic contexts. For example, Marie-Louise Abjean, a woman from La Feuillée in her late sixties, practices as a *guérisseuse,* or healer, curing skin diseases by magical means. To cure warts she engraves the sign of the cross in an onion with a matchstick and rubs the onion over the affected area of the skin. The patient must then go into the garden behind Marie-Louise's house, cross himself and throw the onion over his right shoulder. The wart will disappear when the onion has rotted. Other *guérisseurs* in the Monts d'Arrée, like the Portuguese folk healers described by Cutileiro (1971:273–278), base their cures on the repetition of ritual formulas, called *prières,* or prayers. These nonofficial prayers are not perceived by the healers or their clients to differ qualitatively from those of the church.

Sorcery and witchcraft, which are closely related to magical healing, also borrow Catholic terminology. The spells or incantations used by those who seek to perform harmful magic are, like healing formulas, referred to as *prières*. It is impossible to draw a neat distinction between the Catholic and unorthodox supernatural domains: priests themselves are suspected of having practiced sorcery in the past, and they continue to be consulted on occasion as healers and "unwitchers," or exorcists. Like their lay counterparts, they too recite prayers to cure skin ailments and to lift spells from those who believe themselves bewitched.

It is not easy to initiate conversations about unorthodox manifestations of the supernatural in rural Brittany. Many people who believe in *intersignes*, for example, are unwilling to admit publicly that they do, for fear of being considered "superstitious," "old-fashioned," "stupid," or mentally deranged. However, faith in the non-Catholic aspects of the supernatural remains strong for some groups of people in certain contexts. One such group includes the middle-aged and elderly in the Monts d'Arrée. In the Plouguerneau area, folk beliefs about the supernatural are less openly discussed. Possibly the church has been more successful at imposing its own orthodox definition of the supernatural in this area of the Léon than in the Monts d'Arrée.

Although many people over fifty in the Monts d'Arrée, as well as some in younger age groups, express belief in phenomena such as *intersignes*, the processes of secularization and rationalization have raised doubts about the credibility of these facets of the supernatural, just as the same processes have called official Catholicism into question. The traditional perspective, according to which existence is given meaning through reference to the supernatural, is increasingly being challenged by the perspective of scientific positivism, according to which all explanations are to be found in the natural domain. Paradoxically, only according to the second perspective does the supernatural become something fundamentally "other." From the traditional point of view, the supernatural was so familiar as to be almost "natural." Ariès makes this development clear in his discussion of "tame" precursors of death:

> Strictly speaking, the distinction we are making here between natural signs and supernatural premonitions is probably an anachronism; in those days the boundary between the natural and the super-

natural was indefinite. It is nevertheless remarkable that the signs most often mentioned to indicate imminent death in the Middle Ages were signs that today we would call natural: an obvious routine observation of the common and familiar facts of everyday life. It was later, in more modern and contemporary times, that observers who no longer quite believed in them emphasized the miraculous quality of presentiments, which were henceforth regarded as popular superstitions.

(1982:7)

Traditional Breton worldview has many features in common with the worldview of certain non-Western cultures. As in the African contexts documented by Horton (1967:174–175) and Evans-Pritchard (1937), the notion that tragedy can be a random occurrence is inadmissible. Phenomena are conceived to be interconnected. Thus, the fact that a particular noise was heard prior to a particular death cannot be attributed merely to coincidence. Events must all fit into a pattern, and their significance can be properly understood only in terms of this pattern.

In contrast, the secular perspective is characterized by readiness to admit ignorance of the underlying causes of phenomena or events (compare Horton 1967:173–174), and by faith that technical or scientific explanations always exist, even though they may as yet be undiscovered and one may not personally possess the skills to understand them (Weber 1946:139). Confidence in natural science thus precludes the need for an all-embracing deterministic supernatural pattern. Events, including personal tragedies, can be interpreted as the outcome of natural laws and processes that can be scientifically understood. In this perspective there are no necessary interconnections among events, other than on a purely physical or mechanical level. That the owl calls around one's house for three weeks prior to a death in one's family has no significance. It is viewed as coincidence rather than as proof for the existence of a supernatural guiding force behind nature which predetermines the course of individual lives. Tragedies, according to the scientific perspective, become random occurrences.

In contemporary Brittany the scientific and supernatural perspectives compete. As noted earlier, the degree of adherence to one or the other perspective tends to vary among age groups and geographical locations within Brittany. Moreover, a single individual may choose to privilege the scientific explanatory framework in some circumstances and the supernatural perspective in others. Many people who are skeptical about the supernatural in general terms are nevertheless convinced of the veracity of supernatural phenomena they themselves have encountered, such as *intersignes*.[1]

The tendency to alternate between competing scientific and supernatural explanatory models is not a new development in Brittany. Luzel's *Veillées bretonnes* provides evidence that ambivalence about the credibility of the supernatural perspective also existed during the nineteenth century. First published in 1879, *Veillées bretonnes* is unusual in that Luzel reports the metatexts, or critical discussions among his informants about the legends he collected, as well as the narratives themselves. Many of these conversations include lively debates in which Luzel himself participated about the reality of supernatural manifestations. It is clear from *Veillées bretonnes* that some of the same skeptical attitudes toward the supernatural which are currently expressed in the Monts d'Arrée were also voiced in the late nineteenth century. Luzel's storytellers are unwilling to believe things they have not personally seen or heard but adamantly defend the veracity of their own supernatural experiences (e.g., Luzel [1879] 1980:82–83). Like contemporary Bretons, many of those quoted by Luzel are reticent about such experiences because they fear being mocked by their peers for foolishness or cowardice in the face of the unknown ([1879] 1980:9, 58, 62). Then, as now, natural explanations were advanced for supernatural phenomena. Some of Luzel's more skeptical informants claim that most visions of revenants can be attributed to poor eyesight, excessive drinking, or an overexcited imagination ([1879] 1980:44, 59, 68, 71). Moreover, in the nineteenth-century context described by Luzel, as in present-day Brittany, there is a perception that the dominant society rejects belief in the supernatural, at least in those aspects of it not condoned by the church. The curé, the local mayor, and the schoolteacher were among the authority figures who ridiculed "superstitious" supernatural beliefs in Luzel's time ([1879] 1980:45).

Luzel's material allows us to glimpse the complexity of changing

---

1. This reaction coincides with folklorist Lauri Honko's (1964:10) observation that "in general, informants react critically to supernatural experiences. They want to consider true only that which they themselves saw or which some acquaintance experienced."

patterns of folk belief in Brittany. The supernatural perspective was by no means unquestioned during the nineteenth century. Therefore, it would be incorrect to suggest that the changes in Breton worldview since that time simply involve replacement of one previously unchallenged supernatural paradigm by a new, universally accepted scientific one. Nevertheless, the degree to which the supernatural perspective is critically evaluated has increased. In contemporary Brittany it is impossible to elicit many of the types of narrative which Luzel records, particularly those concerning revenants. Many present-day narrators who do speak about revenants distance themselves from their texts, treating them as historical curiosities rather than chronicles of events inspiring belief. This attitude suggests that a shift toward a scientifically based, naturalistic interpretation of reality has taken place in Brittany over the course of the twentieth century, even though supernatural perspectives continue to be entertained alongside scientific ones. The reasons for this shift are complex and difficult to elucidate, but among them must be included exposure to a naturalistic cosmology disseminated through the state educational system, which has functioned to encourage the integration of Brittany into the larger metropolitan society.

The following discussion focuses on memorates, or personal experience narratives, about *revenants* and *intersignes* recorded in the Monts d'Arrée.² These narratives clearly indicate that although belief in some aspects of the supernatural has declined, supernatural explanations continue to be called upon in the face of tragedy. For many people in the La Feuillée area, the scientific perspective, with its insistence on the random character of events, cannot provide emotionally satisfying interpretations of personal misfortune or

2. Memorates are a genre of narrative about personal experiences with the supernatural which are considered by the narrator to be true. The memorate is thus a subcategory of legend.
Linda Dégh (pers. com. Nov. 22, 1987) has suggested that since the texts included in this discussion were collected in response to questions about experiences with *intersignes*, they should be classified as "interview responses" rather than memorates. I feel, however, that the genre of an item of folklore does not depend on the context of performance. Most of the narratives discussed in this chapter were tape-recorded at afternoon or evening coffee gatherings at homes in the La Feuillée area. Although I made an effort to direct conversation to the topics of death and supernatural beliefs, and the speakers knew they were being taped, these social occasions were not conducted as interviews. The conversations were completely unstructured, informal, and open-ended.

death. It is only through recourse to the supernatural perspective, which emphasizes the interconnectedness of phenomena, that death can be accounted for in a meaningful fashion.

Revenants

The publications of the nineteenth-century folklorists who worked in Brittany are filled with legends about revenants. Reading their collections, one can almost feel the atmosphere in the dimly lit stone cottages where neighbors gathered around the hearth on winter evenings to talk of experiences with *conjurés*, malevolent ghosts changed through exorcism into animal form, or of spirits who return on pilgrimages to shrines they were unable to visit during life (Le Braz 1928:2:89–93, 251–309; Le Men 1870–1872:424–427).

In La Feuillée it is remembered that "old people used to talk of nothing but ghosts. Every time they heard the slightest noise outside at night, they thought it was a revenant." Some of these revenants, or *teuzioù*, as they were known in Breton, appeared in the form of animals. In the *quartier* of Croas Hir in La Feuillée, a bull accompanied by the sound of chains was said to haunt the neighborhood by night.[3] A revenant in the form of a fox was said to frequent *an hent treuz*, one of the footpaths leading across the fields to the *quartier* of Keranheroff. An elderly woman remembers that "they always used to see a cat, always the same one, between the *quartiers* of Roc'h ar C'hezeg and Botbian. My father, who had seen the cat, was timid. Especially when he had to cross the stream, on stepping stones. It was there that they used to see phantoms."[4] Other ghosts, like the tall man wearing a hat seen on the road to Trédudon, assumed human form.

For the most part such apparitions are now dismissed as false. Belief in ghosts has been undermined by, among other factors, the declining influence of the church in Brittany. To some extent the church was able to co-opt popular beliefs concerning revenants by promoting the custom of offering Masses for the souls in purgatory. There are numerous memorates about the dead who return to

---

3. Le Rouzic (1924:49–50, 69–70) describes revenants in the form of bulls in Carnac as well.

4. Le Rouzic (1924:99–100) records a similar belief from the Carnac area, where a cat haunting a ford was said to cause passersby to fall into the watercourse.

demand Masses from the living to shorten their penance in the afterlife, as in the following conversation between two women in their seventies from Berrien:

Marie: There used to be an old man next door who used to say that he too "saw" [revenants], you see. So, he would say, "I have seen so-and-so, and he said to pay for a Mass for him."
Mona: Oh yes, in the old days it was like that, yes.
Marie: He used to say that he had "seen."
Mona: Oh, there was a woman, down at the village of Le Crann, who had seen her mother on the bridge. And her mother said to her, "But you must pay for a Mass for me. As soon as a Mass has been said, I will be happy. Now I am in torment."

The impact of the efforts made by the post-Tridentine church to exercise control over popular eschatological beliefs is witnessed by the widespread distribution of legends concerning revenants who request Masses, which are recorded not only from Brittany but also from many other parts of Catholic Europe (see, for example, Douglass 1969:80–81).

With the disappearance of the traditional hierarchical and supernaturally legitimated social order, clerical authority in Brittany has waned. In the new atmosphere of skepticism and increased social mobility, it is now possible to challenge the church. Part of this process has involved speculation that the tales of revenants told in the past were actually invented and propagated by the clergy in order to increase revenues from Masses for the dead.[5] Both *rouges* and *blancs* in La Feuillée also suggest that the church's former insistence on Judgment, hell, and damnation ensured that thoughts of death were always uppermost in people's minds, conditioning a susceptibility to belief in ghosts and related supernatural phenomena.

The social and political power of the Breton clergy before the 1960s, together with their superior education and their knowledge of French and Latin, gave rise among the poor and illiterate rural classes to anticlerical folklore in which priests were closely identified with sorcery. *Rouges* in the Monts d'Arrée claim that in the past, priests used their privileged access to the supernatural to maintain their position of social dominance and to uphold church-

---

5. In fact, documentary evidence exists from as early as the seventeenth century implicating priests in the encouragement of ghost beliefs for this purpose (Croix 1981:1060).

approved norms of behavior. Using esoteric knowledge learned in the seminary or from books they possessed, priests are said to have caused ghostly apparitions with which they frightened their parishioners into submission. One such supernatural apparition, or *teuz*, is remembered by Yves, a retired farmer in his seventies from Plonévez-du-Faou, fifteen kilometers south of La Feuillée. In the following conversation, Yves describes a *teuz* that he saw as a young man:

Yves: And then, me, I heard, while coming home after a wedding—I was just a young boy at the time; I was perhaps twenty-five-years old—I heard it, and I didn't see it at all. It followed me; it was about two in the morning, you see. Me, I was walking my bicycle, because at that time there weren't any paved roads as there are now. Well, I had to hold on to the bike. I had the bike, and I saw it. It was white. In a village further along the road, you see. I saw it, white, eh? And then I said nothing. I said nothing. Afterward it followed me, not on the road. In the fields, yes, in the fields. It came up on the hedgerow. It made a terrible noise, a terrible noise.

My question: What kind of a noise? Did it cry?

Yves: Well, it didn't say anything. Me neither! Well, in my opinion, it shouldn't have followed me, in my opinion. Because I had seen it first.[6] And when I saw it I was going to push my bike into it and it disappeared. Without a moment's notice. Afterward, it came up on the embankment next to the road. It made a ghastly noise, like an I don't know what! Well, I don't know how or by what route I got home after that. I was terrified. I wanted . . . I didn't know if I had my bike or anything. Because it had followed me and made so much noise. Well, that's a *teuz*. I was pretty brave as a young boy, but after that I wasn't quite so brave.

Henri: There wasn't anyone dead around there, do you know?

Yves: Yes. The father of Georges Roger had been dead for two days.

My question: You never found out what it was?

Yves: No, it was more of an animal to my mind. A white animal, bigger than a cat and smaller, a little smaller than a fox, you see. Between the two.

My question: And it was all white?

---

6. This comment is probably related to a folk belief known from Scotland, that a ghost can do you no harm if you see it before it sees you (Le Braz 1928:2:239n).

Yves: All white, yes. There was someone who had put that there to get me worried, I'm sure. In the old days, the priests used to know certain things. Now they aren't able to terrify people.

Henri: Before, they used to.

Yves: Before, they used to. Now they can't do it anymore.

Maria: They are learned people, eh?

Yves: The priests can do that sort of thing with the learning they have, if there is someone who doesn't believe in them. And yet, me, I had never bothered the curés at all. Me, I found it odd. He had caused that to appear for someone else, maybe. Yes, it was meant for another person. Well, even the family of the man who had died, there they weren't religious at all, eh? It was because of that, maybe.

Yves suggests that the *teuz* that followed him was an apparition caused by the parish priest. In Yves's view it was probably intended to be seen by the family of a neighbor, Georges Roger, who did not support the church. There is some suggestion that the *teuz* may have been the ghost of M. Roger himself in the shape of an animal. It is apparent that for Yves and his listeners, the education or "learning" of the clergy is perceived to have been the key to their ability to control others in the community through fear. Significantly, Yves remarks that priests can no longer practice this type of sorcery. Other people from the Monts d'Arrée concur in this belief, stating that priests have lost their ability to work harmful magic, because they are no longer the only literate people in Breton society. According to this point of view, the increased level of general education in the rural milieu has made it impossible for the clergy to manipulate their parishioners through either natural or supernatural means.

Memorates such as Yves's that link priests to sorcery reflect the resentment and suspicion provoked among the poor by clerical domination. The extent to which clerical authority conditioned belief in all aspects of the supernatural is apparent in another text recorded from Soazic Bihan, an eighty-three-year-old woman living in Botmeur. The legend she recounts combines both the motif of the revenant returning to ask for a Mass and that of the spirit in animal form. Soazic's interpretive comments at the end of the narrative highlight the discrepancy between current social conditions and traditional folk beliefs concerning ghosts.

Soazic recalls that her neighbors used to tell the story of a girl from the *quartier* who was given the task of bringing home her father's cows from the fields at dusk. One day, as she drove her cattle along the road, she saw a mysterious hare, which jumped from the hedgerow at the side of the road into her path.[7] Other people from the village, including Soazic's father, had seen the hare several times at the same place along the road. The girl was frightened and refused to look after the cows anymore or to bring them home at the end of the day. Her parents counseled her to continue minding the cattle, but "if you ever see the hare again, talk to it." Soazic exclaims,

> Talk to a hare! But she saw it again. When it came down onto the road the next time, all of a sudden it took on the form of a man. And it told her, "You mustn't be afraid. I am your godfather. And you tell your parents to go with you to give the price of a Mass for me to Saint Diboan." So, with the horse and carriage, in the middle of the night, they went to the chapel of Saint Diboan to give the price of a Mass for the godfather of the girl.

Commenting on the credibility of her story, Soazic says:

> Perhaps this was true, perhaps. Certain people assumed it to be true. . . . This is one of the tales of the old people from long ago. And the old people long ago were ignorant, so they didn't know any better. That was all they knew. And all the priests then used to be believed, whatever they said. And people believed everything, and now they believe nothing. Or not enough now. Now people don't listen to anything. And then they used to listen to everything!

The connections between the supernatural perspective and acceptance of established authority are clearly delineated in Soazic's assertion that people once "believed everything" and "used to listen to everything" said by the priests. In contrast, the scientific perspective is linked to resistance to such traditional sources of social power. Now people "believe nothing" and "don't listen to anything." Soazic's attitude to this reversal is ambivalent. While she applauds the fact that people are no longer poorly educated and easily manipulated by "all the priests," she also suggests that something has been lost, for people now do not believe "enough." Faced

---

7. Revenants in the form of hares are common in Breton folklore. Compare Le Braz (1928:2:39–41) and Le Rouzic (1924:67, 75, 77, 100, 102, 104–105).

with alternative scientific and supernatural interpretations, Soazic, like many others of her generation, chooses to retain both. Although specific miraculous phenomena such as spirits who return as hares were only "perhaps" true, in her opinion, the supernatural perspective does not totally lack validity.

For Soazic Bihan, World War II was the watershed dividing belief and skepticism. The Occupation had the effect of challenging the immutability of established hierarchical patterns of social relationships in rural Brittany by making all classes, including the elite ones, subject to a dominant outside power. Through their experience of the outside world, in the army or as prisoners of war in Germany, many young men from the Monts d'Arrée returned after the Liberation with new ideas and a desire to modernize both the social and material conditions of life in the region. For those like Soazic who remained in the Monts d'Arrée throughout the Occupation, fears of the supernatural were outweighed by other, more imminent, natural, fears during this period. As Soazic observes, "Since the Germans left, I have never been afraid again. Those living men were worse than any ghosts!"

The decline of belief in ghosts is partly the result of changing social circumstances. In addition, many contemporary Bretons assume that scientific knowledge has progressed to such an extent that all phenomena previously identified as revenants can now be explained with reference to purely natural processes. Such phenomena include *feux follets,* glimmering flamelike lights known in English as will-o'-the-wisps or jack-o'-lanterns and by the Latin term *ignis fatuus.*[8] *Feux follets* were frequently sighted in the Yeun Ellez, a barren, windswept marshland surrounded by the Monts d'Arrée to the south of La Feuillée. According to folk tradition, the entrance to hell is a turbulent greenish pool, known as the Youdic, located in the center of the Yeun Ellez. Here, after exorcism, those malign spirits who tormented the living were said to be consigned

---

8. Thompson (1955–1958: Motif 491, will-o'-the-wisp). The link between the dead and *feux follets* is a general feature of European folk belief. Brandes (1981:181) records that in Andalusia such flames, called *fuegos fatuos,* are believed to be emitted from corpses in the cemetery. Similarly, in an overview of Slavic folklore, Máchal ([1918] 1964:230–231) writes that "the souls of the deceased often appear as jack-o'-lanterns flickering about in churchyards or morasses, leading people astray in swamps or ponds."

for eternity to the otherworld (Le Braz 1928:2:251, 281–293; Le Men 1870–1872:424–425).[9] Legends about the Youdic and the Yeun Ellez continue to be remembered in La Feuillée and neighboring parishes. The *feux follets* seen there were believed to be errant souls completing their penance in this foreboding place. *Feux follets* were also seen in the cemetery, where some claim they can still be observed. On occasion the sighting of *feux follets* was thought to foreshadow an upcoming death. Now, however, the naturalistic interpretation, that these flames are emissions of phosphoric gases from decaying organic matter, is generally accepted. The following narrative, related by seventy-seven-year-old Jannick Le Goff of La Feuillée, illustrates how natural explanations for *feux follets* have been substituted for supernatural ones:

> Oh, in the past people used to be afraid of the dead. . . . I was scared of the dead, scared of the dead. . . . That is to say, one used to be told a lot of things, too. Like that there were revenants. And they never existed. Look, for example, why did we use to see lights in the fields near our place? That was very likely because there were farms. Next to my home there was a big farm. During the war there were only women left to look after the animals. And the animals weren't looked after well, and they would die. So then they used to be buried in the field behind the house. You know, women, when there aren't any men to dig. . . . Well, one month later, you would see the animals' hooves emerging from the ground! And in places where there were bones like that, there used to be a type of *feu follet*. You know, emitted by the bones. And so people saw something like that. . . .
>
> In those days they didn't know about that sort of thing, that bones could cause such flames. And so at that time, people used to have a crazy fear: "Oh, that's the light of so-and-so." "Yes, so-and-so has died and I have seen his sign." And *voilà*, that's how the legend got started. A sign of death. And it was simply the bones that gave off a bit of phosphoric light at night. And it was natural. Those were natural phenomena.

Such scientific explanations for *feux follets* are not recent in rural Brittany. Luzel quotes rural dwellers who had been frightened by these apparitions, only to discover on closer inspection that the light was given off from rotting wood. He himself informs his lis-

---

9. The Yeun Ellez has been partially flooded since the construction of a hydroelectric dam in the 1930s. Ironically, the former "entrance to hell" became the site of a nuclear power station during the 1960s.

teners that phosphorus is the gas responsible for these flamelike emissions ([1879] 1980:62–64). Clearly, like other literate representatives of metropolitan society, folklorists too have contributed to the process of change in Breton worldview.

Although it sounds scientifically credible, the explanation for *feux follets* given by Luzel, which many present-day Bretons believe, is not technically accurate. The light emitted from rotting wood is a form of bioluminescence produced by fungi through a chemical process in which phosphorus plays no part (Wassink 1978:173). *Feux follets* associated with decaying organic matter in swamps or cemeteries are more probably emissions of methane than of phosphorus, although the exact cause of the flames remains unclear (Harvey 1940:19–20).[10] Regardless of its truth value, therefore, the "phosphorus theory" is accepted as a better explanation for *feux follets* than the supernatural "revenant theory." Since few possibilities exist for nonspecialists to test the "scientific" explanation, it must, like supernatural ones, be taken on faith. Thus, the supernatural and scientific perspectives are not radically different. As Weber (1946:139) points out, the disenchanted worldview does not imply that the average individual possesses any specialized knowledge or understanding of the conditions under which he or she lives. Rather, it presupposes acceptance of the principle that all phenomena are amenable to explanation within a naturalistic, technical frame of reference.

Although a "scientific" account for *feux follets* is now generally accepted in the Monts d'Arrée, local people alternate between natural and supernatural explanations for another phenomenon associated with the souls of the dead. This is the *laer amann*, or butter thief. According to folk belief, those who make a pact with the devil can steal the cream from their neighbor's cattle by sending the spirit of the last person to die in the victim's household to milk the cows by magic at night. This magical milking removes only the most valuable portion of the milk, the cream needed for making butter. The milk subsequently produced by the cows becomes thin and watery, and their owner is unable to use it in butter produc-

---

10. See also *McGraw-Hill Encyclopedia of Science and Technology*, 5th ed., s.v. "methane," and *Van Nostrand's Scientific Encyclopedia*, 6th ed., s.v. "methane."

tion. The thief, in contrast, uses the stolen cream to produce large quantities of butter, which permits him to enrich himself at the victim's expense.

The *laer amann* is a variant of the evil-eye tradition documented cross-culturally in association with milking and dairy production (Roberts 1976:241; see also Dionisopoulos-Mass 1976; Kittredge 1929:163–173; Maclagan 1902:89; Maloney 1976; Murgoci 1981; and Vuorela 1967; among others). Similar "magic attacks" are described by Favret-Saada (1980:112) in her study of witchcraft in the Mayenne. In Brittany the *laer amann* fuses magic with ghost beliefs.

A typical experience with the *laer amann* is recounted in the following excerpt from a conversation with Yves, from Plonévez-du-Faou, whose description of a *teuz* has previously been discussed.

> *Yves:* Yes, I've heard . . . I knew the guy well, [the one] who went to look inside his stable at midnight. I knew the guy—he was a bit old-fashioned, he wasn't afraid of anything. But this time he got scared! He saw his dead mother. . . . She had been dead for eight days, perhaps, before that. He was astonished to see his mother.
> *My question:* She was milking the cows?
> *Yves:* Yes, oh yes.

In another memorate, sixty-three-year-old Gérard Bertholoux from La Feuillée explains that the souls of the dead are unable to cross bodies of water. For this reason they must employ a hose (*tuyau*) to siphon off the cream if their victim lives on the opposite side of a river or lake. According to Gérard's narrative, a farmer from Brennilis suspected that his cream was being stolen. Early one morning, he happened to be walking from Brennilis to Loqueffret. When he came to the bridge across the River Ellez, which divides the two communes, he noticed a spiderweb on the bridge. Looking at it, he said to himself: "I wonder if that is the hose of the *laer amann?*" To satisfy his curiosity, when he was halfway across the bridge, the man put his hand through the spiderweb, breaking it. As he did so, cream burst out of it into the water below. His suspicions confirmed, the farmer decided to follow the spider's thread leading away from the web. As he had suspected, it ended in his own cowshed. Following it in the other direction, it led him to the stable of the thief, a man in the *quartier* of Couzanet, several miles away on the other side of the river.

Legends such as Gérard's involving the *laer amann* are rarely told in the present tense. Most incidents involving the magical theft of cream in the Monts d'Arrée are said to have taken place before the 1960s. Significantly, by that period, home butter production had ceased to be economically important in this region. Since the mid-1960s, processing of milk has been centralized in large dairies, which send out trucks several times a week to collect raw milk from farms. Formerly butter merchants made weekly or biweekly visits to *quartiers* in the La Feuillée area, buying home-produced butter for resale in stores or regional markets. Neighbors would sell their butter at the same time, and it was therefore clearly apparent if one household was producing more than others in the *quartier*. Such a situation frequently generated suspicions that the person with the most butter was practicing magic to rob his or her neighbors of their cream.

With the new organization of production, the amount of milk sold by each household has become a private affair, known only to the producer and the dairy. This system, together with the fact that butter is no longer the primary source of cash income for farmers, has contributed to the declining importance of the *laer amann* in folk belief. Nevertheless, even within the changed context of production, the supernatural perspective remains current. In at least one case rumored to have occurred during the 1970s, a farmer from the Monts d'Arrée blamed witchcraft for a sharp drop in the cream content of the milk she was selling to the dairy. The milk controller employed by the dairy accused her of adding water to the milk in order to sell a larger quantity. However, the woman maintained that she had been bewitched, and that the *laer amann* was responsible for the low fat content and watery quality of her milk. The situation was apparently resolved when the woman visited a priest who performed counter-magic to lift the spell from her cattle.

Certain people in the Monts d'Arrée continue to believe firmly in the *laer amann*. Augustine, a La Feuillée woman in her seventies, recalls how her mother used to churn for an entire day without transforming her milk into butter, while their neighbor, who owned fewer cows, produced more butter than everyone else in the *quartier*. Augustine exclaims, "And that is true. It happened in every village!" However, others advance a different explanation for the phenomenon. They argue that prior to the introduction of modern feeds and livestock management techniques, people did not know how to care for their cattle properly. Moreover, the majority of agriculturalists were poor and could not afford good fodder for their animals. According to this technically oriented point of view, it was these factors that caused certain herds to stop producing or to produce only poor quality milk with little cream. The *laer amann*, in the opinion of the skeptical, was simply a supernatural scapegoat, blamed because people were ignorant of the real, natural causes underlying their problems.

The *laer amann* provides a second example of a folk belief involving revenants which has been discredited by the scientific perspective. Not all of those who claim to have suffered as victims of the *laer amann* accept the scientific explanation, however. Some insist that the loss of cream took place even though their cattle were well nourished. While these people accept the general principle that shortages of cream may result from natural causes, they consider such causes insufficient to explain their own particular experiences, which can only be accounted for by reference to the supernatural.

People in the Monts d'Arrée are keenly aware of the cognitive gap dividing the scientific outlook from the supernatural perspective that accepts the existence of ghosts and related phenomena. Augustine, for example, suspects that "educated" people will laugh at her stories of the *laer amann*, although she is convinced of their veracity. The middle-aged and elderly frequently seek to dissociate themselves from the supernatural perspective, with its "old-fashioned" and "superstitious" connotations. This reaction is most likely to occur when they are discussing supernatural phenomena with relative strangers from outside the region, including ethnographers. From the Monts d'Arrée point of view, the dominant contemporary attitude toward revenants is one of disbelief. For this reason it is considered wiser to respond to questions about revenants with stories about supernatural apparitions that were indisputably false than with narratives about experiences with the supernatural which are regarded as true. As a result, tales of "fake" revenants, or hoaxes in which living persons pretended to be ghosts or to have seen them, are eagerly recounted.

One story about a false apparition remembered in the village of Le Crann, Berrien, concerns a group of pious women who routinely gathered in the evening to read religious works. One night a group of young men decided to play a practical joke on the women. They hollowed out a turnip, carved eyes, mouth, and nose in the shell, and placed a lighted candle, jack-o'-lantern fashion, in the interior. One of the young men climbed onto the roof of the house where the women were gathered and lowered the turnip on a string down the chimney until it reached the fireplace, around which the women were sitting. On hearing their startled screams, his accomplices held the door to the house shut from the outside, so that there could be no escape from the *teuz*. One senses anticlerical sentiments behind this prank and the enjoyment produced by retelling the story. Any occasion to ridicule the *blancs* in a predominantly *rouge* community is now, as in the past, highly appreciated.

Another, more widely known, incident involves the "haunted house" at Loqueffret, south of La Feuillée. For a period of several months in the mid-1950s, a poor family in one of the outlying *quartiers* of the parish was able to convince a large proportion of the local population that their house was haunted. The "haunting" took the form of strange noises heard in the night and stones that mysteriously fell down the chimney. The incident was reported in the regional press, and busloads of the curious came from all over Finistère as well as from other departments to see the house. Finally a police investigation revealed that one of the daughters in the family was herself staging the bizarre incidents. At present, several explanations are advanced for this episode. According to some people, the haunting was an attempt by the girl to scare her father, an alcoholic, so that he would give up drinking. Others suggest that the hoax was performed to make money. The family played on the sympathies of the curious visitors in order to receive donations to help them escape from the apparent persecution of the malign spirits. The schoolteacher who ran the communal school in Loqueffret at the time of the "haunting" recalls that many people in the community were convinced that the family was the victim of a magic attack. When the truth was revealed, the former believers became ashamed of their credulity, and open discussion of the incident became extremely difficult.

A third case concerning a fake revenant took place in the woods between the *quartiers* of Kerbargain and Kerberou at La Feuillée, during the winter of 1928–1929. A postcard dated January 2, 1929, from Pierre Briand of La Feuillée to his cousin in Paris recounts the details of the affair:

> My dear cousin:
> I received your card yesterday. Thank you very much; it gave me great pleasure to receive your news. What F. J. told you is true. For eight days we heard someone crying in the woods. Sometimes he called out "Father, I am lost." At other times he let out dismal cries, which made one shiver. But he has been caught, and do you know who it is? You will never guess. It is M. A——. He was afraid that someone would steal his wood, so he decided to stage a haunting.
> I wish you all the best for the New Year . . .
>
> Pierre

Many older people in La Feuillée recount this incident with humor. The entire community was terrorized during the "haunting." In addition to crying out "Father, I am lost," the "revenant" also moaned, "I am a damned man on the road to hell."[11] The "haunting" was all the more credible because a man working in a gravel quarry near the woods had been killed accidentally a short time prior to the incident. When the perpetrator of the hoax was discovered (either by some soldiers or by a young man and a hired hand from a nearby farm, according to different versions of the story), his reputation in the community was ruined. He was nicknamed "the Teuz," the ghost, for the rest of his life. Although the family of "the Teuz" were prosperous and had been respected locally, they were considered "a bit odd." Moreover, their avaricious concern for money and property contrasted with community norms of generosity and reciprocity. As Pierre Briand's postcard suggests, "the Teuz" sought to scare people in order to prevent them from collecting dead wood for fuel on his property.

In contrast to the readiness with which anecdotes are recounted about fake revenants, experiences with revenants which are believed to be true are talked about rarely and in private. The two final memorates to be discussed in this section are thus particularly

---

11. The revenant in the form of a lost child (*bugel noz*) is a common motif in Breton folklore (see Le Braz 1928:2:223).

significant. Both told by Lise Segalen, a La Feuillée woman in her mid-seventies, these memorates differ from many stories about revenants in that they are deeply and sincerely believed. Moreover, they are associated with landmark experiences of bereavement in Lise Segalen's life.

Lise was born in the village of Keranheroff, La Feuillée. Except for brief interludes in Paris and North Africa, where her husband was posted during his military career, Lise has lived most of her life in the *bourg* of La Feuillée. The first incident she describes occurred after the death of her father, when, as a young woman, she was living alone at Keranheroff. Her mother was already dead, and Lise was the only one of her brothers and sisters to remain with her father in the family home. Every night in bed she cast her eyes around the room, and every night she was aware of her father's empty bed opposite her own. It disturbed her to see his vacant place, and she regularly dreamed about her father.

Sometimes in her dreams Lise saw her father leaving the cemetery, emerging from a sort of underground tunnel that passed from his grave under the cemetery wall and surfaced on the opposite side, next to the road leading to Keranheroff, their home village. These emotionally traumatic dreams frightened her. In an effort to put an end to them, she asked the curé to say a Mass for her father's soul. He refused, telling her she had no reason to be afraid. The dreams continued, even after the *messe d'anniversaire*. As Lise recalls, "I had done everything the way it should be done, the *messe d'anniversaire* and a family meal afterward." Thus, in her view, there was nothing remiss in her conduct toward her dead father to explain his persistent "return" in her dreams. Finally, Lise confided in one of the old women from the village. The elderly neighbor suggested that Lise sleep in her father's bed. That way she would no longer be troubled by the vision of his empty place at night. Lise recalls that since the night she started sleeping in her father's bed, she has never dreamed of him again.

Following one line of interpretation, Lise's dreams can be linked to the psychological process of detachment from the dead which follows bereavement. The father's empty bed symbolizes his former status and roles, his place during life. So long as these remain unfilled by another, the dead continue implicitly to occupy them in the minds of the living. Although Lise does not phrase it in this way, it seems she felt that her father was returning nightly from the tomb to sleep in his own bed. As soon as his place had been taken by another, he stopped returning.

While Lise's experience of her father's "return" involves dreams rather than an actual haunting, little distinction is made by people from the Monts d'Arrée between apparitions seen in a waking state and those seen in dreams. In response to a question about legends concerning ghosts, one elderly La Feuillée woman explained: "Revenants? They were mostly dreams." As noted in Chapter 8, dreams are a particularly potent medium for communication between the living and the dead.

The second memorate recounted by Lise Segalen concerns a waking vision of a revenant. This incident took place after the death of her husband in 1972. M. Segalen had been an invalid for almost forty years, since his return from North Africa, where he had contracted tuberculosis. Lise had cared for him at home to the end of his life, refusing to hospitalize him even after he developed cancer, from which he died. As an invalid requiring a great deal of attention, M. Segalen occupied a large part of Lise's emotional energy and time. After his death she had difficulty adjusting to being alone. Possibly because she had been used to thinking about her husband and nursing him continually, she had the sensation that her husband's spirit lingered around her for some time after his funeral.

As Lise describes it, "It's true what they say—your dead track you down, they follow you." Approximately one month after her husband's death, Lise was washing the windows of her house, when she caught a glimpse of a man walking past the house along the path leading toward the cemetery. He was wearing navy blue, as her husband used to, and his gait resembled that of her husband. This vision troubled her. Eight days later, Lise was again doing her housework, cleaning the front door. All of a sudden, she saw the same man she had seen the previous week walk past the house again. "He had the same face as my husband," she recounts. "His face, it was *his* face. He was a thin man, very elegant. He was walking quickly, going toward the cemetery." She rushed outside, but the man had already disappeared along the path. "It was *then* that I understood what it was," she says. "It was an apparition of my husband."[12] Lise continues, "And the old people used to tell us that when you are afraid of your dead, when you see them, you must say a prayer for them." Remembering this advice, she went immediately to the cemetery and said a Latin prayer she had learned in childhood at her husband's grave. Since that time, she remarks, "I have never seen him again, nor dreamed about him, either." This last comment is made with a certain regret and bitterness. As Lise explains, she feels that the prayer she said for her husband in the cemetery acted somewhat like a magic formula to prevent him from reemerging from the grave. "In the past all the prayers were in Latin, and we couldn't understand what the words meant. So we used to condemn our dead to stay there [in the tomb] without knowing what we were doing." Both of Lise Segalen's narratives illustrate the ambivalence the living express toward the dead. One longs for their return, yet should they appear, in visions or dreams, they become a source of fear and uncertainty.

For Lise Segalen, it was her Latin prayer that consigned her husband's spirit eternally to the grave. Others in La Feuillée advance a similar explanation to account for the rarity of revenants in the contemporary world. After recounting several narratives about revenants, eighty-year-old Marie Cousquer remarked, "Now the curés are better educated. They conjure the dead at the funeral to make them stay in the grave. That's why we don't see 'things' anymore." Others share this folk belief, suggesting that the prayers said by the priest at the graveside are now stronger and more efficacious than in the past. Thus, priests are now able to prevent the spirit from wandering out of the grave. It is for this reason that revenants no longer appear very often among the living. Here, as in many other aspects of Breton popular belief, a Catholic ritual is thought to accomplish ends that diverge widely from those intended by the clerical representatives who perform it. It is also striking that this explanation does not rely on the scientific perspective. Instead, the

---

12. Significantly, the Breton word Lise uses to describe this apparition is not *teuz*, the word most often used when speaking of fake revenants, but *spes*. Although both words mean "phantom," *spes* has the connotation of "appearance." *Teuz*—with the additional meanings of specter, goblin, and demon—implies apparitions of a more terrifying nature.

traditional worldview has successfully generated an explanation for the disappearance of a supernatural phenomenon which is consistent with its own—supernatural—terms of reference.

In discussions of revenants, people from La Feuillée frequently expressed the opinion that it is unusual to see the dead return, but that in contrast, experiences with the supernatural prior to a death are common. *Intersignes*, or precursors of death, have greater continuing significance than ghost beliefs for contemporary Bretons in the Monts d'Arrée. Tales of revenants often end on a note of uncertainty or skepticism, as in the case of Soazic Bihan's legend about the revenant in the form of a hare, which, as she comments, was "perhaps" true. However, memorates about *intersignes* are believed. Frequently the speaker concludes such narratives with the phrase, "And *that*, that's true!" The next set of narratives to be discussed concerns *intersignes* and their connection to the concept of destiny or fate.

Intersignes

As the term *intersigne*, meaning "sign between," suggests, these omens bridge two dimensions of time, the present and the future, and two levels of reality, the natural and the supernatural. For those who talk about and have experienced *intersignes*, there are no rigidly defined boundaries between these domains. In many narratives concerning *intersignes* the supernatural expresses itself through the medium of natural phenomena: the actions of birds, dogs, and horses; or noises heard in the night. These "supernatural" signs therefore do not differ greatly from the "natural" signs, such as weather prognosticators, that many people in the Monts d'Arrée are predisposed to recognize. The observation that gulls are flying toward the coast, for example, is interpreted as a sign of good weather. In the same way, the call of the owl is taken to be an indicator of a forthcoming death. The primary difference between weather signs or other "natural" signs and *intersignes* lies in the gravity of the signified. *Intersignes* address profound human issues of death, grief, and loss.

In the Monts d'Arrée the term *intersigne* is generally shortened to *signe*. The Breton word *seblant*, which connotes "semblance" or "apparition," is also used in the region to refer to precursors of death. These signs are described as *huñvreel*, "dreamlike." Both Breton terms imply the surreal, extra-normal quality of such omens.

It is acknowledged in the Monts d'Arrée that some people are more receptive to *intersignes* than others. Le Braz (1928:1:3) records the nineteenth-century belief that children who enter and leave consecrated ground before being baptized are especially likely to develop this ability to "see" the future. Such would be the case if, for example, a child was scheduled to be baptized but the priest was unexpectedly called away, and the ceremony had to be postponed. This explanation, which is still remembered in La Feuillée, again bears witness to the assimilation of Catholic notions of the sacred by less orthodox traditions. It is as though a *rite manqué* generates its own special power.

Several different types of events are recognized in the La Feuillée area as *intersignes*. The most common of these is the call of the "death bird" in the neighborhood of a person who is about to die. This bird, known in Breton as *labous an ankou*, is often identified as an owl or a screech-owl, although some claim it is a sparrow-hawk.[13] Direct species identification of the bird is not of great importance to people in the Monts d'Arrée: the ambiguity attached to its identity stems from its supernatural role as an *intersigne*. Many people in La Feuillée claim that "it's like an owl, but not quite the same."

Other signs interpreted as omens of death in the Monts d'Arrée include the howling of dogs, the crowing of a cock by night, and the repeated appearance of crows or magpies around a house. Magpies are said to "sweep the road" that will soon be taken by a coffin and mourners on the way to a funeral. *Intersignes* also include premonitory dreams, unexplainable noises, and waking visions of funeral processions seen well in advance of an actual death and funeral in the community.[14] As numerous examples attest,

---

13. Sébillot (1906:196) notes that the call of the tawny owl, the *chat-huant*, is considered a sign of death in Lower Brittany.

14. All these phenomena are reported as *intersignes* from nineteenth-century Brittany as well, which demonstrates the continuity over time in folk belief. See Le Braz (1928:1:5–7) for *intersignes* involving sparrow-hawks, magpies, cocks crowing at night, and howling dogs. He also describes visions of funeral processions (1928: 1:67–71). Sauvé (1883–1885) documents most of these and many other *intersignes*. Sébillot (1906:100, 192–196) observes that howling dogs, magpies, crows, and owls

many of these phenomena are standard omens cross-culturally.[15] Similar precursors of death are mentioned in anthropological studies of European rural communities by Danforth (1982:15), Douglass (1969:19–20), and Pina-Cabral (1986:217–218).

The following memorate, told by Maryvonne, describes several typical *intersignes,* including the call of *labous an ankou.* Some of Maryvonne's experiences with the supernatural have already been mentioned, such as her dreams of her deceased mother, discussed in Chapter 4. Here Maryvonne tells of *intersignes* she received in conjunction with her father's death in 1981.

> One thing that I have also noticed: the clock. There used to be, there is still, a clock at my parents' house, and the clock stopped working at the moment my father died. My father died at four o'clock in the morning, and the clock stopped. It had never stopped before. And it stopped at four o'clock in the morning, and it has not worked properly since! I saw it the other day; I was there, and it had stopped at seven forty-five. The clock refuses to start running again. And it stopped—I looked; it had stopped. We spent the night with my father, I was there when he died, and the clock stopped at the moment of my father's death. And since then the clock won't work.
>
> And I had a sign there, too, when my . . . before my father died. There was an owl—or a screech-owl, I don't know what you'd call it—that flew onto the gable of the house. The window of my room was open. The dog howled for more than an hour afterward. The owl let out a piercing cry! So loud, so loud that I thought the room was shaking. A screech, a hideous screech! Only one shriek, but so loud that, I'm telling you, I thought the house was shaking. And the dog started to howl; the whole house was woken up. About two months before the death of my father. Around two months. And so then I went to the window, because I said to myself, "The whole *bourg* will have heard that screech," and I said to myself, "But all those in the *bourg* are surely going to . . ." And I heard everyone speaking in the *bourg.* Yes. I heard lots of people talking in the *bourg.* There, you know, the day of my father's funeral, everyone from the

---

were considered omens of death or disaster in a number of other regions of France besides Brittany, including Normandy, Anjou, the Ardennes, Lorraine, and the Gironde.

15. The owl has been regarded as a bird of ill omen in many cultures at least since classical times. The magpie, cock, and crow are also frequently cited in Indo-European folklore as prophetic birds. The howling of dogs is taken to be an indicator of death in many parts of the world (Thompson 1955–1958: Motifs B143.0.2, magpie as prophetic bird; B143.0.3, owl as prophetic bird; B143.0.8, crow as prophetic bird; B147.2.2.4, owl as bird of ill omen; B733.2, dogs' howling indicates death; B733.2.1, cock hears inaudible voice of dying man; D1812.5.1.12.1, howling of dog as bad omen). Bernabé (1980:31–33) draws attention to the significance in Romania of dreams as precursors of death.

bourg came. There weren't many who didn't come. And it was those people there who were speaking, that I heard speaking. There was no one. I asked my neighbor the next day if she had heard the owl. "But no." No one had heard the owl.

As Maryvonne's narrative reveals, belief in *intersignes* depends on faith in the interconnectedness of phenomena. Human affairs, the actions of animals and natural forces, and the supernatural realm are all perceived to be inextricably linked. Even manmade objects, such as the clock that stopped at Maryvonne's father's death, are integrated into this all-encompassing network of connectedness. In this interpretation of reality, there is no room for random coincidence. The clock stops because, on the supernatural level, its mechanism is influenced by the death of its owner. It is not simply that the clock has worn down independently of the death. Maryvonne's narrative implies that the clock would still be working if her father were alive.

In Maryvonne's memorate the clock stops at the exact moment of death, and therefore, unlike the other signs she describes, it does not provide advance warning. The cry of *labous an ankou* and the howling of the dog, however, serve as precursors. The nonrandom significance of these coincidental events is recognized after the death of Maryvonne's father. Likewise, on the day of his funeral, Maryvonne realizes that the voices she had listened to in the *bourg* two months previously were those of the mourners she was supernaturally enabled to hear in advance. Analysis of other memorates shows that this after-the-fact interpretation of events as omens is a central feature of experiences with *intersignes*.

For Maryvonne, the owl cried outside her house because it knew of her father's upcoming death. She cannot simply interpret the incident as a natural event, explainable by the fact that owls are nocturnal birds that occasionally let out piercing cries around human habitations when startled. Others of her generation in the Monts d'Arrée, influenced by the scientific perspective, are more willing to allow for the possibility that night birds call at random, without reference to deaths that will occur in the human world around them. Anne Rousvoal, a Berrien woman in her early sixties, remarks that in the past, "we didn't consider the nocturnal life of those creatures. We didn't conceive of it. We imagined that they were birds that came here to announce a bad omen. It never occurred to us to think that those animals had their life, their nocturnal life, as the diurnal birds have their life too." This type of explanation clearly stems from a "disenchanted" view of reality, which does not postulate the interconnectedness of phenomena.

In the majority of *intersigne* memorates, as in Maryvonne's narrative, the person whose death is foreshadowed is someone close to the one who receives the advance warning, like a relative or neighbor. Maryvonne's father was not ill at the time she heard the death bird, the howling dog, and the mysterious voices in the *bourg*. However, many experiences with *intersignes* occur when the person about to die is already fatally ill. Then the *intersigne* frequently serves as a message or cue which changes the attitudes of the living toward the dying person. It confirms the fact that he or she is no longer a sick person who may recover, but one who will inevitably die. The *intersigne* thus marks the transition of the dying person into a liminal state, part way between the worlds of the living and the dead. Upon receiving the *intersigne* the living are spurred into action, to prepare themselves and the moribund for imminent death. This response may be seen in the following memorate, told by Jannick Le Goff, the seventy-seven-year-old La Feuillée widow whose description of *feux follets* and their causes has previously been discussed. The narrative she relates concerns the death of her husband. It was recorded during the course of an afternoon coffee gathering with women friends and neighbors of Jannick's generation.

> And *this*, this was true. Because, listen. I had hospitalized my husband. My husband was in the hospital in Saint-Brieuc. In a clinic. And he had cancer. And one month before his death he was still at the clinic. He was like a cadaver. He couldn't stand up any more. Well, enough said. And so, there was a little window in my room—like that, eh? And me, I had a small bed so that I could sleep there. So that I could stay with my husband. I stayed with him so that he wouldn't be alone. In Saint-Brieuc, this was. And so, one night, around . . . I was already in bed. Around ten o'clock at night there was a bird at the window. It made a noise like "cri, cri, cri, cri, bwa, bwa, bwak, bwak!" It sounded just like those birds we used to hear in our village when I was a girl. And then it left. But you know, me, that had a big effect on me. I wasn't going to talk to my husband, because he wasn't asleep. He had heard, he too. Because the noise . . . The window was hooked half open, you see, not closed. Since the bird came right onto the edge of the window, me, I heard it. I didn't mention it to my husband at all.

The next morning the nursing sister said to me, "Oh, Madame Le Goff, you must take your husband home," she said, "because, you know, he is very, very sick." I said, "I know that, Sister. I know only too well that my husband is sick," I said. "It is high time to take him back home, because otherwise he will die here," I said. And the nursing sister had heard that bird, too. And when that bird comes, it's death, you see. It smelled that my husband was moribund. And that's no lie. It was I myself who heard it. And I knew what it was. And in front of the clinic, there were some old pine trees. Big pines, big pines. Perhaps the bird had its nest there. It made only one cry, at the window, and then it left . . . And I didn't mention it to my husband. Without a doubt he heard it; he wasn't deaf. And he didn't say anything to me either. And that is a true . . . it's not . . . But people used to be afraid of that in the past. A sign of death. And it isn't a sign of death, it was the bird who smelled the corpse.

When asked if her husband had died immediately afterward, Jannick replied,

He returned home, and he died one month later. In the clinic they told me that it was time to take him back home. So I said, "Right away. Tomorrow morning we take my husband home," I said, "because he isn't well." The nursing sister said to me, "Yes, Madame, I didn't want to tell you, but it is high time to take him home." I said, "My husband is ready to die. I must take him home." "I thought so," she said, "but I didn't dare tell you." *Eh ben,* the next day he was in the ambulance to come home. He lived another month afterward, even so.

In this memorate Jannick emphasizes that it was the call of the death bird which made her realize the urgent need to transport her husband home from the clinic while he was still capable of traveling. The importance traditionally accorded to dying in one's own home rather than in an institution is underscored throughout the entire narrative, especially in Jannick's phrase "It is high time to take him back home, because otherwise he will die here." The bird's cry acts as a message for the nursing sister also, provoking her to speak to Jannick about the gravity of her husband's condition.

As Jannick's narrative also illustrates, seemingly inconsequential events, such as the cry of a bird at one's window, are interpreted as *intersignes* in the context of a death. Awareness of the environment may be heightened during this period of intense psychological stress, and perhaps only then are bird calls or the howling of a dog, for example, consciously heard and remarked. The owl may call every night, but one is only awake to hear it when caring for a sick relative.

As noted in connection with fake revenants, increasing exposure to the scientific perspective has led numerous middle-aged and elderly people in the Monts d'Arrée to attempt to dissociate themselves from what they think society at large regards as "superstitions." Many of those who distance themselves from the supernatural in this way nevertheless retain a certain measure of faith in it. This apparently contradictory stance is maintained by rationalizing supernatural beliefs to make them consistent with the scientific perspective. To some extent this process has remolded folk tradition. Ideas about *labous an ankou* provide one example of this process. Certain people, like Maryvonne, report that it emits a long, shrill shriek, described as "strident" or "lugubrious," prior to a death. Others, like Jannick, claim that the bird lets out a series of short cries, often likened to the squeaking wheels of a cart. This noise is also identified with *karrigell an Ankou*, the cart or wheelbarrow in which the Ankou carries away the souls of the dead. The sound of the *karrigell an Ankou* (or *karrig an Ankou*, as it is also known) was traditionally recognized as an *intersigne* (Le Braz 1928: 1:114–123). Today many people continue to interpret the noise as a portent of death. For them, however, it is produced not by the Ankou with his cart but by a bird. Discussing *karrig an Ankou*, one frequently hears statements such as, "That's a bird, that noise." Birds are said to be able to smell the odor of the body's decay even before a death occurs, and for this reason they cry around the home of a dying person. This explanation removes the supernatural persona of the Ankou, in whom, it is implied, only the old-fashioned or the simple-minded in the contemporary world would believe.

Jannick Le Goff rationalizes the call of the bird heard before her husband's death by referring to this hypothesis: "But as for the *signes*, like that bird. In the past everyone was afraid, because that was like a sign of death. And in effect . . . But now we are more intelligent. We know that the bird smells the cadaver. They smell it in advance. So they come around." Others in the La Feuillée area agree, observing that "death has an odor, a heavy, heavy odor." Like *labous an ankou*, the dogs that howl before a death are also believed to be alerted by this smell.

Although the "odor theory" seeks to demystify *intersignes*, the explanation relies on the traditional representation of death personified as an animate being with a will of its own. This paradox is implied in the statement "Death has a heavy odor," which suggests that death is imagined to be similar to an animal, like a fox, whose physical presence can be detected by other animals through its distinctive scent.

The odor hypothesis cannot explain all *intersignes* involving the call of the death bird or the howling of a dog, because sometimes these are heard before a sudden or accidental death, when there is no cadaverous odor to be smelled in advance. The following memorate, told by Fanch Tromeur, a man in his forties from the Carhaix area, provides one example. Fanch recalls that his first experience with *labous an ankou* took place in 1970. At that time he was working at the nuclear power station in Brennilis. He and his family lived in housing provided for the power station employees, above the hamlet of Kerflacconier on the outskirts of the *bourg* of Brennilis. One evening he heard the death bird crying in the neighborhood. Jokingly he told his young son that someone in the area was sure to die soon. However, beyond this banter, he thought nothing more about the bird's call. The next evening, when Fanch returned home from work, his son greeted him with the words, "I hope you won't hear that bird very often." A neighbor from Kerflacconier had hanged himself that day.

Fanch's anecdote illustrates two important features characteristic of *intersigne* narratives. First, it conveys the message that one should not joke about *intersignes*. Death is a serious matter. Like the Ankou with his arrow and scythe, it is a force that can strike at any moment, when one least expects it. Second, the narrative demonstrates that, as previously mentioned, the natural event—in this case a bird call—is not interpreted as an *intersigne* until after the fact. It is a signal whose referent remains hidden in the future. Had the neighbor in Kerflacconier not committed suicide the following day, Fanch and his son would most likely have forgotten the call of the death bird. Like many other *intersigne* memorates, Fanch's narrative represents an after-the-fact interpretation whereby a shocking or tragic death is placed in the context of a supernaturally determined, meaningful pattern foreshadowed by signs.

It is faith in this type of deterministic pattern which underlies belief in *intersignes*. The signs preceding a death are interpreted as proof for the existence of fate, or destiny, a supernatural guiding force that controls the course of individual lives. Logically, if certain animals and people know in advance when a death will occur, the future must be preordained. As one woman remarks, reflecting on the accuracy of the *intersignes* that presaged her son's accidental death, "Those things are true, those things that I've just told you. Yes, they're true. So therefore, there is something supernatural above us, don't you believe?" Belief in destiny is associated with a conception of time in which the future already exists as an objective reality waiting to unfold. It is the *intersigne* which connects the domain of the present with that of the predestined future. Through *intersignes* certain persons are permitted by fate to know beforehand what must inevitably occur.

Many people in the Monts d'Arrée believe that destiny regulates all the events that occur during an individual's lifetime. This outlook is succinctly summarized in the Breton proverb quoted in Chapter 2, "Pep hini en deus e blanedenn" (Each person has his destiny) which is well known among the elderly of La Feuillée.[16] The belief that the course of one's life is "written in advance" is frequently expressed in the region. Drawing an imaginary line on the table in front of him, Paul, aged fifty-five, explains, "If your life is going to follow that direction, it will not go any other way, try as you might. What must happen will happen." To clarify, he cites the example of his aunt, the victim of a serious illness, whose doctors gave her only a short time to live. "That was a year ago," he observes. "And now she's running around like a rabbit. It wasn't her destiny to die young." Similar sentiments are voiced by Margit, a Brennilis woman in her sixties, whose mentally handicapped son made an unsuccessful suicide attempt by shooting himself in the head with a hunting rifle. Margit asks rhetorically, "Don't you believe that my son would be dead now if it had been his destiny to die then?" As she concludes, "It was not the hour of his death."

Many elderly people share the attitude that one will not die before one's appointed time.[17] Eighty-six-year-old Marie-Thérèse suf-

---

16. The word *planedenn*, "destiny," also means "planet," suggesting that destiny is astrologically determined.
17. For historical parallels to this attitude, see Le Roy Ladurie (1979:288–290) and Ginzburg (1985:8). In the latter example, Ginzburg quotes a sixteenth-century Friulian peasant who describes how the spirits of certain individuals leave the body by night. The peasant notes that during the time that the spirit is absent, "if the body, seeming to be dead, should be buried, the spirit would have to wander around the world until *the hour fixed for that body to die*" (emphasis mine).

fers from numerous physical problems, which are aggravated by loneliness. On winter days, when her depression matches the grayness of the weather, she asks herself why she remains alive. But she is resigned to the fact that "I must wait until it comes to seek me out. Life is like that." In the same way, eighty-five-year-old Pierre-Louis notes that he is one of the few men left from his age class in the parish. "But I must stay here, because it has not come to get me yet." It is difficult to render the exact sense of such remarks in English, for French makes use of the impersonal form in the third person singular: "Il faut attendre, jusqu'à ce qu'on vienne me chercher," and "On n'est pas venu me chercher." Who or what is this *on* that comes to seek out those who will die?

Statements such as those made by Marie-Thérèse and Pierre-Louis reflect a continuing tendency to personify death or destiny. Even if death is no longer represented in the form of the Ankou with his scythe, it is still conceived to be an animate force that acts on its own volition. Speaking of destiny, an elderly neighbor of Marie-Thérèse explains, "If you are named to go, you must go." Significantly, the Breton verb *gervel*, meaning "to call" or "to name," is also used in connection with *labous an ankou* and *karrig an Ankou*. When asked to describe the Ankou, a La Feuillée woman in her sixties replied, "The Ankou? It's a call." Death calls, and one has no choice but to follow.

By representing death as the inevitable culmination of a predetermined life course, a worldview privileging the concept of destiny provides the bereaved with a meaningful context in terms of which the death of a loved one can be explained. However, people from the Monts d'Arrée do not rely on destiny for explanations in all situations. Reference to destiny is made most frequently in reflections about deaths or personal tragedies that occurred in the past. Just as *intersignes* achieve most of their significance in after-the-fact reconstructions of the events associated with a death, so too is destiny invoked with hindsight as an after-the-fact justification or explanation for tragedies. For rural Bretons, belief in destiny thus coexists with active efforts to control those aspects of life which are perceived as controllable. The idea that one cannot escape the preordained moment of one's death does not prevent people in the Monts d'Arrée from seeking to avoid illness or accidents. Likewise, the same people who express the view that the course of one's life is "written in advance" strive to provide their children with higher education that will permit them to pursue lucrative and satisfying careers. Nonetheless, in the face of, or after, an unavoidable tragedy, such as the death of a close family member, ideas about destiny lend "interpretability" (Geertz 1973c:100) to the experience of personal loss.

The process of referring to destiny as an explanatory medium in the aftermath of a death is poignantly outlined in the following anecdote, recounted by Geneviève Kerannou, a La Feuillée widow in her late seventies. Over morning coffee on All Souls' Day, Geneviève describes the circumstances of her husband's death sixteen years previously. He had suffered from heart problems and high blood pressure. However, he disliked taking his medicine and complained about the diet his doctor had prescribed. Even though he knew fat was bad for his health, M. Kerannou was only happy eating high-cholesterol dishes like pot-au-feu or rich butter cakes. He would deliberately choose the fattiest cuts of meat. Instead of taking his heart pills, he would hide them or throw them away. Geneviève tried to make him eat correctly and take his medicine, to no avail. Finally her husband was hospitalized after a severe heart attack, from which he did not recover. On the day that he died, Geneviève told him, "You know, it's a bit of your own fault if you're here now. You should have listened to me." He replied, "Now I'll listen to you." But it was too late; several minutes afterward he died. Geneviève sighs, "But I believe it was his destiny, to some extent. It's traced out from birth. You can try all you like to go to one side or the other, but you can do nothing." According to her interpretation, her husband was destined to die of a heart attack at sixty-two years of age. All her efforts to prevent this early death, by making him follow his diet and take his medicines, were futile in the face of his unavoidable fate.

Like death, marriage is also "written in advance." Geneviève reminisces that she had no trouble choosing a husband. She was married to her first suitor at age eighteen. In her opinion it makes no difference whether one has looked for years in the hope of finding the ideal spouse; if it is one's destiny to marry a certain person, one will do so. No amount of careful screening will prevent one from making a bad marriage, if that is one's destiny. This point of view is echoed by another elderly La Feuillée woman, commenting on the marriage of an eighteen-year-old girl from the commune who had become pregnant by her boyfriend. While noting that such a marriage, arranged to appease the girl's family, is unlikely to succeed, the woman concludes, "It was her destiny." The girl was fated to become pregnant and marry at eighteen. A Breton phrase frequently used in the Monts d'Arrée expresses this perspective:

> *Er mod-se emañ ar vuhez*
> Life is (persists) that way.

Significantly, those who believe in destiny do not necessarily believe in God. Paul, whose remarks about destiny were quoted earlier, reflects that if God existed, He would intervene to correct the injustices of the world, such as the evils of war and the deaths of children. "All that sort of thing must be traced out at birth," Paul concludes. Likewise, a strongly anticlerical woman in her sixties from the La Feuillée area claims that the *intersignes* she has experienced have convinced her that "there must be a Master. I don't know if it's *le bon Dieu* or another, but I think there must be a Master who forewarns us." As her comment suggests, destiny is not conceived of so much in terms of the Christian concept of God's will as in terms of an ordering force in the universe, which bears no necessary connection to Roman Catholic doctrine.

If all the major crises in life are "written in advance," it is not surprising that some people should be forewarned when a death is about to occur. Such prescience is frequently described in the Monts d'Arrée as a *don*, or gift. Yet the knowledge of the future which is given through *intersignes* is often only partial. When listening to *intersigne* memorates, one is struck by the frequency with which the identity of the person about to die is mistaken. In this mistaken-identity motif an incident, such as the howling of a dog, is initially interpreted as a portent of the death of some person in the community considered likely to die. However, the *intersigne* is in fact followed by another, much more tragic and unexpected, death. The following memorate, told by Odille, the thirty-five-year-old municipal clerk in La Feuillée, is structured around the mistaken-identity motif.

Odille is the daughter of Yann Marc'h, a retired La Feuillée municipal employee. Intending to become a doctor, she started, but later abandoned, university studies in the sciences. To some extent

Odille distances herself from "superstitions" or belief in any aspect of the supernatural. Nevertheless, she recalls an inexplicable event which, she says, "comes to mind every time I hear someone talking about *intersignes.*" The incident occurred on May 7, 1963, when Odille was living with her family in the village of Kerbrann, La Feuillée. Her paternal grandfather was gravely ill at the time, in the hospital at Carhaix. His children would each take turns spending the night with him at the hospital. On the night of May 7 it was Odille's father who had promised to go to the hospital.

After finishing his day's work, Yann was in the courtyard preparing his motorbike for the trip to Carhaix. That evening, Odille remembers, something was wrong with the motorbike and her father was late in leaving. As he worked on the bike, changing a spark plug, he joked and chatted with his good friend and next-door neighbor, Jerome Le Roux. As Odille explains, "We really liked Jerome. He was like a brother to Papa." The two men helped one another in their work and played *boules* together in their spare time. Their outbuildings were built side by side. In fact, Jerome's barn abutted directly onto that of Odille's father. While Yann changed his spark plug, he and Jerome joked about death, as they often did, saying to one another, "If you get to paradise before me, save me a place next to you." Neither man gave a second thought to their jesting. Finally the motorbike was fixed and Yann was ready to leave. Just as he was getting onto the bike, Odille and her mother and the two men heard an owl calling. The bird was perched at the juncture of the two barns, between Jerome's property and that of Odille's family. Upon hearing the owl, Jerome commented to Yann, "You may find some bad news waiting for you at the hospital." Odille's mother responded, "Well, whatever the case, we know that Yann's father is dying." Everyone was expecting the grandfather to die soon, so the *intersigne* came as no surprise.

Throughout the evening Odille's mother kept close to the telephone, waiting for Yann to call from the hospital with the expected message. Finally the family went to bed. In the middle of the night they were awakened with a start by a loud banging at the door. It was a neighbor, come to tell the family about the death—of Jerome Le Roux. "He had lost all his blood," Odille explains. Apparently Jerome suffered from a genetically transmitted blood disease. "We all knew that he had that disease," she says, "but he had been perfectly all right when we talked to him that evening." After the fact, it became obvious to Odille and her parents that the owl had been calling not for Yann's father but for Jerome. The grandfather died, as expected, two days later. Odille concludes, "Frankly, I don't believe in that sort of thing, but even so, that comes back to me; it really marked me." This was Odille's first contact with death, at ten years of age.

In Odille's memorate the sudden death of Jerome Le Roux is far more shocking and tragic than the expected death of her grandfather. Typically *intersignes* are observed in connection with this sort of *triste* death. As noted in Chapter 3, suicides, accidental deaths, sudden deaths, or the deaths of young persons shake the community to a greater extent than the "normal" deaths of the old. Such *triste* deaths are considered unjust and senseless. By setting these tragedies in the context of a predestined pattern beyond human control and foreshadowed through *intersignes,* one can to some extent reconcile their apparent lack of reason with the desire for an ordered, meaningful vision of reality.

The mistaken-identity motif reaffirms the ultimately unknowable and uncontrollable character of destiny. It conveys the message that the supernatural, while permitting some people to glimpse imperfectly into the future, reserves the right to its mysteries. Suzanne, a middle-aged woman who runs a café and store in the *quartier* of Kerelcun at La Feuillée, acknowledges this limitation. Suzanne has experienced a number of premonitions. Yet, she explains, she rarely foresees exactly what the future holds: "I just miss it" (*je tape à côté*). For example, she recounts that several years ago her brother in Paris contracted a fatal disease. Before she knew of his illness, Suzanne experienced a series of recurring dreams in which her daughter, Marie-Jo, died in a car accident. "And it was my brother who was sick in Paris. And who came here to die of his illness. And I dreamed *next to* that (*à côté*). I said it was my daughter in Paris who had had an accident, and that I saw her dying as a result of it. I don't dream exactly what will happen, but next to it; I just miss it."

Suzanne recounts another *intersigne* story, involving her mother. Again dramatic irony reinforces the message that fate is beyond mere human understanding or control.

> And then, you see, me, I had a brother who was killed on the road. And *maman,* she thought that it was herself who was going to die. And so she had said, "We must kill the cock. All he does is sit on

his perch and sing during the night." That's a bad sign, too, eh? So she told her son, the one who was killed on the road, she told him like that, "*Eh ben!* Saturday, you've got to kill that cock, eh? I've had enough of hearing him. All he does is sing on his perch. Me, I'm going to die," she said, *maman*. "He's after me." "Oh," my brother said, like that, "You get these silly ideas in your head, *maman*. That isn't true," Robert [the brother] told her. "Ah, if you don't want to do me a favor," she said, like that. "Well, if you don't kill him this week,"—she'd been asking him for two weeks by then—"if you don't kill him this week, well, that means you want me to die!" "Oh well, then I'll kill him," Robert said, like that, "since you keep going on about it!" *Eh ben*, the week after, the next Saturday, it was *Robert* that was killed on the road! And my poor mother lived on for five or six years after her son. It [the *intersigne*] wasn't for her. She just missed [the meaning], too (*elle tapait à côté aussi*).

Suzanne's mother's comment that the cock was "after her" (*Celui-là me cherche*) is significant. In many *intersigne* narratives, the owl that calls, the magpies that cluster around a house, or the dog that howls are described as "coming to get" or "seeking out" a person who is about to die. Here again, the impression is conveyed that death is an active force operating through certain natural creatures. Suzanne tells of another incident, involving a close neighbor in Kerelcun, who died in 1980:

Eh ben, behind the house there. François Goasguen, he keeps his chickens. *Mah* [interjection], you know, Chan ar Menez, his wife died suddenly? Well, his cock wouldn't stop crowing at night. And me, I told François one day, like that, and he made fun of me, eh? I said to François, "When you have a cock that crows at night like that, me, I don't like that, because I don't know that he isn't after me," I said, "to go to the cemetery." Well, he said to me, "You! You won't be going to the cemetery so soon. You are too healthy!"

Well, you know, his wife died just a little while afterward! She went to have an operation, and she died on the operating table. She hadn't been very sick beforehand, no. So you see, there are certain things like that, eh? *Eh ben,* me, I'm telling you, Chan ar Menez's cock was calling her.

In Suzanne's final comment, we are again reminded of the definition of the Ankou as "a call."

All of the *intersignes* described up to this point have involved unexplainable noises, the actions of animals, or dreams. *Intersignes* also take the form of apparitions seen in a waking state. Several *intersigne* memorates describe visions of funeral processions which appear to one or more persons prior to a death. Typically, the actual funeral procession follows the same route seen earlier in the vision. The following memorate illustrates this kind of *intersigne*. It was recounted by Jean-Marie Trellu, a retired farmer in his early seventies, from Loqueffret, south of La Feuillée. According to Jean-Marie, the incident he describes took place during the early 1920s.

> But me, I knew this man. I knew him very well. And one day he was coming home. Me, I was just a kid at that time. He was coming from the *bourg* with my uncle, with *tonton* Louis, and a neighbor, Pierre Henry. And so, just before they arrived at the road leading to their village, there was a path. There was a little gate in the field, and people used to go through there sometimes. Anyway, they reached that gate, and he stopped. And he said to the others, "Let's go this way." "But why?" "Let's go this way. I will tell you later." And when they had entered the field, just as they were crossing the field, the guy, he kept looking at the road. And he said, "There is a funeral procession passing by there." But the others said, "But where, then?" And there was no one there. "There is a funeral procession passing by there. There is a *char-à-banc* [carriage] and a coffin, and two people behind it and that's all. But I don't know them. I don't know anyone there," he said.
>
> And three days later, in effect, there was a corpse that passed by. It was a policeman. At that time there was a police post at La Feuillée. It was a policeman from La Feuillée who had been killed—but he wasn't dead when the guy saw the coffin—he was killed at Châteauneuf. Because at that time they had horses, the police. And this man had gone up to the granary to get some hay for the horses. And his belt got caught in the twine around the bale of hay. And he fell. He fell onto the pavement below and he died. He died suddenly, by accident. I'd say three days, maybe eight days, later the coffin passed by there, exactly as the guy had seen. Exactly. The same road, two people behind, everything.

Once again, in Jean-Marie's narrative, an *intersigne* is associated with a dramatic, sudden death. Accidental deaths of this kind lack the "normal" indicators that precede the deaths of the elderly or the very ill. For this reason there is a greater need to invoke a supernatural precursor to set the death in a coherent context. Ariès's (1982:6) observation that death in the early Middle Ages never came unannounced holds true as well for traditional Brittany. Anecdotes like Jean-Marie's imply that death *should* not come without warning. Therefore, when the signs of illness or old age are absent, supernatural indicators must be sought in after-the-fact interpretations of the event.

Significantly, Jean-Marie's narrative has a solid base in local history. There was actually a La Feuillée policeman who died in Châteauneuf as a result of a fall during the early 1920s. The widow of the policeman still lives in La Feuillée, as does his goddaughter, Hughette Cadiou. Both women's descriptions of the man's accident coincide exactly with the details of Jean-Marie's account. "He suffered a terrible death," recalls Hughette. When told of the *intersigne* narrative, she confirmed, "That must have been the same person. He was the only one who died in those circumstances." The unexpected death of a public figure, such as a policeman, is certain to have provoked much discussion in the countryside, giving rise to legends about *intersignes*.

People in the Monts d'Arrée are reluctant to discuss *intersignes* involving visions of funeral processions, for they cannot easily be rationalized in terms of the scientific perspective. Whereas one can claim that dogs or birds smell the odor of death, it is more difficult to develop a natural explanation for premonitory visions. Jean-Marie himself speculates that those who see funeral processions in advance derive their power from "a type of magnetism." This theory represents another attempt to integrate supernatural phenomena with scientific modes of explanation.

The final *intersigne* memorate to be considered is of special interest because it illustrates a striking continuity in folk belief from the nineteenth century to the present. Moreover, it shows how a particular folklore motif has changed to correspond to the context of contemporary Brittany. During the nineteenth century, as Le Braz (1928:1:293) records, it was held to be a bad sign should a horse pulling a carriage carrying a coffin stop on the way to a funeral ceremony:

> One must never whip a horse that is pulling a hearse. If it stops, it is necessary to wait until it resumes walking itself, or in any case to stimulate it only with one's voice, speaking softly to it.
> If the vehicle in which the coffin is being transported to the cemetery should stop at any point along the route, it is a sign that in the next eight days, it will perform the same function for another member of the deceased's family, or at least for another person from his village.

Since the 1960s, when use of automobiles became widespread, this belief has been modified. Now in the Monts d'Arrée it is taken by some to be an indicator of a forthcoming death if a car transporting a coffin halts in a funeral procession. Fifty-three-year-old Jacqueline Milin, who discussed this belief, recalls that during her girlhood, whenever someone from her *quartier* died, it was her stepfather who transported the coffin in his wagon to the *bourg* for the funeral. Jacqueline remembers that on such occasions her mother would say, in Breton, "The horse must not stop, that's a bad sign." At one funeral the horse stopped in a neighboring village, and it was only with considerable effort that Jacqueline's stepfather could induce it to continue the route. Shortly afterward, a death occurred in the village where the horse had stopped.

This incident from her childhood came to Jacqueline's mind in 1980, when she attended the funeral of Catherine Paul, an elderly woman from her *quartier* in La Feuillée. This was an unusual funeral, for although the Mass was held in the church at La Feuillée, the family burial plot was located in Huelgoat. Therefore the relatives, close friends, and neighbors of the deceased accompanied the coffin to the cemetery by car after the Mass, a distance of thirteen kilometers. Since Catherine Paul had been a close neighbor of the Milins, Jacqueline and her husband along with another neighbor, Denise, followed directly behind the car carrying the coffin in the funeral procession. This car was driven by *tonton* Pierre, Jacqueline's husband's brother, who lived next door to the Milins. As the procession passed the road leading to the village of Le Crann, approximately two-thirds of the way to Huelgoat, *tonton* Pierre's car blew a tire. The whole cavalcade was forced to stop while the tire was changed. At that time Jacqueline said to her husband and to Denise, "That's a bad sign. A corpse shouldn't stop along the route like that. There will certainly be another death from the *quartier* soon." Jacqueline's husband passed this off as a foolish superstition. Jacqueline did not say anything more on the topic, for privately she suspected that the next person to die from their *quartier* would be Denise's elderly mother, who was not well at the time. Jacqueline did not wish to disturb Denise with such speculations. However, Jacqueline's interpretation of the *intersigne* was mistaken. The next death in the *quartier* was that of *tonton* Pierre, the driver of the car carrying the coffin. His sudden death six months later was shocking, for he was only forty.

Jacqueline concludes her account of this incident with the observation that "they say it is the dead who come to get the dead. It was *she* who came to get him." When asked to elaborate, Jacqueline explained that it was Catherine Paul, as the previous person to die from the *quartier,* who "came to get" *tonton* Pierre at his own passage to the otherworld. Neither Jacqueline nor her forty-four-year-old friend who was present during the conversation questioned the validity of the idea that the dead come for those about to die. This folk belief recalls a tradition collected by Le Braz (1928:1:111), according to which the last person of the year to die and be buried in a parish serves as the Ankou for that parish throughout the upcoming year.[18]

Jacqueline's story reveals important differences with respect to male and female attitudes toward the supernatural. When Jacqueline first mentioned to her husband that the flat tire on the way to the cemetery was a "bad sign," he dismissed her comment as a worthless superstition. Later, when she reminded him of the incident after *tonton* Pierre's death, her husband argued that the apparent intersigne was "only a coincidence." He maintains a skeptical attitude, whereas for Jacqueline this event constitutes proof of the existence of the supernatural and the validity of its signs. Many men, like M. Milin, refuse to give credence to *intersignes* or at least to admit publicly that they believe in such things. In part this is because the supernatural, like religion, is perceived to be a woman's domain. Skepticism is therefore the "manly" reaction. Furthermore, men from the Monts d'Arrée are often more vehemently *rouge* and anticlerical than women. Since little distinction is drawn in this region between faith in Catholicism and faith in such unorthodox manifestations of the supernatural as *intersignes,* belief in any aspect of the supernatural implies belief in all its aspects, including the tenets of the church. Consistent with the materialism characteristic of their political stance, men reject all types of supernatural phenomena, regardless of whether these fall within or outside of the Catholic domain.

Although people in the Monts d'Arrée continue to refer to *intersignes* to provide a framework of significance in which to situate tragic deaths, many claim that the number of *intersignes* observed at present is vastly reduced relative to the past. As M. Le Grall from La Feuillée explains, "No. No, now people no longer hear or see

---

18. This belief varies from locality to locality. In some areas it was held to be the first person to die in the year who acts as Ankou for the following twelve months (Le Braz 1928:1:111n).

the signs or any of those things. You don't hear anymore. No. Now you don't see, either. In the past, *ben*, the old folks, they used to say that they saw, heard, things, you know; but not now." Discussing *labous an ankou*, some suggest that, like so many other species of birds, it has become extinct, the victim of the pesticides used in modern agriculture. Even among the elderly, the supernatural perspective is perceived to be in decline. Two sisters in their seventies from the Carhaix area reflect that "all those things have changed now. No one believes in God or anything anymore." Likewise, Joséphine Kerouac of La Feuillée explains, "The world has become too modern to stop for all those kinds of signs. Now people think that they were only superstition, and that we were persecuted by superstition in the past."

Such nostalgic sentiments may be expressed by the elderly in all societies and at all historical periods. Nostalgic comments therefore should perhaps be read as indicators of attitudes toward perceived changes rather than as reliable guides to transitions that have occurred.[19] Clearly it is impossible to judge whether or not the number of *intersigne*s observed in the 1980s is actually lower than the number observed in the 1920s or the 1880s. However, from the perspective of people in the Monts d'Arrée, there has been a definite decrease in these occurrences. Comparison with the works of the nineteenth-century folklorists also indicates that *intersigne* memorates are now told less frequently and spontaneously than in the past, which suggests that a shift in worldview has occurred.

Some people in the Monts d'Arrée advance the explanation that one now rarely receives premonitions of death because modern life lacks a "rapport with nature." As Jean-Marie Trellu of Loqueffret observes, "People don't pay attention in the same way, and then they don't go anywhere on foot. When they go out to the fields, they're on the tractor, they don't hear anything." Others claim that people are less receptive to *intersignes* now because they listen to the radio or watch television whenever they are alone.

Since the 1950s, innovations such as agricultural machinery, indoor plumbing, and central heating have combined to insulate those living in the rural milieu from the natural environment. Elec-

19. Compare Pina-Cabral's (1987) penetrating discussion of perceptions of time and ideas about the past in rural Portugal, which touches on many of the same issues raised in this chapter.

tric lighting has demystified the night. All these features of the modern lifestyle have made contemporary Bretons less likely than their grandparents to pay attention to such things as bird calls, noises, and the actions of horses or dogs. Nonetheless, the perceived decline of *intersignes* is not simply the result of the fact that such phenomena are no longer noticed. The significance of events in the environment can now be interpreted differently. For example, many from La Feuillée remark that certain dogs in the *bourg* howl frequently; however, their howling is not generally considered a sign of death. Rather, the dogs are said to howl because the sound of the church bells that strike hourly in the *bourg* hurts the animals' ears. The sign is no longer invested with the same significance.

The fact that phenomena formerly interpreted as *intersignes* are now perceived, at least in some cases, to be of only trivial significance can be related in part to changing patterns of social relationships. The majority of *intersigne* memorates deal with the deaths of family members, neighbors, or other close associates of the narrator. Recall Odille's comment that Jerome Le Roux "was like a brother to Papa." Such narratives belong to a social context structured around face-to-face relationships, where the death of one person is experienced as a loss by an entire social network. With the changing character of neighborhood ties in contemporary Brittany, people are now less aware of deaths that occur around them. To a large extent, death has been displaced from the home and local community to the institution. For this reason neighbors are now less actively involved in networks of reciprocal assistance during sickness or tragedy. People from the *quartier* no longer gather in the home of a dying person to recite prayers and to accompany the bereaved family. As one La Feuillée woman states, "In the past when someone died, everyone was in mourning. Now it's not the same." The independence of families and individuals from non-kin based social networks has meant that people are no longer automatically intimately implicated in the deaths of other community members. In this new social context, from which death is being distanced, one is less apt to conceive of natural events as *intersignes*.

The scientific perspective has also influenced *intersigne* beliefs. The scientific outlook has introduced a greater tolerance for randomness and undermined the traditional conception of the interconnectedness of phenomena. Reliance on technical or scientific explanations makes it easier to accept the notion that events are not necessarily linked in an underlying, supernaturally determined pattern. Coincidences, like the stopping of a clock on its owner's death, are not held to provide unambiguous proof of the existence of such a pattern. Increasingly it becomes possible to view the death of a young person in a car crash, for example, not as the outcome of a predestined scheme but as an accident that could have been avoided with rational judgment.

As these last points suggest, the partial disappearance of *intersignes* is linked to the wider issue of waning belief in destiny. In contemporary Brittany the idea that one's life course is supernaturally determined from birth is beginning to be questioned. Anne Rousvoal explains, "Oh, yes. My husband says it often, 'It was written,' he tells me. I don't know. I tell him, 'But you know, destiny, one can go against it, one can improve it, one can often change it' . . . Yes . . . And I believe, I think that a person can forge his destiny himself."

Although the perceived power of the scientific perspective has challenged the concept of fate, it is primarily the disruption of the traditional, rigidly hierarchical class-based system of social organization in Brittany which has undermined belief in destiny. With increased possibilities for social mobility, the trajectory of an individual's career no longer seems preordained. Improved educational opportunities, immigration, and new possibilities for employment outside the agricultural sector have meant that the children of poor farmers do not necessarily follow the lifestyle of their parents and grandparents. The amount of land owned by a family no longer inevitably determines the social status which those born into that family will occupy. Moreover, the attenuation of social control within small rural communities has resulted in greater individual freedom of choice with respect to ethics, social norms, and lifestyle. All these social factors have contributed to a greater sense of personal autonomy and independence in rural Brittany, which is reflected in the idea that one forges one's own destiny. The contemporary emphasis on personal freedom is incompatible with the traditional belief that "everything is traced out from birth." With the gradual weakening of the latter conception the folk beliefs associated with it, including *intersigne* traditions, are also being displaced.

It is important to emphasize that while from the viewpoint of people in the Monts d'Arrée, the number of *intersignes* observed has decreased, *intersignes* have not, for the majority of people, disappeared. Belief in *intersignes* is strongest among the elderly and less accepted by the young. However, people from all age groups tend to alternate between belief and skepticism. There has been no sudden and definitive mass conversion to the scientific perspective. Rather, both scientific and supernatural frames of reference are invoked, and supernatural interpretations are often perceived to be more potent in the face of tragic events. Discussing the scientifically inexplicable character of *intersignes,* Odille, the town clerk from La Feuillée, expresses a blend of faith and rational incredulity. She speaks for many others in the Monts d'Arrée who, like herself, are reluctant to see the world exclusively in terms of either the scientific or the supernatural perspective. Her comment, quoted earlier at the conclusion of her narrative about the death of Jerome Le Roux, bears repeating in this context. "Frankly," she admits, "I don't believe in that sort of thing, but even so . . ."

Conclusion

Both ghost beliefs and *intersignes* are aspects of the supernatural which fall outside the boundaries of orthodox Catholicism. Like more conventional religious faith, however, belief in revenants and *intersignes* enables Bretons in the Monts d'Arrée to interpret the experience of bereavement in a meaningful way. *Intersignes* in particular provide the bereaved with a structure of significance within which a death can be placed. The omens preceding a death prove the existence of destiny, a supernatural force that regulates the course of human lives. According to this perspective, it is impossible either to hasten or to postpone the preordained hour of one's death. The call of the death bird, the howling of a dog, or a premonitory vision signals that death is imminent. Such signs bridge present and future time dimensions, since the future is perceived to be "written in advance." In the Monts d'Arrée *rouges* and *blancs* alike believe in destiny. This supernatural force is not conceived to be identical to the will of God. Belief in destiny exists independently of Catholicism.

Reference both to destiny and to *intersignes* as tokens of this force is generally made with hindsight, after a death has occurred. Omens and destiny are invoked in a process of after-the-fact interpretation which enables the bereaved to come to terms with a death and to endow it with significance. Since ideas about destiny come into play as an explanatory medium primarily after a misfortune has occurred or when a death is recognized to be unavoidable, they do not prevent people in the Monts d'Arrée from attempting actively to direct their lives. It is possible to suggest, modifying slightly Maurice Bloch's (1977) ideas about time and ritual discourse, that Bretons subscribe to notions of destiny in certain contexts but assume a nonfatalistic perspective in others. Beliefs about destiny thus would be relatively unimportant in everyday patterns of behavior, whereas in or after crisis situations involving tragedy or death they would become prominent.[20]

Ghost beliefs are less important than *intersignes* in providing contemporary Bretons with a meaningful way of coping with death. The living experience the immanent presence of the dead primarily through dreams. Tales of ghosts in animal form and of other types of revenants told in nineteenth-century Brittany are now frequently greeted with skepticism. In contrast, many middle-aged and elderly people in the Monts d'Arrée continue to believe that in the past the clergy used supernatural powers to cause ghostly apparitions. By so doing, it is suggested, they manipulated their parishioners through fear to maintain the social power of the church.

In the La Feuillée area, scientific and supernatural modes of explanation compete in discussions about *intersignes* and revenants. Frequently attempts are made to rationalize traditional beliefs in order to make them consistent with the scientific perspective. The significance of these explanations lies not in their truth value but in their status as "scientific," which gives them greater prestige and credibility than supernatural accounts. Those who advance scientific rationalizations share, at least to some degree, a worldview characterized by confidence that naturalistic, technical means of understanding phenomena can be found under all circumstances.

20. I am indebted to Stanley Brandes for suggesting this parallel with Bloch's work.

The displacement of supernatural explanations by naturalistic ones suggests that the process of disenchantment is occurring in the domain of folk belief at the same time as secularization is undermining orthodox Catholicism in Brittany. It would, however, be inaccurate to claim that an inevitable replacement of the supernatural by the scientific perspective is underway. People in the Monts d'Arrée alternate between scientific and supernatural ways of viewing the world. Scientific explanations, like those based on destiny, fit certain contexts, but in experiences of personal tragedy supernatural explanations are often more profoundly meaningful. As Lambert concludes in his discussion of death omens from Limerzel, "The most common attitude is to believe in them without believing, while believing all the same" (Lambert 1985:231). It is unlikely that such ambivalence is exclusively characteristic of worldview in late twentieth-century Brittany. As the accounts of folklorists demonstrate, naturalistic explanations for *feux follets* were being advanced during the nineteenth century and were encouraged by representatives of the dominant intellectual tradition of metropolitan France.

Although the scientific perspective has not replaced the supernatural in present-day Brittany, changing features of social organization have favored the process of disenchantment. With the declining influence of the church since the 1960s, anticlerical folklore concerning priests and sorcery has lost some of its relevance. Moreover, because contemporary predication is not centered on death, Catholicism in Brittany no longer helps to create an atmosphere in which phenomena such as revenants are credible. The breakdown of the traditional rigidly class-based social order has led to a questioning of belief in destiny. New economic conditions have permitted greater class and occupational mobility. Whereas in the past the life course of a child born into a rural community could truly be said to be "written in advance," at least insofar as economic opportunities and lifestyle were concerned, this is no longer the case. The heightened sense of personal autonomy in contemporary Brittany is also related to the diminishing force of informal mechanisms of social control, such as gossip. The decrease of *entraide* and the changing style of neighborhood-based face-to-face social interaction has to some extent freed people from the pressure to conform to social norms which, in small communities, can predetermine the choices an individual may make.

In the Monts d'Arrée many people comment that fewer *intersignes* are observed at present than in previous generations. This perceived decline in the numbers of *intersignes* is partly related to the fact that changing social circumstances favor naturalistic explanations over supernatural ones based on destiny. In addition, as the locale in which death occurs is transferred from the home to the hospital, and as specialized health-care professionals take over the role of caring for the dying from neighbors and family members within local communities, awareness of death decreases. If *intersignes* are indeed becoming less common, this change is perhaps best understood as a product of the contemporary social context, in which people do not always know when those around them are about to die. Discussions about death omens indicate that phenomena from the natural environment are frequently not remarked upon and interpreted as *intersignes* unless a death in the community has occurred or is known to be likely to occur. When one is unaware that one's neighbor is gravely ill, one does not notice the owl calling in the *quartier*.

Intersigne beliefs are closely linked to the tame response to death. As death becomes less familiar an event, people cease to look for and to expect its presages. The interconnectedness of phenomena on natural and supernatural levels, the basis for these omens, is no longer an unquestioned feature of folk belief. Death is increasingly excluded from the world of the living, and at the same time the natural world moves farther away from the supernatural domain.

10

Conclusion

This examination of death in Brittany has been concerned primarily with the complex, mutually reinforcing, and interdependent relationships between responses to death and transformations in Breton social organization. It has focused in detail on death as it is experienced and interpreted in two Breton communities. Throughout, the perspective of the study has been a highly local one, although an effort has been made to fit the changes observed in Plouguerneau and La Feuillée into a more general theoretical framework. At this point it is important to draw together some of the diverse pieces of local evidence described earlier and to review the larger patterns of social change against which they must be contextualized.

Many of the changes that have taken place in Breton deathways since World War II indicate the growth in Brittany of the denial of death which Ariès and other researchers have described for other parts of the contemporary Euro-American world. A number of these developments are related to the growing division of labor in Breton society. The creation of specialized geriatric health care and support services has meant that in many cases the elderly have been separated both residentially and socially from other social groups. With medicalization, both aging as a memento mori and the event of death itself for all age groups is gradually being localized in the context of the institution. Solitary death in a hospital presents a striking contrast with the "public death" of the past. As care for the dying in the nonspecialized environment of the home is replaced by care in specialized facilities with specialized personnel, death is distanced from the social space occupied by the living. Becoming less familiar, death inspires greater fear and horror. Moreover, medicalization in Brittany is promoting a view of death as disease, which can potentially be cured with the aid of technology.

The development of a specialized division of labor is also apparent in the domain of funerary ritual, particularly in urban centers. There employees of the *pompes funèbres,* anonymous, paid specialists, have taken over roles such as that of pallbearer, which were formerly carried out by close associates of the deceased. Also, in Breton cities the *toilette des morts* is now often performed by the *pompes funèbres,* or by medical personnel when death takes place in a hospital. Even in La Feuillée, the resident nurse is frequently called upon to do this task. To some extent reliance on specialized personnel to assume responsibility for the *toilette* has distanced the physical reality of death from the everyday sphere of ordinary people. Furthermore, it suggests a growing repugnance for contact with the dead body.

Other changes in funerary ritual reflect the development of an ethos of individualism and the changing character of face-to-face social interaction at the local level. In the past, pallbearers in rural communities were chosen from the same neighborhood and social category as the deceased. Men were selected to carry the coffins of other men, and women served as pallbearers if the deceased was a woman. Similarly, pallbearers were expected to belong to the same age class as the deceased. Now, however, pallbearers in La Feuillée are almost always male, although an attempt continues to be made to choose people from the approximate age category of the deceased if he or she was a young person. This change reveals the lessening importance of group-based social classification in small communities. Increasingly people are seen, and see themselves, as individuals rather than as members of a particular age cohort or sex category. In addition, depopulation in rural areas frequently makes it difficult to choose pallbearers from the deceased's neighborhood, since many *quartiers* do not have sufficient numbers of men to make up a temporary work group of this kind.

In Plouguerneau, where traditionally it has been the duty of the two male neighbors living closest to the deceased to carry the cross at the head of the funeral procession, these neighbors now sometimes refuse to fulfill this obligation. The decreasing importance of this system of reciprocal mortuary obligations is linked to the fact that the community can no longer exert the same degree of pressure as it did in the past for conformity to social norms through gossip and other informal mechanisms of social control. Moreover, relationships with neighbors and kin are increasingly guided by new individualistic values emphasizing personal autonomy.

The denial of death has also been promoted in Brittany by the process of secularization. Since the 1960s, Catholicism in Brittany has changed from a ritualistic to an ethically based religious system. The church now stresses the need to develop inner personal faith and an intellectual approach to religion. These changes are related to the loosening of community-based mechanisms of social control, the growth of individualism, and the disappearance of a rigidly stratified social order dominated by the clergy and landed proprietors. Fear of death, Judgment, and damnation were used by the church in Brittany from the missions of the seventeenth century through the 1950s to instill a moral program whose effect was to ensure the reproduction of this hierarchical social system. With the demise of this social order, the church's insistence on death has also lost its force.

Moreover, the post–Vatican II Church's deemphasis of ritual has both mirrored and provided a model for a more general devaluation of ritual in Breton society at large. Death-related traditions have been particularly affected by this process. Wakes have been abridged in rural areas and virtually discontinued in urban centers. Funeral attendance, while remaining high in rural communities, has dropped in urban centers. The ceremony of public condolences, at which mourners shake hands with the bereaved following the funeral, has for the most part been abandoned. The value of these public rituals associated with death has been challenged, especially by those under forty-five. The public expression of grief at wakes and funerals is increasingly considered inappropriate. Authentic grief, it is felt, is an inner emotion debased through ritual. For this reason mourning customs have largely been rejected. Whereas attendance at wakes and funerals has traditionally been structured by ties of reciprocal obligation, many young people claim it is hypocritical to attend funerals or wakes simply "out of obligation." Instead they feel that one should attend funerary rituals only when one has a close emotional bond with the deceased or the bereaved.

Throughout Breton history, responses to death have included a combination of public events and private grieving. This remains true in contemporary Brittany. However, the relative importance accorded to public ritual and private grieving is changing. Currently the public ceremonies surrounding death are being set aside in favor of exclusively private expressions of grief. Thus the ritual visits made to the bereaved by neighbors and acquaintances during the wake, and the *café* offered to mourners after the funeral by the family of the deceased are frequently criticized, especially among the young. The same people who oppose the custom of attending funerals out of obligation argue that the celebration of Toussaint, the annual festival of the dead, lacks emotional authenticity. They argue that one should not honor the dead publicly, in a ritually prescribed fashion, on a single day of the year, but privately, through personal remembrance, at all times.

Such questioning of death-related rituals, which reflects the attenuation of face-to-face social ties in urban and rural communities and the growth of individual autonomy, has led in Brittany to the distancing of death. As responses to death become progressively privatized and attendance at funerary rituals declines, death itself becomes less familiar. Children and young people are no longer socialized to confront death through attendance at wakes and funerals, as they were in the past. Likewise, through the removal of cemeteries from the churchyards in the centers of Breton *bourgs*, the community of the dead is being separated from that of the living.

All these changes, consequences of new attitudes toward ritual and the trend toward a specialized division of labor, point to the growth in Brittany of the denial of death. However, close scrutiny of the ethnographic evidence reveals a more complex mosaic in which denial coexists with the traditional familiarity with death. The elderly in La Feuillée make little effort to avoid the reality of death. Many of those nearing death consider it important to organize the details of their own funeral and wake. Women knit the white sweaters they will wear on their *lit de mort*, and the elderly and middle-aged commonly build their own *caveaux* and tomb monuments. For many people in La Feuillée the "good death" remains one which gives advance warning, although this ideal is currently being supplanted by that of the sudden death.

Although funeral attendance has declined in Breton cities, rural funerals and wakes remain important social events, serving as opportunities for family reunions. Despite criticism from the young, attendance at wakes and funerals continues to be structured by reciprocal obligations, and the contemporary force of the obligation to reciprocate for Masses and services is witnessed by the large numbers of these offices which are requested. In Chapter 4 it was suggested that the increase in Masses and services paid for at funerals since the 1950s may indicate the commoditization of social relationships in Brittany and a disinclination on the part of associates of the deceased to engage in more active, time-consuming forms of support for the bereaved. However, the same phenomenon can also be interpreted as evidence for the continuing importance of death as a focus for displaying and validating reciprocal social networks in Breton communities.

The complexity of contemporary Breton attitudes toward death is especially apparent with respect to the cemetery. On the one hand the relocation of cemeteries suggests the growth of a new conception of community in Brittany from which the dead are being excluded. On the other, however, people do not wish to have their relatives buried in cemeteries that have been relocated beyond walking distance from town centers. It is said that no one will bother to visit the graves in these new cemeteries and that the dead will consequently be forgotten. Such comments make it clear that the cemetery continues to be conceived of as a familiar place that should be visited. In fact, visits to the tombs of deceased kin are an important part of the weekly routine for elderly and recently bereaved persons in communities like Plouguerneau and La Feuillée. The lack of support for cremation in contemporary Brittany stems in part from the persistence of the romantic desire to maintain ongoing relationships with the deceased through communion at the tomb. Moreover, it is significant that funerary architecture is one of the most important status markers in contemporary Brittany. Were they not highly visible, tomb monuments would have little value as symbols of social distinction. They fulfill this function precisely because the cemetery remains a frequently visited public space.

The ongoing importance of death and the dead as central themes in Breton culture is further evidenced by the role of death as an occasion for the most important family reunions, those at wakes and funerals and the annual reunions at Toussaint. The dead, at least those who died in the French armed forces and the Resistance, also serve to legitimate the contemporary political order. On a more personal and private level, there is a willingness among middle-aged and elderly Bretons to speak of the dead and to keep souvenirs of deceased family members, such as photographs, on view rather than to hide them and repress the memories they evoke. In spite of the trend toward contraction of the family in contemporary Brittany, the dead continue to be accorded a special place in the kin group.

Clearly the response of repression and denial is accompanied in contemporary Brittany by the familiar acceptance of death. In addition a third possibility, which differs from both the "tame" death of the past and the denial response, is emerging among medical professionals and those involved in providing geriatric care. The promotion of death-awareness training for hospital personnel as well as the home-helper program for the elderly created by the ADMR represent attempts to create a new kind of acceptance of death under social-structural conditions that are not conducive to familiarity with it as a natural element of the life cycle. Unlike the "tame" death, this new rapprochement with death is being self-consciously constructed by the medical community together with social workers and employees of social welfare agencies, all of whom have been influenced by the reexamination of death in Western culture in the social-science literature since the 1970s.

The complex pattern of continuity and change which typifies responses to death in Brittany is also apparent in the realm of orthodox Catholic and folk beliefs concerning the supernatural and the afterlife. The process of disenchantment has occurred in both of these domains. The aspect of traditional Breton folk eschatology which has lost most credibility over the forty years since World War II is belief in revenants. Legends concerning the dead who return in animal form or who in human form demand Masses for their release from purgatory are now viewed with skepticism. Naturalistic explanations are frequently advanced for phenomena previously identified with the spirit world, such as the theft of cream. For many contemporary Bretons it is only through dreams that the dead continue to manifest their presence among the living.

In contrast to revenants, supernatural precursors of death, or *intersignes,* remain important in providing the bereaved with meaningful explanations for personal tragedy. Signs linking present and future as well as the natural and supernatural domains, *intersignes* are closely associated with belief in destiny, an extrahuman force that predetermines the direction of human affairs. For those who believe in *intersignes*, death continues to be conceived of as an animate power with a will of its own, even though it is no longer represented as the Ankou of nineteenth-century folklore.

In contemporary Brittany, scientific and supernatural interpretations of the world compete. Under some circumstances scientific models predominate, but in other situations, particularly in the face of death, supernatural explanations carry greater weight. Often supernatural beliefs are rationalized to make them conform to the scientific perspective. In the case of *intersignes*, certain individuals are said to possess a type of "magnetism" enabling them to have premonitory visions. Dogs that howl and birds that call before a death are believed to smell the odor emitted as death begins to cause the body of a moribund to decay. Belief in the *laer amann*, or magical theft of cream by the souls of the dead, is now challenged by the skeptical, who contend that the cream content of cows' milk depends only on the type of nourishment the animals are given. In the same fashion *feux follets*, formerly interpreted as revenants, are now held to be caused by emissions of phosphoric gas from decaying organic matter. Although this explanation is not completely accurate, verifying the details of the scientific account is not particularly important for contemporary Bretons. The credibility of such explanations does not depend on their technical validity but rather derives from belief in the possibility of achieving a naturalistic, "scientific" understanding of causality. Reliance on the scientific perspective should not be read as evidence for the inevitable triumph of reason and Enlightenment thought. Most contemporary Bretons who espouse scientific explanations do so with faith (and not empirical proof) that these explanations are somehow "better" than supernatural ones. In this respect there is little difference between the natural and supernatural views of the world.

In her review of Keith Thomas's (1971) study of religion and magic in Tudor and Stuart England, Hildred Geertz makes the point that the plausibility of magical beliefs "derives not so much from empirical testing but from the fact that a particular notion is set within a general pattern of cultural concepts, a conventional cognitive map in terms of which thinking and willing, being anxious and wishing, are carried out" (1975:84). The same characterization applies to the plausibility of scientific explanations for twentieth-century Bretons and, indeed, probably for the majority of people in contemporary Western society. Discussing the decline of magic in sixteenth-century England, Geertz also argues that beliefs change when the culturally specific "cognitive map" or "substratum of convictions about the nature of the universe" to which they belong begins to disintegrate (1975:83–84). This is exactly the process that is occurring with respect to supernatural beliefs in present-day Brittany. Moreover, the weakening of the traditional Breton cosmological system is coming about in conjunction with, and is being reinforced by, social-structural changes, which are in turn being bolstered and promoted by the changes in worldview.

It is important to stress, however, that there is no clear-cut rejection of the supernatural in contemporary Brittany. To some extent the supernatural perspective remains more credible and meaningful for middle-aged and elderly persons than for the young. Nonetheless, people of all generations tend to alternate between scientific and supernatural views of the world. Most believe while not believing, maintaining an attitude of faith mixed with skepticism toward phenomena such as *intersignes* that defy easy explanation. This complex and apparently contradictory stance is by no means unique to Brittany, nor does it seem in Brittany to be exclusively a product of the late twentieth century. Rather, as the comments of Luzel's informants about the natural causes of *feux follets* demonstrate, the alternative scientific and supernatural modes of interpreting reality have coexisted in Breton culture at least since the nineteenth century.[1]

1. Likewise, a continuity in *mentalités* is suggested by Devlin (1987), who argues in her detailed examination of French popular belief that twentieth-century society has not abandoned the "irrational" but has merely changed the vocabulary with which discourse about it is conducted. The problem with Devlin's analysis is that while arguing that nineteenth-century supernatural beliefs were "reasonable," in that they served important social and psychological functions, she nonetheless implies that—like contemporary psychoanalysis, totalitarian political movements, and "quack" cures, which she claims serve analogous functions—they were fundamentally misguided and self-deceiving. A more fruitful line of inquiry would be to look at all these nineteenth- and twentieth-century phenomena as parts of coherent culturally embedded systems of meaning which generate a sense of order in the world. It should be noted that this approach does not inevitably lead to moral tolerance of totalitarianism.

The dramatic decrease in church attendance in Brittany since the 1950s can be interpreted as evidence for the secularization of Breton society. However, in making this analysis it is important to remember that the decline in public observance is not necessarily correlated with an overall loss of religious faith. Religious expression may be becoming more privatized, less restricted to formal settings (and, consequently, more resistant to scrutiny by the ethnographer!). In addition, new forms of spirituality—such as yoga, Rosicrucianism, and an interest in the occult, which are particularly popular among the young—should not be overlooked. Even the Breton revival movement, although essentially concerned with issues of politics and language, provides for its adherents some of the sense of belonging to a community with shared values and aspirations which the church formerly offered. In addition, the cultural revival has involved a growth of interest in ancient Celtic forms of spirituality.[2]

The correspondence we have seen between changes in responses to death and changes in the structure and organization of Breton society over the twentieth century cannot be reduced to a simple model of social determinism. Changes have occurred both in the realm of worldview and in the realm of society, and these changes have supported one another. The interdependent and mutually reinforcing patterns of change in social organization, eschatological beliefs, and attitudes toward death which have been outlined for Brittany may also be characteristic of a wide range of cultures experiencing rapid social transformations. Further cross-cultural studies would help to determine whether the theoretical framework presented here is useful for understanding death in other ethnographic contexts. Certainly the tame response to death is by no means exclusive to Brittany. Familiarity with death and its rituals prevails in many other contemporary cultural settings where face-to-face social interaction predominates: Latin America (Kelly 1975), rural Africa (Goody 1962; Thomas 1982), Madagascar (Bloch 1971),

---

2. Whether some of these forms, such as contemporary druidic rites, are truly "ancient" or "Celtic" is a matter of debate. As I shall explain, it is my position that their historical authenticity matters little. Even if they are in fact not linked to prehistory or to the Celts, they are believed to be, and as such they provide an underlying system of significance wherein individuals can meaningfully situate their lives.

southern and eastern Europe (Bernabé 1980; Douglass 1969; Pina-Cabral 1986:214–238), as well as certain regional or ethnic communities in the United States (Ablon 1970; Garrity and Wyss 1976; Moore 1970). Moreover, in some of these contexts the same types of changes documented for Brittany since World War II have taken place over roughly the same period of time (Thomas 1982:251–253).

These last points raise the issue of whether Breton responses to death are in fact as distinctive as many of the earlier researchers in this area have suggested. Is Brittany more preoccupied with death than other regions of France or Europe? Are the comments of writers like Hélias, who credits Bretons with "an obsession with death," justified? While recognizing that the death-related traditions of every culture are to some degree unique, it is probably incorrect to claim that Brittany is radically different in this respect from certain other parts of Europe. Devotion to the dead has been recognized as a characteristic cultural feature throughout the European Atlantic fringe, from Ireland to Galicia (Christian 1972:94). Present-day death rituals are clearly more elaborate in Greece and Romania than in Brittany (Danforth 1982; Kligman 1988), and the acceptance of destiny which typifies the traditional Breton worldview has also been noted in other contexts, including rural Portugal (Riegelhaupt 1984:110–111). It is true that Breton deathlore is marked by the fusion of Catholic concepts with unorthodox folk beliefs, some of which may be pre-Christian in origin, but this syncretism is equally typical of folk religion elsewhere, as the examples of Ireland, Portugal, Greece, and the Basque country suggest. Many of the same customs and certain of the folk beliefs recorded from Brittany exist or existed elsewhere in France, although they may have been maintained somewhat longer in the isolated Armorican peninsula.[3] Even the Ankou, an indisputably Celtic figure, has analogues in the iconography of other folk and literate traditions elsewhere in Europe.

These similarities call to mind another question. Is the preoccupation with death attributed to Brittany by Le Braz and his contemporaries, as well as by later researchers, simply another case of the

3. Indeed, according to Weber (1976:372–374), the period between 1870 and 1914 marks the disappearance elsewhere in France of the kinds of folk rituals and customs which I have argued are associated with a tame response to death, and which are documented for Brittany up to the mid-twentieth century.

"invention of tradition" (Hobsbawm and Ranger 1983) by nineteenth-century intellectuals? Its Celtic exoticism drew folklorists to Brittany during the romantic era, and consequently, oral traditions relating to death were more thoroughly studied here than in other areas of France (Sébillot 1904:146). Brittany may therefore *appear* to have more deathlore than the Midi or Alsace, for example, simply because more efforts were concentrated on collecting folklore of all kinds in this region.

The nineteenth-century folklorists may have been more active in Brittany, but those on whose works I rely do not seem to have fabricated their materials. Le Braz, for instance, identifies his informants by name and place of residence for the majority of folklore items he records. As he states in his introduction to the second edition of *La légende de la mort chez les Bretons armoricains*,

> At least I have worked hard, even at the risk of seeming incorrect or ungrammatical, to stay as close as possible to the Breton text. Because it is in Breton that almost all of these documents were first written down, and, with the exception of some information about rites or beliefs that I owe to the help of trustworthy correspondents, they were all collected directly by me as dictated by the storytellers.
>
> (1928:1:lxvii–lxviii)[4]

Souvestre, whose works I have not used, probably invented some of his texts and certainly added material to others to evoke an impression of the cultural context from which they were collected (Postic 1987:359; Senn 1981:31–32). Controversy has surrounded La Villemarqué's *Barzaz Breiz*, a work in which invention in the style of Macpherson's *Ossian* has been suspected (Gourvil 1959; McDonald 1986:336).[5] However, recent scholarship suggests that the texts published in the *Barzaz Breiz* were in fact collected in fieldwork by La Villemarqué, although he altered certain formal details of their presentation (Croix 1981:926; Laurent 1987).

---

4. In addition to his folklore publications, Le Braz wrote several novellas, which are works of the imagination based on folkloristic themes. However, his scholarly and literary works are strictly separate. See Dottin (1928:7–8), Marillier (1928:398–399), and Postic (1987:363) for discussion of the accuracy of Le Braz's work in *La légende de la mort chez les Bretons armoricains*.

5. See Trevor-Roper (1983) for a history of the invention of tradition in nineteenth-century Scotland, which includes discussion of the supposed Gaelic epic *Ossian*.

In any event, the issue of "invention" leads into somewhat of a blind alley. As anthropologists in the postmodern world are well aware, ethnic groups are engaged in a continual process of cultural construction and reconstruction. Thus, to some degree, all traditions are "invented." Even if, in some positivistic fashion, it were possible analytically to separate those which are "invented" from those which are "authentic," the results would not provide much useful information. Ethnic actors themselves would not make such a distinction. From the emic point of view, "invented" and "authentic" traditions are equally potent symbolic rallying points in the process of self-definition, and both provide important models for action in everyday life.

It is not inconceivable that the Breton "obsession with death" has been reinforced and elaborated over the course of the nineteenth and early twentieth centuries as a result of having become the object of self-conscious reflection on the part of literate academics.[6] Some of the academics in question were themselves Breton in origin, while others were attracted by the folkloric image that Brittany has long held in the eyes of metropolitan France. Even those who were born in Brittany, like Le Braz and Luzel, were educated in Paris and influenced by the point of view of the wider society. Like all peripheral regions in centralized nation-states, Brittany has not existed in a vacuum over the past two or three centuries but has influenced and been influenced by the larger social universe of which it is a part. The folklorists with their metropolitan perspective may have helped to construct Breton responses to death during the nineteenth century, but this process was not unprecedented. Rather, it parallels the shaping of those same responses by another metropolitan institution, the Catholic church, starting in the seventeenth century.

In present-day Brittany, the outside force that seems to have the greatest impact on worldview is scientific empiricism, which rural Bretons perceive to be the dominant explanatory paradigm of

---

6. In this connection it is important to note that with the revival of local culture in the context of the ethnoregionalist movement of the 1960s and 1970s, popular publications about Brittany based on the works of the early folklorists, as well as the original scholarly collections themselves, have sparked widespread interest.

French and Euro-American society. The persuasiveness of this paradigm and the prestige accorded it by the larger society challenge both Catholicism in Brittany and the supernatural folk beliefs that attracted the folklorists. The scientific perspective is not, however, new to Brittany. As they have done in the past, Bretons continue in the late twentieth century to manipulate both scientific and supernatural models to construct meaningful explanations in the face of death.

Bibliography

Ablon, Joan. 1970. The Samoan Funeral in Urban America. *Ethnology* 9: 209–227.
AELF. 1977. *Rencontrer le Seigneur Jésus*. 3d ed. Paris: Centre National de Pastorale Liturgique.
Ariès, Philippe. 1977. *L'homme devant la mort*. Paris: Seuil.
———. 1982. *The Hour of Our Death*. Trans. Helen Weaver. New York: Vintage Books.
Badone, Ellen. 1987. Ethnicity, Folklore and Local Identity in Rural Brittany. *Journal of American Folklore* 396:161–190.
Balanant, Abbé. 1899. *Taolennou ar Mision*. Quimper: Ar. de Kerangel, Diocesan Printer.
Behar, Ruth. 1986. *Santa María del Monte: The Presence of the Past in a Spanish Village*. Princeton: Princeton University Press.
———. Forthcoming. The Struggle for the Church: Popular Anticlericalism and Religiosity in Post-Franco Spain. In *Religious Orthodoxy and Popular Faith in European Society*, ed. Ellen Badone. Princeton: Princeton University Press.
Benson, Saler. 1977. Supernatural as a Western Category. *Ethos* 5:31–53.
Berger, Peter. 1967. *The Sacred Canopy: Elements of a Sociological Theory of Religion*. Garden City, N.Y.: Doubleday.
Berger, Suzanne. 1972. *Peasants Against Politics: Rural Organization in Brittany, 1911–1967*. Cambridge: Harvard University Press.
———. 1977. Bretons and Jacobins: Reflections on French Regional Identity. In *Ethnic Conflict in the Western World*, ed. Milton J. Esman, 159–178. Ithaca: Cornell University Press.
Bernabé, Jean. 1980. *Le symbolisme de la mort: Croyances et rites roumains*. Ghent: Communication and Cognition.
Beuchet, Jacques. 1982. Regards sur le peuplement des communes bretonnes. *Octant: Cahiers statistiques de la Bretagne* 11:5–20.
Blauner, Robert. 1966. Death and Social Structure. *Psychiatry* 29:378–394.
Bloch, Maurice. 1971. *Placing the Dead: Tombs, Ancestral Villages and Kinship Organization in Madagascar*. London: Seminar Press.
———. 1977. The Past and the Present in the Present. *Man* 12:278–292.
Bloch, Maurice, and Jonathan Parry. 1982. *Death and the Regeneration of Life*. Cambridge: Cambridge University Press.

Bossy, John. 1970. The Counter-Reformation and the People of Catholic Europe. *Past and Present* 47:51–70.
Bowman, Leroy. 1959. *The American Funeral: A Study in Guilt, Extravagance and Sublimity.* Washington, D.C.: Public Affairs Press.
Brandes, Stanley H. 1976. The Priest as Agent of Secularization in Rural Spain. In *Economic Transformations and Steady-State Values*, ed. J. B. Aceves, E. C. Hansen, and G. Levitas, 22–29. Flushing, N.Y.: Queen's College Press.
———. 1980. *Metaphors of Masculinity.* Philadelphia: University of Pennsylvania Press.
———. 1981. Gender Distinctions in Monteros Mortuary Ritual. *Ethnology* 20:177–190.
Brousmiche, Jean-François. 1977. *Voyage dans le Finistère en 1829, 1830 et 1831.* Vol. 2. Quimper: Morvran.
Bulletin de Liaison (ADMR newsletter). 1984. Plabennec: Fédération Départementale des Associations Locales de l'Aide à Domicile en Milieu Rural. March issue.
Burguière, André. 1977. *Bretons de Plozévet.* Paris: Flammarion.
Cambry, Jacques. [1836] 1979. *Voyage dans le Finistère.* Geneva: Slatkine Reprints.
Canaan, T. 1929. Water and the "Water of Life" in Palestinian Superstition. *Journal of the Palestinian Oriental Society* 9:57–69.
Carson, Katherine. 1900. Burial Customs. *Folklore* 11:210.
Chadwick, Nora K. 1969. *Early Brittany.* Cardiff: University of Wales Press.
Chaussy, M., R. Emeillat, and G. Messager. 1976. *Monographie communale: La Feuillée.* Angers: Ecole Supérieure d'Agriculture.
Chevalier, Jacques. 1983. Les nouvelles conditions de la production agricole. In *L'Ouest, bouge-t-il? Son changement social et culturel depuis trente ans. Synthèse des recherches de l'ATP du CNRS dans le Grand Ouest*, 81–99. Nantes: Vivant.
Christian, William A., Jr. 1972. *Person and God in a Spanish Valley.* New York: Seminar Press.
———. 1981. *Local Religion in Sixteenth-Century Spain.* Princeton: Princeton University Press.
Christiansen, Reidar. 1946. The Dead and the Living. *Studia Norvegica* 2:1–96.
Colclough, N. T. 1971. Social Mobility and Social Control in an Italian Village. In *Gifts and Poison*, ed. F. G. Bailey, 212–230. New York: Schocken Books.
Cormier, Hervé. 1979. Côtes-du-Nord: Le retour au pays. In *Retour aux pays: Aquitaine, Bretagne, Limousin, Pays de la Loire, Poitou-Charentes.* INSEE: Directions régionales de Bordeaux, Limoges, Nantes, Poitiers, Rennes.
Croix, Alain. 1981. *La Bretagne aux 16e et 17e siècles: La vie, la mort, la foi.* Vol. 2. Paris: Maloine.

Croix, Alain, and Fanch Roudaut. 1984. *Les Bretons, la mort et Dieu: De 1600 à nos jours*. Paris: Messidor–Temps Actuels.
Curtin, Jeremiah. 1895. *Tales of the Fairies and of the Ghost World, Collected from Oral Tradition in Southwest Munster*. Boston: Little, Brown.
Cutileiro, José. 1971. *A Portuguese Rural Society*. Oxford: Clarendon Press.
Danforth, Loring. 1982. *The Death Rituals of Rural Greece*. Princeton: Princeton University Press.
Dante Alighieri. 1971. *Dante's Inferno*. Trans. Mark Musa. Bloomington: Indiana University Press.
Debidour, Victor Henry. 1979. *L'art de Bretagne*. Paris: Arthaud.
Deeney, Daniel. 1900. *Peasant Lore from Gaelic Ireland*. London: Nutt.
Delumeau, Jean. 1977. *Catholicism from Luther to Voltaire: A New View of the Counter-Reformation*. Philadelphia: Westminster Press.
Dempsey, David. 1975. *The Way We Die: An Investigation of Death and Dying in America Today*. New York: Macmillan.
Deonna, Waldemar. 1939. Croyances funéraires: La soif des morts; le mort musicien. *Revue de l'Histoire des Religions* 119:53–81.
Devlin, Judith. 1987. *The Superstitious Mind: French Peasants and the Supernatural in the Nineteenth Century*. New Haven: Yale University Press.
Diocèse de Quimper. 1975. Hymnbook.
Dionisopoulos-Mass, Regina. 1976. The Evil Eye and Bewitchment in a Peasant Village. In *The Evil Eye*, ed. Clarence Maloney, 42–62. New York: Columbia University Press.
Dottin, Georges. 1928. Anatole Le Braz. Foreword to *La légende de la mort chez les Bretons armoricains*, by Anatole Le Braz, 5th ed., 1:1–24. Paris: Honoré Champion.
Douglas, Mary. [1970] 1978. *Natural Symbols*. Harmondsworth: Penguin Books.
Douglass, William A. 1969. *Death in Murelaga: Funerary Ritual in a Spanish Basque Village*. Seattle: University of Washington Press.
Dundes, Alan. 1980. Wet and Dry, the Evil Eye: An Essay in Indo-European and Semitic Worldview. In *Interpreting Folklore*, 93–133. Bloomington: Indiana University Press.
Durkheim, Emile. 1933. *The Division of Labor in Society*. Trans. George Simpson. Glencoe, Ill.: Free Press.
Eichenberg, Fritz. 1983. *Dance of Death: A Graphic Commentary on the Danse Macabre through the Centuries*. New York: Abbeville Press.
Elégoët, Fanch. 1983. Populations et structures sociales. In *L'Ouest, bouge-t-il? Son changement social et culturel depuis trente ans. Synthèse des recherches de l'ATP du CNRS dans le Grand Ouest*, 100–114. Nantes: Vivant.
Eskopti Kemper ha Leon. 1953. *Kantikou Brezonek Eskopti Kemper ha Leon*. Quimper: Imprimerie Cornouaillaise.
Evans-Pritchard, E. E. 1937. *Witchcraft, Oracles and Magic among the Azande*. Oxford: Clarendon Press.
Favret-Saada, Jeanne. 1980. *Deadly Words: Witchcraft in the Bocage*. Trans. Catherine Cullen. Cambridge: Cambridge University Press.

Fortier, David H. 1980. Brittany: "Breiz Atao." In *Nations without a State: Ethnic Minorities in Western Europe*, ed. Charles R. Foster, 136–152. New York: Praeger.

Fox, James J. 1973. On Bad Death and the Left Hand. In *Right and Left: Essays on Dual Symbolic Classification*, ed. Rodney Needham, 342–368. Chicago: University of Chicago Press.

Freeman, Susan Tax. 1968. Religious Aspects of the Social Organization of a Castilian Village. *American Anthropologist* 70:34–49.

———. 1978. Faith and Fashion in Spanish Religion: Notes on the Observance of Observance. *Peasant Studies* 7:101–123.

———. 1987. Egalitarian Structures in Iberian Social Systems: The Contexts of Turn-Taking in Town and Country. *American Ethnologist* 14: 470–490.

Garrity, Thomas F., and James Wyss. 1976. Death, Funeral and Bereavement Practices in Appalachian and Non-Appalachian Kentucky. *Omega: Journal of Death and Dying* 7:209–228.

Geertz, Clifford. 1973a. Thick Description: Toward an Interpretive Theory of Culture. In *The Interpretation of Cultures*, 3–30. New York: Basic Books.

———. 1973b. Ritual and Social Change: A Javanese Example. In *The Interpretation of Cultures*, 142–169. New York: Basic Books.

———. 1973c. Religion as a Cultural System. In *The Interpretation of Cultures*, 87–125. New York: Basic Books.

Geertz, Hildred. 1975. An Anthropology of Religion and Magic, I. *Journal of Interdisciplinary History* 6(1):71–89.

Gilmore, David. 1984. Andalusian Anti-Clericalism: An Eroticized Rural Protest. *Anthropology* 8:31–44.

Ginzburg, Carlo. 1985. *The Night Battles: Witchcraft and Agrarian Cults in the Sixteenth and Seventeenth Centuries*. Trans. John and Anne Tedeschi. Harmondsworth: Penguin Books.

Goldey, Patricia. 1983. The Good Death: Personal Salvation and Community Identity. In *Death in Portugal*, ed. Rui Feijo, Herminio Martins, and João de Pina-Cabral, 1–16. Journal of the Anthropological Society of Oxford Occasional Papers, no. 2.

Goodrich-Freer, A. 1902. More Folklore from the Hebrides. *Folklore* 13: 29–62.

Goody, Jack. 1962. *Death, Property and the Ancestors: A Study of the Mortuary Customs of the LoDagaa of West Africa*. Stanford: Stanford University Press.

———. 1975. Death and the Interpretation of Culture: A Bibliographic Overview. In *Death in America*, ed. David E. Stannard, 1–8. Philadelphia: University of Pennsylvania Press.

Gorer, Geoffrey. [1965] 1967. *Death, Grief and Mourning in Contemporary Britain*. Garden City, N.Y.: Doubleday Anchor Books.

Gourvil, Francis. 1959. *Théodore-Claude-Henri Hersart de La Villemarqué (1815–1895) et le "Barzaz Breiz" (1839-1845-1867)*. Rennes: Imprimerie Oberthur.

Go, Yeun ar. 1945. *Ar grasoù pe ar pedennoù evit ar re varo.* Roscoff: Ar Vuhez Kristen.
Griffin, Graeme M., and Des Tobin. 1982. *In the Midst of Life . . . The Australian Response to Death.* Melbourne: Melbourne University Press.
Grignon, J. M. 1983. Déclin des mariages: En Bretagne comme ailleurs. *Octant: Cahiers statistiques de la Bretagne* 14:22–25.
Gröger, Lisa. 1981. Of Men and Machines: Co-operation among French Family Farmers. *Ethnology* 20:163–176.
Gueusquin-Barbichon, Marie-France. 1981. Protection des personnes et des espaces dans un village du Morvan. *Ethnologie française* 11:225–232.
Haddon, A. C. 1893. A Batch of Irish Folk-Lore. *Folklore* 4:349–364.
Harvey, Edmund Newton. 1940. *Living Light.* Princeton: Princeton University Press.
Hélias, Pierre-Jakez. 1975. *Le cheval d'orgueil: mémoires d'un Breton du pays bigouden.* Paris: Plon.
———. 1978. *The Horse of Pride: Life in a Breton Village.* Translated and abridged by June Guicharnaud. New Haven: Yale University Press.
Hemon, Roparz. 1978. *Nouveau dictionnaire breton-français.* 6th edition. Brest: Al Liamm.
Hernin, R. 1983. Les lieux du changement social. In *L'Ouest, bouge-t-il? Son changement social et culturel depuis trente ans. Synthèse des recherches de l'ATP du CNRS dans le Grand Ouest,* 9–40. Nantes: Vivant.
Hertz, Robert. 1907. Contribution à une étude sur la représentation collective de la mort. *Année Sociologique* 10:48–137.
Hobsbawm, Eric, and Terence Ranger. 1983. *The Invention of Tradition.* Cambridge: Cambridge University Press.
Holbein, Hans. [1538] 1947. *Holbein's Dance of Death and Bible Woodcuts.* New York: The Sylvan Press.
Honko, Lauri. 1964. Memorates and the Study of Folk Beliefs. *Journal of the Folklore Institute* 1:5–19.
Horton, Robin. 1967. African Traditional Thought and Western Science. Parts I and II. *Africa* 37:50–71, 155–187.
Huntington, Richard, and Peter Metcalf. 1979. *Celebrations of Death: The Anthropology of Mortuary Ritual.* Cambridge: Cambridge University Press.
Hutson, Susan. 1971. Social Ranking in a French Alpine Community. In *Gifts and Poison,* ed. F. G. Bailey, 41–68. New York: Schocken Books.
INSEE. 1979. Vieillir en Bretagne. *Octant: Cahiers statistiques de la Bretagne* 3:1–16.
———. 1980. *Annuaire statistique régional—Bretagne.* Rennes: Le Colbert.
Isambert, François-A. 1975. Les transformations du rituel catholique des mourants. *Archives de sciences sociales des religions* 39:89–100.
Jackson, Charles O. 1977. Death in American Life. In *Passing: The Vision of Death in America,* ed. Charles O. Jackson, 229–243. Westport, Conn.: Greenwood Press.
Jones, Ernest. 1923. The Symbolic Significance of Salt in Folklore and Su-

perstition. In *Essays in Applied Psycho-Analysis*, 112–203. London: International Psychoanalytical Press.

Jorion, Paul. 1982. The Priest and the Fishermen: Sundays and Weekdays in a Former "Theocracy." *Man* 17:275–286.

Kastenbaum, Robert J. 1977. *Death, Society and Human Experience*. St. Louis: C. V. Mosby.

Kelly, Patricia Fernandez. 1975. Death in Mexican Folk Culture. In *Death in America*, ed. David E. Stannard, 92–111. Philadelphia: University of Pennsylvania Press.

Kertzer, David I. 1980. *Comrades and Christians: Religion and Political Struggle in Communist Italy*. Cambridge: Cambridge University Press.

Kittredge, George Lyman. 1929. *Witchcraft in Old and New England*. Cambridge: Harvard University Press.

Kligman, Gail. 1988. *The Wedding of the Dead: Ritual, Poetics, and Popular Culture in Transylvania*. Berkeley: University of California Press.

Kroeber, Alfred Louis. 1963. *Anthropology: Culture Patterns and Processes*. New York: Harcourt, Brace and World.

Kübler-Ross, Elisabeth. 1969. *On Death and Dying*. New York: Macmillan.

———. 1974. *Questions and Answers on Death and Dying*. New York: Macmillan.

———. 1975. *Death: The Final Stage of Growth*. Englewood Cliffs, N.J.: Prentice-Hall.

Kuter, Lois. 1985. Labeling People: Who are the Bretons? *Anthropological Quarterly* 58:13–29.

Lambert, Yves. 1983. Famille, politique et religion. In *L'Ouest, bouge-t-il? Son changement social et culturel depuis trente ans. Synthèse des recherches de l'ATP du CNRS dans le grand Ouest*, 195–232. Nantes: Vivant.

———. 1985. *Dieu change en Bretagne*. Paris: Cerf.

Laurent, Donatien. 1987. Des antiquaires aux folkloristes: Découverte et promotion des littératures orales. 1. Le temps des précurseurs (1815–1870). In *Histoire littéraire et culturelle de la Bretagne*, ed. Jean Balcou and Yves Le Gallo, 2:335–354. Paris: Champion.

La Villemarqué, vicomte Hersart de. [1839] 1963. *Barzaz Breiz: Chants populaires de la Bretagne*. Paris: Librairie Académique Perrin.

Lawson, John Cuthbert. 1964. *Modern Greek Folklore and Ancient Greek Religion*. New York: University Books.

Leach, Edmund R. 1961. Two Essays Concerning the Symbolic Representation of Time. In *Rethinking Anthropology*, 124–136. London: The Athlone Press.

Lebesque, Morvan. 1970. *Comment peut-on être breton?* Paris: Seuil.

Le Bras, Gabriel. 1955. *Etudes de sociologie religieuse*. Vol. 1, *Sociologie de la pratique religieuse dans les campagnes françaises*. Paris: Presses Universitaires de France.

———. 1976. *L'église et le village*. Paris: Flammarion.

Le Braz, Anatole. 1928. *La légende de la mort chez les Bretons armoricains*. 5th ed. 2 vols. (Notes by Georges Dottin.) Paris: Honoré Champion.

Le Calvez, M. G. 1888. Rites et usages funéraires: La mort en Basse-Bretagne. *Revue des traditions populaires* 3:45-51.
Le Corre, René. 1982. *Bretagne: Le clos et l'ouvert*. Paris: Cerf.
Le Gallo, Yves. 1980. Prêtres et prélats du diocèse de Quimper, de la fin du 18e siècle à 1830. Thèse d'Etat, Université de Paris.
Le Goff, Jacques. 1984. *The Birth of Purgatory*. Trans. Arthur Goldhammer. Chicago: University of Chicago Press.
Le Guirriec, Patrick. 1984. Parents, paysans, partisans: L'ordre social dans une commune bretonne. Thèse de troisième cycle, Université de Paris X, Nanterre.
———. 1986. Communisme local, Résistance et PCF: Les trois éléments du pouvoir dans une commune bretonne. *Etudes rurales* 101-102:219-230.
Le Men, R. F. 1870-1872. Traditions et superstitions de la Basse-Bretagne. *Revue celtique* 1:226-242, 414-435.
Le Menn, Gwennole. 1979. La mort dans la littérature bretonne. *Mémoires de la Société d'histoire et d'archéologie de Bretagne* 56:5-40.
Le Rouzic, Zacharie. 1924. *Carnac: Légendes, traditions, coutumes et contes du pays*. 3d ed. Vannes: Lafolye.
Le Roy Ladurie, Emmanuel. 1979. *Montaillou: The Promised Land of Error*. Trans. Barbara Bray. New York: Vintage Books.
Le Scouëzec, Gwenc'hlan, and Jean-Robert Masson. 1983. *Pierres sacrées de Bretagne: Croix et sanctuaires*. Paris: Seuil.
Linebaugh, Peter. 1975. The Tyburn Riot Against the Surgeons. In *Albion's Fatal Tree: Crime and Society in Eighteenth-Century England*, ed. Douglas Hay, Peter Linebaugh, John G. Rule, E. P. Thompson, and Cal Winslow, 65-117. New York: Pantheon.
Luzel, François-Marie. 1868-1874. *Gwerziou Breiz-Izel: Chants populaires de la Basse Bretagne*. 2 vols. Lorient: E. Corfmat.
———. [1879] 1980. *Veillées bretonnes*. Paris: Jean Picollec.
———. 1887. *Contes populaires de Basse-Bretagne*. 3 vols. Paris: Maisonneuve et C. Leclerc.
———. 1890. *Soniou Breiz-Izel: Chansons populaires de la Basse-Bretagne*. With A. Le Braz. 2 vols. Paris: E. Bouillon.
McDonald, Maryon. 1986. Celtic Ethnic Kinship and the Problem of Being English. *Current Anthropology* 27:333-347.
Máchal, Jan. [1918] 1964. Slavic Mythology. In *The Mythology of All Races*, ed. Louis Herbert Gray and John A. MacCulloch, 3:215-314. New York: Cooper Square.
Maclagan, Robert Craig. 1902. *Evil Eye in the Western Highlands*. London: D. Nutt.
McManners, John. 1981. Death and the French Historians. In *Mirrors of Mortality: Studies in the Social History of Death*, ed. Joachim Whaley, 106-130. New York: St. Martin's Press.
MacNeill, Máire. 1962. *The Festival of Lughnasa: A Study of the Survival of the Celtic Festival of the Beginning of Harvest*. London: Oxford University Press.

Mâle, Emile. 1958. *Religious Art from the Twelfth to the Eighteenth Century*. New York: Farrar, Straus.
Maloney, Clarence. 1976. Don't Say "Pretty Baby" Lest You Zap It with Your Eye: The Evil Eye in South Asia. In *The Evil Eye*, ed. Clarence Maloney, 102–148. New York: Columbia University Press.
Marillier, Léon. 1928. Introduction à la première édition (1893). Appendix to *La légende de la mort chez les Bretons armoricains*, by Anatole Le Braz, 5th ed., 2:393–450. Paris: Honoré Champion.
Middleton, John. 1982. Lugbara Death. In *Death and the Regeneration of Life*, ed. Maurice Bloch and Jonathan Parry, 134–154. Cambridge: Cambridge University Press.
Moore, Joan. 1970. The Death Culture of Mexico and Mexican-Americans. *Omega: Journal of Death and Dying* 1:271–291.
Morin, Edgar. 1970. *The Red and the White: Report from a French Village*. Trans. A. M. Sheridan-Smith. New York: Pantheon Books.
Murgoci, A. 1981. The Evil Eye in Roumania and Its Antidotes. In *The Evil Eye: A Folklore Casebook*, ed. Alan Dundes, 124–129. New York: Garland.
Onians, Richard B. 1951. *The Origins of European Thought about the Body, the Mind, the Soul, the World, Time and Fate*. Cambridge: Cambridge University Press.
Ott, Sandra. 1981. *The Circle of Mountains: A Basque Shepherding Community*. Oxford: Clarendon Press.
Panofsky, Erwin. 1964. *Tomb Sculpture*. New York: Harry N. Abrams.
Pérennès, Chanoine. 1924. *La mort en Basse-Bretagne*. Quimper: Direction diocésaine des oeuvres catholiques de jeunesse.
———. 1925. *Les hymnes de la Fête des Morts en Basse-Bretagne*. Brest: Administrateur de ESI.
Pina-Cabral, João de. 1986. *Sons of Adam, Daughters of Eve: The Peasant Worldview of the Alto Minho*. Oxford: Clarendon Press.
———. 1987. Paved Roads and Enchanted Mooresses: The Perception of the Past among the Peasant Population of the Alto Minho. *Man* 22:715–735.
Postic, François. 1987. Des antiquaires aux folkloristes: Découverte et promotion des littératures orales. 2. L'ère des collectes critiques (1870–1914). In *Histoire littéraire et culturelle de la Bretagne*, ed. Jean Balcou and Yves Le Gallo, 2:355–365. Paris: Champion.
Reece, Jack. 1977. *The Bretons against France: Ethnic Minority Nationalism in Twentieth-Century Brittany*. Chapel Hill: University of North Carolina Press.
———. 1979. Internal Colonialism: The Case of Brittany. *Ethnic and Racial Studies* 2(3):275–292.
Rhŷs, John. 1901. *Celtic Folklore: Welsh and Manx*. 2 vols. Oxford: Clarendon Press.
Riegelhaupt, Joyce. 1973. Festas and Padres: The Organization of Religious Action in a Portuguese Parish. *American Anthropologist* 75:835–852.

———. 1984. Popular Anti-Clericalism and Religiosity in pre-1974 Portugal. In *Religion, Power and Protest in Local Communities: The North Shore of the Mediterranean*, ed. Eric R. Wolf, 93–114. New York: Mouton.
Roberts, John M. 1976. Belief in the Evil Eye in World Perspective. In *The Evil Eye*, ed. Clarence Maloney, 223–278. New York: Columbia University Press.
Rodwin, Victor G. 1984. *The Health Planning Predicament: France, Québec, England, and the United States.* Berkeley: University of California Press.
Rosaldo, Renato. 1984. Grief and a Headhunter's Rage: On the Cultural Force of Emotions. In *Text, Play and Story: The Construction and Reconstruction of Self and Society*, ed. Edward M. Brunner, 178–195. 1983 Proceedings of the American Ethnological Society. Washington: American Ethnological Society.
Salvador, Mari-Lyn. 1981. *Festas Açoreanas: Portuguese Religious Celebrations in California and the Azores.* Oakland: Oakland Museum History Department.
Sauvé, L. F. 1883–1885. Traditions populaires de la Basse-Bretagne: Intersignes et présages de mort. *Revue celtique* 6:495–499.
Schneider, Jane. Forthcoming. Spirits and the Spirit of Capitalism. In *Religious Orthodoxy and Popular Faith in European Society*, ed. Ellen Badone. Princeton: Princeton University Press.
Sébillot, Paul. 1882. *Traditions et superstitions de la Haute-Bretagne.* Paris: Maisonneuve.
———. 1886. *Coutumes populaires de la Haute-Bretagne.* Paris: Maisonneuve frères et C. Leclerc.
———. 1899–1900. *Légendes locales de la Haute-Bretagne.* Nantes: Société des bibliophiles bretons et de l'histoire de Bretagne.
———. 1904. *Le folk-lore de France.* Vol. 1, *Le ciel et la terre.* Paris: Guilmoto.
———. 1905. *Le folk-lore de France.* Vol. 2, *La mer et les eaux douces.* Paris: Guilmoto.
———. 1906. *Le folk-lore de France.* Vol. 3, *La faune et la flore.* Paris: Guilmoto.
Segalen, Martine. 1984. Nuclear Is Not Independent: Organization of the Household in the Pays Bigouden Sud in the Nineteenth and Twentieth Centuries. In *Households: Comparative Studies of the Domestic Group*, ed. Robert McC. Netting, Richard R. Wilk, and Eric J. Arnould, 163–186. Berkeley: University of California Press.
———. 1985. *Quinze générations de Bas-Bretons. Parenté et société dans le pays bigouden sud, 1720–1980.* Paris: Presses Universitaires de France.
La Semaine Religieuse du Diocèse de Quimper et de Léon. 1899. La Feuillée—mission. 716–17.
———. 1926. La Feuillée—mission. 346.
Senn, Harry. 1981. Folklore Beginnings in France, the Académie Celtique: 1804–1813. *Journal of the Folklore Institute* 18:23–33.
Siegfried, André. 1913. *Tableau politique de la France de l'ouest sous la troisième République.* Paris: Armand Colin.

Silverman, Sydel F. 1975. *Three Bells of Civilization: The Life of an Italian Hill Town*. New York: Columbia University Press.
Simon, Pierre-Jean. 1979. Aspects de l'ethnicité bretonne. *Pluriel* 19:23-43.
Souvestre, Emile. 1843. *Les derniers Bretons*. Paris: W. Coquebert.
―――. [1844] 1887. *Le foyer breton*. Rev. ed. 2 vols. Paris: Calmann Lévy.
Stannard, David E. 1975. Introduction. In *Death in America*, ed. David E. Stannard, vii–xv. Philadelphia: University of Pennsylvania Press.
Stone, Lawrence. 1981. Death. In *The Past and the Present*, 242–259. London: Routledge and Kegan Paul.
Strowski, Stéphane. 1948. Le caractère breton dans le culte des morts et la religion des saints. *Revue de psychologie des peuples* 3:366–378.
Tenenti, Alberto. 1952. *La vie et la mort à travers le XVe siècle*. Paris: A. Colin.
Thomas, Keith. 1971. *Religion and the Decline of Magic*. London: Weidenfeld and Nicolson.
Thomas, Louis-Vincent. 1982. *La mort africaine: Idéologie funéraire en Afrique noire*. Paris: Payot.
Thompson, Stith. 1955–1958. *Motif-Index of Folk Literature*. Bloomington: Indiana University Press.
Timm, Lenora. 1973. Modernization and Language Shift. *Anthropological Linguistics* 15:281–298.
Trégouët, Bruno. 1982. La diaspora bretonne. *Octant: Cahiers statistiques de la Bretagne* 11:25–36.
Trevor-Roper, Hugh. 1983. The Invention of Tradition: The Highland Tradition of Scotland. In *The Invention of Tradition*, ed. Eric Hobsbawm and Terence Ranger, 15–41. Cambridge: Cambridge University Press.
Turner, Victor. 1969. The Ritual Process. Ithaca, N.Y.: Cornell University Press.
van Gennep, Arnold. 1946. *Manuel de folklore français contemporain*. Vol. 1, part 2, *Du berceau à la tombe (fin): Mariage—funérailles*. Paris: Picard.
―――. 1947. *Manuel de folklore français contemporain*. Vol. 1, part 3, *Les cérémonies périodiques cycliques et saisonnières, 1: Carnaval—Carême—Pâques*. Paris: Picard.
―――. 1949. *Manuel de folklore français contemporain*. Vol. 1, part 4, *Les cérémonies périodiques cycliques et saisonnières, 2: Cycle de Mai, la Saint-Jean*. Paris: Picard.
―――. 1953. *Manuel de folklore français contemporain*. Vol. 1, part 6, *Les cérémonies périodiques cycliques et saisonnières: Les cérémonies agricoles et pastorales de l'automne*. Paris: Picard.
―――. 1960. *The Rites of Passage*. Trans. Monika B. Vizedom and Gabrielle L. Caffee. London: Routledge and Kegan Paul.
Verdier, Yvonne. 1976. La femme-qui-aide et laveuse. *Homme* 16(2–3): 103–128.
―――. 1979. *Façons de dire, façons de faire: La laveuse, la couturière, la cuisinière*. Paris: Gallimard.
Vuorela, Toivo. 1967. *Der böse Blick im Lichte der finnischen Überlieferung*.

Folklore Fellows Communications, no. 201. Helsinki: Academia Scientiarum Fennica.
Waquet, Henri. 1960. *Art breton*. Paris: Arthaud.
Wassink, E. C. 1978. Luminescence in Fungi. In *Bioluminescence in Action*, ed. Peter J. Herring, 171–197. London: Academic Press.
Weber, Eugen. 1976. *Peasants into Frenchmen: The Modernization of Rural France, 1870–1914*. Stanford: Stanford University Press.
Weber, Max. 1946. Science as a Vocation. In *From Max Weber: Essays in Sociology*, ed. and trans. H. H. Gerth and C. Wright Mills, 129–156. New York: Oxford University Press.
———. 1958. *The Protestant Ethic and the Spirit of Capitalism*. Trans. Talcott Parsons. New York: Charles Scribner's Sons.
Weingrod, Alex, and Emma Morin. 1971. Post-Peasants: The Character of Contemporary Sardinian Society. *Comparative Studies in Society and History* 13:301–324.
Whaley, Joachim. 1981. Introduction. In *Mirrors of Mortality: Studies in the Social History of Death*, ed. Joachim Whaley, 1–14. New York: St. Martin's Press.
Wilde, Lady Jane Francesca. 1973. *Ancient Legends, Mystic Charms and Superstitions of Ireland*. Reprint of 1925 edition. New York: Lemma Publishing Corporation.
Zonabend, Françoise. 1973. Les morts et les vivants. Le cimetière de Minot en Châtillonais. *Etudes Rurales* 52:7–23.
———. 1980. *La mémoire longue*. Paris: Presses Universitaires de France.

Index

Absolution, 190, 197, 198
Acceptance of death. *See* Tame death
Action Catholique, 43, 185, 217, 234
ADMR (Aide à Domicile en Milieu Rural), 43–44, 46–47, 50, 333
Aesthetics: in funerary rites, 62–63, 86–87, 100, 108; religious vehicles for, 193; in Toussaint cemetery floral arrangements, 264–65
Affectivity, family, 13, 14, 137, 230–31
Africa, 283, 336
Afterlife, 13, 32, 229–38; Catholicism and, 53, 65, 101, 103, 108, 116, 117, 187–94 passim, 225–26, 244 (*see also* Damnation; Heaven; Purgatory); cemetery, 132–33, 142, 149–52, 156, 251; collective vision of, 133, 135, 156, 269–70 (*see also* Anaon); dying process worse than, 170; family reunion in, 13, 32, 137, 142–43, 156, 226, 230–31
Age: of pallbearers, 79–80. *See also* Children; Elderly; Middle-aged persons; Young people
Age classes, 35–36, 79–80, 329
Aging, 35, 42, 44, 48, 49–50, 328. *See also* Elderly
Agriculture, 5–7, 22, 244; and Catholic morality, 196, 197–98; family structure and, 8, 197–98; Jeunesse Agricole Chrétienne and, 240–41; labor in, 5–7, 9, 21, 81, 83, 221; mechanization in, 5–6, 20, 45, 198, 221, 244, 321–22; and political differences, 207; reciprocity in, 5–7, 9, 81, 84, 110, 240; and state health insurance, 41
Aide à Domicile en Milieu Rural (ADMR), 43–44, 46–47, 50, 333
Aides-ménagères (home helpers), for elderly, 43–44, 46–47, 50, 77, 262
Alcohol serving: in funerary rites, 63, 85, 97, 100; for Toussaint collectors, 276. *See also* Drunkenness
All Saints' Day. *See* Toussaint

All Souls' Day (Fête des Morts), 122, 164, 253, 258–65, 274–75
America. *See* Latin America; United States
Anaon (community of the dead), 3–4, 17, 97, 157, 245–50; and cemetery location, 153–54, 331; and cemetery visits, 251–52, 265, 332; dreams communicating with, 85, 120–21, 255–56, 258, 279, 299, 300, 333; and festival of Saint John, 165–66; incorporation into, 51, 84, 97, 112–23 passim, 129–30; missionaries and, 179; mourning and, 123; prayers for, 69–71, 257–58, 267–68, 279, 301 (*see also* Masses); Toussaint–Fête des Morts and, 122, 203, 265, 269–70, 274–77, 279, 332. *See also* Cemeteries; Revenants
Andalusia, 140 n, 149 n, 251 n, 252 n, 262 n, 291 n
Animals: in cemeteries, 134, 135; civil funerals and, 210–11
Ankou (Death), 4–5, 17, 160–62, 267 n, 320, 334; analogues of in other traditions, 161–62, 187, 337; call of, 311, 316; cart of, 5, 308; warning by, 5, 55–56, 308
Anticlericalism, 26, 201–9, 213, 239, 241, 243–44, 326; and afterlife, 231–32; and burial, 152, 209, 212, 213, 241; and classed funerals, 95; and destiny, 313; and funeral behavior, 91, 108–9; and giving Masses and services, 108–9, 111; and "ladies in black," 199; of men, 320; and *messe d'anniversaire* and *messe de huitaine*, 119; and mourning traditions, 127; and political celebration, 278; and sexuality of priest, 220; and supernatural, 287–89, 297; and Toussaint, 164, 279; of young people, 219
Architecture, in cemeteries, 136, 140–41, 156–57, 332. *See also* *Caveaux*; Tomb monuments

353

Ariès, Philippe, 11–15, 44, 211; and afterlife beliefs, 132–33, 142, 156, 243, 251; and cemeteries, 132–33, 135–36, 137, 138, 142, 147, 156, 157, 250–51; and denial of death, 12, 13–14, 15, 16, 18–19, 243, 328; and hospital death, 45–46; and mourning, 98; and ostracism of bereaved, 107; and romantic cult of the dead, 13, 32, 50, 137, 138, 142, 147, 157, 251, 257, 279; and tame death, 12–13, 15, 18, 47–48, 50, 137, 157, 282–83; and warnings of death, 55, 317
Art, ephemeral, 265. *See also* Aesthetics
Astrology, 239
Atheists, 212, 219
Attendance: church, 17, 110, 116, 174, 192–93, 207, 214–22, 238, 242, 253, 336; civil burial, 209; funeral service, 87–89, 95, 330, 331–32; at Masses and services for dead, 110, 116–17, 122; wake, 67–68, 330, 331–32; wedding, 88–89
Autumn, and death, 36

"Bad deaths," 57n–58n
Balanant, Abbé, 183
Baptism, 59, 93, 100, 211, 216, 222
Barzaz Breiz (La Villemarqué), 338
Basque country: funerary rites in, 66, 74n, 84n, 98n, 111n–12n, 114n, 163n; *ogistie* in, 119n, 123n; reciprocal mortuary obligations in, 111n–12n; and reunion with dead, 143n; Saint John's Day in, 166; Spanish, 188n; syncretism of Christianity with folk beliefs in, 337
Belief/Believers, 163, 168, 238, 281
Benson, Saler, 10–11
Bereavement. *See* Grief
Berger, Peter, 15
Bioluminescence, of *feux follets*, 293
Bird *intersignes*, 5, 303–9, 314–16, 321, 334
Birth control, 9, 196, 211–12
Birth rituals, parallels with funerary rites, 59–60, 93, 100
Blancs (whites), 27–28, 202–9, 212, 297; and afterlife, 232, 287; cross carried by, 82; and destiny, 324; hymn singing by, 91; and political celebrations, 278–79
Blessed bread, 84n
Blessing: boxwood, 63, 64–65, 167–68; of catafalque, 115–16; of coffin at funeral service, 92–94; at Rameaux, 64–65, 167–68; at Toussaint, 260, 261; at wake, 63–65, 73
Bloch, Maurice, 100, 325
Bonfires: festival, 164, 165–66; mission, 186
Bossy, John, 188
Boundary stones, 4
Boxwood, 63, 64–65, 167–68, 169
Brandes, Stanley H., 140n, 149n, 220, 225n, 262n, 291n
Breton language, 1, 10, 178, 198, 336
British Isles, 159n–63 passim, 170, 272, 334–35. *See also* Ireland
Brousmiche, Jean-François, 1–2
Burial, 84, 97, 100, 131–57; alternatives to, 154–56, 332; civil, 209–13, 241, 277; communal, 135; kinship and, 30–33, 47, 141–47, 148; premature, 13; secondary, 112–14, 119, 123, 129, 135, 146, 147, 151. *See also* Cemeteries
Butter thief (*laer amann*), 293–96, 333, 334

Café, as antichurch, 92
Café meal, after funeral, 97–100, 331
Calvin, John, 13
Cambry, Jacques, 272
Candle lighting, for dying, 171
Capitalism, 188, 208, 209, 215
Capuchins, 70–71, 177, 182
Carpenter, funerary activities of, 58, 78, 85, 86, 89, 97, 99
Catafalques, 114–15, 117, 225, 261
Catechism, 190, 191–92, 217, 225; and afterlife, 232, 235–36; and *communion solennelle*, 217, 218; missions and, 176, 182, 183
Catholicism, 7–8, 17, 27–28, 158–244, 257–58, 281, 326, 330, 333, 339, 340; and afterlife, 53, 65, 101, 108, 116, 117, 187–94 passim, 225–26, 242, 243, 244 (*see also* Damnation; Hell; Purgatory); alternatives to, 238–41 (*see also* Secularization); and burial, 132–33, 138, 151–52; changing patterns of, 53, 108, 213–29, 242–44 (*see also* Vatican II); and Counter-Reformation, 13, 53–54, 173–88 (*see also* Missions); and cremation, 155; and cult of the dead, 169, 251, 253, 257, 279; and destiny, 324; and festivals, 258–77 (*see also* Saints); and funerary rites, 52–55, 64–71 passim, 82, 90–94, 101, 210, 211, 212–13, 220; and gender differences, 219–21, 320; and *intersignes*, 303, 324; and mourning traditions, 127, 128;

regional boundaries and, 25; and revenants, 286–89, 301, 324, 326; and social services, 43; syncretism with folk beliefs of, 64, 69, 158–73, 186–87, 188, 243, 277, 281–82, 337; traditional, 109–10, 189–94. *See also* Clergy; Masses; Services
Caveaux (cement-lined burial vaults), 34, 132, 137–57 passim, 261
Celibacy, 197, 220
Celtic traditions, 1, 239, 336, 337, 338; Samhain festival of, 163–64, 271–72, 276, 279; syncretism with Catholicism of, 159–64, 187. *See also* Folk religious beliefs
Cemeteries, 12, 32, 131–57, 279; enclosure of, 176; funeral procession to, 82–84, 86, 89, 94, 96, 256, 318–19, 329; missions and, 176, 186; Rameaux procession to, 168; relocation of, 153–54, 156–57, 206, 331, 332; Toussaint and, 168–69, 259–60, 261–67, 270, 277; visits to, 20, 168–69, 250–55, 257, 265, 277, 280, 332
Chapelle blanche (white chapel), 62
Charnel houses. *See* Ossuaries
Childbearing: Catholic morality encouraging, 196–98; Saint Margaret and, 193–94. *See also* Birth control
Children: burial of, 144–45, 146; funeral attendance by, 331; rituals involving, 216, 222, 224 (*see also* Baptism); and wakes, 74, 101, 126, 331
Christian, William A., 193, 211n, 220, 242–43
Christianity, 59, 208, 238–39. *See also* Catholicism; Protestantism
Christianization, 173–82
Christiansen, Reidar, 170, 272
Church. *See* Catholicism
Churching, of new mothers, 211
Civil burials, 209–13, 241, 277
Civil weddings, 212
Class, social, 7, 27, 194, 195–96
Classed funerary rites, 94–95, 107
Clergy, 214; Counter-Reformation and, 174, 175, 182 (*see also* Missionaries); and male parishioners, 220–21; politics and, 26, 27–28, 194, 201, 204–5; regional preferences of, 200–201; social power of, 27–28, 176, 191, 194–99, 202, 220; and supernatural (unorthodox), 178–79, 199, 282, 287–89, 325, 326; and Vatican II, 222, 223–24, 225–26, 242. *See also* Anticlericalism; Masses

"Clerical model," 213, 239
Clothing. *See* Dress
Clubs du troisième âge (senior citizen's clubs), 29–30, 38–39, 128, 220
Coffin, 78; blessing of, 92–94; pallbearers for, 78–82, 86, 97, 99, 329; placing in, 84–86; transport without, 67
Cold: of dead, 159, 248–49, 272; of hell, 159–60, 187
Collections. *See* Money collections
Collectivity. *See* Community
Commune unit, 21
Communications media: access to, 9, 20; clergy denouncing, 198; obituaries page in, 75–77, 199. *See also* Television
Communion, 206; for dead, 179, 185; first (*petite*), 217, 224; *solennelle*, 216, 217–18
Communists, 26–27, 201, 204–5, 208–9; and burial, 132, 138, 152, 209–10, 213; and clergy, 198; and earth symbol, 209; and funerary rites, 65, 91–92, 108–9; and giving Masses and services, 104; and mourning traditions, 127; national vs. regional, 205n; and political celebrations, 278–79; and Toussaint, 277. *See also Rouges*
Communitas, 68, 221, 227
Community, 336; Catholicism and, 221–22, 234, 241, 242; of dead, 133, 135, 156, 269–70 (*see also* Anaon; Reunions); and individualism, 13, 135, 221–22, 330; of living (*see* Social networks)
Condolences, 95–96, 98, 101, 330
Confirmation, 216, 217
Consumer economy, 9–10, 139–40, 198
Cooperation. *See* Reciprocity
Cooperatives, agricultural, 6n, 7, 240
Coopératives d'Utilisation de Matériel Agricole (CUMAs), 6n
Cornwall, 159n, 161, 170
Corpus Christi festival, 224–25
Costs: of *caveaux*, 139, 143; of flowers, 108, 263–64; of Masses and services, 91, 104–11 passim, 119, 129, 202, 204, 226, 258; of *pompes funèbres*, 81; of *prière prônale*, 268; of tomb monuments, 139; of transport to crematorium, 155. *See also* Gifts
Council of Trent, 173
Counter-Reformation, 13, 53–54, 173–88. *See also* Missions
Credit, bank and government, 139

356   Index

Cremation, 154–55, 156, 332
Croix, Alain, 2, 10, 64n, 226; and anticlericalism, 213; and Counter-Reformation missions, 173, 176, 184, 188, 224n–25n; on devil, 183; and extreme unction, 52n; on mirrors, 62n; on skull boxes, 136n; and social function of cemeteries, 134; and syncretism of folk and Catholic beliefs, 159, 160, 161n, 162, 163, 169, 173; on Toussaint, 271; and Vatican II, 225, 226
Cross carrying: in funeral procession, 82–83, 86, 97, 99, 101, 329; in Toussaint procession, 260
Croyants (believers), 104, 163, 168, 238, 281
Cult of the dead, 2, 271, 280; Catholicism and, 169, 251, 253, 257, 279. *See also* Romantic cult of the dead
Culture: material (*see* Material culture); nature and, 11–12, 211, 277; social (*see* Social organization)
Cutileiro, José, 281

Damnation, 71, 106, 108, 189, 198, 230, 232, 237, 243; missions and, 174, 175, 187–88; Vatican II and, 117, 128, 225, 230, 242. *See also* Hell
Dancing: clergy against, 176, 182, 198–99, 225n; festival, 174–75; forbidden during mourning, 123, 124, 127, 128
Danforth, Loring, 51–52, 113, 119, 122, 123, 304
Dante Alighieri, 160
Death-awareness training, 47, 50, 333
Death bird (*labous an ankou*), 5, 303–9, 314–16, 321, 334
Death knell (*glas*), 75, 259, 261, 274
Decomposition, physical, 60, 150–52, 155, 156, 233
Decree of Prairial Year XII, 206
Dégh, Linda, 285n
Delumeau, Jean, 164, 173, 174n, 175n
Denial of death, 18–20, 25, 49–50, 214–15, 328, 330, 331, 333; afterlife beliefs and, 243; Ariès on, 12, 13–14, 15, 16, 18–19, 243, 328; cemeteries and, 149–52, 154, 156–57, 252; funerary rites and, 52, 54, 74, 95, 101; and *messe de huitaine*, 117; mourning behavior and, 130; and specialized care of elderly and dying, 43, 47, 48
Depopulation, rural. See *Exode rural*
Deritualization, 16–17, 88; of death, 73, 96, 117, 128; weddings and, 88
Destiny, 18–19, 47, 281, 326–27, 337;
and *intersignes*, 302, 310–15, 316, 323, 324–25, 334; and *triste* deaths, 58, 315
Devil, 178, 180, 181, 183–84, 185, 186
Devlin, Judith, 17n, 335n
Dioceses, 25–26
Diptychs, 269
Disenchantment/Rationalization, 17–18, 241, 242; and afterlife, 101, 228, 333; and funerary rites, 90, 96, 101, 102; and supernatural, 17–18, 19, 102, 249–50, 282, 293, 306, 326, 333. *See also* Scientific perspective
Diseuses/Diseurs de grâces, 69–70
Distancing of death, 331; and burial, 156–57; in funerary rituals, 58, 78, 96–97, 100, 329; with medicalization of dying, 328; and mourning behavior, 128, 130; and supernatural, 249–50, 322, 327; Toussaint rituals and, 260. *See also* Denial of death
Division of labor: in funerary rites, 52, 58, 82, 100–101, 329; in health care and social services for elderly and dying, 36–50, 81–82, 100–101, 328
Divorce, 196, 237
Dogs, howling, as *intersignes*, 5, 303, 309, 324, 334
Donation of body to research, 154–56
Douglas, Mary, 16–17, 18, 54, 74, 128
Douglass, William A., 66, 74n, 111n–12n, 119n, 304
Dreams, dead appearing in, 85, 120–22, 255–56, 258, 279, 299, 300, 333
Dress: of dead, 61; at funeral services, 87, 125, 126–27; at *messe de huitaine*, 125; mourning, 123–28, 129, 130; for nuns and priests, 222, 223
Drunkenness, missions and, 174, 182
Durkheim, Emile, 15, 20
Dying, 44–47, 48, 49–50; fear of, 33–34, 35; at home, 46, 56, 307, 328; in the hospital, 45–46, 48, 56n, 67, 150, 327, 328, 329; neighbors involved with, 44–45, 47, 48, 56n; in retirement homes, 42–43; syncretism of folk and Catholic rituals for, 169–73, 187

Economics: of *blancs* and *rouges*, 26, 119, 195, 207, 208, 209; capitalist, 188, 208, 209, 215. *See also* Agriculture; Class; Costs; Labor; Money collections
Education: of laity, 176 (*see also* Catechism); of priests, 204; in scientific view, 236; state, 201–2, 285

Egalitarianism, 26, 95, 101, 195, 243
Elderly, the, 24, 29–50; afterlife beliefs of, 232–34; and Catholic practice, 217, 239; cemetery visits by, 252; in family structure, 8, 39, 42, 43; funeral attendance of, 87–88; health care for, 36–37, 39, 40–44, 49, 328, 333; *maison-caveau* link among, 148–49; missions and, 188; preparation for death by, 34, 331; and supernatural perspective, 20, 282, 296, 308, 321, 324, 335; young people missed by, 222
Electricity, 9, 321–22
Embalming, 60, 78
Emotion: internalization of, 128, 130. See also Affectivity; Grief
Empiricism. See Scientific perspective
Employment, 26. See also Labor; Occupations
Enclos paroissial (parish enclosure), 136
England, 159n, 161, 170, 334–35
Enterrements. See Funerals
Entraide, 6, 7, 81–82, 221, 326–27. See also Reciprocity
Erasmus, 13
Eschatology. See Afterlife
Ethics. See Morality/Ethics
Eulogy, funeral service, 91
Euthanasia, 35, 171
Evans-Pritchard, E. E., 283
Evil, 13–14, 190
Evil eye, 294
Evolution, 236
Exhumation, 113–14, 119, 122, 123, 146, 147, 151, 153
Exode rural (rural depopulation), 7, 254, 329; from La Feuillée, 23, 26, 28, 30, 31, 39, 42, 48, 80, 145; from Plouguerneau, 21; Toussaint and, 266, 279
Exorcism, 282, 291–92
Extreme unction, 52–55, 169–70, 172, 227

Face-to-face social interaction, 10, 19, 326–27; and attendance at Sunday Mass, and Masses and services, 110, 242; and funerary rituals, 68, 74, 80–81, 95, 101, 108, 329, 331; *intersignes* and, 322; and tame death, 18, 336–37
Fairies, 272
Fall, doctrine of, 190
Family, 8–9, 39, 42, 333; affectivity channeled within, 13, 14, 137, 230–31; and burial, 141–47, 148; and Catholic morality, 196–98; and cemetery visits, 252–53; dying accompanied by, 45–49 passim; elderly in, 8, 39, 42, 43; extended (stem), 8; in funerary rites, 58–59, 81, 84n, 86, 88–90, 97; *juloded* and, 27; at *messe de huitaine*, 117; mourning period of, 123; nuclear, 8, 9, 13, 148; obituary notices and, 76–77; and *octaves*, 105; residential autonomy of, 148; reunions with (*see* Reunions); and seating in church, 192, 195; at Toussaint/ Fête des Morts, 122, 265–71, 279
Farming. See Agriculture
Fasting, 125
Fate. See Destiny
Favret-Saada, Jeanne, 294
Fear: Catholicism and, 90, 174, 175, 184–98 passim, 225, 227–28, 237, 242, 243, 330; of dead, 72–73; of death, 13, 35, 175, 228, 243, 330; of dying, 33–34, 35; of night, 245–46; World War II and, 291
Fees: clergy resented for, 202–4, 208, 239. See also Costs
Femme-qui-aide ("helping woman"), 60
Ferry, Jules, 201
Festivals, 163–69, 187; and cemetery visits, 253–54, 265–67, 277, 280; Fête-Dieu (Corpus Christi), 224–25; money collections at, 203, 204, 276–77; New Year's, 191; patron saint's (*pardon*), 193–94, 195, 224, 254; processions at, 168, 224–25, 229, 259–60; Rameaux, 64–65, 167–69, 187; of Saint John the Baptist, 164–67, 187, 254; secular, 278–79, 280. See also Fête des Morts; Toussaint
Festoù-noz, 128
Fête des Morts (All Souls' Day), 122, 164, 253, 258–65, 274–75
Fête des muguets (May 1), 254
Fête-Dieu (Corpus Christi) festival, 224–25
Feux follets, 291–93, 326, 334, 335
Flowers: artificial, 255, 265; for civil burials, 209, 277; for festivals, 254, 263–65, 267, 277, 279; at funerals, 80, 99, 108–9, 209; tombs decorated with, 169, 252, 253, 255, 263–65, 267, 277; for *triste* deaths, 57; for wakes, 63
Folklorization, 164–65
Folk religious beliefs, 2–5, 10–11, 17, 25, 239, 281–327, 333, 336–39, 340; on community of dead, 3–4, 17,

Folk religious beliefs (*continued*)
245–50, 279 (*see also* Anaon); dying rituals of, 169–73; and funerary rites, 69, 85–86, 94, 96–97, 156n; on *intersignes*, 5, 17, 281, 302–25; on respect for dead, 66; on revenants, 3–4, 67, 73, 246–47, 248–49, 271–77, 286–302, 324, 325, 333; syncretism with Catholicism of, 64, 69, 158–73, 186–87, 188, 243, 277, 281–82, 337; weddings and funerals associated with, 82n, 88–89, 99n
Fox, James J., 57n
Freeman, Susan Tax, 17, 163, 193, 238
Funerals, 12, 20, 24, 51, 52, 84–97, 100; attendance at service of, 87–89, 95, 330, 331–32; *café* meal after, 97–100, 331; changes in form of, 94–97; dress at, 87, 125, 126–27; flowers at, 80, 99, 108–9, 209; Greek, 51–52, 64n; "last night" and, 72; Mass at, 90–94, 210, 211; Masses and services offered at, 57, 84n, 92, 97, 99, 103–11, 129, 232; *messe de huitaine* compared with, 117; nonreligious, 209–13; organizing, 75–84; processions at, 82–84, 86, 89, 94, 96, 256, 318–19, 329; *triste*, 57, 106; urban, 52, 95; visions of processions of, 303n, 316–17, 318
Funerary rites, 51–130, 212–13, 218–19, 241, 329–31. *See also* Funerals; Wakes

Geertz, Clifford, 15, 16
Geertz, Hildred, 334–35
Gender: church seating by, 192; and *club du troisième âge*, 220; death knell indicating, 75; of pallbearers, 79–80; and religious practice, 219–21. *See also* Men; Women
Genealogies, 76, 252. *See also* Kinship
Ghosts. *See* Revenants
Gifts: for *communion solennelle*, 218; of Masses and services, 57, 84n, 92, 97, 99, 103–11, 118, 129, 232, 257, 258, 286, 332; at Toussaint, 263, 276–77. *See also* Flowers
Gilmore, David, 220
Ginzburg, Carlo, 310n
Glas (death knell), 75, 259, 261, 274
Good death, 12, 55–58, 192, 331
Gorer, Geoffrey, 107, 108
Gossip, 83, 101, 128, 270, 326, 329–30
Grâces, 69–70, 184
Grave markers, 135. See also *Caveaux*; Tomb monuments

Greece: exhumation in, 113, 119, 122, 123, 151; funerary rites in, 51–52, 64n; and attitudes toward physical decomposition in, 151; syncretism of Christianity with folk beliefs in, 337
Grief, 24, 107–8; at *mise en bière*, 85; and ritual, 112, 117–30 passim, 265, 330–31; Toussaint and, 262, 265
Guarding the house, during funeral, 96–97
Gueusquin-Barbichon, Marie-France, 169n
Guilt: Catholicism and, 189–90, 196–97, 225; Toussaint and, 270; toward dead, 255

Halloween, American, 265, 277n
Hares, revenants as, 4, 290
Healers, magical, 281, 282
Health care, 49; for elderly, 36–37, 39, 40–44, 49, 328, 333; extreme unction and, 53; reciprocity in, 83–84
Health-care professionals: care of dying by, 46, 47, 327, 328, 333; interest in death and dying, 14, 47, 50, 333; *toilette des morts* by, 59, 329
Heaven, 230, 231, 233, 234, 235, 264; missions and, 181, 185, 186–87, 229
Hélias, Pierre-Jakez, 2, 36, 180, 183, 337
Hell, 71, 188, 190, 229–37 passim, 243; cold, 159–60, 187; and cremation, 155; Fête des Morts and, 258; *feux follets* and, 291–92; missions and, 174, 175, 179–88 passim, 229, 230; Vatican II and, 242
Herbs, Saint John's festival and, 165n–66n
Hertz, Robert, 112–13, 129
Heuriou brezonnec ha latin (Book of Hours), 69, 70
Hierarchy. *See* Social hierarchy
Holidays. *See* Festivals
Home: and *caveaux*, 147–49; dying at, 46, 56n, 307, 328; guarding, 96–97; material culture at, 9–10, 150, 198, 321–22; retirement (*maison de retraite*), 39–40, 41–43, 48, 205. *See also* Family; Wakes
Home helpers (*aides-ménagères*), for elderly, 43–44, 46–47, 50, 77
Homo totus, survival of, 133, 142, 155, 156
Honko, Lauri, 284n
Horton, Robin, 283
Hospitals, 41, 48; death-awareness training for personnel of, 333; dying

in, 45–46, 48, 56 n, 67, 150, 327, 328, 329; elderly in, 41–42, 45–46, 48
Houat, 158, 220–21
House, family. *See* Home
Huntington, Richard, 47 n, 113
Hymns: for festival of Saint Houardon, 162–63; funeral service, 90, 91, 94; missions and, 176–77; Toussaint, 260, 275–76, 277 n

Ifern yen (cold hell), 159–60
Illegitimacy, 196
Illness, care of. *See* Health care
Immortality, 168
Incorporation, rites of, 51, 52, 84, 97–100, 112–23 passim, 129–30
Indemnité viagère de départ, 37
Individualism, 13, 14, 20, 326, 330, 331; and agricultural modernization, 240–41; and Catholic practice, 221–22; and cemeteries, 133–34, 135–37, 156; Counter-Reformation and, 188; and destiny, 323, 326; diptychs and, 269; and funerary rituals, 88, 101, 329; and young Catholics, 218. *See also* Privacy
Indonesia, 113, 119
Indulgences, 184, 190, 274
Inferno (Dante), 160
Inheritance, 144–45, 197
Institutions: for dying, 45–47, 49, 50, 56 n, 67, 150, 327, 328, 329; for elderly, 39–40, 41–43, 45–46, 48, 50, 56 n, 205
Insurance, health, 41, 42 n
Intellectual approach, to religion, 185, 222, 242, 330
Interconnectedness: of phenomena, 283, 305, 309–10, 327. *See also* Destiny; Nature; Supernatural
Intersignes (omens of death): 5, 12, 17, 241, 281–86 passim, 302–25, 326, 333–34; decline in numbers of, 321–22, 324, 327; good death and, 12, 331
"Invention of tradition," 338–39
Ireland, 159 n; revenants in, 249 n, 271–72, 276; social power of clergy in, 194; syncretism of Christianity with folk beliefs in, 166, 170, 337
Isambert, François-A., 56
Italian Communist party, 205 n

Jack-o'-lanterns. *See Feux follets*
Jehovah's Witnesses, 239
Jesuits, 177, 182
Jeunesse Agricole Chrétienne (JAC), 8, 185, 240–41, 244

John Paul II, Pope, 196
Jorion, Paul, 158, 220–21
Judgment, Last, 90, 155, 170, 181, 194, 225, 236, 330
Juloded (upper peasantry), 27, 194, 195

Kertzer, David I., 205 n
Kest an Anaon, 203, 276–77
Kinship, 8–9, 330, 333; and burial, 30–33, 47, 141–47, 148; and funerary rites, 86, 88–89, 92; obituary notices and, 76–77; women looking after, 252. *See also* Family
Kübler-Ross, Elisabeth, 14, 47

Labor, 21, 22, 26; agricultural, 5–7, 9, 21, 81, 83, 221; wage, 42, 110, 116, 139, 201–2, 244. *See also* Division of labor; Occupations
Labous an ankou (death bird), 5, 303–9, 314–16, 321, 334
"Ladies in black," 198–99
Laer amann (butter/cream thief), 293–96, 333, 334
Lambert, Yves: and alternatives to Catholicism, 240; and church social functions, 221–22; and civil burials, 211, 212; and death omens, 326; and Rameaux rituals, 168 n; and giving Masses and services, 106 n, 107; and levels of religious practice, 214; on traditional Catholicism, 189–90; and Vatican II, 242
Landlords, social obligations to, 105
Land ownership, 7, 144–45, 195, 244
Language, 1, 10, 336; and Catholicism, 178, 190, 198, 222, 223, 242
Latin America, 336
Latin language, 190, 222, 223, 242
La Villemarqué, vicomte Hersart de, 2, 338
Laying out, of corpse, 58–61
Le Braz, Anatole, 2–5, 10, 337–38, 339; and Ankou, 4–5, 55–56, 320; and cemetery location, 153; and funeral processions, 318; and good death, 55–56; on guarding the home, 96–97; and *intersignes*, 5, 303; on pallbearers, 79; and revenants, 3–4, 58 n, 67, 159, 246–47, 248–49, 272, 274, 276; and rituals for dying, 170, 171–72; and Saint John's festival, 166; on touching deceased, 85–86; and Toussaint/All Souls' Day, 164, 272, 273 n, 274, 276
Le Corre, René, 109–10, 158–59, 215, 216–17, 237

Lefebvre, Marcel, 223
Le Gallo, Yves, 194
Légende de la mort chez les Bretons armoricains (Le Braz), 3–5, 153, 338
Legends: about Ankou, 55–56; about revenants, 3, 67, 73, 289–91, 292, 294–95, 333
Le Guirriec, Patrick, 205n
Le Menn, Gwennole, 160
Le Nobletz, Michel, 177–80 passim, 186, 188, 189, 200, 219
Le Rouzic, Zacharie, 286n
Le Roy Ladurie, Emmanuel, 310n
Liberation, of France, 278, 291
Lit de mort, 60–63, 74, 84
Local identity, 10, 221, 241, 242
Loneliness, of elderly, 38
Love: brotherly, 243; God of, 71, 225, 230, 242
Luzel, François-Marie, 2, 284–85, 292–93, 335, 339

McDonald, Maryon, 159n
Máchal, Jan, 291n
Machinery, agricultural, 5–6, 20, 45, 198, 221, 244, 321–22
Macpherson, James, 338
Madagascar, 336
Magical beliefs, 334–35; healing with, 281, 282. *See also* Supernatural; Witchcraft
Marriage, 88, 216, 312–13. *See also* Weddings
Masses, 216; attendance at (*see* Attendance); cemetery visits after, 253; cost of, 91, 104–11 passim, 119, 129, 202, 204, 226, 258; funeral, 90–94, 210, 211; giving of, 57, 84n, 92, 97, 99, 103–11, 118, 129, 232, 257, 258, 286, 332; High, 125, 192; Low, 192; on May 8, 278; *messe d'anniversaire*, 111–14, 118–22, 123, 129, 185, 299; *messe de huitaine*, 109, 111–22, 125, 129, 185; *messe pour tous les défunts*, 122; missions and, 174, 175, 185; on November 11, 278; Rameaux, 168; to Saint Diboan, 171; *services de continuation*, 226–27; Sunday, 192–93, 215–16; on television, 238; Toussaint, 164, 259–60, 267–68; Vatican II changes in, 222–23, 242; wedding, 249
Material culture, 20, 28, 139–40; church, 190–91; home, 9–10, 150, 198, 321–22. *See also* Economics; Technology
Maunoir, Julien, 176, 177–78, 179, 180, 182, 185, 188, 189

May 8, 278–79, 280
Meals: after funeral, 97–100, 331; after *messe d'anniversaire*, 118, 121; after *messe de huitaine*, 117; for Toussaint revenants, 272
Mechanization, agricultural, 5–6, 20, 45, 198, 221, 244, 321–22
Mediators, between man and God, 193–94, 243. *See also* Saints
Medicalization, of death, 14, 40–46, 48, 56n, 59, 100–101, 328, 333
Medical services, 40–42, 49; for elderly, 36–37, 40–44, 49; extreme unction and, 53; personnel offering (*see* Health-care professionals); reciprocity and, 83–84
Mel beniguet (blessed mallet), 170
Memorates (personal experience narratives), 285; of *intersignes*, 302, 304–5, 306–7, 313–17, 318–20, 321; of revenants, 288–89, 294–95, 298–301, 302
Men: and *café* after funeral, 97, 99; cemetery visits by, 252; and *club du troisième âge*, 220; funeral attendance of, 87; as pallbearers, 79–80, 329; religious practice by, 219–21; seating in church of, 192; supernatural rejected by, 320; in Toussaint procession, 260
Mentalités, 20; and afterlife, 133; Ariès and, 11, 133; and capitalism, 188, 215; regional differences in, 20, 25, 199; and the supernatural, 335n. *See also* Worldview
Metatexts, 284
Metcalf, Peter, 47n, 113
Middle-aged persons: and Catholicism, 239; cemetery visits by, 252; funeral attendance by, 87–88; and supernatural, 282, 296, 308, 335
Middle Ages: dioceses established during, 25; *Miroirs des âmes* during, 180; *prière prônale* and, 269; public death in, 44; tame death during, 12, 13, 55, 98
Middleton, John, 57n
Migration. *See Exode rural; Retour au pays*
Mirrors, during wake, 61–62
Mise en bière, 84–86
Missionaries: in Brittany, 173–74, 177–80, 182, 188, 196–97; money for Masses and services sent to, 110; overseas, 214. *See also* Missions
Missions, 173–88, 189, 224n–25n, 243, 330; and hell, 174, 175, 179–88 pas-

sim, 229, 230; and purgatory, 181, 185, 229, 230; *tableaux* of, 103, 179–87 passim, 229; twentieth-century, 182–87, 188
Mistaken identity, *intersignes* and, 313–15, 319
Money collections: by clergy, 202–4; during funeral service, 91, 204; Toussaint (*kest an Anaon*), 203, 276–77. *See also* Fees
Montfort, Grignion de, 178
Montfort Fathers, 178, 182
Monument aux morts, in town square, 278
Monuments, in cemeteries. *See* Tomb monuments
Morality/Ethics, 16, 17n, 19; and afterlife, 231–32, 236–37; of *blancs*, 207, 208; Catholic, 101, 108, 116, 176, 191, 196–98, 236–37, 242, 243–44, 330 (*see also* Sin); of *rouges*, 208, 231
Morin, Edgar, 266
Mortality rates, 30, 36n
Mourning, public, 12, 112, 117, 122–28, 129–30, 330; full (*grand deuil*), 123–24, 125, 129; half/partial (*demi-deuil*), 123, 124, 125, 128, 129; length of period of, 123. *See also* Grief
Mutual assistance. *See Entraide*; Reciprocity

Narratives: about supernatural, 24–25, 284, 285–86, 309. *See also* Legends; Memorates
Nature, 10–11, 18, 19, 211, 232, 250, 282–86; and acceptance of death, 36, 47–48, 277; and culture, 11–12, 211, 277; supernatural expressed in, 5, 302, 303–9, 314–16, 321, 324, 334; and supernatural phenomena, 282–85, 291–93, 295–96, 305–6, 318, 326, 327, 333, 334 (*see also* Disenchantment/Rationalization); technology and, 13–14, 295–96, 321–22
Neighbors: dying accompanied by, 44–45, 47, 48, 56n; and elderly, 39; and *entraide*, 6, 7, 81–82, 221, 326 (*see also* Reciprocity); face-to-face interaction with (*see* Face-to-face social interaction); in funerary rites, 58–59, 68, 79, 80–83, 84n, 86, 87, 93–94, 329; individualism and, 221, 330; *messe de huitaine* and, 118; obligations of (*see* Obligations)
New Year, 191
Night, 4, 245–47, 321–22

Nobility, local, 194, 195
November 11, 278–79, 280
Nuclear power station, 292n
Nuns, 197, 222, 223, 226

Obituaries page, 75–77, 119
Oblates of Mary Immaculate, 182
Obligations, 16, 19; of attendance at Masses and services, 110, 117; to the dead, 119, 122, 129; in funerary rituals, 82–84, 93–94, 95, 209, 330, 331, 332; of giving Masses and services, 104–6, 107; of mourning, 123–24. *See also* Reciprocity
Occult sciences, 239, 336. *See also* Supernatural
Occupation, World War II, 291
Occupations, 21, 22, 26, 83, 201–2; navy, 21, 22, 26, 76, 79, 83; of pallbearers, 79
Octaves, 105
Odor, of death, 308–9, 334
Omens of death. *See Intersignes*
Onction des malades, 53–55, 101, 227
Organs, donation of, 154–56
Ossian (Macpherson), 338
Ossuaries, 113–14, 135–36, 153, 156, 176, 225
Ostracism, of bereaved, 107–8. *See also* Privacy
Otherworld. *See* Afterlife; Anaon
Owl calls, as *intersignes*, 5, 303, 304–5, 314–15
Ownership: car, 9; land, 7, 144–45, 195, 244; machinery, 6

Pallbearers, 78–82, 86, 97, 99, 329
Palm Sunday (Rameaux), 64–65, 167–69, 187
Panofsky, Erwin, 108
Paradise. *See* Heaven
Parapsychology, 239
Pardon de saint Michel, 195
Pardon (patron saint's festival), 193–94, 195, 224, 254
Parishes, 21–22; identification with, 10, 221, 241, 242
Parry, Jonathan, 100
Parti Communiste Français (PCF), 26–27, 104, 127, 201, 204–5, 209. *See also* Communists
Parti Socialiste (PS), 27, 198, 201, 278–79
Patronage: supernatural, 193–94. *See also* Saints
Pensions, 37

Pérennès, Chanoine, 61n, 69n
Perrot, Abbé, 205
Physical decomposition, 60, 150–52, 155, 156, 233
Pina-Cabral, João de, 239n, 304, 321n
Politics, 10, 26–28, 332–33, 336; clergy and, 26, 27–28, 194, 201, 204–5; and May 8 celebrations, 278–79, 280; as men's realm, 220; and November 11 celebrations, 278–79, 280; *tableaux* and, 181–82. See also *Blancs*; *Rouges*
Pompes funèbres, 59, 77–78, 81, 100, 329
Population: decrease in, 7, 21, 329 (see also *Exode rural*); of elderly, 37; of La Feuillée, 22, 23, 37; of Plouguerneau, 21
Portugal, 17, 321n; destiny in, 337; festival flowers in, 265; folk healers in, 281; good death in, 56n; nontraditional spirituality in, 239n; and attitudes toward physical decomposition, 151
Positivism, 236, 251, 282. See also Scientific perspective
Poverty, 26, 106, 119, 195, 207
Prayers: in curing rites, 281, 282; for dead, 69–71, 257–58, 267–68, 279, 301; at Toussaint, 267–69, 279; at wakes, 69–71. See also Masses
Pregnancy: Catholic morality encouraging, 196–98; Saint Margaret and, 193–94. See also Birth control
Premonitions. See *Intersignes*
Preparation, for death, 34, 55, 101, 150, 191–92, 331
Present orientation, of worldview, 240
Preservation, of body, 60, 78, 150–52, 155. See also *Homo totus*
Prière prônale (prayer from the pulpit), 267–69, 279
Priests. See Clergy
Privacy: of dying, 45 (see also Solitary death); of faith and religious experience, 238, 330, 336; of funerary rites, 73, 74, 95, 96, 98, 101, 330–31; of grief, 107–8, 128, 130, 330–31; of Masses and services for dead, 110
Processions: class and, 195; festival, 168, 224–25, 229, 259–60; funeral, 82–84, 86, 89, 94, 96, 256, 318–19, 329; mission, 186; visions of funeral, 303n, 316–17, 318
Protestantism, 13, 53–54, 202, 238–39
Proverbs, 25; quoted, 31–32, 33, 35, 57, 66, 148n, 167, 229, 248, 310
Public death, 44–45, 46, 48, 328

Public ritual: funerary, 95, 96, 98, 101, 330–31. See also Mourning
Purgatory, 190, 229–38 passim, 243; cremation and, 155; and Fête des Morts, 258, 274, 275; and giving Masses and services, 103–4, 129, 257, 264; and Masses to Saint Diboan, 171; missions and, 181, 185, 229, 230; mourning dress and, 124; and revenants, 286–87; *services de continuation* and, 226; Vatican II and, 128, 242
Purification, of new mothers, 211

Quartiers, 21, 23. See also Neighbors
Quêtes, 203–4, 208; *de la moisson*, 203; *du beurre*, 203

Rameaux (Palm Sunday), 64–65, 167–69, 187
Rassemblement pour la République (RPR), 27
Rationalization. See Disenchantment/Rationalization
Readings, funeral service, 90–91, 92, 106–7
Reciprocity, 83–84, 221, 322, 326–27; in agricultural work, 5–7, 9, 81, 84, 110, 240; in attendance at civil burials, 209; in child care and housework, 8–9; in funerary rites, 58–59, 63, 81–84, 88, 99, 101, 111n–12n, 117, 329–30, 332; in giving Masses and services, 105, 106, 107, 108, 111, 129, 332; and *intersignes*, 322; toward saints, 193; *services de continuation* and, 226
Reformation, 53–54
Regeneration, 63–65, 167, 168
Regional differences, 25–28; in *mentalités*, 20, 25, 199; in religious traditions, 199–202
Regional identity, Breton, 10, 336
Regional politics, 10, 26. See also *Blancs*; *Rouges*
Reincarnation, 239
Religion, 7–8, 13–19 passim, 28, 199–202, 336; definitions of, 17; rationalization of (*see* Disenchantment/Rationalization). See also Catholicism; Folk religious beliefs; Protestantism
Religious orders, 197. See also Capuchins; Jesuits; Nuns
Remembering the dead: private, 331; at Toussaint, 267–70
Republicanism, 26
Resistance, French, 205, 210, 278–79, 280, 333

Resurrection, physical, 155, 231–32, 234. See also *Homo totus*
Retirement. See *Retour au pays*
Retirement homes (*maisons de retraite*), 39–40, 41–43, 48, 205
Retour au pays (return migration), 26, 30–33, 37, 47, 145, 147
Retribution, divine, 55, 228–29, 233, 243. See also Damnation
Reunions, family: with deceased, 13, 32, 47, 137, 142–43, 156, 226, 230–31; at funerals, 331–32; in natal commune, 32; at Toussaint, 265–71, 279, 332; at wakes, 331–32
Revenants (ghosts), 3–4, 24, 73, 281, 286–302, 324, 325, 333; cold of, 159, 248–49, 272; fake, 296–98; funeral procession indicated by, 256n; legends about, 3, 67, 73, 289–91, 292, 294–95, 333; at night, 246–47; scientific views and, 284, 285–86, 291–93, 295–96, 301–2, 325, 326, 334, 335; at Toussaint, 271–77; of *triste* deaths, 58n
Rhŷs, John, 272
Riegelhaupt, Joyce, 17, 193, 208
Rituals, 12–19 passim, 24, 241, 257–58, 281; for children, 216, 222, 224 (*see also* Baptism); of death, preparation for, 34, 191–92, 331; for dying, 169–73; extreme unction, 52–55, 169–70, 172, 227; funerary, 51–130, 212–13, 218–19, 241, 329–31 (*see also* Funerals); and grief, 112, 117–30 passim, 265, 330–31; of incorporation, 51, 52, 84, 97–100, 112–23 passim, 129–30; for salvation, 53, 93, 229; of separation, 51–59 passim, 84–85, 100, 119, 122–23; of transition, 51, 52, 53, 84, 100, 117, 118, 131; Vatican II and, 54, 110, 117, 222–29, 242, 260, 330. *See also* Deritualization; Festivals; Masses
Roads, 9, 23
Rodwin, Victor G., 42n
Rogation Days, 229
Romania, 337
Romantic cult of the dead, 13, 50, 257, 279; and burial, 32, 47, 137, 138, 142–43, 147, 156, 157, 251, 279, 332; and reunion with family, 32, 47, 137, 142–43, 156, 230–31
Rosaldo, Renato, 112
Rosicrucianism, 239, 336
Rotation, in obligations to neighbors, 84n
Roudaut, Fanch, 2, 226; and anticlericalism, 213; on devil, 183; and missions, 173, 176, 184; and social function of cemeteries, 134; and syncretism of folk and Catholic beliefs, 159, 160, 162, 163, 169, 173; on Toussaint, 271; and Vatican II, 225, 226
Rouges (reds), 26–27, 28, 202–9, 238, 241; and afterlife, 231–32; and *caveau* burial, 152; and civil burials, 209–10, 212–13; and destiny, 324; flowers rather than Masses and services given by, 108–9; at funeral service, 91–92, 204; men as, 320; and political celebrations, 278–79; and supernatural, 287

Sacred: Catholicism and, 174, 175–76, 182, 190–91, 242–43; cemeteries and, 135; civil burials and, 212; in funerary rituals, 61–63, 73, 85. *See also* Religion
Sacrifice, in mourning ritual, 124–25
Saint Anne, 193
Saint Diboan, 171
Saint Houardon, 162–63
Saint John the Baptist, festival of, 164–67, 187, 254
Saint Joseph, 192
Saint Margaret, 193–94
Saint Pol Aurelian, 162
Saint Ronan, 162
Saints, 162, 193–94, 243, 258; *petits*, 195. *See also* Festivals; *individual saints*
Saint Samson, 162
Saint Yves, 193
Salvador, Mari-Lyn, 265
Salvation, 106, 189, 190, 229, 243; baptism for, 93; ethics vs., 108; extreme unction for, 53; missions and, 174, 175; Vatican II and, 128
Samhain, 163–64, 271–72, 276, 279
Sauvé, L. F., 303n
Scandinavia, 170, 272
Scientific perspective, 17–18, 19, 236, 282–86, 326, 334, 339–40; and *intersignes*, 284, 285–86, 305–6, 308–9, 318, 322–23, 324, 325, 334; and revenants, 284, 285–86, 291–93, 295–96, 301–2, 325, 326, 334, 335
Scotland, 159n, 170
Seating, church, 192, 195
Sébillot, Paul, 2, 303n–4n
Secularization, 16–20, 201, 240–41, 249–50, 283, 326, 330, 336; and festivals, 277, 278–79, 280; and funerary rites, 52, 54, 74, 101; and supernatural, 282

Segalen, Martine, 6, 9, 38, 89n, 144n, 154n, 262n
Segregation: of aging, 39–40, 48; of dying, 44–47, 48. *See also* Distancing of death
Separation, rites of, 51–59 passim, 84–85, 100, 119, 122–23
Separatism, Breton political, 10
Services, religious: cost of, 91, 104, 109, 202, 204, 226; *de continuation*, 226–27; funeral, 86–94, 95, 330, 331–32; giving of, 57, 84n, 92, 97, 99, 103–11, 118, 129, 232, 332; *grands*, 109; *petits*, 109
Sexual activity: Catholicism and, 176, 196–98, 199, 220; culture and, 11–12, 211
Siegfried, André, 25, 26, 27
Sin: and afterlife, 236–37; extreme unction and, 53; Fall and, 190; secularization and, 16; *tableaux* and, 180–81; and tame death, 18; Vatican II and, 242
Sins, 106, 243
Skull boxes, 136, 156
Slavic folklore, 291n
Social activities, 242; in cemeteries, 134; church, 192–93, 221–22, 242; of elderly, 29–30, 38–39, 48, 128, 220; funerals as, 331–32; wakes as, 65–71, 331–32
Social change, 5–11, 15–20, 28, 326–27, 328, 333, 336–37; and afterlife beliefs, 133–34, 333; and changes in Catholicism, 243–44, 330 (*see also* Vatican II); funerary ritual influenced by, 52, 74, 101, 329–32. *See also* Division of labor; Individualism; Material culture; Secularization; Social control; Social hierarchy; Worldview
Social control, 16, 52, 83–84, 133; and carrying cross, 83, 101; clergy exerting, 27–28, 176, 191, 194–99, 202, 220; and destiny, 18–19, 323, 326–27; face-to-face social interaction and, 18–19, 74, 326–27, 329–30; individualism and, 19, 326–27, 329–30; and mourning, 128
Social hierarchy, 16, 20, 201, 330; Catholicism and, 95, 330; and destiny, 323, 326. *See also* Class
Socialists, 27, 198, 201, 278–79
Social mobility, 201, 323
Social networks, 20–21, 242; and giving of Masses and services, 92, 104, 108, 111, 112n, 332; and *intersignes*, 322;

Toussaint and, 265–71, 279, 332. *See also* Face-to-face social interaction; Family; Neighbors; Parishes; Reciprocity
Social obligations. *See* Obligations
Social organization. *See* Social change; Social networks; Social status
Social ostracism, of bereaved, 107–8. *See also* Privacy
Social scientists, interest in death and dying, 14
Social services: for elderly, 36–37, 41–44, 328. *See also* Health care
Social status: tomb monuments and, 140–42, 157. *See also* Gender; Social hierarchy
Solidarity, mechanical and organic, 20
Solitary death, 44–47, 48, 328
Solitary households, elderly, 8, 39–40
Sorcery, 24, 182, 281, 282, 287–88, 326
Souvestre, Emile, 2, 338
Spain, 17, 188n, 211, 243; and clergy, 220, 225n; private faith in, 238; and supernatural, 163. *See also* Andalusia
Specialization: in funerary rites, 52, 58, 82, 100–101, 329; of health care and social services for elderly and dying, 36–50, 81–82, 100–101, 328
Spirituality: alternatives to Catholicism, 238–41, 336; definition of religion and, 17n. *See also* Religion
Sterilization, of death, 150–51
Storytelling, about supernatural, 24–25, 284. *See also* Narratives
Strowski, Stéphane, 2
Succession, and inheritance, 144–45
Sudden death, 55, 56, 331
Supernatural, 18, 250, 281–327, 333–35, 340; clergy and, 178–79, 199, 282, 287–89, 325, 326; *croyants* in, 163, 168, 281; defined, 10–11; and funeral ritual, 72, 101–2; narratives about, 24–25, 284, 285–86, 309 (*see also* Legends; Memorates); naturalistic explanations for, 282–85, 291–93, 295–96, 305–6, 318, 326, 327, 333, 334 (*see also* Disenchantment/Rationalization); nature expressing, 15, 302, 303–9, 314–16, 321, 324, 334; and Toussaint, 279. *See also* Destiny; *Intersignes*; Religion; Revenants
Sweeping, after dark, 246–47
Symbols, 15; in blessing the dead, 65, 92–93; on catafalques, 115; in cemeteries, 131, 136, 137, 140–41, 157; Christian, on prehistoric monu-

ments, 162; culture/nature, 211; diptychs and, 269; dreams of dead and, 255, 258; for dying, 170; earth, 209; festival, 165–67, 266, 277, 279; flowers as, 108; lists of givers of Masses and services as, 111; in *maison-caveau* link, 148; prospective, 108; Resistance as, 205 n; retrospective, 108; *tableaux*, 103, 179–80
Syncretism, of Catholic and folk beliefs, 64, 69, 158–73, 186–87, 188, 243, 277, 281–82, 337
Syndicates, agricultural, 7, 240

Tableaux, 103, 179–87 passim, 229, 235
Tame death (acceptance), 12–13, 14, 33–36, 333, 336–37; Ariès on, 12–13, 15, 18, 47–48, 50, 137, 157, 282–83; and cemeteries, 132–34, 137, 149–52, 157; diptychs and, 269; funerary rites and, 52, 98; and good death, 12, 55, 56; *intersignes* and, 282–83, 327
Technology: and nature, 13–14, 295–96, 321–22; and supernatural, 295–96, 321–22. *See also* Mechanization; Medicalization
Television, 9, 45, 218, 221, 238
Thomas, Keith, 334–35
Toilette des morts, 58–61, 63, 78, 84 n, 100–101, 329
Tomb monuments, 20, 131–32, 137–41, 149–50, 153, 332; advance preparation of, 34, 149–50; cleaning of, 168, 261–63, 265; cremation and, 155, 156; romanticism and, 138, 251. *See also Caveaux*
Touching the dead, 85–86
Tourism, Plouguerneau, 21, 22
Toussaint (All Saints' Day), 122, 163–64, 175, 187, 258–77, 279, 280, 331; cemetery visits during, 168–69, 253, 265, 277, 280; and donation of body to research, 156; family reunions at, 332; and *kest an Anaon*, 203, 276–77
Tragedy: as divine retribution, 228; secular perspective on, 283; supernatural explanations for, 58, 285–86, 311–12, 315, 325, 326, 333–34. *See also Triste* deaths
Transition, rites of, 51, 52, 53, 84, 100, 117, 118, 131
Triste (sad) deaths, 57–58, 106, 210, 211, 267, 315
Troisième âge, 36–40, 48; *clubs du*, 29–30, 38–39, 128, 220. *See also* Elderly
Turner, Victor, 100

Undertaker service (*pompes funèbres*), 59, 77–78, 81, 100, 329
Union pour la Démocratie Française (UDF), 27
United States, 14, 47 n, 133, 265, 277 n, 336
Université de Bretagne Occidentale, Brest, 47
Urban areas, influence of, 26, 28, 31; and Catholicism, 217; and condolences, 96; and denial of death, 152; and funerals, 52, 95; and migration (see *Exode rural*; *Retour au pays*); and mourning traditions, 127; and *pompes funèbres*, 78

van Gennep, Arnold, 112–13, 159; and festivals, 64 n, 163–64, 165, 167, 169 n, 277; and hell, 160; on mourning, 122–23; and rites of incorporation, 51, 98, 100, 117 n, 123; and rites of separation, 51, 52–53, 100, 122–23; and rites of transition, 51, 100
Vatican II, 110, 114, 222–29, 330; and afterlife, 117, 128, 225–26, 230, 242; and fasting, 125; and meat eating, 16; and mediators, 242–43; and *onction des malades*, 54, 227; Toussaint rituals and, 260
Vaults, burial. *See Caveaux*
Vegetarianism, 239
Veillées (neighborhood evening gatherings), 9
Veillées mortuaires. See Wakes
Verdier, Yvonne, 59–60
Villages. *See Quartiers*
Visions, premonitory, 12, 303 n, 316–17, 318, 324
Visits: cemetery, 20, 168–69, 250–55, 257, 265, 277, 280, 332; wake, 63–65, 73–74, 331
Voluntary associations, obituary notices by, 76
Voting patterns, 26–27

Wage labor, 42, 110, 116, 139, 201–2, 244
Wakes (*veillées mortuaires*), 24, 58–74, 100, 101; attendance at, 67–68, 330, 331–32; boxwood at, 63, 64–65, 168; changes in, 71–74, 330; funeral arrangements during, 75, 78; and *triste* deaths, 57; visits during, 63–65, 73–74, 331
Wales, 159 n, 161, 272
Warnings of death, 12, 55–56. *See also Intersignes*; Visions

Washing: at birth, 59–60; of dead, 58–61; of tombs, 168, 261–63, 265
Water: baptism, 93; blessing dead with, 63–65, 92–93, 100, 115–16, 117, 260, 261; running, 9–10, 150
Weber, Eugen, 202n, 337n
Weber, Max, 17, 19, 241, 250, 293
Weddings, 82n, 88–89, 99n, 212, 216, 249
Widowers, cemetery visits by, 252
Wilde, Lady Jane Francesca, 271–72
Will-o'-the-wisps. See *Feux follets*
Witchcraft, 24, 182, 281, 282, 287–88, 326
Women: and burial, 145, 149; and Catholic morality, 196–97; cemetery visits by, 252; clergy exerting social control through, 194–95; and *club du troisième âge*, 220; elderly cared for by, 49; after funeral, 99; as pallbearers, 79–80, 329; religious practice by, 219–20; seating in church of, 192; supernatural as domain of, 320; in Toussaint activities, 260, 261–63; wage labor by, 42
Worldview, 18–19, 20, 28, 172–73, 213, 214–15, 237, 326, 336, 339–40; alternative to Catholicism, 240 (*see also* Anticlericalism; Secularization); and catafalque position, 115; of civil funerals, 211; of elderly, 31, 47–48; and supernatural, 3–4, 10–11, 20, 72, 102, 250, 283, 285, 291–93, 301–2, 325–26, 335 (*see also* Disenchantment/Rationalization). *See also* Destiny; Morality/Ethics; Folk religious beliefs; Religion
World War I, 278, 280
World War II, 291. *See also* Resistance, French
Wrapping, of body, 60

Yoga, 239, 336
Young people: afterlife conceptions of, 235–36; and cemetery visits, 252–53, 280; funeral attendance of, 87, 95, 330; and *intersignes*, 324; and Jeunesse Agricole Chrétienne, 240–41; and mourning, 124, 126, 127–28, 330; as pallbearers, 80; and public rituals, 95, 330; and religion, 217–19, 223, 235–36, 239; residences of, 148; and Toussaint, 270–71, 280. *See also* Children; *Exode rural*

Zonabend, Françoise, 157, 168–69, 255, 263n

Compositor:	G&S Typesetters, Inc.
Text:	10/13 Palatino
Display:	Palatino
Printer:	Braun-Brumfield, Inc.
Binder:	Braun-Brumfield, Inc.

ACC-0934

WITHDRAWN
From Bertrand Library

DATE DUE			
DEC 30 1991			
MAY 23 1994			
DEC 1 1993			
GAYLORD			PRINTED IN U.S.A.